SWITCHING TECHNOLOGY IN THE LOCAL NETWORK:

FROM LAN TO SWITCHED LAN
TO VIRTUAL LAN

SWITCHING TECHNOLOGY IN THE LOCAL NETWORK:

FROM LAN TO SWITCHED LAN TO VIRTUAL LAN

MATHIAS HEIN
AND
DAVID GRIFFITHS

London • Bonn • Boston • Johannesburg • Madrid • Melbourne • Mexico City • New York • Paris
Singapore • Tokyo • Toronto • Albany, NY • Belmont, CA • Cincinnati, OH • Detroit, MI

Switching Technology in the Local Network: From LAN to Switched LAN to Virtual LAN

Copyright ©1997 International Thomson Publishing

 A division of International Thomson Publishing Inc.
The ITP Logo is a trademark under license.

For more information, contact:

International Thomson Computer Press
Berkshire House
168–173 High Holborn
London WCIV 7AA
United Kingdom

International Thomson Computer Press
20 Park Plaza, 13th Floor
Boston, MA 02116
USA

Thomas Nelson Australia
102 Dodds Street
South Melbourne, 3205
Victoria
Australia

Nelson Canada
1120 Birchmount Road
Scarborough, Ontario
Canada M1K 5G4

International Thomson Publishing Southern Africa
Bldg. 19, Constantia Park
239 Old Pretoria Road, P.O. Box 2459
Halfway House, 1685 South Africa

International Thomson Publishing GmbH
Königswinterer Strasse 418
53227 Bonn
Germany

International Thomson Publishing Asia
221 Henderson Road #05-10
Henderson Building
Singapore 0315

International Thomson Publishing Japan
Hirakawacho Kyowa Building, 3F
2-2-1 Hirakawacho
Chiyoda-ku, 102 Tokyo
Japan

International Thomson Editores
Campos Eliseos 385, Piso 7
Col. Polanco
11560 Mexico D.F. Mexico

International Thomson Publishing France
1, rue st. Georges
75 009 Paris France

British Library Cataloging-in-Publication Data
A catalogue record for this book is available from the British Library

Library of Congress Cataloging-in-Publication Data
A catalog record for this book is available from the Library of Congress

ISBN: 1-85032-166-3

Commissioning Editor: Liz Israel Oppedijk   Publisher/Vice President: Jim DeWolf, ITCP/Boston
Project Director: Chris Grisonich, ITCP/Boston   Manufacturing Manager: Sandra Sabathy Carr, ITCP/Boston
Marketing Manager: Kathleen Raftery, ITCP/Boston

Cover Designed by: Button Eventures, London
Production: Jo-Ann Campbell • *mle design* • 562 Milford Point Road • Milford, CT 06460

Printed in the U.S.

There is a theory that says if anyone ever finds out exactly how data communication can be used with good results, and why this technology is discussed with such euphoria, then this technology will disappear straight away and will be replaced by something even more bizarre and even more incomprehensible.

For Joachim and Gabi Dreher

According to another theory, all this has already happened.

Mathias Hein

*Hindsight benefits from 20/20 vision. Most peoples' eyes are focused on how life used to be, not where its going. Visionaries don't look too hard on the failures of the past, they can't afford to. **Real** visionaries have three eyes: one out there on the horizon, one on the middle ground, and a third positioned just under their nose.*

For Alison, Andrew and Alex, my three three-eyed children

David Griffiths

Contents

Foreword

The information superhighway, the Internet, online services, video conferencing, interactive multimedia—if the reader has confidence in these catch phrases which, thanks to hyperactive marketing departments, are dominating public discussion, then we, both as private individuals and in the world of business communication, are currently going through an evolution—one might even say a revolution—in communication technology. This process has already left Marshall McLuhan's vision of the "global village" far behind and is set to change our living and working conditions more radically than the invention of the printing press, the typewriter and the telephone put together. Novell aims to network over a billion nodes world-wide within a few years; what is more, we can expect all manner of "intelligent" machines—from the car that navigates itself, to the drinks machine that automatically orders a new supply of lemonade on time. For business communication, this not only presents opportunities for conducting multimedia-based, synchronous communication with complete freedom of location (the "virtual team" concept), but the integration of "intelligent" machines also heralds the arrival of completely new applications, for example in logistics, in which "just-in-time" manufacturing is a key concept.

Network operators are uneasy about this development, yet it is they who have to provide the necessary bandwidths in LAN and WAN in the near future. This is not a matter of choosing the fastest technology; what is required is the protection of investment in equipment which has already been installed and planned, as well as an optimum price/performance ratio—in short, a strategy for migration to new, high-speed technologies that satisfies technical and economic necessities.

If all (or nearly all) experts agree that ATM will be the solution in both the WAN and LAN areas in the medium-term, this has been of no use to network operators, who are looking for gentle migration strategies and solutions to performance problems arising in their real, existing networks. Ethernet switches, with their modular ports, promise to provide the answer here—even for rival high-speed technologies. As a means of retaining existing installations on the user side, Ethernet switching in particular is an attractive alternative to shared media solutions, which are gradually becoming "too narrow." This is because a dedicated bandwidth of 10 Mbit/s is currently more than sufficient for the majority of users. The hubs that are now flooding onto the market promise a gentle migration to all forward-looking high-speed technologies. After all, in economic terms, evolution is more acceptable than revolution.

Dr. Dirk R. Glogau
Oberhausen

1 Foundation Stones

This book is about adaptation, one of human kind's greatest attributes. When we examine the impact created by the computer and network infrastructure over the past 20 years, we see that adaptation has worked hand-in-hand with invention. Even so, much is taken for granted. Perhaps that's how it should be. As systems become more complex, it follows that they are less likely to be fixed or extended by users. In fact, the user has come to depend on the specialist.

Users should not be concerned with how data moves from their computer or workstation to another; this should happen with the minimum of effort on the users' part. Software vendors have come a long way from the days when a manual as large as a city telephone directory was needed to understand even the simplest commands. Now, users often don't know where the recipient of a message or file is located. The destination may be in the same building or on another continent; senders know the recipient's name; that's all they really need to know. How it gets from here to there is not important to many—they just want to know that it gets there.

Our children have adapted to the PC more quickly than we have. They are not fazed with the technology the way some of the executives of today are.

Believe it or not, a large percentage of middle and senior management above the age of 45 are scared of computers.

Even networks are no problem to the younger generation. Their relatively uncluttered minds readily grasp networking principles. They have grown up with "TLAs," or Three Letter Acronyms, which are in abundance in this industry. More and more students are signing up for networking and IT courses than ever before. We are raising a new generation of network, and network management cognizant individuals who will accept computing and networking without hesitation.

There's Nothing New Under the Sun

The evolution of the LAN (Local Area Network) can be compared with the development of the telephone system. Not too many years ago, to call anyone outside of one's local area meant speaking with at least one operator who would handle the call on behalf of the caller. If the call was routed from one village on the outskirts of one town to a village on the outskirts of a town hundreds of miles away, several operators would be involved. Each one would have some knowledge of his or her own switched network, or domain. It was not possible for the caller to speak to the other party without the cooperation and knowledge of these disembodied people. Now, we take it for granted that a call can be initiated without the personal touch. Even transcontinental calls can be made from a phone in one country to almost anywhere around the world without the need to speak with an intermediary.

How would Alexander Graham Bell have felt on March 10th 1876 when he initiated the first call, to be told that just over a century later, one could call from the United States to Europe by just pushing a sequence of buttons. Also, thanks to switching technology, the callers can hear each other as if they are in the same town.

If we look at the growth of LANs and WANs (Wide Area Networks) over the last 20 years, their uptake has been phenomenal. Almost no section of society has escaped the installation of some network component or system. Compare this with the installation of electricity in the home. In 1882, Thomas Edison began to deliver electricity on a commercial scale, yet by 1946, less than half of American homes were still without electricity.

What effect has the network had on the computer and communications market? For one thing, it has freed us from the ties of the corporate environment. Terms like "telecommuting," "telecottage," "mobile networking," and "remote access" have been adopted into the language. One large computer company allows some employees up to 40% of their working week to be spent at home, still providing them access to corporate resources via WAN and LAN connections. For some, it's great. Free from traffic jams, parking problems, snatched lunch breaks, some find working at home increases their output. Others cannot function outside of the company of fellow workers. Whatever we think of working at home, it's sure to increase. Less travel implies less pollution. Think how much time most people spend travelling to and from their place of work every week, and how that time could be used for more profitable activities.

Whatever our views on working at home, there has been a marked trend over the past few years of organizations moving staff out of expensive, city-based corporate centers, to remote branch offices where land prices and parking are less expensive, and parking is less expensive. Branch offices need LANs. Their LAN traffic, carried to the headquarters by whatever WAN technology, adds more load to the corporate LAN. Staff who work from home and mobile users connect to the branch offices and the corporate center, adding further demands on the corporate and branch LAN.

The information technology industry is growing at an exponential rate. The computer and network sector employs millions of people around the world. Research and development funding is continuously needed by vendors to push the speed barriers and keep ahead of, or at least alongside, the competition. If the reader cares to take a moment to review the sales figures of the top 10 LAN vendors, the question must come up—where is this product going? Isn't the market saturated? Well, it seems not. Vendors are still selling product; network churn rates are high. As with any market, there are victors and victims. Switched LAN is no exception to this rule.

Network Dependency

We have become almost entirely dependent upon computers and networking. Most organizations hold their data on computer, not on paper. Many have no backup procedures in the event of a computer or network failure. Airlines, insurance companies, banks, governments, even small companies would grind to a halt if the systems failed. In the case of large organizations, redundant systems can handle major network failures; those running small organizations just hope that the worst never happens.

We have become so dependent on the LAN that in many sites, an Ethernet segment failure (here we use an example where switched LAN is not used), can result in hundreds of users denied access to the network. How often have we called an airline, credit card company, and so on, to be told that they can't help us at the moment "because they system is down." When that occurs, it can cost millions of dollars of lost revenue per hour. With the judicious application of switched LAN, putting hundreds off-line at one time is less likely. We believe that switched LAN will be adopted in two directions. First, down from the high level, sub-dividing (or micro-segmenting) large networks, and secondly, from the workstation group and up.

Another factor many organizations have had to face over the recent years is sabotage and terrorism. No longer can multinationals afford to risk putting all their computing resources in one computer room or even on one site. Terrorists are becoming more computer literate. By this we mean that they have begun to realize how vital computers and networks are to government, commerce, and industry. Computer systems and networks have to be designed to accommodate worst case scenarios which would have been unthinkable 30 years ago. Parallel networks increase network complexity and add load to the system. Switched networks, correctly designed and implemented, can provide a more resilient framework in the event of attack.

Major system outages caused by other factors such as fire, floods, and lightning strikes can create financial disaster to organizations that are dependent upon computing. Again, well thought-out networks with computing and switched resources backed up with network management pay for themselves the first time a disaster occurs. The reader should take a moment to consider how reliant his or her organization is with respect to computing and networking. How would the organization manage if the above events occurred? Is the network able to handle fire, flood or sabotage? We are not saying that switched LAN is the answer to the problem. We know, however, that a well-designed and implemented network which utilizes switched components can often minimize complete system failure.

Development Parallels

The development of the switched LAN can be compared with Alexander Graham Bell and the telephone. When Bell showed his device to one of America's largest telegraph companies, they were singularly unimpressed. At the end of the demonstration, the executives of Western Union simply told Bell, "after careful consideration of your invention, while it is a very interesting novelty, we have come to the conclusion that it has no commercial possibilities." Budding inventors please note. As a result of Western Union's rejection, Bell went on to found what later was to become the largest American corporation, the American Telephone and Telegraph, more well known today by the acronym AT&T.

When switched LAN first appeared on the market, it was ignored by many, lambasted by some. Even network "gurus" saw no sense in switching on broadcast mediums like Ethernet. What was wrong with a 10Mbit/s broadcast LAN? Perhaps these individuals had never heard of the "Elastic Band" principle of marketing.

Elastic Technology

The growth of twentieth-century technology seems to have been founded on the "Elastic Band" marketing principle. Imagine someone taking a strong elastic band, looping it around his or her thumb and first finger, then putting his or her hand, fingers extended, down onto a table. Keeping his or her thumb anchored to the table, the person extends his or her index finger away from the thumb. After a short distance (depending on the elasticity and size of the band), the thumb will be "encouraged" to follow the index finger. In fact, if allowed, the thumb could pass the finger and continue along the table. Try the process yourself, keeping the index finger anchored and increase the gap by drawing the thumb further away. This is one of the simplest models of marketing. Consider the index finger to be the marketing team, and the thumb the market.

In the beginning, the marketeers do all they can to persuade or pull the market in their direction. Initially, the market is unwilling to commit to this new product or service. Inertia caused by fear, lack of understanding, financial restraints, anchors the market. Eventually (not in all cases), inertia is slowly overcome. When it is, the hoped-for efforts of the marketing department pay off. The market takes up the product or service, business accelerates, the thumb passes the index finger and now strains the index finger, the marketing team. Before the marketeers know it, the customers are demanding enhancements. The only trouble is, the marketing people have only just convinced the investors that the idea was a success. Now they have to convince conservative accountants that the demands of the market are needed right away in order to maintain market leadership or presence.

If we compare the elastic band principle to the LAN market, it fits all too readily. In the early days of Ethernet, the developers saw the need for an easy to install broadcast-based network. The market didn't respond quickly, even though peripherals were costly. Even today, it is possible to find small organizations where LANs have not been established. In this age of standards-based networking, some still hold on to the belief that proprietary networking products are superior to the more widely accepted standards-based devices. In some cases they may be right. Unfortunately, maintaining an air of exclusivism often results in high network downtime. Obtaining proprietary components is also more difficult than buying off-the-shelf standards-based products.

As LAN technology developed, along came applications to stretch the elastic band. If we go back only a few years to the Intel 8-bit processor, the 8080 and the 8085, applications were designed around the limitations of memory. As CPUs and memory have become more efficient and less expensive, application sizes have almost gone out of control. At one time, a word-processing application probably took up less than 200 Kb of memory. Today, it's normal to find that a package needs more than 12Mb.

The Tail That Wags The Dog

As applications have become more memory intensive and complex, they have put pressure on the infrastructure. Now we hear of computers with CPU clock speeds above 200Mhz, data transfer rates between disk and memory of over 30Mb per second, yet many overlook the network. In reality, a well-designed network is "the tail that wags the dog," not the other way around. The difference between a good and bad network is easily seen by the specialist, not by the user. For example, as networks grow, many users experience a gradual speed degradation in data transfer. They may not notice the change, they just get used to it. In fact, they may believe it's not the network, but other factors, such as the latest version of an application, or the addition of new utilities. Indeed, these things may negatively affect the efficiency of the network, but it takes a specialist with diagnostic equipment to identify the bottlenecks and restore the network to full efficient operation.

When switched Ethernet first appeared, many just saw it as yet another way to sell snake oil. Why should anyone need a dedicated 10Mbit/s channel; surely, that's what Ethernet already provided wasn't it? Well, that's what the salesperson told them, and they must be telling the truth! In fact, when Ethernet switching first appeared, it is more than likely that dedicated 10Mb/s bandwidth was not required in most installations. However, in just four years, that metric has changed. While many small-to-medium sized organizations have yet to install switched LANs, it is only a matter of time. Faster and faster PCs and workstations are replacing the machines of the early part of this decade. Along with the computers come more and more network-intensive applications. The Internet, video conferencing, and widespread database activity demands more network bandwidth. Consequently, users are less willing to wait for their machines to spit out the answers. The thumb will again fly past the index finger, more marketing teams will burn the midnight oil to keep control of their market sector.

For the moment, let's turn to areas where LAN technology hasn't yet made a significant impact. Until recently office equipment, for example photocopiers and fax machines, were regarded as "islands of technology." With the introduction of embedded intelligence like Novell's NEST (Novell Embedded System Technology), these products plus scanners, energy management systems, even the vending machine can be managed via a LAN. This will put a further burden on the network infrastructure and strengthen the argument to make the most use of an existing cabling system. Another recent technology guaranteed to put strain on the LAN is the intranet.

Intranets (as distinct from the Internet), are essentially server-based systems which hold information in the same form as the World Wide Web holds information on the Internet. Pages of information can be made available to staff (or to the public as in the case of stations, libraries, or museums), which can be reviewed by client-based browser software (such as Netscape). Pages are encoded in HTML (Hypertext Markup Language), and can come from the Internet or from internal resources. For example, corporate announcements, press releases, news items, spreadsheets, database records, almost anything can be converted to HTML, stored, and retrieved. As intranets become more popular, network loads will increase. Intranets are growing quickly, as executives recognize that they not only perform a useful internal function, they can be used by staff at remote locations. Switched LAN, plus external WAN links can provide quick and easy access for internal and external data.

Where else do we expect switched LAN to be adopted? In the place where the LAN has so far not been established. In the home environment. Embedded communications interfaces with a LAN could be installed in many places around the home. Central heating, lighting, security systems, the oven, VCR, all are still "islands of technology." The domestic market has been waiting for a low-cost, standards-based interface for home automation to become a reality. Now with NEST and Java (Sun Microsystems) embedded technology, new domestic products could be hooked up to a switched LAN and controlled by an in-house computer or externally by the user via the telephone. All we are waiting for is a new index finger beckoning the market.

2 | Roller Skating and Tapdancing–The Market

S witched LAN is clearly an adaptation with enormous market potential. Like all technologies, the LAN switching market has fallen into a number of well-recognized architecture camps. Interestingly enough, the company to deliver the first Ethernet switch, Kalpana, designed its product around a more efficient architecture than many that followed. (See Figure 6.8.)

The Market and Performance Claims

As the market recognized that Ethernet switching was not a passing fad, existing and new manufacturers poured resources into development. By the middle of 1994, nearly 70 vendors either had a deliverable product, claimed to have one ready for delivery "next month," or were in some phase of a development program. Along with this came the claims and counterclaims on performance. The performance claims made by some vendors were, in most cases, impossible for the customers to refute; how could they? There was no defined performance benchmark, and few independent test houses knew how to test them. At the same time, few network consultants knew enough about Ethernet switching to challenge the claims of some less scrupulous vendors.

The president of one switched Ethernet manufacturer used to enjoy peering into the innards of competitors products at trade shows, then challenging the competitors to prove the claims made on their data sheets. More than one competitor lost the argument. Knowing the wire-speed of Ethernet, the throughput of CPUs and RISC architecture, the internal contention and buffering (a degree as a statistician may have helped), the vendors were glad when she left their stand. One competitor, when faced with the facts, resolutely stood by his data sheet, saying that it didn't matter what the facts were, his switch somehow transcended physics and worked in accordance with the data sheet!

The "smoke and mirrors" technique of some manufacturers made it difficult for the customer to determine what was real and what wasn't. "Full wire speed on all ports" seemed (and in some cases still seems) to deny the fact that if all the ports were activated continuously, the claim, based on the architecture, is impossible. That doesn't prevent the claims continuing. The problem is—if an organization installs one or more LAN switches, can they really measure the expected gain in throughput? In many cases, the answer is no. The reason is simple. Many organizations (even large ones) still have no form of network management installed. They cannot measure the "before" and "after" the installation of a switched LAN. Psychologically, they may believe that the installation has improved network performance (and it should), but they cannot determine this in reality. It is fair to say that, as with any network component, a LAN switch installed in the wrong place could (and sometimes does) degrade the performance of the network.

Depending on one's viewpoint, network management is either a vital system component or it is a waste of money. Those who think it's a waste of money need to review how much it cost the last time there was a network failure. It wasn't just the cost of the technician called in to find the fault. Think of the lost revenue and lack of customer service when the system is down.

The installation of an SNMP-based network management system can pay for itself in a number of ways. First, if part of the network fails, and the system has been designed properly, the management system can limit the outage to the minimum number of devices. Second, fault and operation logs can help network administrators determine where, when, and how networks should be expanded or reconfigured. Third, organizational changes result in frequent equipment moves. Approximately 80% of network failures are cable-related. A network management administrator can save his or her organization a fortune and prevent its staff a lot of frustration. The combination of network management and switched micro-segmented LANs pays for itself by virtue of its flexibility and ease of installation.

With a correctly designed and managed network, the effects of switched LAN can be determined in a short time. Comparing pre-switched LAN with the new configuration allows the network administrator to see the effects of the installation. If necessary, LAN switches can be moved around the network to fine-tune the system. With a structured cabling system, this should not create prolonged network downtime.

Installation of a switched LAN device on workgroups generate a performance increase. When large files are moved between workstations in a workgroup, a well-designed LAN switch cuts transfer delays to the minimum. The result is an increase in productivity.

Switched Ethernet was expensive when first introduced. This was partly due to the small number of products shipped, the high research and development costs which needed to be recovered, and the need to promote what was an under-appreciated technology from the customer perspective. Some vendors, recognizing that high performance was vital, designed switches which were wholly transparent to the network. In other words, if their switches received a "bad" data packet, they forwarded it anyway. Others, believing that passing suspect data frames around a network was not a good idea, designed their devices with frame checking software. The result was the battle between the "cut-through" and the "store and forward" brigades (more on that subject later). Some Ethernet switches could be configured to pass or check suspect frames, allowing the network administrator to let the switch act as it should, or act as a "fast" bridge.

As the demand for switched LAN increased, some vendors adopted the "quick and easy" approach, adapting bridge technology to create store and forward switches. The battle between the "cut-through" and the "check it before passing it on" vendors increased. Both designs have their merits, however, since Ethernet switches operate on the lower layers of the ISO 7-layer model (see Chapter 3 for details), they should switch data. Error checking in most cases can be handled by communication protocols, leaving the switch to perform their function. Not everyone agrees with this point, and price/performance also needs to be taken into consideration when deciding what switched LAN is right for a system.

Some in the industry say that a store and forward Ethernet switch is an anachronism; it's just a glorified multiport bridge. Whatever the viewpoint, it has not prevented sales of store and forward switches in the market. Later in the book, we review the two basic architectures, their strengths and weaknesses, and where they are best suited.

What the market needed was a more clear definition of terms relevant to switching, and how the prospective buyers could evaluate switch performance.

Testing the claims

From the independent viewpoint, Scott Bradner in the USA is a well-known and respected evaluator of switched LAN devices. So is Bob Mandeville of the European Network Test Labs in France. From the vendor viewpoint, Elon Littwitz, Joint President of Ornet in Israel, has provided much guidance on how switches should be definitively tested. For more information on switch testing, see Chapter 6. Evaluation networks have been assembled at independent laboratories, and with the help of test equipment companies like Wandel and Goltermann, comparisons between switches have been made. Even so, the most efficient switched LAN component is only a link in a complex system, and reader please note, Murphy's Law still applies.

Fortunately, more and more trade magazines publish comparison tests of switched LAN products, and it is hoped that eventually, technical terms will be less subject to manufacturers interpretation. What must daunt many buyers is the choice of switched LAN, and is there merit in paying approximately $600 per port for cut-through switches when another vendor (with similar claims of 100% throughput under all conditions), sells its switch at less than $200 per port.

The Downward Price Spiral

As often occurs in the high technology market, when switched LAN became available, prices were in the order of $1500 per port and higher. With the introduction of low port-count store and forward switches, this dropped below $200 per port and is still showing a downward trend. The shakeout of the market has already begun. Some vendors have been bought out by companies acquiring the technology rather than developing it. Others have pulled out or simply vanished.

Currently, the switched LAN market is still in a state of flux. This is good for the customer and not so good for the switch vendors. It does, however, guarantee that prices will continue to fall, while performance is expected to increase. Furthermore, the addition of hardware routing, virtual LAN, extended network management in the form of RMON (Remote Monitoring), and ATM will guarantee the LAN switch lifecycle for many years to come. Faster CPUs and RISC (Reduced Instruction Set Computers), more vendors committing their designs to ASIC (Application Specific Integrated Circuits), will provide faster, more flexible switched products to an ever-more demanding market.

What Goes Up Doesn't Always Go Down

Readers of this book will no doubt be familiar with the word "vaporware," defining products that have been announced and not yet delivered. Switched LAN is no exception. One vendor, a well-known LAN hub manufacturer, announced a LAN switch, took over 100 forward orders, but was unable to deliver production devices for almost one year following the official "rollout" of the product.

Another word, coined by Mathias Hein is "wonderware" (no connection with the company Wonderware Software). The authors have used this word on many occasions over the past years. It refers to products that began as vaporware, but never appeared, so we "wonderware" the product went. Sometimes, vendors just couldn't get the product to work, (this has happened where companies designed LAN switches based on ASIC designs). Get it wrong first time, and it could be expensive. Get it wrong the second time, and it could be fatal. Few switched LAN vendors developed an ASIC-based switch and got it right first time. We know one team that succeeded. To achieve this they sacrificed their comfy beds and slept at their workstations for many months. When the ASIC was proved to be "right first time," even the silicon foundry who delivered the first chips were astounded.

Product Lifecycles—The Industry Myth

One myth about computing and networking is the lifecycle of a product or technology. A prime example is ISDN (Integrated Services Digital Network). This four letter acronym has been humorously decoded as "I Still Don't kNow" (meaning that it will be adopted), "I See Dollars Now" (a hopeful attitude from some U.S. vendors), and "It's Slow, Dumb and No-good" from the occasional critic. At the end of the 1970s, ISDN was hailed by some as the technology to kill the modem within two years. Any modem manufacturer with any sense should shut shop now and go home, they said. Try telling that to companies like US Robotics, with ever increasing sales of modems. Yes, ISDN is now a well-established and growing technology, but it has taken almost 20 years to come of age.

Switched LAN has already taken off far faster than ISDN. Even so, sales will not peak for some considerable time (see Chapter 7 for more definitive information). There is a vast installed base of half-duplex Ethernet. With the slow, but sure implementation of ATM (Asynchronous Transfer Mode), to augment conventional unswitched LAN traffic, switched LAN has a bright future.

A distinct advantage of switched LAN is that in many cases, it can be installed with the minimum amount of network disruption. In the Ethernet environment, LAN switches can often be installed in a matter of hours, depending on the cabling infrastructure. Assuming the correct switch has been chosen, and the device installed in the most optimal position of the network, the performance increase will be gained for a relatively low cost. The thought of having to rip out a cabling infrastructure just to provide a performance increase can be imagined. The cost of cabling is a sizable proportion of the overall cost of a network.

3 | An Introduction to Switching Technology

Over twenty years ago, Ethernet revolutionized the world of in-house communication. Hierarchically organized computer concepts were superseded by distributed computer networks based on LANs (client server architectures). This development resulted in a rapid quantitative and qualitative growth in the performance of data processing end systems. Slogans such as Open Systems Interconnection (OSI) were used to describe the new communications technologies made possible to manage large volumes of data sensibly and provide a fast distribution of the available information. There arose manufacturer-dependent, generally available solutions, which followed international standards both in communications software and hardware components. The availability of comparable machines resulting from this development significantly accelerated the general fall in prices and enabled the broad spread of LAN components. The local data networks have today become a permanent feature of every communication concept. They enable the integration of mainframes, terminals and PCs into one general network, in which the computing power is distributed and can, in principle, be used by all the end systems. The computer and communications industries have become the engine of worldwide economic development in recent years.

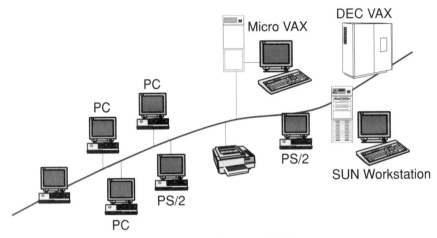

Figure 3.1: Traditional LAN

LAN technology requirements are changing continually as a result of technological development. The use of ever more powerful end systems, for example, and the increased use of client/server applications means that the load on networks is increasing rapidly. The traditional LANs, in which the bandwidth on the shared medium was divided between all attached end systems, no longer provides the necessary transmission capacity. The integration of new applications (video, audio or high resolution graphics applications) in the traditional networks mean an increase in the demands on available bandwidth, throughput and delay times. The traditional LANs cannot meet these requirements for optimum bandwidth. For this reason, new technologies must inevitably be developed and implemented.

From Newcomer to Network Standard

The early Ethernet networks were constructed on the bus-type Yellow Cable (10Base5) or Cheapernet Standard (10Base2). Not until the Ethernet on Twisted Pair (10BaseT) standard became available did it become possible to restructure the networks to a star-type cabling topology. The star-type cabling systems simplified the installation of servers and workstations significantly. In addition to this, there was a dramatic fall in the price of Ethernet adapters. At the end of the 1980s, this led to around two out of every three installed data networks being based on the IEEE 802.3 standard. At the start of the 1990s, however, this success was suddenly halted. The availability of high performance PCs and bandwidth-hungry applications meant that applications no longer had sufficient bandwidth available on the traditional 10 Mbit/s Ethernet. Network operators therefore began to seek for a new LAN technology which supported the significantly higher data rates.

The first high speed solution for users was FDDI on fiber optics. Using this technology, networks could be constructed of up to 200 km in size. Because of the complexity and high installation costs for fiber optic components, FDDI was relatively slow to establish itself in the market. Although the availability of FDDI on copper cable has led to prices falling by half in the last three years, network operators must still pay 5 to 10 times as much for FDDI components compared to 10BaseT solutions. When making the transition between an Ethernet and FDDI network, the Ethernet packets must also be converted into FDDI formats. This transition is achieved via translation bridges or routers. This software-intensive task leads to the fact that over 50% of the available bandwidth is lost, particularly with short data packets.

A totally new technology was presented by the US company, Kalpana, at the start of 1991, with the first Ethernet switch. This new Ethernet technology was based on the fundamental principles of telephone technology. In normal Ethernet technology, all devices must divide the available bandwidth of 10 Mbit/s between one another. This led to the fact that more machines activated on the network meant less bandwidth available to the individual stations. If the Ethernet stations are attached to a switch, this device ensures that an exclusive 10 Mbit/s data highway is made available individually to each port. The switch constructs a quasi-exclusive 10 Mbit/s connection between any two end systems using the source and destination addresses of the packet via the internal bus. The first switch launched on the market by Kalpana was capable of guaranteeing a simultaneous 10 Mbit/s connection to all of its 15 ports. Subsequently, Ethernet switches were developed by other manufacturers with a larger number of ports (e.g., 128 Ethernet ports) with a theoretical transmission capacity of several Gbit/s.

By using switches, the overall throughput of the network depends only on the maximum speed of the internal logic of the switch. The switching technology has meanwhile developed in several different directions. The user is confused by a variety of new terms (store-and-forward, cut-through-forwarding and cellbus switches). The architecture of the switch is the key feature for the performance of the attached end systems. The Ethernet switches are offered either as standalone switches or as modules for existing hub systems. The standalone switches have currently established themselves as market leaders, since these devices have been developed specially for the specific functions. The switch functions in hub systems are achieved by plugging modules in the basic housing. Since the hub systems were designed for a general use scenario, the technology which they contain is not configured in an optimal manner for these applications with the integration of switches. The bus architectures in the hubs must firstly be redesigned to meet the new requirements. It is generally anticipated that the new hub generations of the manufacturers (e.g., 3Com, Cabletron, Bay Networks) will meet the new challenges and soon support all switching functions in the relevant systems at an optimum level.

Since the market players are not afraid of extolling their merits, this book is intended to offer the reader a guide for evaluating switching technology and criteria, which will facilitate selection of the correct switch.

3.1   Evolution of Ethernet

Ethernet is still one of the most frequently-installed local networks worldwide. Its appeal is simple installation, flexibility, a multifaceted nature and ease of use. The underlying open system architecture is the key to its success and created the basis for a network concept penetrating into all areas of data processing. Ethernet enables a range of users to use any information and data efficiently in a distributed information system. Ethernet also has a tradition of breaking new ground. Circuit switching products have been replaced largely by packet switching technology. Since all stations have equal privileges on the network, packet switching technology enables multiple exploitation of the medium by different devices and protocols. A high data rate (10 Mbit/s, 20 Mbit/s, 100 Mbit/s and 200 Mbit/s), high fault tolerance, and the relatively load-independent nature of the technology with a simultaneously high number of end stations have led to a reduction in operating costs and constitute the key to market acceptance of the Ethernet system.

The development of Ethernet began at the start of the 1970s. The transmission system became known worldwide, when the IEEE 802.3 group standardized this process. The IEEE architecture is based on the definition of functions provided in the lower two sublayers of the OSI reference model. The IEEE 802.3 standard defines the CSMA/CD (Carrier Sense Multiple Access with Collision Detection) mechanism as the access process for the network and the physical characteristics of the network components. All specifications beyond that are undertaken in other IEEE standards (e.g., IEEE 802.2 LLC or IEEE 802.1 Layer Management) or other protocols (e.g., TCP/IP).

2a	Link layer	Media Access Control
1	Physical layer	

Figure 3.2: Working levels of Ethernet

The Ethernet standard is composed of the following components: the Media Access Control protocol (MAC), Physical Signalling (PLS), the Attachment Unit Interface (AUI), the Medium Dependent Interface (MDI) and the Physical Medium Attachment (PMA).

3.2 The IEEE 802.3 Standard

The working group 802 of the American Institute of Electrical & Electronic Engineers (IEEE) officially started defining the first LAN standard in February 1980. This standard converted the specifications of the DIX consortium (DEC, Intel, and Xerox), Ethernet Version 1 into an internationally recognized standard. In December 1982, the IEEE 802.3 document first saw the light of day as "Carrier Sense Multiple Access with Collision Detection (CSMA/CD)" for yellow Ethernet (10Base5) as an unapproved standard. In the same month, the DIX group published the specifications for Ethernet Version 2. Ethernet V.2 is considered an adaptation of Ethernet V.1 to the IEEE draft. Work began on the Cheapernet Standard (10Base2). In June 1983, 802.3 was ratified as an unapproved standard by the IEEE Standards Board and in December 1984 by the American National Standards Institute. In the same year, work began on Ethernet on Broadband (10Base36) and on the StarLAN (1Base5) specifications. In 1985, the Ethernet Standard was published worldwide as the ISO/DIS

8802/3 standard. The magic number of 100 manufacturers supporting this standard was exceeded in this year. In 1986, several smaller companies began to transmit Ethernet data on four-wire lines. Work began in the IEEE 802.3 committee for the new Ethernet on Twisted Pair standard. At the same time, a new working group was created, which was intended to investigate Ethernet communication on fiber optic lines. In 1988, Ethernet on Twisted Pair (Pre Standard) products and multi-protocol routers were marketed in Europe. In February 1990, the IEEE 802.3 standard was published as an international ISO standard. In 1991, the 10BaseT standard (Ethernet on Twisted Pair) was approved after lengthy discussions. The first promising products for the wireless (radio) LAN appeared in the Ethernet sector. This technology enabled wireless communication in the in-house sector between Ethernet devices and offered a genuine alternative to conventional cabling at a time when cable ducts were full and installation costs were rising. In the following year (1992), the 10BaseF standard followed (Ethernet on fiber optic). At the start of 1995, the 100 Bit/s standard for Ethernet was published.

3.2.1 Physical Signalling Services

The MAC layer and the Physical layer communicate with one another via a common interface. This interface is not specified as a logical or physical interface but defined in the form of service primitives and parameters. The exchange of data between two MAC layers is controlled via these service primitives.

3.2.2 Physical Line Signalling

Physical Line Signalling (PLS) serves to exchange data between two MAC layers. This sublayer is used to control medium access (CSMA/CD) and signals special conditions of the physical medium (e.g., medium occupied/idle, collision occurred, etc.). These functions were implemented in the transceiver, also known as the Media Access Unit (MAU).

The IEEE 802.3 standard specifies that the end systems, PCs and workstations, can be installed at a certain distance from the actual connection point to the transmission medium. In a typical Ethernet configuration, only an absolute minimum of electronics is required directly at the access point to the transmission medium. The Ethernet MAU contains only the functions which are required for access to the medium. This means that the MAU can be constructed relatively simply (chipset). The repair and maintenance of the MAU are reduced to a minimum or dispensed with entirely. By standardizing the Attachment Unit Interface, the actual end system becomes independent of the physical medium. The entire IEEE 802.3 logic can therefore be implemented in one or more chipsets directly on the Ethernet controller. This model reduces the costs of the relevant products significantly.

The AUI and MAU do not have to be designed as individual separate components in all cases. As can be seen also in the example of the 10Base2 and 10BaseT standards, the MAU and AUI are located directly on the actual Ethernet controller.

The MAU assumes the following functions under IEEE 802.3:

- Transmission of the signals onto the medium

- Reception of the signals from the medium

- Determining freedom to signal on the medium

- Monitoring the data for collisions

The Attachment Unit Interface consists physically of the following five pairs of conductors:

- Data Out: transmits the data from the station to the MAU

- Data In: transmits the data from the MAU to the end system

- Control In: used to transmit control signals from the MAU to the end system

- Control Out: optional signal for the transmission of control signals between the end system and MAU

- Voltage: voltage supply to the MAU via the end system

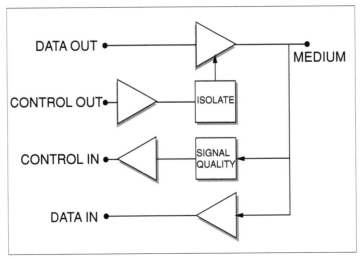

Figure 3.3: General diagram of the MAU model

3.2.3 The AUI Interface

The connection between the transceiver and the end system is made via the Attachment Unit Interface (AUI). This connection is always made between the Ethernet controller (Network Interface Card: NIC) of the end system and the transceiver via a transceiver cable (drop cable). The following interface characteristics were established in the IEEE 802.3 specifications:

End system: socket (DTE)

Transceiver: plug (DCE)

A 15 pin subminiature D plug connector with slide locking was specified as the plug. This lockable plug connector of the AUI interface is specified by the military standard MIL-C-24308-1972.

3.2.4 The Manchester Code

The data prepared by the interface is coded according to the Manchester process. In the Manchester code, the first half of the bit value always contains the complementary value, while the second half contains the true value of the bit to be represented. This process ensures that there is no identical signal resulting on the cable, even when transmitting several identical bits in succession.

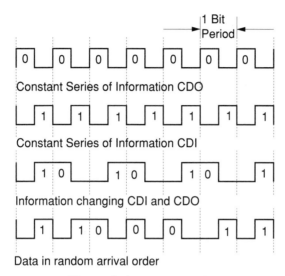

Figure 3.4: Manchester Code

The length of a bit period is 100 nanoseconds. Since in the baseband tech-nology, no clock is available for synchronization between the transmitter and receiver, Manchester encoding is used to generate the clock signals. For this reason, the Manchester code is also termed the self-clocking code. In the CSMA/CD mechanism, an occupied medium is established by means of a car-rier on the cable. Since no separate carrier frequency is used in the baseband process, the carrier must be generated from the signals on the cable. The car-rier is determined using the level values after 0.75 and/or 1.25 bit periods. If a level change occurs after this time, there is a carrier on the cable. In all other cases, the medium is considered unoccupied.

The voltage on Ethernet cable is between –2.2 Volt and 0 Volt with a current of between –90 mA and 0 mA. By using the Manchester code, it is ensured that there is no identical signal resulting on the cable, even when transmitting sev-eral identical bits in succession.

3.2.5 The AUI Cable

The AUI cable is composed of four (with the option of five) individually shield-ed symmetrical twisted pairs of conductors. A general cable shield (S) is also offered for protection against radiation from outside and/or inversely protects the environment from high-frequency radiation, which is emitted as a result of the datastreams. The impedance of the cable is 78 Ohm. The maximum length of the transceiver cable is limited to 50m. Some manufacturers (e.g., DEC) in the Ethernet field reduce the maximum cable lengths for security reasons to 40 m. Some hardware installations (e.g., PC cards) dispense with the use of this type of cable. In these solutions, the transceiver is integrated directly into the Ethernet controller.

3.2.6 Physical Medium Attachment (PMA)

The Physical Medium Attachment (PMA) and the Medium Dependent Interface (MDI) together form the actual transceiver in the IEEE 802.3 standard. The Physical Medium Attachment here represents the functional interface to the medium.

The Physical Medium Attachment (PMA) interface provides the following functions:

Transmit Function

The transmission of serial data bit streams onto the medium. When transmitting data packets, it must be ensured that a maximum of only two complete bit cells are lost, despite the low pass behavior of the medium. If possible, the second bit transmitted onto the cable should already correspond to the time conditions and the relevant signal levels. The delay occurring in the transmission of bits between the MAU interface (Data Out; DO) and the cable must not be greater than half a bit cell. It must also be ensured that the collision function is activated by the MAU after the Data Output conductor is in idle mode.

Receive Function

The reception of serial data bit streams via the medium. The MAU receiver and the end system must have an AC connection via a coupler. When transmitting data packets from the medium to the end system, it must be ensured that a maximum of only five complete bit cells are lost, despite the low pass behavior of the medium. If possible, the second bit transmitted onto the cable should already correspond to the time conditions specified in the standard and the relevant signal levels. The delay occurring in the transmission of bits between the cable and the receiver circuit must not be greater than half a bit cell. The bandwidth of the receiver function is restricted to 50 MHz.

Collision Function

This function is used to detect collisions on the medium. The Signal Quality Error (SQE) is transmitted by the MAU via the Control In (CI) lines. The SQE signal is represented by a negative frequency with half the bit rate (BR/2). In the case of standard Ethernet, this frequency is 2.5 MHz. The SQE mechanism makes it possible for the MAU to report the following conditions to the end system:

- An invalid signal was received on the medium.

- A collision was detected.

The collision signal must be present on the CI line at the latest 9 bit periods after the voltage level on the medium has exceeded the collision detection mark. Exceeding of the collision detection mark on the medium, however requires that at least two or more MAUs are transmitting on the cable at the same time. The possibility must be avoided under all circumstances that the collision level may be exceeded with only one active MAU.

Jabber Function

The jabber function was integrated into the IEEE 802.3 standard in order to prevent one station from occupying the medium for an impermissibly long period of time. This interruption mechanism guarantees that no MAU transmits data onto the medium for longer than 30 successive milliseconds. If this transmission window is exceeded, the data transfer onto the medium is interrupted automatically by the MAU hardware. At the same time, SQE signals are transmitted continuously to the end system. The SQE signals have the effect that the Ethernet end system interrupts the transmission procedure. The jabber function in the MAU is suspended either by breaking off transmission or by deactivating the power supply to the MAU.

Monitor Function

The optional monitor function enables the transmission function onto the medium to be deactivated. The collision detection and reception functions are retained, however. Using the isolate message, the end system informs the MAU either that it should remain in monitor mode or transfer into this mode. The isolate mode must be entered at the latest 20 ms after receipt of the signal. The isolate signal is represented by a negative frequency with half the bit rate (BR/2). In the case of standard Ethernet, this frequency is 2.5 MHz.

3.2.7 Medium Dependent Interface (MDI)

The Physical Medium Attachment (PMA) and Medium Dependent Interface (MDI) together form the actual transceiver (MAU) in the IEEE 802.3 standard. The Medium Dependent Interface (MDI) here assumes the physical interface to the medium. The transceiver is the link between the end system and the actual medium via which the data is transferred. This interface is designed differently in the various substandards. For this reason, the relevant specifications are given in separate medium-specific publications.

3.3   10Base5

In the 10Base5 standard (Yellow Cable), the connection to the cable is made via standard N connectors or taps. The outer shielding and insulation of the coaxial cable are removed down to the copper core (inner conductor) with the aid of a special tool (drill) during tap assembly. By using this method, the inner conductor is connected to the transceiver by means of a thin contact tip on the tap. The cable shielding and the earth conductor of the transceiver are connected to the cable by means of small clamping claws in the tap. The installation of a tap can be performed without affecting continuous operation of the network, in contrast to the screw process for the standard N connectors.

3.4   10Base2

In the 10Base2 standard, the transceiver is installed directly on the Ethernet controller of the end station. The connection of the end station to the thin Ethernet is made directly via BNC sockets and tees. Certain authors claim repeatedly in the literature that because of the small physical distances between components and conductors on the controller card, integration of the transceiver leads to considerable risks for the network. The standard clearly defines a voltage dielectric strength for the transceiver of up to 2.5 kV. It must not be possible, even under the most unfavorable conditions conceivable, for mains voltage to cross over onto the card and the network because of a defect in the computer.

3.5 Media Access Control

The Media Access Control (MAC) layer is to be found on layer 2A of the OSI reference model and forms the intermediate layer between the Physical layer and the higher protocols. The MAC layer defines the access process onto the medium and establishes the transmission and reception procedures. The Media Access Control standard is totally independent of the underlying physical circumstances of the transmission medium (e.g., coaxial, twisted pair, broadband, fiber optics). The Carrier Sense Multiple Access with Collision Detection (CSMA/CD) mechanism contained in the Media Access Control standard guarantees the equal privileges (Multiple Access) of all stations on the network. All Ethernet stations have unrestricted access to the network at all times and on every occasion. The CSMA/CD mechanism controls access to the medium. Before every transmission, a check is made as to whether the medium is free for the transmission of data (Carrier Sense) or occupied. Since no carrier frequency can be used in the Ethernet baseband process, it is also not possible to detect a carrier.

The presence of a carrier in the baseband process is achieved using a special mechanism. The following specifications are made for that purpose: the signals of a transmitting station are evaluated as quasi-carriers. This may lead to a station detecting that the medium is free, although another Ethernet station at the other end of the cable has already transmitted data onto the medium. For this reason, it takes a certain time until a collision is clearly detected. In the Ethernet broadband process, the Ethernet data is modulated onto the carrier frequencies. For this reason, it is possible to talk clearly of a Carrier Sense Mechanism in this process.

If the medium was already occupied by another station, the station defers transmission of the data to a later time. If the idle state was established, in which the medium is recognized as free, transmission of the data occurs after a defined period of time has elapsed. This period of time is described as the interframe gap and is 9.6 µs (96 bit periods) long. The interframe gap describes the smallest interval permissible between two data packets on the network. The data is transmitted onto the medium in a bit serial process. The transmitted signal is received once more on the receiver conductor for checks, after a delay of 18 bits (1.8 µs). The cable used for transmission is a transmission medium with a low pass characteristic. For this reason, some bits are lost in transmission onto the cable and in the transient reaction in the receiver. These bits are termed dribbling bits. Because these bits are lost only from the first bits of the 7-8 byte long preamble, these missing bits go unnoticed.

MAC Layer Transmission Function

1. A datagram is transported from a higher layer (LLC or another protocol) to the receiver section of the MAC layer.

2. Next, the MAC layer creates the data packet from the following components:

   - Preamble
   - Start frame delimiter
   - Destination address
   - Source address
   - Type field (for Ethernet), length field (for IEEE 802.3)
   - Data field with the protocol information from the higher layers
   - If less than a 48 byte data field is transmitted, the data field is filled out to the minimum length using the padding function

3. After the data packet has been generated, the transmission MAC module calculates the value of the Cyclic Redundancy Check and inserts this into the CRC field.

4. The entire data packet is transported to the transmission MAC management module.

5. The transmission MAC management module prepares a serial datastream for transmission onto the medium.

6. Afterwards, a check is made as to whether the medium is free for transmission of serial information.

7. If the medium is occupied, transmission of the serial information is deferred.

8. If a medium is free, the interframe gap time (9.6 µs) is waited and then the serial data is transmitted onto the network.

9. During transmission, a check is made, as to whether a collision has occurred.

10. If the transmission ends without a collision, the transmission procedure is considered complete, and the next data packet can be transmitted.

11. If a collision occurs, further steps are taken:

    • Transmission of the bit serial datastream is interrupted immediately.

    • A jam signal is transmitted onto the medium.

    • After a waiting period, the serial data is prepared once more for transmission onto the medium.

    • After 16 failed attempts, transmission of this data packet is broken off and the data discarded.

    • An error message is then passed to the higher layers.

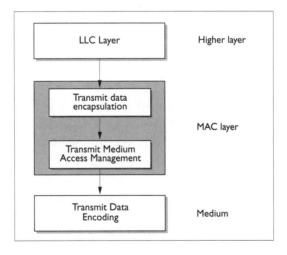

Figure 3.5: MAC layer transmission function

MAC Layer Reception Function

1. All data packets are received from the network. Only those data packets which are intended for the local receiver are processed further; all other data packets are discarded.

2. Next, the received data packet is checked for errors by the receiver MAC module using the CRC value. If an error is established, the data packet is discarded.

3. In the event of a valid data packet, the following components are separated from the data packet:

   - Preamble
   - Start frame delimiter
   - Destination address
   - Source address
   - Type field (for Ethernet), length field (for IEEE 802.3)
   - Any padding characters contained in the data field

4. The following checks are made on the remaining data field:

   - Check whether the data field has the correct length (IEEE 802.3)
   - Check the length of the data field is a multiple of 8 bits

If an error is determined, the data field is discarded.

5. In the case of a valid data field, the data field is transported to the relevant higher protocol with the specific protocol information.

The CSMA/CD mechanism can mean that two or more stations determine at the same time that the medium is free. This leads to these stations accessing the medium and transmitting their data simultaneously. This inevitably leads to the electrical signals colliding on the medium and the transmitted information being lost through the signal collision. The collision of the signals leads to the current and voltage on the cable increasing. This increase is evaluated by the collision detection mechanism in the transceiver. Collisions occur only during a relatively short period after transmitting the data. This time connection corresponds to the CSMA/CD parameter slot time (= 52 bit periods). The slot time defines the maximum period until the unambiguous occupation of the medium by a station, after this period no other collision may occur on Ethernet.

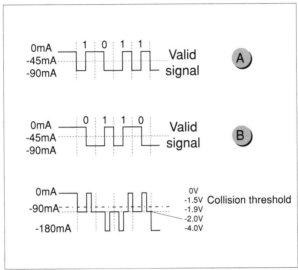

Figure 3.6: Collision on coaxial cable

If a threshold value of -1.5 Volt is exceeded on the cable, the transceiver generates a collision signal (constant 10 MHz signal). The transmitter thereby interrupts the transmission procedure and generates a 32-48 bit long jam signal. This jam signal is used to make it clear that a collision has occurred and consists of the following 10101010-10101010-10101010-10101010 (10101010-10101010) bit combination. After breaking off transmission and after transmitting the jam signal, a particular time must be waited (truncated binary exponential backoff) before a new transmission attempt can be made. It can of course occur that there is a further collision when transmitting data in a repeated transmission attempt. The transmission attempt is suspended once more. The waiting time, which determines at what time the medium can be accessed again, is changed dynamically. This process sets the maximum number of attempts at 16 (attempt limit). From the tenth attempt onwards, the waiting time is kept constant (backoff limit). This process ensures that several stations do not attempt to occupy the medium at one and the same time in a recurring sequence. This mechanism can be described most simply using the following example: After the first collision, each station participating in the collision tosses a two-sided coin and attempts to access the medium using the value established. If a collision occurs again, each station participating in the collision tosses a four-sided coin and attempts are made to access the medium using the value obtained. This process is continued up to the tossing of a 1024 sided coin.

3.6 Collision Mechanism

The maximum round trip delay must not be exceeded, using the round trip delay for the individual components in the overall data path between the transmitter and receiver. The IEEE 802.3 standard defines a Maximum Round Trip Delay (RTD) in the LAN of 64 + 512 = 576 bit periods. The period defined as the Maximum Round Trip Delay is the time which an Ethernet packet requires within a particular network topology in order to cover the distance to the furthest station and back to the transmitter station. The RTD value fundamentally determines the restriction of the physical expanse of the network. If this value is exceeded (RTD > 576 bits), the collision mechanism fails to function and the stations on the network can no longer establish clearly that the medium is occupied. This leads to the fact that communication can no longer function unambiguously under certain circumstances. This is generally expressed by the occurrence of "late collisions." Late collisions are collisions which occur after the first 64 bytes (512 bits) have been transmitted onto the network.

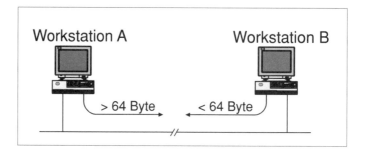

Figure 3.7: Late Collision

The recommended planning base for a network planner is therefore a value of RTD < 480 bits.

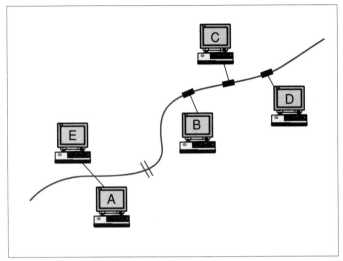

Figure 3.8: Network structure

In the network configuration shown in the Figure 3.8, communication proceeds as follows:

1. Station A begins to transmit.

2. After transmitting 64 bits, the collision mechanism is activated.

3. The signal propagates in the direction of station D.

4. Station D begins to transmit just before the signal from station A is detected.

5. The signals collide on the network medium.

6. Station A continues to transmit the signals, since the signal has not yet been received by station D.

7. Station D activates the collision detection mechanism after transmission of the first 64 bits and detects the collision. Station D thereupon transmits a jam signal.

8. Station D interrupts the transmission procedure and moves into the backoff mechanism. This leads to a delay in a repeated attempt to access the medium.

9. Station A detects the collision and transmits a jam signal itself.

10. Station A then interrupts transmission of the data.

11. Station A receives no further signal from station D and initiates the transmission delay before a fresh transmission attempt for the data packet in question.

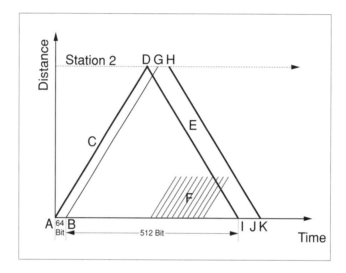

Figure 3.9: Collision mechanism 1

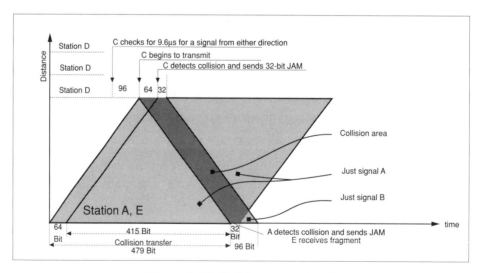

Figure 3.10: Collision mechanism 2

In the network configuration shown in Figure 3.10, communication proceeds as follows:

1. Station A begins to transmit.

2. After transmitting 64 bits, the collision mechanism is activated.

3. The signal propagates in the direction of station B.

4. Station B begins to transmit just before the signal from station A is detected.

5. The signals collide on the network medium.

6. Station B activates the collision detection mechanism after transmission of the first 64 bits and detects the collision. Station B thereupon transmits a jam signal.

7. Station B interrupts the transmission procedure and moves into the backoff mechanism.

8. Station A detects the collision and transmits a jam signal itself, interrupts transmission of the data and initiates the transmission delay before a fresh transmission attempt for the data packet in question.

9. Station E receives a data fragment following the collision

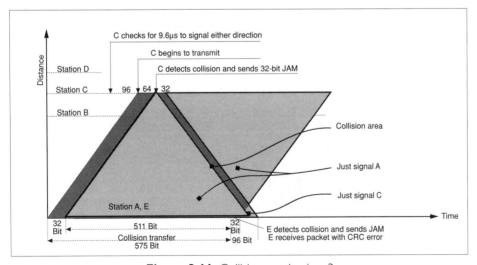

Figure 3.11: Collision mechanism 3

In the network configuration shown in Figure 3.11, communication proceeds as follows:

1. Station A begins to transmit.

2. After transmitting 64 bits, the collision mechanism is activated.

3. The signal propagates in the direction of station D.

4. Station C begins to transmit just before the signal from station A is detected.

5. The signals collide on the network medium.

6. Station A continues to transmit the signals, since the signal from station C has not yet been received.

7. Station C activates the collision detection mechanism after transmission of the first 64 bits and detects the collision. Station C thereupon transmits a jam signal.

8. Station C interrupts the transmission procedure and moves into the backoff mechanism.

9. Station A detects the collision and transmits a jam signal itself, interrupts transmission of the data and initiates the transmission delay before a fresh transmission attempt for the data packet in question.

10. Station E receives a data packet with CRC errors.

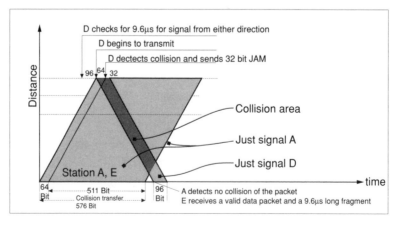

Figure 3.12: Collision mechanism 4

In the network configuration shown in Figure 3.12, communication proceeds as follows:

1. Station A begins to transmit.

2. After transmitting 64 bits, the collision mechanism is activated.

3. The signal propagates in the direction of station D.

4. Station D begins to transmit just before the signal from station A is detected.

5. The signals collide on the network medium.

6. Station A continues to transmit the signals.

7. After the transmission of 576 bits, the medium is considered occupied and the collision mechanism of station A is deactivated.

8. Station D activates the collision detection mechanism after transmission of the first 64 bits and detects the collision. Station D thereupon transmits a jam signal.

9. Station D interrupts the transmission procedure and moves into the backoff mechanism.

10. Station A continues to transmit data and does not detect the collision.

11. Station E receives a valid data packet and a 9.6 µs long fragment.

In order to find out whether the network design has a permissible configuration, the delay times of all components located in the communication path must be determined. The following guide values apply for the delay times of Ethernet components currently available on the market:

Ethernet controller transmitting direction:	3 bits
Ethernet controller receiving direction:	7 bits
Transceiver cable:	2.5 bits
Transceiver transmitting direction:	3 bits
Transceiver receiving direction:	5 bits
Network segment:	22 bits

Repeater: 8 bits

Inter-repeater link: 25 bits

Only by calculating the delay times precisely, can it be predicted with certainty whether the configuration in a network is valid or invalid.

3.7 Physical Medium

The IEEE 802.3 (Ethernet) standard initially supported only transmission on coaxial cable. Over the years, this standard was adapted to the widest possible range of media. The relevant substandard specifies the particular characteristics of the Physical layer. Various reference values arise independently of the medium (cable type, modulation) and transmission speed. A simple code here enables allocation to the relevant implementations. This code is composed of three components, the transmission rate (in Mbit/s), the transmission type (baseband/broadband) and the maximum segment length (x 100m) (or of the medium used)

10Base5   Standard Ethernet (Yellow Cable)

10Base2   Cheapernet or Thin Ethernet

10BaseT   Ethernet on Twisted Pair

10BaseF   Ethernet on Fiber Optics

10Base36   Ethernet on broadband

1Base5   StarLAN

100BaseX   Fast Ethernet

3.7.1 Standard Ethernet

The Ethernet process was first established as a standard in the 10Base5 implementation. The maximum data rate is 10 Mbit/s in this baseband transmission process. The data is encoded on the medium according to the Manchester process. A Mean Time Between Failures (MTBF) value was established at 1 million hours in the standard for the 10Base5 MAU. The bit error rate for the physical medium is 10^{-8}. Thick Ethernet was used as the cable for the network medium. Since the standard specifies the color yellow for this cable, it is often referred to in the literature as Yellow Cable. An Ethernet segment for the 10Base5 standard may be a maximum of 500m. Such a cable segment may consist of several individual sections, which are connected to one another via connector plugs. Up to a maximum of 5 cable segments (total length 2.5 km) can be connected using repeaters as interconnection components. The standard defines a maximum Round Trip Delay (RTD) for such a configuration over the entire LAN of 64 + 512 = 576 bit periods. If this value (RTD > 576 bits) is exceeded, the collision mechanism fails to function. A recommended planning basis for this value is RTD < 480 bits. The yellow cable must be prepared using "N" standard connector plugs and a terminator must be provided at both ends (50 Ohm + 1% with an output of 1 Watt). The terminators prevent possible signal reflections. The cable segments must be earthed on one side (terminator) according to the standard.

The end station attachment onto the cable is always performed via transceivers (taps or N connectors). There are markings on the cable at 2.5 m intervals for transceiver fitting. The distance between two transceivers should be n*2.5 m. A maximum of 100 transceivers can be attached per cable segment. The connection between the transceiver and the end station is achieved via the AUI interface and the Ethernet drop cable.

The essential reference figures of the 10Base5 standard are:

Table 3.1: Key features of the 10 Broad 5 standard

- 50 Ohm coaxial cable

- signalling technology: baseband

- topology: bus

- maximum transmission rate: 10 Mbit/s

- encoding: Manchester code

- maximum segment length: 500 m

- maximum network distance between two stations 2800 m

- maximum number of stations per segment: 100

- minimum distance between two stations: 2.5 m

- connection to the medium: AUI interface via transceiver cable

3.7.2 The 10Base2 Standard

The 10Base2 implementation was developed in the years 1983-1984 and published in 1987 as an annex to the IEEE 802.3 standard. The maximum data rate in this baseband transmission process is 10 Mbit/s. The data is encoded on the medium according to the Manchester process. A Mean Time Between Failures (MTBF) value was established in the standard at 100,000 hours. The bit error rate for the physical medium is 10^{-7}. Thin Ethernet (RG-58 A/U or RG-58 C/U) was used as the cable for the network medium. The length of an Ethernet segment is only 185 m because of the maximum permissible attenuation of 8.5 dB at 10 MHz. Such a cable segment may consist of several individual sections, which are connected to one another via BNC connector plugs. Up to a maximum of 5 cable segments (total length 925 m) can be connected using repeaters as interconnection components. The standard defines a maximum Round Trip Delay (RTD) for such a configuration over the entire LAN of 64 + 512 = 576 bit periods. If this value (RTD > 576 bits) is exceeded, the collision mechanism fails to function. A fixed component of this physical standard is the integration of transceiver functions into the 10Base2 devices. The Cheapernet cable is prepared using "BNC" standard connector plugs, and a terminator must be provided at both ends of 0.5 Watt 50 Ohm (+ 1%). The terminators prevent possible signal reflections. The cable segments must be earthed on one side (terminator) according to the standard.

Table 3.2: Key features of the 10 Broad 2 standard

* 50 Ohm coaxial cable
* signalling technology: baseband
* maximum transmission rate: 10 Mbit/s
* encoding: Manchester code
* topology: bus
* maximum segment length: 185 m
* maximum number of stations per segment: 30
* minimum distance between two stations: 0.5 m
* connection to the medium: direct via BNC plug or via AUI interface

3.7.3 Ethernet on Twisted Pair Cables

As early as 1986, some smaller US companies started to achieve transmission of Ethernet data on four-wire lines. Standardization was achieved in the IEEE 802.3 committee in the Ethernet on Twisted Pair working group. The

Ethernet on Twisted Pair standard (10BaseT) was published in 1991. The following objectives were pursued by the 10BaseT standardization committee:

- It was intended to create an opportunity by means of which Ethernet would be extended onto the physical medium of twisted pair cable.

- The twisted pair products were intended to be not only cheaper but also easier to install and to use.

- The twisted pair products had to be compatible with the Ethernet standards already in widespread use. This guaranteed protection for investment which had already been made.

- It was intended to make the transition from the twisted pair technology to other products using simple interconnection techniques (e.g., repeaters).

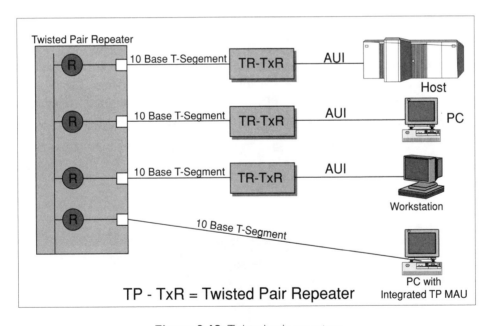

Figure 3.13: Twisted pair repeaters

The maximum data rate is 10 Mbit/s in the 10BaseT standard. The baseband transmission process is also used on the twisted pair cables. The data is encoded on the medium according to the Manchester process. A Mean Time Between Failure (MTBF) value was established in the standard for the 10BaseT MAU at 100 000 hours. The bit error rate for the physical medium is 10^{-7}. An Unshielded Twisted Pair (UTP) cable was used as the cable with an impedance of 100 Ohm + 15%. The length of a twisted pair Ethernet segment is only 100 m because of the maximum permissible attenuation of 11.5 dB at 10 MHz (UTP cable with 0.5 mm core diameter = AWG 24). The Round Trip Delay for such a link segment is a maximum of 1000 ns. The maximum jitter is 5 ns per twisted pair connection. The 10BaseT cabling is structurally star-shaped cabling. A link status test was integrated for each 10BaseT port. The 10BaseT repeaters must be capable of separating network segments if failures occur in that segment. Since each attachment point is separately amplified, this means that in the event of a failure behind this attachment point, the relevant port must be switched off automatically. This ensures that the continued functional ability of the remaining ports is not affected.

The 10BaseT MAU is divided into the following fields as with all other Ethernet standards: the Physical Medium Attachment (PMA) and the Medium Dependent Interface (MDI). The Physical Medium Attachment here assumes the functional interface and the Medium Dependent Interface provides the physical interface to the medium. RJ-45 technology was specified for standard connectors in Ethernet on Twisted Pair. An 8 pin RJ-45 socket is provided as a standard MDI interface.

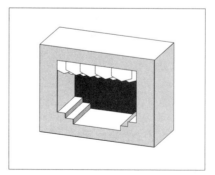

Figure 3.14: MAU MDI socket

The only standard plug for twisted pair cabling in the Ethernet field is the 8 pin RJ-45 plug (also termed the Western plug). This plug is known from telephone technology. It is available in a shielded and unshielded design. Assembly is performed using insulation piercing techniques with a special crimping clip.

The individual contacts of the 8 pin RJ-45 plug are used as follows:

Contact	Signal
1	Transmit +
2	Transmit -
3	Receive +
4	Unused
5	Unused
6	Receive -
7	Unused
8	Unused

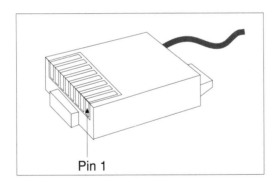

Pin 1

Figure 3.15: RJ-45 plug

Link Integrity Function

The link integrity test is a permanent component of the 10BaseT standard. Since the transmission process over the twisted pair lines is a purely simplex process, it must be ensured that the connection between the two end stations is active in both directions. Link integrity signals are transmitted, in addition to the actual data signals, to the relevant opposite MAUs at regular intervals by the twisted pair repeater as well as by the twisted pair connected end station. The frequency of the link integrity signals is 1 MHz. After a data packet has been sent, it takes 16 + 8 ms until the transmitter generates a link integrity signal. If a TP port receives no link integrity signals over a period of between 50 ms and 150 ms, this connection is considered broken and an error message is generated. If 2 - 10 successive link integrity signals are received from the other communication partner, the connection is reactivated and the regular data can be transmitted. This function is triggered by the auto-partition/reconnection algorithm defined in the 10BaseT standard. The algorithm allows the repeater to switch off a port automatically, if the latter shows a fault and reactivate the port automatically if the fault is remedied. In this way, the defective port is deactivated and not the entire repeater.

The essential reference values for the 10BaseT standard are:

Table 3.3: Key features of the 10BaseT standard

- 100 Ohm twisted pair cable
- signalling technology: baseband
- maximum transmission rate: 10 Mbit/s
- encoding: Manchester code
- topology: star
- maximum segment length: 100 m
- monitoring of link connection by idle signal
- plug construction: 8 pin RJ-45
- connection to the medium: directly via RJ-45 plug or via AUI interface

3.7.4 Ethernet on Fiber Optics

Fiber optics have been used on the lowest layer of the OSI reference model for over 10 years as a transmission medium. The data is not transmitted as with copper conductors in the form of electrical signals but instead in the form of light. Ethernet on fiber optics has been established definitively in the IEEE 802.3 standard (10BaseF) since 1993. The IEEE specifications can be divided into the following three subgroups: the 10BaseFP, 10BaseFL and 10BaseFB specifications.

Passive Technology (10BaseFP)

The 10BaseFP standard describes all the functions necessary for data transmission between end station using passive fiber optics technology. The 10BaseFP standard is divided into the following components:

- 10BaseFP Medium Attachment Unit (MAU)

- 10BaseFP passive star coupler

- 10BaseFP repeater

10BaseFP Medium Attachment Unit (MAU)

The 10BaseFP MAU (transceiver) connects the end station (DTE) or repeater via fiber optics with a passive star coupler. The attachment of this end station to the 10BaseFP fiber optic cable is performed either directly via the 10BaseFP Ethernet transceiver integrated on the Ethernet controller or via an AUI interface (drop cable), whereby external the transceiver enables adaptation to the 10BaseFP standard. The maximum length of the attached 10BaseFP link segment is 500 m. The data rate for the 10BaseFP standard is set at 10 Mbit/s.

10BaseFP Star Coupler

The maximum length of the link segment between the MAU and the passive star coupler is 500 m. The maximum communication path via the passive star coupler between two 10BaseFP MAUs is 1000 m. The use of passive star couplers is recommended only in data networks, for which there are no supplies or only a reliable voltage supply guaranteed on the site. The ports of a passive star coupler may show a maximum throughput attenuation of 16 to 20 dB between input and output. Because of the passive technology, this means that the star coupler can be equipped with a maximum of only 33 ports. A mean time between failure (MTBF) was established in the IEEE 802.3 standard at 10 million hours. The optical transmission output of a passive port is –15 dB to –11 dB. The input sensitivity of a port is between –27 dB and –41 dB. The maximum attenuation of a connection and of all components connected in that connection is between 16 dB and 26 dB.

10BaseFP Repeater

A repeater is defined as a 10BaseFP repeater if it has at least a 10BaseFP MAU. Since the light signals transmitted by 10BaseFP standard components are not compatible with the 10BaseFL and 10BaseFB standards, connection between the individual standards on the Physical layer can therefore be achieved only via a repeater.

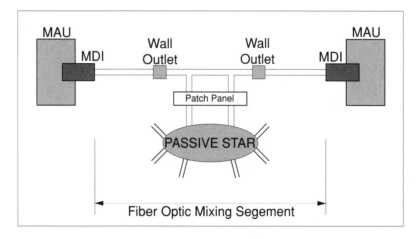

Figure 3.16: 10BaseFP components in a network

PMA-MDI Signal Coding

When transporting data from the Physical Medium Attachment sublayer to the Medium Dependent Interface, the first 40 bits of the preamble are recoded. The reason for this additional mechanism lies in the guarantee of synchronization and the detection of collisions in passive systems. The first 40 bits of a preamble are replaced by the following bit patterns:

•   Synchronization pattern

•   Packet header code rule violation

•   Unique word

Synchronization Pattern

The 4 bit long synchronization pattern is encoded according to the Manchester process and contains the following bit pattern: 1010

Packet Header Code Rule Violation

Using the 4 bit long packet header code rule violation field, a special bit pattern is created differing from the Manchester process. The field contains the following: 1, MV0, 0, 1. The Manchester Code Violation Zero (MV0) bit is encoded according to the rules of the Manchester process. In this case, the first half of the bit value does not contain the complementary value of the second bit half of the bit to be represented. The MV0 bit is the only bit which does not correspond to the Manchester conditions during a valid data transmission.

Unique Word

The 32 bit long Unique Word field ensures that the preambles of the MAUs attached to the 10BaseFP star coupler are constructed differently. The 32 bits can be divided as follows:

- 12 bit Organizationally Unique Identifier (OUI)

- 20 bit 10BaseFP MAU ID

The OUI identifier is issued centrally by the IEEE committee to the relevant manufacturer. The MAU identification number (ID) must be used by the relevant manufacturer as a unique feature.

There then follow the remaining 16 bits of the preamble (10101010 10101010), the start frame delimiter (10101011) and the actual Ethernet header information.

10BaseFP Collisions

The 10BaseFP standard also ensures that collisions are detected unambiguously and propagated across the network. If a collision is established, the transmitter interrupts transmission of the data packet. The transmitter next generates a 33 bit long data packet with the following structure: <MV0> <Unique Word>.

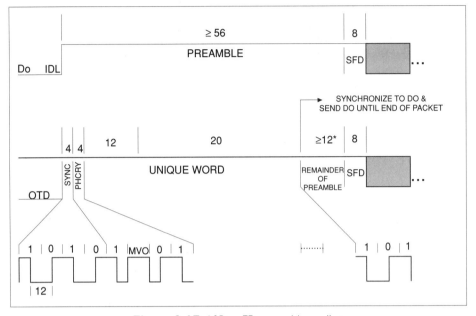

Figure 3.17: 10BaseFP preamble coding

Table 3.4: Key points of the 10 Broad FP Standard

- fiber optic cable
- signalling technology: baseband
- maximum transmission rate: 10 Mbit/s
- encoding: Manchester code
- topology: star
- maximum segment length: 500 m
- transmission type: asynchronous
- connection to the medium: directly via fiber optic plugs (ST) or via AUI interface

The 10BaseFL Standard

The 10BaseFL standard describes all the functions required for data transmission between end stations using active fiber optics technology. The data is transmitted asynchronously, as in the 10BaseFL standard, and corresponds essentially to the provisions specified in the Fiber Optic Inter Repeater Link

(FOIRL) standard. The 10BaseFL standard is divided into the following components:

- 10BaseFL Medium Attachment Unit
- 10BaseFL repeater

The 10BaseFL MAU (transceiver) connects the end station (DTE) or repeater with the fiber optic medium. The attachment of this end station to the 10BaseFL fiber optic cable is performed either directly via the 10BaseFL Ethernet transceiver integrated on the Ethernet controller or via an AUI interface (drop cable), whereby the external transceiver enables adaptation to the 10BaseFL standard. The 10BaseFL standard guarantees that the signals are generated to full power in each device attached to the network. Each port of a 10BaseFL star coupler has an integrated fully compliant 10BaseFL MAU. The maximum length of the attached 10BaseFL link segment between two 10BaseFL MAUs is 2000 m. The maximum length of a 10BaseFL link segment between a 10BaseFL MAU and an FOIRL MAU is 1000 m. The data rate for the 10BaseFL standard is set at 10 Mbit/s. The 10BaseFL MAU must provide the following functions: transmission and reception of data, collision detection, jabber, and link integrity test. A mean time between failure (MTBF) was established in the IEEE 802.3 standard for the 10BaseFL MAU at 10 million hours. The optical transmission output of a port is –20 dB to –12 dB. The input sensitivity of a port is between –12 dB and –32.5 dB. Because of the active technology of the 10BaseFL components, the maximum attenuation of a connection and of all components connected in that configuration is between 0 dB and 20.5 dB.

10BaseFL Repeater

A repeater is defined as a 10BaseFL repeater, if it has at least an integrated 10BaseFL MAU. Since a repeater operates on the Physical layer, all higher protocols are ignored and the function is merely signal regeneration of the bit streams. According to the valid IEEE 802.3 specifications, it is never possible to cascade more than 4 repeaters. The standard defines a maximum round trip delay time in the LAN of 64 + 512 = 576 bit periods. If this value (RTD > 576 bits) is exceeded, the collision mechanism fails to function. Since the light signals transmitted by 10BaseFL standard components are not compatible with the 10BaseFP and 10BaseFB standards, connection between the individual 10BaseF standards on the Physical layer can therefore be achieved only via a repeater.

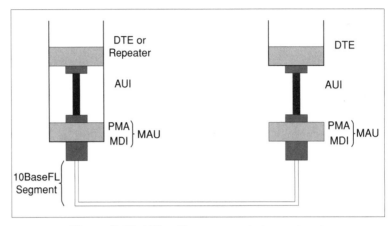

Figure 3.18: 10BaseFL components in a network

10BaseFL Collisions

Collisions in the 10BaseFL standard are defined as the presence of a signal on the reception channel during the transmission of data via the transmission channel. If a collision is established, the transmitter interrupts transmission of the data packet and generates a jam signal.

10BaseFL Jabber

The jabber function was integrated into the 10BaseFL standard in order to prevent one station from occupying the medium for an impermissibly long period of time. This interruption mechanism guarantees that no MAU transmits data onto the medium for longer than 30 successive milliseconds. If this transmission window is exceeded, the data transfer onto the medium is interrupted automatically by the 10BaseFL MAU hardware. At the same time, SQE signals are transmitted continuously to the end station. The SQE signals have the effect that the Ethernet end station interrupts the transmission procedure. The jabber function in the MAU is suspended either by breaking off transmission or by deactivating the power supply to the MAU.

10BaseFL Link Integrity Test

A link integrity test was defined for the 10BaseFL ports. Since Ethernet transmission over fiber optics is a purely simplex process, it must be ensured that the connection between both end stations is active in both directions. In addition to the actual data signals, link integrity signals are transmitted to the relevant opposite MAUs at regular intervals by 10BaseFL repeaters as well as by the 10BaseFL end station. The frequency of the link integrity signals is 1 MHz. After a data packet has been sent, it takes 16 + 8 ms until the transmitter generates a link integrity signal. If a 10BaseFL port receives no link integrity signals over a period of between 50 ms and 150 ms, this connection is considered broken and an error message is generated. If 2–10 successive link integrity signals are received from the other communication partner, the connection is reactivated and the regular data can be transmitted.

Table 3.5: Key points of the 10 Broad FL Standard

- fiber optic cable
- signalling technology: baseband
- maximum transmission rate: 10 Mbit/s
- encoding: Manchester code
- topology: star
- maximum segment length: 2000 / 1000 m
- transmission type: asynchronous
- connection to the medium: directly via fiber optic plugs (ST) or via AUI interface

The 10BaseFB Standard

The 10BaseFB standard describes all the functions required for data transmission between active star couplers. This standard can also be used as a connection of FB MAUs (transceivers) to active star couplers. Synchronous optical transmission technology is used in the 10BaseFB standard. This mechanism means that the star coupler does not have any integrated repeater functions and merely regenerates the incoming information. Because of this, a number of 10BaseFB star couplers can be cascaded and the repeater rules can be ignored. This technology forms the basis for the construction of repeater-free backbone structures. The 10BaseFB standard is divided into the following components:

- 10BaseFB Medium Attachment Unit

- 10BaseFB repeater

10BaseFB MAU

The 10BaseFB MAU (transceiver) connects the end station (DTE) or repeater with the fiber optic medium. The attachment of this end station to the 10BaseFB fiber optic cable is performed either directly via the 10BaseFB Ethernet transceiver integrated on the Ethernet controller or via an AUI interface (drop cable), whereby the external transceiver enables adaptation to the 10BaseFB standard. The 10BaseFB standard guarantees that the signals are generated to full power in each device attached to the network. Each port of a 10BaseFB star coupler has an integrated fully functional 10BaseFB MAU. The maximum length of the attached 10BaseFB link segment between two 10BaseFB MAUs is 2000 m. The maximum data path via a 10BaseFB star coupler between two 10BaseFB MAUs is 4000 m. The data is transmitted according to the synchronous process. Idle signals are transmitted onto the linked segment in the pauses between the data packets. This has the effect that the transmitter and receiver are always synchronized to one another and no data bits are lost in the transmission through the transient reaction. The data rate for the 10BaseFB standard is set at 10 Mbit/s. The 10BaseFB MAU must provide the following functions: transmission and reception of data, collision detection, jabber, and link integrity test. A mean time between failure (MTBF) was established in the IEEE 802.3 standard for the 10BaseFB MAU at 10 million hours. The optical transmission output of a port is –20 dB to –12 dB. The input sensitivity of a port is between –12 dB and –32.5 dB. Because of the active technology of the 10BaseFB components, the maximum attenuation of a connection and of all components connected in that configuration is between 0 dB and 20.5 dB.

10BaseFB Repeater

A repeater is defined as a 10BaseFB repeater if it has at least an integrated 10BaseFB MAU. Since a repeater operates on the Physical layer, all higher protocols are ignored and the function is merely signal regeneration of the bit streams. Since the light signals transmitted by 10BaseFB standard components are not compatible with the 10BaseFP and 10BaseFL standards, connection between the individual 10BaseF standards on the Physical layer can therefore be achieved only via a repeater.

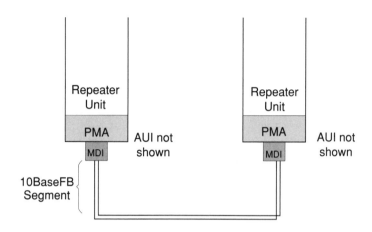

Figure 3.19: 10BaseFB components in a network

Additional Signals

The 10BaseFB standard defines the following additional signal sequences:

- Manchester Code Violation One (MV1)
- Manchester Code Violation Zero (MV0)
- Synchronous Idle (SIDL)
- Remote Fault (RF)

Manchester Code Violation One (MV1)

The Manchester Code Violation One (MV1) bit is encoded according to the rules of the Manchester process. In the case of the MV1 bit, a complete bit cell is set to the value 1.

Manchester Code Violation Zero (MV0)

The Manchester Code Violation Zero (MV0) bit is encoded according to the rules of the Manchester process. In the case of the MV0 bit, a complete bit cell is set to the value 0.

Synchronous Idle (SIDL)

The synchronous idle (SIDL) sequence is formed from the concatenation of MV1, MV1, MV0, and MV0 bits. This sequence results in a frequency of 2.5 MHz. This frequency is used to represent communication pauses between the data packets. The transmission of SIDL symbols is begun immediately after the last data bit of a data packet.

Remote Fault (RF)

The remote fault (RF) sequence is formed from the concatenation of MV1, MV1, MV1, MV0, MV0, and MV0 bits. This sequence results in a frequency of 1.667 MHz. This frequency is used for the notification of remote faults.

Collisions

Collisions in the 10BaseFB standard are defined as the presence of a signal on the reception channel during the transmission of data via the transmission channel. If a collision is established, the transmitter interrupts transmission of the data packet and generates a jam signal.

10BaseFB Jabber

The jabber function was integrated into the 10BaseFB standard in order to prevent one station from occupying the medium for an impermissibly long period of time. This interruption mechanism guarantees that no MAU transmits data onto the medium for longer than 12 successive milliseconds. If this transmission window is exceeded, the data transfer onto the medium is interrupted automatically by the 10BaseFB MAU hardware. At the same time, SQE signals are transmitted continuously to the end station. The SQE signals have the effect that the Ethernet end station interrupts the transmission procedure. The jabber function in the MAU is suspended either by breaking off transmission or by deactivating the power supply to the MAU.

Since Ethernet transmission over fiber optics is a purely simplex process, it must be ensured that the connection between the two end stations is active in both directions. A series of fault conditions were defined for 10BaseFB ports, which are evaluated by the relevant stations and transmitted to the link partner. The faults are divided into local and remote faults. The local faults include the Low Light Function (failure to attain the light level below the maximum input level of –32.5 dB over more than 30 bit periods), Receive Jabber, and the receipt of invalid data. The remote status signals are the correct reception of SIDL signals and of remote faults. The table below shows the faults and the associated signals in detail:

Table 3.6:

Fault type	Transmitted signal
Low Light	RF
Receive Jabber	RF
Invalid Data	RF
Receipt of the RF	SIDL

3.8 Throughput Considerations

The throughput consideration of an Ethernet segment is based on the following prerequisites:

- The transmitting station is capable of exploiting the entire transmission bandwidth.

- There is no other transmitter attached to the segment. This means that no collisions occur and that the network is not affected by any additional signals such as jam packets.

In order to calculate the overall performance, all transmitted bits of the Ethernet data packet must be added and divided by twice the maximum transmission frequency. An Ethernet data packet is composed as follows:

Preamble:	7 bytes
Start frame delimiter:	1 byte
Destination address:	6 bytes
Source address:	6 bytes

Length field/type field: 2 bytes

Data field: 46–1500 bytes

CRC field: 4 bytes

This results in a minimum packet length of 72 bytes and a maximum packet length of 1526 bytes. The literature always refers to a minimum packet length of 64 bytes and a maximum packet length of 1518 bytes, since the preamble and the start frame delimiter field are not counted.

A period of 100 nanoseconds is required for the transmission of a bit using 10 Mbit/s Ethernet. Before a data packet can be transmitted onto the network, a minimum waiting time of 9.6 μs must be observed after the last packet on the network. In order to determine how many data packets can be transported via the network using the Ethernet process, the following calculations must be made:

Calculation 1: minimum packet size

$$9.6 \text{ μs} + 8 \times (72) \text{ bit} \times \frac{100 \text{ ns}}{\text{bit}} = 0.0672 \text{ milliseconds}$$

In order to transmit a minimum data packet of 72 bytes via the network, a period of 0.0672 milliseconds is required in the Ethernet process. 1/0.0672 milliseconds = 14880 packets can therefore be transmitted in one second.

Calculation 2: maximum packet size

$$9.6 \text{ μs} + 8 \times (1526) \text{ bit} \times \frac{100 \text{ ns}}{\text{bit}} = 1.23 \text{ milliseconds}$$

In order to transmit a maximum data packet of 1526 bytes via the network, a period of 1.23 milliseconds is required in the Ethernet process. 1/1.23 milliseconds = 813 packets can therefore be transmitted in one second.

As can be seen from the two calculations, the maximum packet rate for Ethernet clearly depends upon the length of the data packets. Each data packet therefore contains an Ethernet overhead of 26 bytes. The size of the overhead in comparison to the payload data (higher protocols) has a significantly more negative effect in small packets than in the transmission of maximum size packets. Some protocols (e.g., LAT) transport only one character of user information in a minimum data packet. The remainder of the packet is filled up with the protocol header and padding. If such a packet is examined in detail and the total overhead is calculated in comparison to the payload data, an overhead is arrived at of 98.61%.

Table 3.7: Ethernet capacity utilization

Packet Size in Bytes	Network load in data packet(s)				Overhead in %
64/72	3720	7440	11160	14880	36.111
92/100	2790	5580	8370	11160	26.000
128/136	2339	4678	7017	9356	19.117
142/150	1929	3825	5787	7716	17.333
192/200	1474	2948	4422	5896	13.000
256/264	1183.5	2367	3550.5	4734	9.848
292/300	1001.5	2003	3004.35	4006	8.666
392/400	758.25	1516.5	2274.75	3033	6.500
492/500	610.25	1220.5	1830.75	2441	5.200
592/600	512	1024	1536	2042	4.333
692/700	438.75	877.5	1316.25	1755	3.714
792/800	384.75	769.5	1154.25	1539	3.250
892/900	342.5	685	1027.5	1370	2.888
992/1000	308.75	617.5	926.25	1235	2.600
1092/1100	281	562	843	1124	2.363
1192/1200	257.75	515.5	773.25	1031	2.166
1292/1300	233.5	467	700.5	934	2.000
1392/1400	221.25	442.5	663.75	885	1.857
1442/1450	213.5	427	640.5	854	1.793
1467/1475	210	420	630	840	1.762
1492/1500	206.5	413	619.5	826	1.733
1518/1526	203	406	609	812	1.703

4 LAN Cabling

Local data networks have become a permanent feature of every communication concept. They enable the integration of mainframes, terminals and PCs into one general network in which computing power is distributed and, in principle, can be used by all the end systems. Arguments as to the better transmission procedure went on for years—chiefly between defenders of Ethernet and those of the Token Ring. However, the choice has become largely a matter of taste since the arrival of the 16 Mbit/s Token Ring and the FDDI ring network. In the final analysis, the application is important to the user regardless of the transport procedure used. The extremely wide variety of transmission mechanisms used by individual data networks have settled on the lowest two layers of the often quoted 7-layer model or ISO reference model. In the case of all the procedures (Ethernet, Token Ring, Token Bus and FDDI), only the Data Link Layer (Layer 2) and the Physical Layer (Layer 1) are defined.

Layer 3	Higher-Layer protocols			
Layer 2B	IEEE 802.2			
Layer 2A	Ethernet MAC	Token Ring MAC	ATM MAC	FDDI MAC
Layer 1	Ethernet	Token Ring	ATM	FDDI

Figure 4.1: Lower Layers of the ISO Reference Model

Connections between the individual LAN components are achieved by a wide variety of transmission media. Planners must be familiar with the characteristics and limits of physical transmission media in order to plan LAN systems.

4.1 Distributed LANs

Data networks were based on the technology of distributed LANs for many years. Using this technology, all the stations in a network are connected to the same physical medium. The best known forms of distributed LANs are the bus and the ring.

Ring Networks

With ring topology, the end stations are interconnected as a physical ring so that each end station has a precisely defined predecessor and successor. The expense of cabling is relatively low for ring topology. All stations that are active in the ring are evenly loaded by the total traffic. With the most common access techniques, messages are passed on by the individual stations. The failure of one cable or of one station can result in the breakdown of all communication. A dual ring is often used in order to overcome this serious drawback. Using the dual ring method, such errors are intercepted by active network components. The most well known forms of ring network are the Token Ring (4 Mbit/s and 16 Mbit/s) and FDDI (100 Mbit/s). The cables in a ring network are always designed as point-to-point lines in practice. These cables are interconnected through loop cable distributors or concentrators as a logical ring. Each station connected to the ring provides active signal regeneration. This means that received signals are automatically forwarded on the transmit side of the interface.

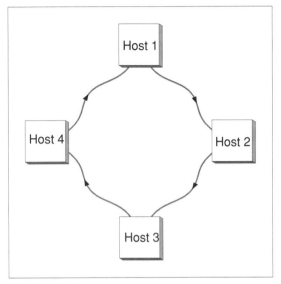

Figure 4.2: Principle of a ring network

Bus Networks

With bus topology, all the end stations are connected one after the other like pearls on a necklace. This technique is encountered inside computers (e.g., VME bus) and for connecting peripherals (e.g., IEC Bus, HP IB Bus), not just in computer networks (Ethernet). Using this method, all destination entities (terminals, computer cards, peripheral devices) are electrically connected in parallel so that all devices can register all signals on the line (almost) simultaneously. This method is very important for LAN access procedures. This technique has one major advantage: the capacity of all stations is utilized evenly. The expense of laying lines is reduced to a minimum. In addition, it is not a problem to expand the network at any time. However, a fault in the bus cable can disrupt the entire network and faulty stations may affect each other. Another disadvantage of this technique is the fact that even stations that have a low traffic volume have to process the entire network traffic continuously. With the Ethernet procedure, before a packet is sent by the transmitter, the transmission medium is checked for the presence of a signal (Carrier Sense). If a signal is detected, the medium is deemed to be occupied and transmission is deferred to a later time. If no signal is detected, the medium is free and the data can be transferred. This procedure (Multiple Access) may result in two stations transmitting simultaneously. The information is superimposed on the cable, the data packets collide and the data they contain is lost. Collisions are detected by special logic circuitry in the receiver (Collision Detection) and reported to the end station. The devices involved in the collision must send the data again after a wait time has elapsed. The Carrier Sense Multiple Access/ Collision Detection (CSMA/CD) mechanism used by Ethernet is capable of identifying all collisions, but the procedure cannot prevent collisions. In networks containing many stations, this can result in a significant increase in response time as soon as traffic loads exceed just 40%. Even with the theoretical 10 Mbit/s data rate available to the user, there may be problems in practice well below this data rate.

With bus and ring-type network distributed LANs, all data is monitored by all active network users. The available network bandwidth is allocated to the active network users on the basis of a network fairness rule. In purely statistical terms, this means that the higher the number of devices that communicate via the network, the less bandwidth is available to an individual station per unit of time. This inevitably leads to significant problems in the case of bandwidth-hungry applications.

Advantages: Distributed LAN Procedure

- The medium can be installed simply and quickly.

- Expansion can be carried out at an affordable cost.

- The costs of network infrastructure are relatively low.

Disadvantages: Distributed LAN Procedure

- Cabling structures can only be converted to future LAN technologies with difficulty and at considerable expense.

- Bandwidth varies depending on the number of end stations connected.

- There is hardly any possibility of implementing a security mechanism.

- Exacting availability requirements are imposed on the medium and on active components.

- Security functions can only be integrated at considerable expense.

4.2   Point-to-point LANs

The star topology is one of the oldest forms of connection in communication networks. Using this method, all the connecting lines of all the end stations communicate via a central node. In practice, such star-type networks are often connected to each other hierarchically. The central switching node of one area is itself connected to other star nodes in a star configuration. The telephone network with its various switching nodes is the best known example of point-to-point networks. The advantage of such networks is the ease with which they can be expanded and modified and the relatively small effect that the failure of one end station has on the network. The major disadvantage of this topology has proved to be the fact that the network is completely dependent upon the central node. Failure of a central node results in loss of communication in the area affected or, under some circumstances, failure of the entire network. In addition, the central nodes decisively determine the throughput of the network. A performance bottleneck in central nodes inevitably results in a reduction in the bandwidth available for transmission purposes in the end stations. Another disadvantage of star-shaped cabling is the length of cable needed because even adjacent end stations cannot be connected to each other directly and always have to be connected via the "central station." However, strictly point-to-point connections make it possible to create a service-independent infrastructure. Nowadays, the primary goal when establishing a network infrastructure is to install a high-performance, future-proof cabling system. Point-to-point cable structures have the following important features:

- There is no problem in using the cabling for future transmission technologies.

- Cables allow flexible use of new products and applications.

- The entire cable system can be installed so that it is based on standards and is non-proprietary.

- Selecting high-quality cables ensures that the network operator has sufficient capacity to meet future requirements in terms of transmission bandwidth.

- The cables are easy to install and require no maintenance.

- Important end stations can be designed so that they are redundant.

Star-type Token Rings/FDDI Networks

In star-type networks, the individual cables of end stations are interconnected in a ring topology at a logical level. This means that each terminal has a precisely defined predecessor and successor. A token (a precisely defined bit pattern) is received by each active station and passed on to the next station. If the station that holds the token has data to transmit, it changes the token to a busy token and sends its data over the cable. This information is passed on from one station to another without modification until it reaches the receiver. The latter copies the data to its receive buffer, adds a confirmation flag to the token, and returns this bit pattern to the cable. The bit pattern is then forwarded to the station that originally transmitted the data. This station checks that the data was transmitted correctly and removes the data and the busy token from the network. A new free token is then generated in the network. In the best case, a station that wishes to transmit must wait for the time taken to transit the entire ring network until it can send data to the network again. The Token Ring method is therefore a deterministic procedure in which it is possible to state precisely the maximum duration until a station can send data to the network. However, considerable bandwidth is lost due to unnecessary circulation of the token. In order to remedy this drawback, Early Token Release is used in newer token techniques (e.g., the FDDI Ring). With Early Token Release, a new free token is added immediately a data packet has been sent. This means that there can be more than one data packet in the ring.

In the same way as with the bus topology, all stations are uniformly loaded by the entire data traffic over the network. All ring networks are based on a structured cabling system. Individual twisted-pair cables to end stations are connected directly to loop cable distributors or concentrators. The components of the loop cable distributors or concentrators take care of interconnection as a ring.

Star-type Ethernets

As early as 1986, some US companies began to transmit Ethernet data on four-wire lines. Standardization was achieved in IEEE Committee 802.3 as Ethernet on Twisted Pair (10BaseT) and as Fast Ethernet (100BaseTx, 100BaseT4). The baseband transmission process is used on the cables used. The data is encoded according to the Manchester process in the case of the 10BaseT standard, according to the 4B/5B process in the case of the 100BaseTx standard and according to the 8B6T process in the case of the 100BaseT4 standard. A 4-core Unshielded Twisted Pair (UTP) cable is defined for 10BaseT and 100BaseTx and an 8-core cable was specified for the 100BaseT4 procedure.

Ethernet on twisted-pair cabling is generally star shaped. A link integrity test is an integral part of this standard. Because the transmission method using twisted-pair lines is a strictly simplex procedure, it is necessary to ensure that the link between the two end stations is active in both directions. The twisted-pair repeater, as well as the twisted-pair terminal, send link integrity signals in addition to the actual data signals to their opposite MAU at regular intervals. If a TP port receives no link integrity signals for a specific period, the link is deemed to have failed and an error message is generated.

If both communication partners receive 2-10 successive link integrity signals, the link is reactivated and regular data can be transferred. This function is triggered by the auto-partition/reconnection algorithm. The algorithm allows the central repeater to switch off a port automatically if it is affected by a fault and to reactivate the port automatically when the fault has been cleared. In this way, only the faulty port is deactivated and not the entire repeater.

In all previously commercially available star-type network structures, the physical links are connected to a central unit (repeater, loop cable distributor or concentrator). The task of these components is to transmit all the data traffic to the cable or to forward it from the cable to the next station. One result of this method is to significantly reduce the full bandwidth that is theoretically available to an end station over the cable.

Advantages of Point-to-point LANs

- Between the workstation and the network attachment point, a separate cable for data communication is available to each end station.

- In theory, the entire transmission bandwidth is available to each terminal.

- Modifications can be made extremely quickly.

- New techniques can be integrated quickly.

Disadvantages of Point-to-point LANs

- The number of cables is the same as the number of planned end stations. Therefore, a relatively large number of cables must be laid.

- The high cable density demands high initial investment in network infrastructure.

- The number of connection ports in the central components (repeaters, loop cable distributors, or concentrators) is the same as the number of end stations that are to be connected.

- Star-type networks are only suitable for spanning relatively short distances (in the 100 meter range).

4.3   Structured Cabling

Because both bus and ring-type data networks proved inflexible, network operators demanded a widely available, flexible cabling structure that was not tied to any particular technology. The introduction of structured networks took these requirements into account. The International Standards Organization for Standardization (ISO) defined a universal cabling structure for blocks of buildings in its Generic Cabling for Customer Premises—Specifications (ISO/IEC DIS 11801). The idea of structured cabling is to create a service-independent infrastructure. The type of cabling is selected so that, regardless of the network components used, a cable structure is installed which can be used to set up Ethernet, Token Ring, or FDDI configuration or point-to-point connections. In practice, this means that it must be possible to operate all services and LANs over the installed cable. This hierarchical communication infrastructure is split up into the following three levels:

- Primary cabling:
  Premises cabling (cabling between individual buildings).

- Secondary cabling:
  Building cabling (cabling between floor distribution frames inside buildings).

- Tertiary cabling:
  Connection cabling (cabling between floor distribution frames and end stations).

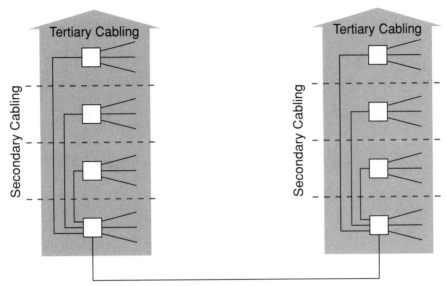

Figure 4.3: Structured cabling

4.3.1 Primary Cabling

The term "primary cabling" defines the connection between individual buildings on a site. The end points of the premises cabling are produced as points of termination into the individual buildings. There may be several concentration points depending on the size of the building. In practice, primary cabling is nowadays installed in either a ring or star configuration. One concentration point is created on the premises (e.g., the computer center) where the campus backbone is laid in a star shape. All control and monitoring of the cabling is performed by a Network Management System from this central node. Because a star-shaped cabling structure is relatively susceptible to faults (cable breaks, failure of central node), designing the infrastructure to ensure redundancy (dual star) is a crucial precaution. This is the only way to guarantee that this resource is always available. The only transmission medium that currently satisfies such high requirements in terms of electrical safety and high transmission rates is optical fiber. This is why optical links based on graded-index or single-mode optical fibers are used in the primary area.

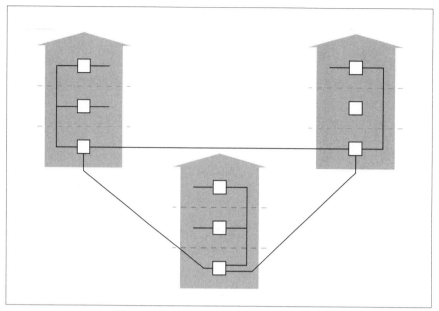

Figure 4.4: Ring-type primary cabling

4.3.2 Secondary Cabling

The secondary area is defined as the connection between the primary and tertiary cabling. This cabling provides the link between the building concentrator and the concentrators on the individual floors. The distribution links can either be laid in a star configuration as point-to-point connections or in a ring configuration. Large buildings may require several secondary concentration points. The area between the individual floors of a building is characterized by relatively high volumes of data traffic. Because the individual data networks on the floors are linked via these cable runs, exacting requirements are inevitably imposed on availability. This is why only optical fiber cables are used nowadays in this area. In the secondary area the cables are laid either as a ring or bus (Distributed backbone) or as a star (Collapsed backbone) as a rule. Depending upon redundancy requirements, the backbone may also be duplicated. The cabling in the secondary area must be planned so that modifications only have to be made exceptionally rarely. Both the primary and secondary areas are usually designed as backbone cabling.

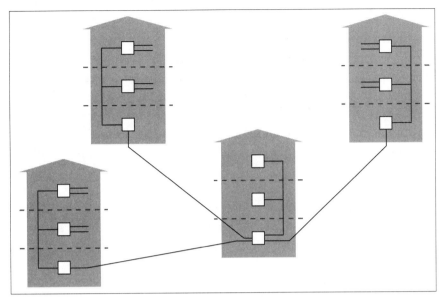

Figure 4.5: Star-type primary cabling

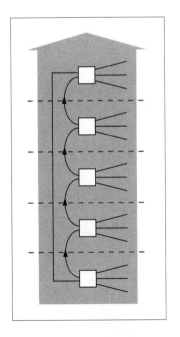
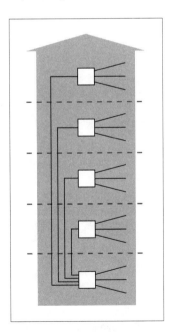

Figure 4.6: Distributed backbone *(on left)*

Figure 4.7: Collapsed backbone *(on right)*

4.3.3 Tertiary Cabling

The tertiary cabling defines the area of the connection wiring to the end stations (e.g., computers, workstations, PCs, terminals, and printers). The cable infrastructure in this area must therefore offer a high degree of flexibility so that different devices having special-purpose interfaces can be included into the overall concept. The cable installed to the end stations must be capable of supporting all LAN and modem (V.24, V.11) devices as well as normal communications equipment such as telephones and faxes. This involves the integration of an extremely wide variety of communication services by installing just one communication medium. The high priority assigned to universal use and flexibility of the cabling in the tertiary area excludes ring or bus type LAN infrastructures. Only star-type cabling is capable of supporting a very wide range of protocols and requirements in a service-independent manner.

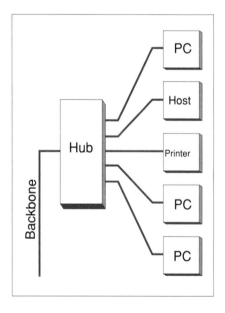

Figure 4.8: Tertiary cabling

Given the present state of the art, copper cable is used as the ideal transmission medium in the tertiary area on cost grounds. These cables are suitable for Local Area Networks in the vicinity of workstations, e.g., between floor distribution frames and workstations. Completely unshielded cables are susceptible to external interference and may also constitute a source of interference themselves. These cables do not satisfy telecommunication engineering regulations. Another alternative is the screened UTP cable. This cable has at least one static shield, but the pairs themselves are unshielded. The screened unshielded twisted-pair cable is suitable for single-channel transmission systems up to a data transmission rate of 100 Mbit/s. Cable according to the IEEE Standard 802.3 is used in the vicinity of the workstation (up to 100 m).

In the past, the requirements imposed on cabling components were defined by maximum transmission rates of 10 Mbit/s (Ethernet area) or 16 Mbit/s (Token Ring area). Fast Ethernet, FDDI Twisted Pair, and the Asynchronous Transfer Mode (ATM) made the requirements imposed on a universal, future-oriented, and, above all, open system drastically more exacting. There is no simple yardstick for defining system performance that can be precisely grasped and this forces planners to specify their cabling system in accordance with telecommunication engineering aspects and values. Compliance with applicable EMC specifications is another important criterion for the cabling concept. Class B limit of interference as specified in Standard EN 55022 is the most important parameter. It is crucial that the network operator complies with Class B limit of interference in order to obtain a general operating license without the need for additional testing of the EMC characteristics of the cable system. A general operating license can only be granted if the cabling system is shielded end to end. The position in law is that the system operator must shut down the entire installation if it causes interference to third parties and compliance with the limiting interference level cannot be ensured. The standard regulates the EMC law which came into force in October 1992.

4.3.4 Cabling Standards

The technical guidelines prepared by the Electronic Industries Association/ Telecommunications Industry Association in Technical Systems Bulletin 36 (EIA/TIA TSB 36) form the basis of all specifications for the cabling of end stations. These guidelines rely on practical experience acquired by American specialists in dealing with cabling techniques. These guidelines are therefore optimized only for requirements that are applicable in the United States of

America. The new feature of this guideline is that, for the first time, no consideration is given to any cable made by a specific manufacturer. The 4-pair UTP cable with an impedance of 100 W ±15% is taken as the basis for this directive. Attenuation and near-end crosstalk were specified as the most important values for this cable. Table 1 shows these values as a function of transmission frequency (varies from 64 kHz to 100 MHz). These values can be used to classify cables into five categories. The EIA/TIA TSB 36 Guideline only deals with upper Categories 3, 4, and 5 because these are the only cables that offer adequate quality for data transmission. For the first time, this provided generally understandable and usable standards of quality for assessing the quality of a cable.

Table 4.1: Maximum permissible attenuation according to EIA/TIA TSB 36 (in dB per 100 m)

Frequency (MHz)	Cat 3	Cat 4	Cat 5
0.064	0.918	0.754	0.721
0.256	1.311	1.114	1.049
0.512	1.836	1.508	1.475
0.772	2.229	1.868	1.803
1.0	5.573	4.262	4.262
8.0	8.524	6.229	5.901
10.0	9.836	7.213	6.557
16.0	13.114	8.852	8.196
20.0		10.163	9.180
31.25			11.803
62.5			17.049
100			21.967

Table 4.2: Minimum near-end crosstalk values to be achieved according to EIA/TIA TSB 36 (in dB)

Frequency (MHz)	Cat 3	Cat 4	Cat 5
0.772	43	58	64
1.0	41	56	62
4.0	32	47	53

(continued)

Table 4.2: (continued)

Frequency (MHz)	Cat 3	Cat 4	Cat 5
8.0	28	42	48
10.0	26	41	47
16.0	23	38	44
20.0		36	42
31.25			40
62.5			35
100			32

The values are calculated using the following formula: NEXT (F) > NEXT (0.772) - 15 * log (F/0.772). The following assumptions are made for the basic values at 0.772 MHz:

- Category 3: 43 dB,

- Category 4: 58 dB,

- Category 5: 64 dB.

Although EIA/TIA TSB 36 represents an important step towards the standardization of cable infrastructure, this directive only covers part of a high-capacity network infrastructure in the vicinity of end stations. For instance, the directive contains no value for the shielding factor of a cable, a parameter that is indispensable for assessing the EMC qualities of a cable. The overall system performance of a system (plug-in connector and jumper cable) is also not taken into account. Because the EIA/TIA TSB 36 Guidelines only deal with some topics, such as material quality and material selection, but ignore the entire question of installation quality and the final resulting overall system performance and its appraisal by tests, these Directives should be regarded as a first step in the right direction. The standards published by the ISO for universal cabling stipulate that the distance between distribution frame and connection box must not exceed 90 meters. A total of ten meters is allowed for the incoming cables (on the distribution frame and in the vicinity of end stations). This gives a maximum distance of 100 meters from the distribution frame to the end station. In this cabling scheme, the following cables are regarded as standard for connecting end stations:

- 100 W cable with two or four pairs (UTP),

- 120 W cable with two or four pairs (UTP),

- 150 W cable with two pairs (STP),

- 2-core optical fiber cable (62.5/125 mm).

The 100 W UTP cable is the preferred cable type in this specification.

The standard also lays down four classes of transmission systems:

Class A

Transmissions involving low requirements over long distances are specified in this class. Examples include analogue voice transmissions. A frequency of 100 kHz is defined as the maximum transmission rate for class A.

Class B

This system class is suitable for communication at medium bit rates over medium distances. It includes equipment for voice transmission with digital private branch exchanges (S0 interfaces).

Class C

This class is suitable for transmission at high bit rates (up to 20 MHz) over short distances. Typical representatives of this group include the CSMA/CD (10BaseT) or the Token Ring procedure (up to 16 Mbit/s).

Class D

The highest class defines communication at very high data rates (up to 100 MHz) over short distances. This includes Fast Ethernet, FDDI, and the ATM procedure on copper.

4.4   Distributed Backbone Versus Collapsed Backbone

In structured cabling systems, all cables necessarily converge at one or more points in a building or on a floor. The data networks or connections to end stations that originate from these concentration points therefore communicate exclusively via a strictly point-to-point link. The individual distribution points are connected to each other via the backbone (premises or building backbone). The following backbone design strategies have achieved dominance: distributed backbones and collapsed backbones.

4.5.1 Distributed Backbone

With a distributed backbone, all buildings on the premises or the individual floor distribution frames in a building are successively connected in series. This series connection of backbones requires only short lengths of connecting cable between individual distribution frames (Ethernet = 2 wires, Token-Ring and FDDI = 2 or 4 wires). Nevertheless, the need for one input port and one output port for each distribution frame to be connected to the backbone has an adverse affect on cost.

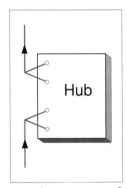

Figure 4.9: Input and output ports for the backbone

Because all cables in a distributed backbone are looped from one distribution center to another, at floor level it is no longer possible to assign cables to individual LANs. If there is a requirement to implement several parallel LANs and several parallel LAN techniques (Ethernet, Token Ring, FDDI, etc.) in a distributed backbone, resources must be provided in the form of multicore connecting cables and the corresponding input and output ports. Because the available bandwidth is shared by all the devices connected to the distributed backbone, precautions must be taken to ensure that communication between all distribution frames is achieved without bottlenecks. The file servers or other computer resources are therefore always connected on the individual stories in the case of a distributed backbone concept. Users then only communicate via the backbone if they want to exchange information with resources outside their department.

A distributed backbone is relatively susceptible to faults. Failure of a distribution frame or a link inevitably prevent the rest of the system downstream from accessing the backbone. Even pure transmission errors are passed on from one distribution frame to another and can have a significant effect on the performance of the system. Safeguarding a distributed-backbone structure against faults involves enormous expense. The following precautionary measures are recommended:

- Equip the distribution rooms with a UPS system.

- Check the hubs are fitted with duplicated power supply units.

- Locate the interfaces to the backbone on different cards of a plug-in unit.

- Lay cables in a ring configuration so that a redundant path is available even with Ethernet.

- Connect important network resources to a parallel backbone if necessary.

Advantages of Distributed Backbones

- Only a small number of conductors are required in the cable between individual buildings and/or floors.

- Fault redundancy can be achieved simply and affordably thanks to the connection of buildings or floors in a ring configuration.

- The low cable density reduces the investment cost of the backbone.

Disadvantages of Distributed Backbones

- New techniques can only be integrated with difficulty.

- Twice the number of input/output ports must be provided in order to connect the distribution frames to the backbone.

- The bandwidth available to an individual device diminishes as the number of connected active stations increases.

- It is very expensive to make modifications.

Collapsed Backbone

With a collapsed backbone, all the building distribution frames on the premises are connected directly to a central premises distribution frame, and all floor distribution frames are connected directly to a building distribution frame via a separate cable. A direct multicore cable is laid from the central distribution center to the relevant secondary distribution frame as a strictly point-to-point connection. If sufficient conductors are available over this route, several parallel LANs and several parallel LAN techniques (Ethernet, Token Ring, FDDI, etc.) can be implemented without any problem. Using this technique, new transmission methods (e.g., ATM) can be quickly integrated alongside existing services. The need for more cables does, however, have an adverse impact on cost. Obviously, this means significantly more space is needed in cable ducts and requires additional expense on laying cables. The probability of a fault can be significantly reduced even further by duplicating the connecting cables between the central distribution frame and the secondary distribution frame and laying cables along separate routes. In a collapsed backbone structure, the full bandwidth is available for each point-to-point connection. This bandwidth is shared among the devices connected to the particular segment of the network. File servers or other computer resources can therefore be connected to the central distribution frame in the case of a collapsed backbone concept. Although the point-to-point structure of a collapsed backbone makes it relatively susceptible to faults, the failure of a distribution frame or a link only causes one line of communication to fail. All other connections remain unaffected by the failure. This makes troubleshooting significantly easier. Obviously, the core, the central distribution frames, must be protected against failure. The following precautions are recommended:

- Equip the central distribution rooms with UPS systems.

- Fit the hubs with duplicated power supply units.

- Connect important network resources to parallel backbone .

- Locate the interfaces to the relevant backbone on different cards of a plug-in unit.

Advantages of Collapsed Backbones

- A separate cable is available for data communication between the hub and the secondary distribution frame.

- In theory, the entire transmission bandwidth is available for each connection.

- Modifications can be made very quickly.

- New techniques can be integrated quickly.

Disadvantages of Collapsed Backbone

- There is a separate cable from the hub to each secondary distribution frame.

- The number of ports required in the central components (repeater, loop cable distributor, or concentrators) is the same as the number of secondary distribution frames to be connected.

- Fault redundancy can only be achieved at considerable expense due to the connection of the buildings or floors in a star configuration.

- The relatively high cable density inevitably increases the investment cost for the backbone.

5 | An Introduction to Switching Technology

In the past, data networks were connected by a large number of different interconnection components. These interconnection components fulfill the functions defined in the relevant ISO Layer. Before attempting to classify the components, we should first consider the particular objectives of the relevant layer.

Layer 1

The lowest layer of the ISO reference model defines the transmission medium and the physical environment for data transmission. Actual physical transmission of data in the form of a transparent, non-structured bit stream takes place at this level. The topology and encoding or modulation methods, and access mechanisms are located in this layer. In addition to modems and transceivers, repeaters also operate at Layer 1. A repeater provides a purely electrical connection between two LAN segments. The signals are merely amplified and the signal shape is regenerated. Various models of repeaters are currently available as star couplers or hubs.

Layer 2

The purpose of the so-called Data Link Layer is error-free transmission of the Layer 1 bit stream which is split into packets at this level. Flow control and error connection take place at this level. In LANs, the Data Link Layer is split into two parts: a Medium Access Control (MAC) Layer to which parts of IEEE Standards 802.3, 802.4 and 802.5 (CSMA/CD, Token Bus, Token Ring) relate, and a Logical Link Control (LLC) Layer that is described by IEEE 802.2.

Bridges operate on Layer 2. These devices link two or more LAN segments at a logical level. In contrast to the repeater, packets are not only electrically processed, they are also loaded in a memory where they are interpreted by bridge logic circuitry.

Layer 3

This is the Network Layer which essentially provides routing functions. Several networks can be linked at this Layer 1 as a combined logical network. This makes it possible to build up logically-structured, hierarchical networks. Transit systems that operate at Layer 3 are referred to as routers. Routers always operate exclusively with one of the protocols based on Layer 3. An IP router will therefore not handle any non-IP protocols (e.g., XNS, DECnet). Because a router "disassembles" each packet down to Layer 3, these devices are ideally suitable for connecting different network topologies (e.g., Ethernet with Token Ring (802.5), FDDI or X.25).

Each device has characteristic features. This is why familiarity with the specific details of the components is necessary in order to understand their particular functionality. A network can only be correctly planned and implemented if one has an in-depth understanding of the components.

5.1 Repeaters

For the transition between two different Ethernet secondary standards (e.g., 10 Base 5 <-> 10 Base 2, 10 Base 5 <-> 10 Base T), interconnection must be obtained by means of a repeater in accordance with IEEE Standard 802.3. Repeaters are best known from Ethernet applications. A repeater operates at the lowest level, the Physical layer, of the ISO reference model and is therefore a purely hardware-oriented product. No software components of any kind are needed in order to operate a repeater. This results in relatively low-priced repeater components. Because a repeater operates at the Physical layer, all higher-layer protocols are ignored and only signal regeneration for bit streams is performed. This is why it is not possible to use a repeater for interconnection where two different access methods (e.g., Ethernet <-> Token-Ring) are used. Such interconnection is achieved using a translation bridge which operates on Layer 2. In the case of a repeater, each signal is transferred to the connected network segment without taking into account losses. Because the repeater works at the Physical layer, the traffic load cannot be split up in the LAN.

A repeater is used exclusively to adapt and regenerate signals. Most slide-in units for hub systems (e.g., connection cards for 10 Base T cabling) use a repeater function for data preparation during communication between individual ports or between modules.

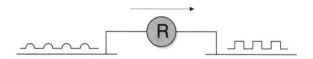

Figure 5.1: Signal conditioning

Repeaters are also used to extend Ethernet segments. This makes it possible to circumvent purely cable-related restrictions (lengths, signal attenuation) within a collision domain. In this case the repeater is connected to the cable run with the aid of a transceiver cable and a transceiver. Repeaters are not just used to connect two cable runs; it is also possible to link several segments to each other. Such systems involve multiport repeaters. Repeaters are capable of automatically disconnecting defective network segments in order to isolate network errors. This prevents effects on other segments.

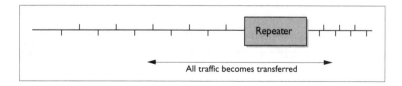

Figure 5.2: Extension of physical network segments

The functions and method of operation of a repeater can be divided into the following main groups:

- Signal generation in synchronization with clock
- Collision detection
- Generating the JAM signal
- Generating the preamble
- Extending data fragments to at least 96 bits
- Isolation of defective network segments

Signal Generation in Synchronization with Clock

Because a repeater operates on the Physical layer, it only receives or transmits bit-serial data streams. In practice this means that a repeater cannot "monitor" the transmitted data content. A repeater simply regenerates the data signal in terms of timing and amplitude and makes sure the preamble, which takes care of synchronizing the receiver to the transmit clock before the actual data packet, is the required length.

Using repeaters increases the signal delay in a data network. The delay introduced by a repeater must not exceed 7.5-9 bit times.

Collision Detection

A dedicated collision-detection function is available in a repeater for each connected network interface. This makes it possible to detect collisions on individual network segments very quickly and to inform all segments of the collision by means of a JAM signal.

Generating the JAM Signal

If the repeater detects a collision in one of the connected data networks, it immediately sends the so-called Jam(ming) signal. The JAM signal is used to make the collision that has occurred apparent and consists of sixteen 1-0 bit combinations.

Generating the Preamble

The preamble enables the receiver to synchronize itself to the start of the frame (Start Frame Delimiter). Due to the lowpass characteristic of a cable, 1-3 bits of every transmission are lost when the cable is "loaded." After receiving a valid data packet, a repeater inserts a new preamble (10101010) before the existing preamble fragment and sends this "new" data packet to the connected network.

Extending Data Fragments to at least 96 Bits

Data fragments occur due to collisions in a network. It is the task of a repeater to extend data fragments to at least 512 bits (Minimum Packet Size).

Isolation of Defective Network Segments

Modern repeaters have a self-test function and also detect erroneous signals on one of the connected segments (e.g., short circuit, no terminating resistor). This results in automatic separation (partitioning) of the network segment affected by the fault so that such faults cannot affect the rest of the data network. Once the fault has been cleared, partitioning is automatically cancelled.

Repeater Design Rules

According to the applicable IEEE Specification 802.3, no more than 4 repeaters must never be cascade connected in succession. The reason for this stipulation is the delay performance of the individual components. The standard defines a maximum Round Trip Delay (RTD) in the LAN of 64 + 512 = 576 bit periods. If this value (RTD > 576 bits) is exceeded, the collision mechanism fails to function. A recommended planning basis for this value is RTD < 480 bits. If the maximum Round Trip Delay is exceeded, unambiguous detection of a collision is no longer possible.

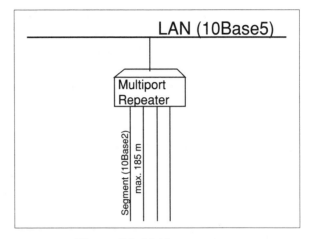

Figure 5.3: Multiport repeater

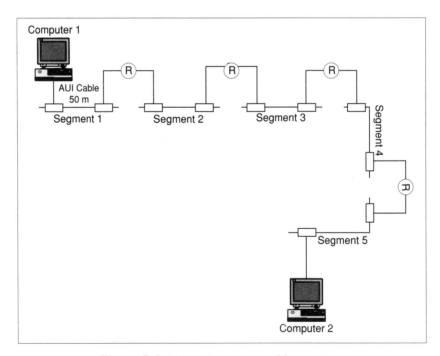

Figure 5.4: Network segments with repeaters

As shown in Figure 5.4, station 1 attempts to communicate with the most distant station 2. In order to find out whether the network design has a permissible configuration, the delay times of all components located in the communication path must be determined.

The following guide values apply for the delay times of Ethernet components currently available on the market:

Ethernet controller transmitting direction:	3 bits
Ethernet controller receiving direction:	7 bits
Transceiver cable:	2.5 bits
Transceiver transmitting direction:	3 bits
Transceiver receiving direction:	5 bits
Network segment:	22 bits
Repeater:	8 bits
Inter-repeater link:	25 bits

This gives the following RTD calculation:

Total:

3+2,5+3+22+5+2,5+8+2,5+3+25+5+2,5+8+2,5+3+22+5+2,5+8+2,5+3+25+5+2,5+ 8+2,5+3+22+5+2,5+7 = 223 bit periods

Round Trip Delay: 223 x 2 = 446 < 480 bit periods

As of 1996, repeaters are classified in two functional groups: local repeaters and remote repeaters.

5.1.1 Local repeaters

Local repeaters can be used to extend Ethernet segments at the lowest level (10 Base 5 and 10 Base 2). A 10 Base 5 repeater is always connected to each cable segment with the aid of transceiver cables and one transceiver per repeater. 10Base2 segments are connected directly to the BNC interface of the repeater. When using local repeaters to interconnect network segments, the following rules apply when determining the maximum distance between two Ethernet end stations:

- There must be no more than five coaxial cable segments (according to the 10 Base 5 standard: 500 m max.) on the communication path.

- Two of the five coaxial cable segments may only be used purely as link segments.

- There must be no more than four local repeaters on the communication path between two Ethernet end stations.

- The length of each transceiver cable must be 50 m max. (in the case of end stations and repeaters).

Situation 1: Maximum Configuration with Coaxial Link Segments

Two of the five coaxial cable segments are used purely as link segments. This means that no end stations are connected to these link segments. This gives the following maximum values between station A and station B:

Number	Description	Length	Total length
2	End station AUI drop cable	50 m	100 m
5	Coaxial segments	500 m	2500 m
8	Repeater AUI drop cable	50 m	400 m
Total length =			3000 m

Situation 2: Calculation without Link Segments

If no link segments are present in a network configuration, only three coaxial cable segments can be connected by two repeaters. This gives the following maximum values between the terminals.

Number	Description	Length	Total length
2	End station AUI drop cable	50 m	100 m
3	Coaxial segments	500 m	1500 m
6	Repeater AUI drop cable	50 m	300 m
Total length =			1800 m

Multiport Repeaters

Connection between two Ethernet segments is normally effected using a local repeater. There is a solution that allows affordable interconnection of many Ethernet cable segments for connecting Cheapernet (10 Base 2) and Twisted Pair (10 Base T). With this solution, a multiple repeater chip is used to build a multiport repeater. Up to eight network segments can typically be connected to these devices. Nevertheless, these simple components are now a days very rarely used in practice. The availability of modular hub components means that these functions can be implemented in the relevant plug-in modules.

5.1.2 Fast Ethernet Repeater

The functions of repeaters are also defined in the Fast Ethernet Standard. Fast Ethernet Repeaters operate on the Physical layer. Because repeaters are a hardware-oriented product, these devices are only used to extend and connect Fast Ethernet segments (100BaseTx, 100BaseT4 and 100BaseFx). The maximum extension of the segments depends primarily on the Round Trip Propagation Time. This value defines the maximum extension that a network configuration can have and still detect a collision within the transmission time window (collision window) as a valid value. This is also called the collision domain. Different collision domains constructed using Fast Ethernet or standard Ethernet components are connected to each other with the help of bridges or switches.

The Fast Ethernet Standard makes a distinction between two classes of repeaters:

- Class I repeaters
- Class II repeaters

Class I Repeaters

Devices that have a maximum delay time of 168 bit times between the input port and the output port are designated as Class I repeaters.

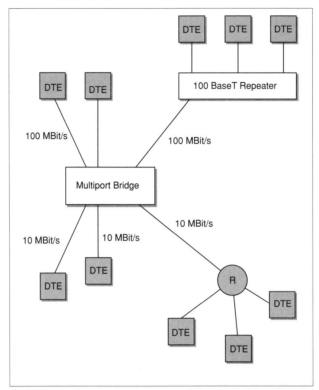

Figure 5.5: Connection between different collision domains

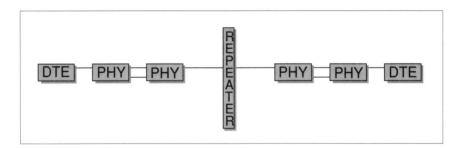

Figure 5.6: Class I repeater in network

Class I repeaters are always used where different physical standards (e.g., 100BaseTx <–> 100BaseFx, 100BaseTx <–> 100BaseT4) have to communicate with each other. Only one Class I repeater may be inserted in a communication path between two Fast Ethernet end stations where full use is made of maximum cable lengths.

Class II Repeaters

Devices that have a maximum delay time of 92 bit times between the input port and output port are designated as Class II repeaters.

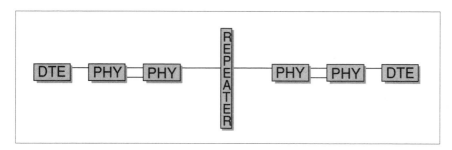

Figure 5.7: Class II repeater in network

Class II repeaters are used in those configurations where only one physical standard (e.g., 100BaseTx) is used. Due to the shorter delay times of Class II repeaters, two Class II repeaters may be inserted in a communication path between two Fast Ethernet end stations where full use is made of maximum cable lengths.

Table 5.1: Maximum extension of collision domains

Medium	Max. number of PHY segment	Max. segment length (in m) per segment	Max. delay caused by medium (in ns)
Copper link Segment: 100 Base T	2	100	1140
Optical fiber link Segment: 100 Base T	2	400	4080

By shortening the length of cable between individual components, the maximum delay can be reduced sufficiently to permit the insertion of additional repeater components in the communication path between two Fast Ethernet end stations. The worst-case Path Delay value (PDV) is a crucial value for checking a valid network configuration. Accordingly, a network configuration comprising several repeaters must be designed in accordance with the following formula:

PDV = (total of all link delays) + (total of all repeater delays) + (total of all MII cable delays) + (total of DTE delays) + margin.

The values in the formula are composed as follows:

The total of all link delays consists of the values of all delays (Link Segment Delay Value [LSDV]) including all inter-repeater links.

LSDV = 2 x segment length x delay for this segment.

The segment length defines the distance between the PHY interface of the repeater and the furthest end stations as well as the length of the inter-repeater link.

The delays caused by the cable are normally quoted by the relevant manufacturer. The cable delay is normally defined in bit times per meter (bit/m). If only the wave propagation velocity is defined as the function x^*c (c = velocity of light), Tables 5.2 and 5.3 can be used as a basis for conversion.

Table 5.2: Conversion table for delays in cables

Wave propagation velocity: $x * c$ (c = velocity of light)	ns/m	Bit/m
0.4	8.34	0.834
0.5	6.67	0.667
0.51	6.54	0.654
0.52	6.41	0.641
0.53	6.29	0.629
0.54	6.18	0.618
0.55	6.06	0.606
0.56	5.96	0.696
0.57	5.85	0.685
0.58	5.75	0.675

(continued)

Table 5.2: (continued)

Wave propagation velocity: x * c (c = velocity of light)	ns/m	Bit/m
0.59	5.65	0.565
0.6	5.56	0.556
0.61	5.47	0.547
0.62	5.38	0.538
0.63	5.29	0.529
0.64	5.21	0.521
0.65	5.13	0.513
0.66	5.05	0.505
0.67	4.89	0.498
0.68	4.91	0.491
0.69	4.83	0.483
0.7	4.77	0.477
0.8	4.17	0.417
0.9	3.71	0.371

Table 5.3: Delay times of Fast Ethernet components

Components	Delay in bit times per meter	Max. delay in bit times
Two DTEs	–	100
Cat 3 cable	0.57	114
Cat 4 cable	0.57	114
Cat 5 cable	0.556	111.2
STP cable	0.556	111.2
Fiber-optic cable	0.501	408
Repeater Class I	–	168
Repeater Class II	–	92

- The total of all repeater delays is calculated from the delay times quoted by the relevant manufacturer. If the user does not know the actual repeater delays, it is advisable to calculate on the basis of default values (Class I repeater = 168 bit times, Class II repeater = 92 bit times).

- The length (in meters) of all MII cables in the communication path gives the total of all delays of these cables (in bit times).

- Because the end station introduces a delay in the communication path when transmitting over the cable, this value must be introduced into the formula stated above. If the relevant manufacturer publishes no timing data in respect of individual components, it is advisable to adopt the default delay times for DTEs (100 bit times) as a basis.

- Allowance for certain minimum margins, (e.g., for poor connections, long connecting cables) must always made when making calculations for a communication path. The standard recommends a margin of 4 bit times.

If calculating the PDV value gives a value that is less than/equal to 511 bit times, the configuration is acceptable.

If late collisions or CRC errors occur during operation, it can be assumed that the maximum delay of 511 bit times was exceeded on the communication path.

5.2 Ethernet Bridges

Ethernet LANs operate using the broadcast procedure in principle. In practice, this means that all information is transferred over the entire network segment to all stations. Only the station that is addressed by its hardware address analyzes the information. This mechanism inevitably results in increased data traffic as the number of connected stations rises. However, Local Area Networks continuously grow due to the pressure of users' demands. One quickly comes up against the logical and physical limits of the networks. This can lead to overloading of the network and unacceptable response times between applications. In the past, it was sufficient to connect individual Ethernet segments via repeaters. Today, LAN segments are linked by using bridges.

By virtue of their function, bridges operate at the Media Access Control (MAC) layer and split a data network into smaller, more manageable units. As a result, only transparent bridges that are used to link LANs to each other are used in the world of Ethernet. Data packets are passed on when transferred via Ethernet bridges without any modification to their data structure. Because Ethernet bridges operate on Layer 2, unlike repeaters, these bridges do not transfer the entire data traffic to the connected network. As shown in Figure 5.8, bridges divide the network into various collision domains.

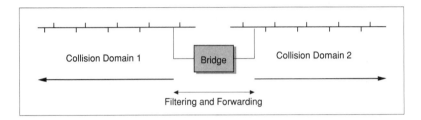

Figure 5.8: Division into different collision domains

Store-and-Forward Mechanism

All MAC-layer bridges operate on the basis of store-and-forward technology. A bridge monitors all data packets in the connected LANs. Each data packet is read in by the Ethernet controller and copied to a buffer. The bridge then checks the destination address for each received packet. The bridge uses the destination address to decide whether the data packet should be forwarded to a connected LAN or whether it involves local data traffic. If a data packet has to be forwarded to a different LAN segment of the bridge, this information is forwarded to the memory of the Ethernet transmission controller. This controller sends the data packet as soon as the network is available for a transfer. If the destination device is in the local network, the received data packet is not passed on to the other Ethernet controllers of the bridge. The store-and-forward function of the bridge takes a relatively long time to perform processing. This delay is called "latency" in technical terminology. By definition, the term "latency" describes the period of time that elapses between the first bit of a data packet received by the bridge port and the time at which that bit leaves the destination port of the bridge. In the case of normal bridges the delay time is approximately 150-300 ms. This delay becomes very significant, especially in the case of applications or protocols where the communication partners confirm each transmitted data packet. The IPX protocol developed by Novell is a typical example of such a protocol. The Novell client sends a data packet to the server. The latter responds to receipt of the packet by a confirmation packet. The client cannot send the next data packet until it has received a confirmation packet from the server. If communication involves five bridges, for example (delay per bridge = 200 ms), this results in a total delay of two seconds between two packets. If large applications (e.g., Windows) are downloaded from a central file server to the client over such a segment, this can result in unreasonable time delays.

A guaranteed or a variable delay time is a further important aspect when considering latency. Multimedia applications generally require a short delay time. If possible, the delay time must be permanently defined and never vary. The transmission of voice and data over a network is made simpler if there is a predictable fixed delay between the transmitter and the receiver. Because significantly more short packets than long packets can be transferred per unit of time, the total throughput of a bridge is always stated in terms of the quantity of smallest Ethernet packets (64 bytes) that can be transferred. Nevertheless, it is precisely such short packets that cause a bridge to hit its processing limits.

Throughput at Maximum Traffic Load

The throughput of a bridge depends on the architecture in many ways. Some bridge architectures claim "full-wire speed" throughput for every port. The existence of difference types of data (unicasts, multicasts and broadcasts) means that total throughput can sometimes drop to 80% of the quoted capacity due to internal wait loops and blocking situations. In a network there is a series of defined criteria for the bridge that can lead to extreme loading and possibly overloading of the device. These critical situations include the following:

- Invalid data packets
- Broadcasts/multicasts
- Overload situations.

Invalid Data Packets

During communication over a network, data transferred over the transport path may be destroyed or mutilated. This results in packet fragments or data packets that have an invalid CRC value. The bridge could forward such packets, without further checking, to the destination device as soon as it detected a valid destination address. The receiver would detect the error and discard the data packet. Higher-level protocol layers would ensure that the discarded data packet was retransmitted. However, the transfer of erroneous packets would pointlessly waste valuable bandwidth. This is why a bridge must be capable of filtering out all invalid data packets that are sent by the end station. This error checking mechanism involves an increase in the delay time under some circumstances.

Broadcasts/Multicasts

If broadcast or multicast packets are sent by an end station, it is the bridge's task to make this information available to all ports or a group of ports. The traffic load therefore increases drastically over the internal communication paths of the bridge. The overall performance of some bridges deteriorates drastically with these types of packets.

Ethernet bridges may have more than two Ethernet controllers in practice. Several hundred end stations may be operating on the segments connected to these controllers. In practice, a situation can occur in which many users want to access a segment. The bridge controller connected to this port has a theoretical throughput of 10 Mbit/s. However, this throughput is split between the devices that communicate via this port. If many data packets (possibly at the maximum data rate) are sent to the bridge to this one port by many computers, this will inevitably lead to data packet overflow or congestion (increased latency). Such an overload situation can be used to draw additional conclusions regarding the quality of a bridge architecture.

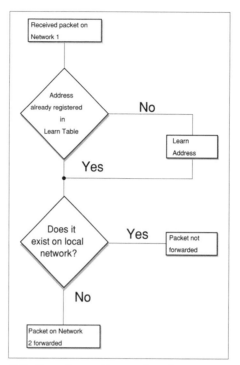

Figure 5.9: Flow chart with transfer of packets via bridges

5.2.1 Learning, Filtering, Forwarding

An Ethernet bridge uses stored address lists to transfer data packets. These address lists are formed by an address algorithm. The bridge monitors all data packets on the connected LANs. When examining the data packets, the bridge reads all the transmit (source) addresses contained in them. These addresses are stored in the relevant address lists of the ports. These address lists are used as transport tables for data packets. Because the address lists are automatically mapped to the connected sub-networks by monitoring the source addresses of all data packets, specialists refer to this mechanism as a learning mechanism. Such bridges are sometimes also called self-learning bridges because of this mechanism.

When a device sends a data packet over the network, the bridge reads in the information. The destination address contained in the packet is compared with the entries in the learned table. If there is an entry in the local table, the bridge recognizes that the receiver is located in the local network. The data packet is therefore not forwarded. This process is also called Filtering. If there is no entry for the destination address, the packet is passed on to the packet switching module of the bridge. The packet switching module of the bridge ascertains whether the destination device is in one of the connected LANs. If this module finds the address in one of the other address tables, the data packet is passed on to the relevant Ethernet controller in the bridge. This Ethernet controller switches the packet to the local network segment. This process is also called Forwarding. If no entry is found, a copy of the data packet is forwarded to all Ethernet controllers in the bridge. In this case, these controllers each transfer one data packet to the local network segment. If the previously unknown device responds to the received data packet, the source address contained in the packet is included in the address table.

After they are entered in the address tables, individual address entries are time stamped. The time stamp is reset to 0 each time the address occurs. All addresses that have been learned but are not being used by a communication partner at that moment are aged by means of a timer. The address tables are always sorted by the age of the entries. As a consequence, addresses that are currently in use are always located at the start of the table and searching takes relatively little time. The bridge in Figure 5.10 sorts the addresses in the tables in accordance with the following criteria for example:

0-180 seconds = young

180-300 seconds = middle aged

300-600 seconds = old

Example:

Address	Time group
080002001234	Old
080123405678	Old
08000AA23434	Old
0800020ABCD4	Old
08000200AFFE	Old
08000234567F	Middle
0800AAAAAA34	Middle

080002BBAAFF	Middle
080201298ADE	Young
080012567812	Young
080FFFFF1231	Young
0800DDDEAF45	Young
081234501256	Young
080056789002	Young

After the maximum time (10 minutes) has elapsed and no communication partner having the computer address 080002001234 has exchanged data, this address is deleted from the address list. This mechanism keeps the address lists in the bridges relatively small and they can be searched through very quickly. This mechanism is referred to as an "aging mechanism" in technical terminology.

The aging mechanism also ensures that devices are removed from the tables after relocation or due to the replacement of an Ethernet controller (defect) after a defined time.

Some bridges also allow permanent entry of addresses in the tables. The Network Administrator has the facility to switch off the learning mechanism and make entries in the table manually. This means that bridge can only switch addresses specified by manual entries. All other addresses or devices cannot communicate with each other.

A <—> X,Y

B, only local communication possible

C <—> X,Y

D, only local communication possible

E, only local communication possible

F <—> X,Y

Z, only local communication possible

T, only local communication possible

Figure 5.10: Bridge with manual address entries

Thanks to the manual entries, only computers A, C, F, X and Y can communicate with each other via the bridge. All other devices operate on the local network segment only.

Forwarding

By making a logical decision using the address tables, an individual check is performed for each data packet to ascertain whether it involves local data traffic or a packet for a user on one of the other connected networks. Local data traffic remains concentrated on these units, and only information that it actually intended for stations on other units is transported by the bridge. This gives real load separation between connected network segments. The broadcast address FF-FF-FF-FF-FF-FF-FF-FF occupies a special position. Most LAN protocols use a broadcast method for communication or connection set-up. In practice, this means that all information is transferred via all network segments to all stations. Only those stations that are addressed by their higher-layer address analyze the information. This mechanism unavoidably results in increased broadcast traffic as the number of connected stations rises. Since the bridge and all other devices on all network segments respond to the broadcast address, this address cannot be deleted from the address table. In the case of faulty configurations, or if there is a very large number of devices in the network, this broadcast mechanism can lead to an extremely high base load throughout the entire network.

Because Ethernet bridges operate on Layer 2 (MAC layer), these devices isolate two networks into two independent collision domains at a logical level. If a collision occurs in one network segment, this signal is not transmitted via the bridge. In addition, the signal transit times are always relevant to only one collision domain. The linking of network segments by bridges creates two completely separate parts of the network that have signal transit times that are independent of each other. One problem that repeatedly occurs when installing fiber-optic based Ethernets is that the maximum distance (using active star couplers) is 4 km. If a repeater is used in the connected coaxial segments, e.g., in order to connect floor systems to the main cable, this drastically reduces the maximum distance of the fiber-optic run. If a bridge is used at the transition from optical fiber to coaxial, communication is possible without any restriction on network extension. All data to be transmitted is buffered in bridges, and no data regeneration is performed. In principle, bridges can be cascade connected endlessly and the usual 2.5 km or 4.0 km maximum range of Ethernet networks can be increased many times by installing bridges. At that point, the data communication timeout does not depend solely on the timers in the end stations. Bridges make worldwide communication extending beyond one country or continent possible using a logical network.

5.2.2 Filter Mechanisms

An additional mechanism allows bridges to filter data or specific events. This gives a network operator the opportunity to implement individual communication structures. Because a bridge operates on OSI Layer 2, these devices are capable of checking all bits/bytes in a data packet down to the lowest level. In the case of bridges it may be necessary to support a large number of filter capabilities. For instance, it should be possible to filter Ethernet addresses, the type field and, if applicable, an SSAP/DSAP or SNAP field in an Ethernet. Under some circumstances it may be important to be able to filter Layer 3 addresses (IP addresses). It is also useful to be able to match any random byte (or even bit) in the packet.

A bridge has the facility to filter each information item in the data packet. Each Ethernet data packet contains a 6-byte destination address, a 6-byte source address, a 2-byte type or length field and 38-1492 bytes of user data (protocol header and data).

Example 1

Computers on subnetwork 1 can communicate with each other using the Novell IPX protocol and the TCP/IP protocol. Computers on subnetwork 2 only use TCP/IP protocols. TCP/IP protocols are also used in subnetwork 3. Because the Novell IPX protocol has to be installed for a test in sub-network 3, but there is no intention to purchase a new server license for the Novell software, all the Network Administrator needs to do is to prevent communication of both the Novell networks through filters. To achieve this, the corresponding type field is masked in the filters.

Filter 1 = bytes: 12, 13 value: 8137

Filter 2 = bytes: 12, 13 value: 8138

Example 2

Access to a subnetwork can be prevented for a specific hardware address, for example, by a combination of a source and destination address filter. This means that a selected device can no longer be reached or can no longer communicate via the bridge. This filter mechanism prevents unauthorized access to specific resources of other network segments.

Filter 1 = bytes: 1-6, 7-12, value: 080002001234, 08001234568137

5.2.3 Throughput Considerations

In terms of its transmission method, Ethernet is half-duplex transmission technology. In practice, this means that before an Ethernet packet is sent, the station that wishes to transmit checks the transmission medium for the presence of a signal. If a signal is detected, the medium is deemed to be busy and the transmit process is postponed. If no signal is detected, the medium is free, and the data can be transferred. With this procedure, two stations may sometimes transmit simultaneously. The information is superimposed on the cable, the data packets collide, and the data they contain is lost. It is the task of the devices involved in the collision to re-transmit the data after a wait time. The CSMA/CD method used by Ethernet is capable of detecting all collisions but cannot prevent collisions. In networks containing many stations, this can lead to a significant increase in response times as soon as traffic loads exceed 40%. Despite the theoretical 10 Mbit/s data rate that is available to the user, in practice problems may occur far below this transmission rate.

One significant cause that affects the performance of a LAN application can be attributed to the delay time of the bridge. This delay is referred to as "latency." By definition, the term "latency" describes the period of time that elapses between the first bit of a data packet received by the bridge port and the time at which this bit leaves the destination port of the bridge. With normal bridges the delay time is roughly 150-300 ms. This delay becomes very important, especially in the case of applications or protocols that require the communication partners to confirm each transmitted data packet. The IPX protocol developed by Novell is a typical example of such a protocol.

Performance as a Function of Delay

Performance depends essentially on all delays on the route between the transmitter and receiver. The computers in the network are as follows: computer 1 = DOS/Windows PC, computer 2 = Sun Workstation. The TCP/IP protocol is used as a communication protocol between the transmitter and receiver.

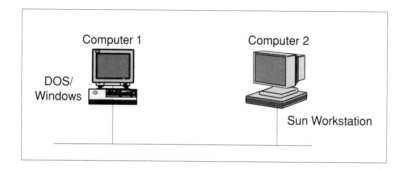

Figure 5.11: Bridge test set-up

The following values were determined by measurements on the Ethernet test-up:

Length of data packets (in bytes)	Delay (in ms)	Round Trip Delay (in ms)
64	281	563
128	537	1075
256	1047	2099
512	2070	4147
768	3070	6195
1024	4120	8243
1280	5145	10291
1500	6025	12051

As is obvious from the measurements, the response time delay depends on the relevant packet size. This means that with an interactive terminal protocol such as TELNET for example (which only transmits 64-byte long packets) response times remain within limits. In the case of a file transfer or when downloading large applications (e.g., Windows) from a central file server to clients, packets that are as large as possible are always transmitted. Under certain circumstances this can lead to intolerable time delays.

5.3 Routers

At the hardware level, LANs operate essentially using the broadcast procedure. In practice, this means that all information is transferred via the entire network to all stations. Only the station that is addressed by its hardware address analyzes the information. This mechanism unavoidably leads to increased data traffic as the number of connected stations rises. This can result in overloading the network and hence unacceptable response times in applications. In addition, there are restrictions that only permit a specific number of stations within one physical network. In the case of Ethernet there can be 1024 stations in a network, with Token Ring the maximum number of stations is 256. Until the mid-1980s it was sufficient to configure the computers in segments and connect them by means of repeaters. A few years later, physical LANs were split up into more manageable smaller structures by bridges. When data traffic in LANs started to explode in the early 1990s, routers were used to create segmentation of LANs which were becoming increasingly larger. The use of routers enabled large full-coverage LAN/WAN configurations that could be operated using a large number of parallel protocol environments. Naturally, the complexity of data networks increased due to the technology.

Different and sometimes confusing terms are increasingly being used in the literature for routers. For example, the terms "Gateway," "Intermediate Node (IMP)," or "Internetwork Nodal Processor (INP)" are used to describe devices that operate on Layer 3 of the ISO/OSI reference model. In this document the term "router" is used exclusively for these devices because, in the authors' view, this term unambiguously describes the function of such devices.

Several separate networks are interconnected as one logical combined overall network at Layer 3. It is the task of this layer to provide the necessary address functions and routing between the separate data networks. This makes it possible to build logically structured, hierarchical networks. Only the bottom two layers are specified in the appropriate standards for all data networks (Ethernet, FDDI, Token Ring). Beyond Layer 3, the functions of higher-layer protocols and their standards and specifications are covered. The Internet Protocol (IP), the Xerox Network System (XNS), the Novell NetWare (IPX), and DECnet protocol are some of the most well-known protocols. All devices that operate on Layer 3 must be capable of understanding the relevant specific protocols, correctly interpreting the content of the received data, and, if necessary, forwarding it to the receiver. All routers only operate with a protocol based on Layer 3. If a router only supports the Internet Protocol (IP), the device is not able to use other protocols (e.g., XNY, DECnet). A router unpacks each data packet down to Layer 3. The data packet is switched using the address information contained in the packet. This is why routers are ideally suitable for connecting different network topologies such as Ethernet to FDDI or Token Ring.

Routable protocols	Non-routable protocols
DECnet	LAT
OSI/ISO	SNA
TCP/IP	NetBIOS
XNS	Xodiac
IPX	NetBUI
XTP	LAN Manager
Vines	ARP RARP

One of the basic functions of a router is to find paths within a meshed network. Routers find the path to adjacent routers and to destination networks by using routing information. This routing information can be entered in routing tables either manually or dynamically through router-to-router protocols. With dynamic routing, cyclic routing information is sent between the routers that are connected to the network. Each router uses the routing packets to learn the existing paths between individual data networks. In the TCP/IP environment, large meshed networks can be split up into individual routing domains. Within a routing domain, the routers use Interior Gateway Protocols (IGP) among themselves. The best known IGP protocols are the Routing Information Protocol (RIP) and the Open Shortest Path First Protocol (OSPF). The routing domains communicate the accessibility of networks among themselves through Exterior Gateway Protocols. These include the Exterior Gateway Protocol (EGP) and the Border Gateway Protocol (BGP). This division into various routing domains reduces the number of routing updates between individual domains significantly.

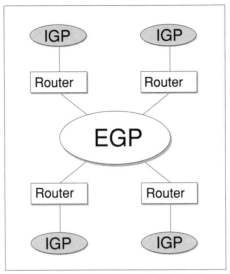

Figure 5.12: Division into routing domains

Fragmentation

Along the path between the transmitter and receiver, data packets may be routed via networks whose maximum permissible packet length is shorter than the length of the datagram to be transported. For instance, this applies in the case of transition from FDDI (4495 bytes) to Ethernet (1518 bytes). If an FDDI datagram has to be transported to the Ethernet by an FDDI/Ethernet router, the original datagram has to be split into several parts. As noted earlier, splitting into smaller data units is referred to as Fragmentation. The length of the resulting datagram fragments is then suitable for transmission over the Ethernet. Each packet fragment is transmitted as an independent data packet. These fragments may be transported to the destination network and reach the destination computer in a different sequence, so the receiver must be capable of passing these data fragments to the higher-level protocol layer in an orderly fashion. This process is referred to as the Reassembly Mechanism.

The following list gives an overview of the maximum packet length in a wide variety of networks:

Network name	Max. packet length in bytes
Ethernet	1512
Token Ring	8000
FDDI	4495
ARPANET	1024
X.25 (Maximum)	1024
X.25 (Standard)	128
ARPA Packet-Radio	256
ALOHANET	80
Bell Lab's Spider	32

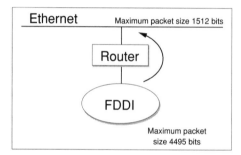

Figure 5.13: Fragmentation between networks

Application Areas for Routers

A router connects two or more data networks to each other by taking care of addressing (matching of addresses) at the Network Layer through physically and logically separate networks. In relation to the connected networks, the router acts as an independent network node. During transmission and reception, the router matches the data packets to network-specific circumstances, such as packet length and maximum transmission time. The data in a router is not simply forwarded transparently; it is buffered and only passed on to the receiver during a subsequent operation. The use of routers is the most effective type of network connection in order to link Ethernets and Token Rings to an FDDI network. When routers are used, the network and the computers connected to it must be planned and configured in greater detail compared with translation bridges (address tables, default routes, etc.). In addition, because of the implementation of different protocols on the software side, a router is always a potential source of errors. It is therefore advisable to make a precise expenditure estimate on a case-by-case basis. As an initial appraisal, it is true to say that routing invariably reduces complexity and problems in the case of meshed networks that have a change of topology (e.g., Ethernet to FDDI) or when connecting slow WAN routes (64 Kbit/s). In contrast, a router is of less benefit in purely Ethernet-to-Ethernet connections. In the event of doubt, one can initially start with connection via bridges and upgrade to routing if necessary. Using bridges that can be enhanced with routing functions by loading new software is ideal for this purpose. The decision whether to use routing or bridging in a multi-protocol environment is particularly difficult. In multi-protocol environments, it is often impossible to route all protocols. Bridging Routers (BRouters) were developed for these situations. BRouters have parallel connected bridge components as well as a fully operational router section. These bridge components bridge all those data packets that cannot be routed using the activated Layer 3 protocols by using translation bridging rules. All routable data packets are transferred by the router by using routing mechanisms. This makes it possible to route the LAT or SNA protocol in a network that is equipped with routers, even though these protocols are inherently non routable because of their structure.

Application Areas for Routers

In the past, routers were always used where connections had to be produced via the local area of data networks. In recent years, routers have been increasingly replaced by bridges because bridges operate in a protocol-transparent manner and are not tied to a particular protocol. Nevertheless, there are still clearly delineated task and/or application areas that can only be sensibly dealt with by routers. Nowadays, routers are installed for the following reasons:

- Compartmentalization of broadcasts

In contrast to bridges, routers do not transport any hardware-specific broadcasts to connected networks. Broadcasts are received by each station in the network, and the information they contain is interpreted. Depending upon the hardware and software architecture of a device, high broadcast traffic rapidly results in overloading of devices. Routers connect networks at Layer 3 and are therefore impermeable to hardware broadcasts.

- Increasing the address space

Let us assume than an official IP network address (e.g., Class C) has been reserved for an organization. Only 254 IP end stations can be connected in such a network. This address space is quickly used up due to a rapid increase in the number of IP devices and no addresses are available for new devices. The only way out of this situation is to apply for additional IP network addresses. These different address spaces are connected to each other via routers.

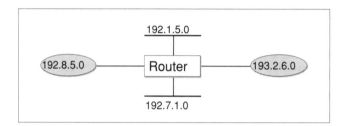

Figure 5.14: Connecting several IP networks via routers

- Segmentation of address space

A company operates a worldwide network. The individual network segments are linked to each other via private services (WAN circuits). The firm is allocated an official IP network address (e.g., Class A or Class B). Because the combined network with all its existing configuration is intended to remain in place, the individual segments are connected to each other via routers with sub-network addresses. Viewed externally, the combined network acts as though it is one completely cohesive address space. Viewed internally, this network is split into smaller configurations.

It is the task of routers to segment address spaces.

- Connecting WAN services

The individual networks in a combined network are linked to each other by WAN services (dedicated lines, X.25, Frame Relay, SMDS, ATM). The routers take care of matching the LAN data streams to the WAN services.

- Company policy reasons

A company has a large number of data networks that are not intended to communicate with each other directly via bridges. Possible reasons for this include:

- Security reasons;

Only local services are available to the users of one data network.

The services of other networks can only be accessed via routers.

Because only end systems of individual stations are configured for routing, only these stations can access these remote resources.

- Administration reasons;

The network is structured into smaller administration units.

Each network is managed and administered through its own management station.

How Does a Router Function?

Network 1 includes end systems A and B and a router having the device address C. The default router address C is entered in a special routing table in devices A and B. Network 2 was configured with correspondingly different addresses to network 1.

Case 1:

Device A attempts to establish a connection to device B.

- Device A detects that device B is in the local network (network 1) and immediately establishes the connection to device B through the local network.

Case 2:

Device A attempts to establish a connection to device Y.

- Device A detects that device Y is not in the local network. It checks its local routing table for an entry concerning network 2. Computer A finds an entry in the routing table that states that all data packets to network 2 must be sent via router C. The data is packed in datagrams and sent to the router's controller C. After receiving the data packet, device C checks the destination address it contains. This destination address informs the router that the data must be transferred to device Y in network 2. For this reason, the router forwards the data to Ethernet Controller Z. Controller Z then sends the data to device Y.

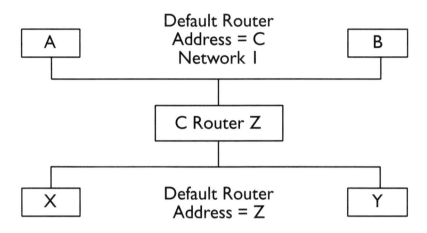

Figure 5.15: Simplified diagram of routing

Protocol-specific Details

The routing function can only be performed between different networks (network addresses, domains or areas). The basic functions of TCP/IP routing is explained in the following example which uses a simple TCP/IP network.

As shown in Figure 5.16, host 1 on the Ethernet (IP address = 193.23.24.1) attempts to establish a connection to a workstation on the FDDI ring (IP address = 194.67.68.1). The Ethernet (193.23.24.0) and the FDDI network (194.67.68.0) are connected via the following three routers: router 1 (IP 1 address = 193.23.24.2, IP 2 address = 195.3.56.2) via the Token Ring network 195.3.56.0; router 3 (IP 1 address = 195.3.56.1, IP 2 address = 194.67.68.2); and router 2 (IP 1 address = 193.23.24.3, IP 2 address = 194.67.68.3). After the user enters the command "TELNET 194.67.68.1" on host 1 (IP = 193.23.24.1) to establish a connection to the workstation (IP = 194.67.68.1), the transmitting computer compares the destination address with the local network address and the sub-network mask. In doing so, it ascertains that this address is not in its local network. Because of an internal entry, the transmitting computer knows which router that is connected to the local network has the path to the destination network. The packet is sent to this router. In a fully functional network, the packet may be sent to both router 1 and router 2. Therefore, it is sensible to only have one router entry in the routing table. TCP/IP protocols offer the following three configuration options for this purpose:

• Static routing

• Default routing

• Dynamic routing

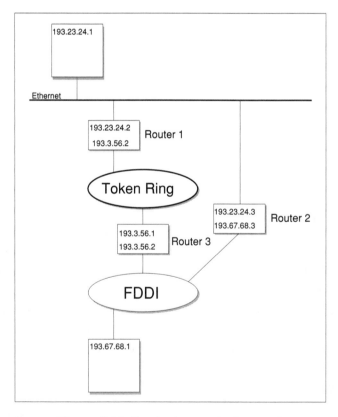

Figure 5.16: Routing in a meshed network

Static Routing

With static routing, the Network Administrator makes one entry for each IP network in each routing table in each router and computer. In practice this means that each path to each IP network, as well as all alternative routes including the number of hops and the subsequent router, have to be entered manually. With UNIX computers, static routing tables are created by using the following command in the /etc/route directory: add route (<network-/host address> <router address> <hopmetric>). The use of static routes makes fault-finding significantly simpler. The path of a data packet through the routed network is made more transparent by the permanent entries and can be traced precisely. The maintenance of static tables is one drawback of static routing. Each new route in a routed network inevitably results in modification and/or updating of all routing tables.

Default Routing

A default router is used to define the exit from the local network in the routing tables of all computers that are to be involved in communication over the local network. All packets that are not intended for communication partners in the local network are sent to this default router. With UNIX computers, the default router is entered using the following command in the /etc/route directory: add default <router address> <hopmetric>). It is the default router's task to decide, for every data packet sent to it, which is the best path for that packet to the destination network. The advantage of default routing is the fact that few entries need to be made in the routing tables. A disadvantage is the effect a failed default router has in a network which has several routers. Failure of the default router is enough to disrupt communication with external networks and computers. As shown in Figure 5.17, router 1 acts as the default router for host 1. If router 1 fails, connection to the workstation is impossible.

Dynamic Routing

With dynamic routing the routers and computers swap routing information packets with each other. In the TCP/IP and Novell environment, the Routing Information Protocol (RIP) is mainly used as a dynamic routing protocol. Routing tables are automatically created and updated in the routers and end systems. With dynamic routing, the path of a packet is not defined as one path and may change continuously in line with existing network resources. The advantage of dynamic routing compared with other mechanisms is the fact that it requires no manual maintenance of routing tables. Each packet is sent via the optimum path with automatic path changes in response to partial failures or resource bottlenecks. The drawback of dynamic routing is the fact that the routing tables in end systems and routers can be significantly longer than with static and default routing. It is not possible to predict the path of an individual packet through the network. This problem is not trivial when fault-finding in relatively large meshed networks because it is impossible to accurately reproduce the paths taken by packets. Dynamic routing also generates an additional network traffic load due to the routing of information packets.

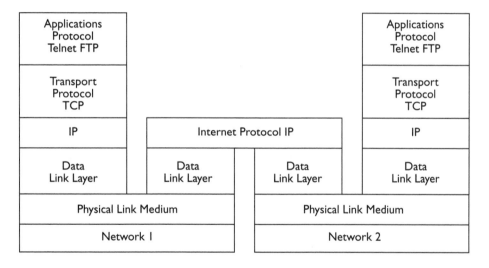

Figure 5.17: Connection between two TCP/IP networks via an IP router

Table 5.4: Bridges versus routers

Function	Bridge	Router
Operating Layer	2	3
Independent of network protocol	No	Yes
Dependent upon higher-layer communication protocol	No	Yes
Ethernet-FDDI connection	Possible	Possible
Token Ring-FDDI connection	Problematic	Possible
LAN-WAN connection	Problematic	Possible
Filtering of network broadcasts	No	Yes
Does not support protocols with routing capability such as LAT or SNA	Yes	No
Supports fragmentation mechanisms	No	Yes
Supports redundant network topologies	No	Yes
Dynamic routing	Limited	Yes
Switchover time to redundant connection	Long	Medium

6 Demands on LANs

Data networks have been installed and operated in a big way for approximately a decade. These networks are continually changing as a result of technological development. The use of increasingly more powerful end systems and the growing use of client/server applications means that the load on networks is rapidly increasing. When Ethernet was introduced, the 10 Mbit/s data rate available on the network offered more transmission capacity than was required. The integration of new applications (e.g., video, audio, or high-resolution graphics applications) into the range of network services means that the demands on available bandwidth, throughput, and delay times are significantly increased. Moreover, the bandwidth available for each workstation decreases as the number of stations active in the network increases.

Example:

Ten intercommunicating workstations are connected on a bus-type Ethernet. Since all data from all devices is distributed over the entire LAN, seen over time in purely statistical terms, each workstation has only 1 Mbit/s available for data transmission. Even the installation of faster processors does not improve performance. If the number of end systems is increased to 100 workstations, each individual station is still left with only 100 kbit/s of the 10

Mbit/s total bandwidth. These observations are based on "best case" scenarios, since delays caused by collisions are not taken into account.

In order to meet these demands for greater bandwidth availability in LANs, network operators have adopted either of the following approaches: installation of a faster LAN technology, or distribution of data traffic in several smaller LAN segments.

Installation of a Faster LAN Technology

The explosion in the development of data networks (Ethernet and Token Ring) in the end systems sector resulted in an ever increasing data load on intersite and floor-to-floor backbones. The technologies available until then no longer satisfied the increasing demands in the backbone sector. Network operators are being forced to increase backbone performance. The effect of the performance bottleneck is particularly dramatic between the individual networks at peak times. One of the options for increasing the available bandwidth for the individual stations is migration to a high-speed network standard (Fast Ethernet, FDDI, or ATM). The following strategies for migration to high-speed data networks have gained acceptance among network operators: total migration and partial migration.

Total Migration

Migration of all end systems to a faster transmission system (e.g., FDDI) is frequently proposed as a means of escaping from the performance/delay deadlock. This strategy of migrating all end systems means that all LAN adapters in the end stations (workstations, hosts, and file servers) and also those in interconnection components (gateways, routers, bridges, etc.) must be replaced. The replacement of all LAN adapters involves

- high investment costs,
- replacement of cabling, and
- a flat network design.

Investment Costs

At any event, it is necessary to invest in a number of areas in order to convert an entire network to a new technology. Examples include LAN adapters, the appropriate drivers, and possibly the communication protocols. The conversion not only requires staff, it also requires a well thought-out migration strategy. The migration of a network to a new transmission technology is rarely completed quickly. Network conversion is usually carried out over a period of several weeks, during which time the network administrators can learn about the new technology and become familiar with the functions and snags of the individual products in detail. Since the new transmission system (e.g., FDDI) no longer allows direct communication with the old components (e.g., Ethernet), an interim strategy must be developed by the planners. In most cases, bridges or routers are used to link the old LAN segments to the new networks for the transitional period. These interconnection components result in additional outlay which causes the transition to the new network to be delayed even further.

Replacement of Cabling

The existing cabling is another important aspect to be considered in the migration to a new transmission system. If traditional Ethernet systems (10Base5 and 10Base2) are transferred to an FDDI network, the existing bus-type cable structures must be completely replaced. Replacement of the cabling must have been allowed for at the planning stage, and cabling replacement plays a major part in increasing the costs and the length of time needed to complete the project.

Network Design

If a network is to be completely converted to a high-speed transmission system, the planning team must consider how the new network design is to be implemented. Direct connection of all end stations to an FDDI network would result in a completely flat network structure. This would mean that the bandwidth available on the transmission medium would be shared among all end stations and interconnection components. In a fully configured FDDI network with 500 end stations, each FDDI station would statistically only have 200 kbit/s of the total 100 Mbit/s bandwidth. This 200 kbit/s bandwidth may well be sufficient for standard applications such as word processing, e-mail, or file transfers, but the use of data-intensive applications (such as graphics, audio, or video) with this network design would result in an immediate bottleneck and cause users to be dissatisfied with network performance. For this reason, high-speed networks are frequently divided into smaller subnetworks. Communication via the common backbone structure takes place via bridges and routers. Since these interconnection components still require a certain amount of transfer time in order to process the data packets, such devices create a time delay in the communication path and therefore cause the performance of the connection using them to be drastically reduced.

Partial Migration

The existing data networks (Ethernet and Token Ring) are retained and are linked to the backbone via bridges and routers. The advantage of using bridges is that every user can access all resources throughout the network on a protocol-transparent basis. In addition, all non-routeable protocols, such as NetBUI, NetBIOS, and LAT, can easily be transmitted. If a fault occurs on a segment, it is possible to trace the cause quickly by deactivating the bridges and to maintain operation. The backbone structure (for a building or site) is replaced by high-speed network technology. The main computer resources are connected to this backbone gradually. In the case of FDDI or Fast Ethernet technology, this approach makes a transmission speed of 100 Mbit/s available between the networks.

Bridges

If the central backbone is implemented on the basis of FDDI technology, the existing LANs are linked via bridges or routers. Direct conversion of LAN data formats (Ethernet, Token Ring) to FDDI packets on Layer 2 takes place via translation bridges. The task of the translation bridge is to convert the various address, protocol, and platform formats. The packet format of the connected Ethernet networks (1512 bytes) does not correspond to the packet length used in FDDI networks (4500 bytes). Since the translation bridges do not have any fragmentation mechanisms, it is necessary to ensure that the maximum packet length is reduced to 1512 bytes on the FDDI network. Consequently, the computers connected on the FDDI network can no longer communicate with the maximum packet length during file transfer, and so the efficiency of the FDDI system is reduced.

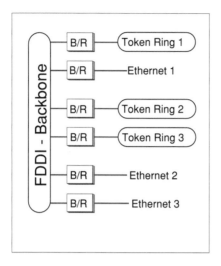

Figure 6.1: Connection of LANs and central resources to the high-speed backbone

The data transfer rate between the connected network segments is called the forwarding rate (expressed in packets per second). The forwarding rate mainly depends upon the access time to the address tables and on the internal processing time of the bridge. In manufacturers' details, the rate stated usually refers to the smallest possible data packets to be transported. The forwarding rate for a bridge is reduced considerably for larger data packets. Since the bridges link the networks on Layer 2, the bridges interconnect all the network segments into a global broadcast domain. This means that all broadcasts are distributed throughout the network. An increase in the broadcast load can thus cause the connected network resources to become overloaded.

Routers

Direct conversion of LAN data formats (Ethernet, Token Ring) to FDDI packets on Layer 3 takes place via routers. The router is the ideal device for converting the various address, protocol, and packet formats to the corresponding transport mechanisms in the other system. Moreover, routers have the appropriate protocol-specific fragmentation mechanisms. A router can therefore transfer the packet formats used in the connected Ethernet networks (1512 bytes) to the packet formats used in the FDDI network (4500 bytes) without the maximum packet length on the FDDI network needing to be reduced. The data transfer rate between the connected network segments is also measured in packets per second in the case of routers. The forwarding rate mainly depends on the processing efficiency of the protocols and on the internal processing time. In manufacturers' details, the rate stated usually refers to the smallest data packets to be transferred. The forwarding rate for routers, as for bridges, is also reduced for larger data packets. However, routers have a significant drawback in that they operate on a protocol-dependent basis. A multiprotocol router may well be capable of processing all routeable protocols (e.g., XNS, IPX, DECnet, or TCP/IP), but, for all non-routeable protocols (e.g., NetBIOS, NetBUI, LAT, and ARP), a router creates an insurmountable obstacle. For this reason router manufacturers have incorporated a router functionality that enables all routeable protocols to be switched via Layer 3 and all non-routeable protocols via Layer 2.

Response Times

As explained above, bridges and routers reduce network performance. Each data packet transfer costs a certain amount of processing time. In general, the cost to performance of a transfer via a bridge/router using the store-and-forward mechanism is between 10% and 15%. If several bridges are cascaded one after the other, the response time is reduced by the total performance loss for all the bridges.

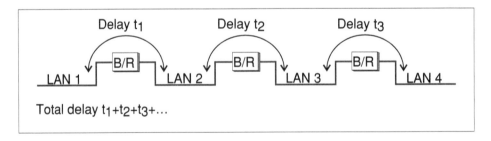

Figure 6.2: Addition of throughput delays

Performance

Another important factor is the availability of bandwidth on the FDDI network. If four Ethernet networks are connected to an FDDI backbone via bridges/routers, then the transmission capacity available to each bridge, in purely statistical terms, is 25 Mbit/s. Even connecting ten segments brings the bandwidth down to the level of Ethernet. Since a number of important network resources (file servers, etc.) are often connected to the central FDDI backbone, the actual bandwidth for all connected end stations is reduced still further.

Criteria for Modern Network Design

If the backbone and the individual LAN segments are connected via MAC-layer bridges or routers, then, with sensible planning, the individual LAN segments can be expanded to almost any size. The following criteria must be taken into account during planning:

- *Bridge/router transit delays*

Each data packet received by the bridge or router must be buffered as a complete packet and, depending upon the bridge/router criteria, either discarded or forwarded to the relevant bridge/router port. Since this processing operation takes some time, long delays can result if bridges and routers are connected in a cascade.

- *Planning note*

If bridges or routers are installed on the path between file servers and the workstations, the effective throughput rate is reduced by the processing speed of the bridge or the router. In straight Novell installations in particular, this can cause undesirable delays in response times.

- *Peak load operation*

If additional users are connected to the network, the quantity of data traffic increases. This inevitably results in a heavier load on the bridge or router and may cause the data packets to be further delayed.

- *Installation location*

In the past bridges or routers were installed primarily in order to divide high data loads between Ethernet segments. Consequently these bridges or routers could not be installed at a central location, such as the room in which the processors or file servers are sited. If the networks are restructured so that these devices can be installed centrally, substantial costs in the form of new or modified cabling would be necessary.

Growth

In order to guarantee that the networks continue to grow and that the future requirements of users can be accommodated, the performance available to each station must inevitably be increased. A number of factors must be taken into account here:

- *Minimizing change*

The installation of bridges and routers often results in substantial changes to the network design and to the network cabling. Measures to enhance network performance should therefore affect the existing network structure as little as possible.

- *Network monitoring*

Performance enhancement measures must not also necessitate the introduction of new methods for network diagnostics and network management.

- *Reducing bottlenecks*

Bridges (particularly some multiport versions) and routers increase the response time between end stations. The new technology must ensure that the response times remain the same even if the load is increased.

- *Data integrity*

Routers have the major drawback of being unable to switch unknown or non-routeable protocols (such as LAT, NetBIOS). Bridges (especially multiport bridges with low memory or a weak CPU) discard packets under heavy load conditions.

6.1 Evolution of Ethernet Switching

Worldwide, approximately 80 million PCs and workstations have been connected to LANs and WANs. Approximately 70% of all networked PCs intercommunicate via Ethernet LAN. A study published in July 1994 by the American company Strategic Networks Consulting shows that the rising use of client/server applications will cause LAN capacity to increase annually by about 30% to 50% per user. The total number of users per network is also increasing by between 25% and 200% annually. The study concludes that standard LAN technologies are no longer able to provide sufficient bandwidth for the drastic increase in data traffic. Because of the large sums invested by companies in LAN technologies, LAN protocols, and LAN infrastructure over the last ten years, operators are now trying to find possible ways of putting these resources to better use and are seeking an opportunity for migration to future technologies (ATM). In a survey on new product requirements, the following key points were named by network administrators:

- Increase in LAN capacity (90%)

- Reduction of operating costs (80%)

- Expandability to accommodate future technological developments (60%)

- Efficiency in meeting customer requirements (60%)

- Reduction of initial purchasing cost for products (60%)

From the above list of criteria for new products, it may be concluded that the current requirement in many networks is for products that can significantly increase the capacity of the LAN in the short to medium term. This increase in capacity affects the desktop computing sector as well as the backbone sector. Although networks are set to expand dramatically over the next few years and the demands on the available bandwidth will be drastically increased by new applications, the budget for employing essential, well-trained network specialists for planning, installation, and technical support is not rising at the same rate. At best, staff budgets are increasing in the order of 3% to 5% annually. Network operators are therefore looking for technologies and products which are able to satisfy the performance requirements of users quickly and easily, which guarantee continuous growth of networks through scalable products, and which require only minimum staff and support resources for their operation. The product requirements can be defined as follows:

1. Increase in network capacity in the end station area

2. Increase in backbone capacity

3. Expansion of network management functions

4. Expansion of security functions in the LAN

5. Independence of the LAN technology

6. Reduction of costs involved in restructuring LANs

7. Minimization of costs for continuous network growth

8. Maximum flexibility in the location of servers and workstations in the network

9. Reduction of router-specific functions and router administration

10. Integration of virtual networks and virtual workgroups

Increase in Network Capacities

One of the biggest problems facing a network administrator is to ensure that the network always matches the performance requirements of the users. Performance bottlenecks in workgroups are particularly difficult to analyze since the users can only ever describe the symptoms, such as long response times, timeout situations, or non-availability of an application on the server. Once the users' network problems have been analyzed in detail, the network administrator can begin to resolve them using one of three possible approaches:

- Division of networks into smaller subnetworks

- Installation of a faster network technology

- Migration to ATM

Division of Networks into Smaller Subnetworks

The traditional approach to improving performance in the network is to divide the entire network into smaller subnetworks. By reducing the number of users per subnetwork, response times are dramatically reduced, timeout situations are minimized, and the number of users accessing the applications on the server is limited. If a subnetwork were to consist of only one user, the end station for that user would inevitably have the entire performance available to it.

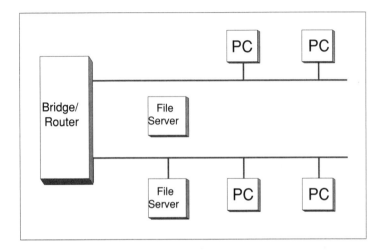

Figure 6.3: Division into smaller network segments

Installation of a Faster Network Technology

The second option for improving network performance is to integrate a high-speed LAN technology (FDDI or Fast Ethernet) in the workgroup area. As explained in the previous section, full migration to a new technology is always associated with high costs, time-consuming planning, and a relatively lengthy restructuring phase.

Migration to ATM

ATM technology is based on high-speed switching. This technology supports transmission speeds of 25 Mbit/s, 100 Mbit/s, 155 Mbit/s, and 622 Mbit/s. Meanwhile there are even plans to take the speed up into the Gigabit/s sphere.

For cost reasons, ATM technology initially is becoming established in the backbone and WAN sectors only. If prices fall drastically in future and place all functionalities within reach, ATM will also move into the workgroup sector.

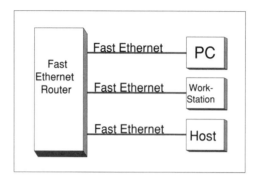

Figure 6.4: Installation of a faster network technology

Of the solutions described above, the only one that can be implemented cost-effectively and quickly is the reduction of networks to a few users. This division into so-called microsegments is used by switching technology, and currently this choice offers the highest possible performance and the most attractive cost/benefit structure.

Table 6.1: Comparison of high-performance LAN technologies.

	ATM	Fast Ethernet	FDDI	LAN switching
Data rate	25-622 Mbit/s	100 Mbit/s	100 Mbit/s	10, 4/16 Mbit/s
Access method	Cells	CSMA/CD	Token passing	LAN-based switching
Packet size	53 bytes	64-1512 bytes	64-4500 bytes	64-8000 bytes
Services	Isochronous	Asynchronous	Asynchronous	Asynchronous
Extent of network	100 meters to 1,000 kilometers	100 meters to 2.5 kilometers	100 meters to 30 kilometers	100 meters to several kilometers
Management	Proprietary MIBs and SNMP	Ethernet MIBs and SNMP	FDDI MIBs and SMT, SNMP	Ethernet and Token-Ring MIBs and SNMP
Costs	High	Low	Moderate	Low

(continued)

Table 6.1: (continued)

	ATM	**Fast Ethernet**	**FDDI**	**LAN switching**
Fault tolerance	–	Spanning Tree	Dual Homing	MAC Ring and Spanning Tree
Application	Backbone and WAN	LAN and backbone	LAN and backbone	LAN and backbone

Ethernet Switching

The transmission procedure used by Ethernet makes it a half-duplex transmission technology. In practice, this means that the transmitting station checks for the presence of a signal on the transmission medium before it transmits an Ethernet packet. This process is called Carrier Sense. If a signal is detected, it means that the medium is occupied and the transmission process is deferred until later. If no signal is found on the network, then the medium is available and the data can be transmitted. With this procedure (Multiple Access) a situation can arise in which two stations transmit their data simultaneously. The information signals overlap on the cable, i.e., the data packets collide, and the data contained in them is lost. Collisions are detected by special logic in the receiving station (Collision Detection) and reported to the end station. The devices involved in the collision have to retransmit the data after a waiting period. The CSMA/CD (Carrier Sense Multiple Access/ Collision Detection) procedure used in Ethernet is able to detect all collisions but cannot prevent them. In networks with a large number of end stations this can lead to a substantial increase in response times, even from a load of 40%. Although the data rate available to users is theoretically 10 Mbit/s, problems occur in practice even at speeds well below the theoretical maximum performance level. The Tx part actively transmits the data in the standard Ethernet interface of the transmitting station. All the data is read via the RX part. The data is received at the receiving device via the RX part of the interface. If two stations transmit data to the network simultaneously, a collision is detected, and the Ethernet controller interrupts the data communication. In Ethernet technologies, such as 10BaseT and 100BaseTx (Ethernet on Twisted Pair), or 10BaseF and 100BaseFx (Ethernet on Fiber Optics), the transmit and receive directions are on a separate cable. The 10/100BaseF and 10/100BaseT technologies are only used in straight point-to-point applications.

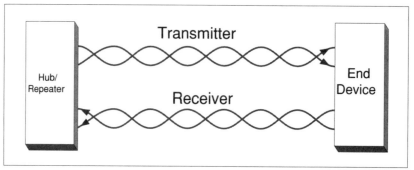

Figure 6.5: Send and receive pairs on the cable

Because the two transmission channels are separate, collisions cannot occur on the transmission medium. However, if the cables are connected in a concentration point (e.g., a hub) via a repeater card, the link between all cables is implemented via Layer 1 (repeater function). All cables connected to the repeater form a common collision domain.

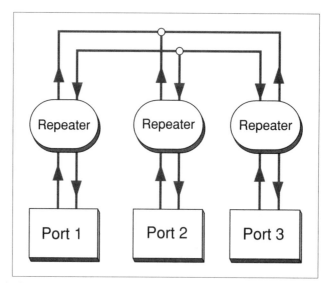

Figure 6.6: Circuit diagram showing function of Ethernet Twisted Pair repeater card

However, connection of all cables on the Physical layer causes all the data transmitted via the transmit line to appear on all receive lines of all connected end stations. This inevitably results in collisions occurring at the connected end stations despite the separation of the send and receive channels on the cable. Any errors (short packets, packet fragments) are also passed on to all lines.

If a multiport bridge is installed in the concentration point instead of a repeater, each data cable connected to the bridge port is treated as a separate segment. In this case, the individual segments are separated or switched on Layer 2. All cables connected to the bridge port thus form a separate collision domain. The bridge automatically learns all the source addresses occurring on the ports and builds up a common address table from these addresses. The information is forwarded only from the transmit port to the relevant receive port in accordance with the destination and originating addresses of the received data packet. In this way an exclusive, collision-free data channel is set up between the transmitter and the receiver.

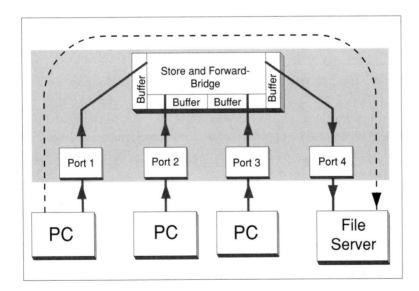

Figure 6.7: Exclusive connection between receive and transmit port via a bridge

However, the drawback of multiport bridges was that these devices operated relatively slowly and were relatively expensive. Nor were multiport bridges geared for handling a high broadcast load. Broadcasts must be transmitted to each available port; this can result in the data traffic on the connected network segments being considerably reduced if the broadcast load is too high.

Switches

The first switches were introduced in the early 1990s by an American company, Kalpana. These devices operated on Layer 2 and were the logical development of multiport bridges. The difference between multiport bridges and the first switches had more to do with the creation of a new marketing term than with technical differences. Since then the hardware and software of switches has been optimized to meet the special requirements. The individual switch ports have been configured so that each connected data cable maps directly to an individual segment. The switch learns all the source addresses occurring on the ports through an integral learning mechanism and builds up a common address table from these addresses. The information is forwarded only from the transmit port to the relevant receive port in accordance with the destination and originating addresses of the received data packet. In this way an exclusive, collision-free data channel is set up between the transmitter and the receiver. The packets concerned are said to be switched via this connection. The original multiport bridges and the switches were set up on straightforward CPU architectures. The task of the CPU was to maintain the address tables, the filter and forward process, and the management processes (Spanning Tree protocol, SNMP protocol). In the meantime the hardware configuration of the switches has been further optimized and replaced with super high-speed ASICs (Application Specific Integrated Circuits). This has drastically reduced the packet throughput speed so that the full network performance is available to every port in an Ethernet network.

6.2   Demands on Ethernet Switches

Over the years, Ethernet has proved to have a solution ready for all necessary expansions and innovations. Whilst the early PC networks were still constructed with Yellow Cable (10Base5) or Cheapernet (10Base2), these network structures were replaced over the next few years with low-cost 10BaseT cabling. The star-type cabling systems greatly simplified the installation of servers and workstations. In addition to this, there was a dramatic fall in the price of Ethernet adapters. The availability of high-performance PCs and band-width-hungry applications (DTP and graphics applications) meant that the individual applications no longer had sufficient bandwidth available on the traditional 10 Mbit/s Ethernet. Network operators therefore looked for a LAN technology which supported significantly higher data rates. Ethernet switches offer a way out of the performance deadlock. This new Ethernet procedure is based on the principles of telephone technology. If the Ethernet stations are connected to a switch, this device ensures that an exclusive 10 Mbit/s pipeline is available to each individual port. The switch sets up a quasi-exclusive 10 Mbit/s connection between the two end stations via the internal bus, using the source and destination addresses of the packet. Switches are required to meet the following criteria:

- High port density

- High performance

- Elimination of bottlenecks in the servers

- Support for Fast Ethernet

- High-speed data pipelines

- Transparency of technology

High Port Density

The first multiport bridges had 4 to 6 ports. This low port density meant that only a relatively small number of end stations could be connected to these components. The first switch launched on the market by Kalpana was capable of guaranteeing simultaneous 10 Mbit/s connections for all 15 twisted-pair ports. Ethernet switches, with a larger number of ports, were introduced as second-generation devices. In these devices, the individual plug-in switching cards communicate via a common bus. Today's switches have to be designed for the workgroup sector and for the so-called enterprise sector.

Workgroup Switches

Today, workgroup switches are based either on straightforward software switch architectures or on ASIC architectures. These workgroup switches are used for interconnecting a small number of high-speed workstations (up to 16 ports). Workgroup switches are designed to support only a small number of MAC addresses per port.

Enterprise Switches

The main feature that distinguishes enterprise switches from other switches is their ability to support a large number of connection ports. The number of ports supported in enterprise switches ranges from 48 to 128. The central core of the enterprise switch is formed mainly by an ultra high-speed central bus. The available bandwidth of this bus depends on the bus width (32-bit or 64-bit) and the frequency (16, 20, 32 MHz, or higher). At a frequency of 25 MHz, a bus with a width of 64 bits can achieve a data throughput rate in the realms of Gigabits. This makes it possible for up to 128 Ethernet devices (10 Mbit/s) to communicate simultaneously via the bus. Enterprise switches must also support a large number of MAC addresses per device. A minimum of 1024 MAC addresses is supported by virtually all manufacturers. Some devices, however, can handle 4000 or even 64,000 MAC addresses. Most enterprise switches are now able to integrate FDDI, Fast Ethernet, 100VG-AnyLAN, or ATM networks via the internal bus. In this way the network operator can integrate individual high-speed Ethernet segments, high-speed servers, or even a high-speed backbone into the overall concept.

High Performance

An important difference between bridges and switches is in the delay time known as latency. Latency is measured in microseconds and is defined as the interval that elapses between the receipt of the first bit of a data packet by the switch port to the point at which this bit leaves the destination port of the switch. The difference in latency between bridges and switches is several hundred microseconds. This difference in latency on the communication path means that switches are able to transfer packets more quickly and have a faster response time. This is particularly important for applications or protocols which require every data packet transmitted to be confirmed by the communication partner. Another important aspect with regard to latency is whether the duration of the delay is guaranteed or variable. Multimedia applications generally require a low latency. Where possible, this latency should be fixed and should never vary. Voice and data transfer via a network is simplified if there is a predictable, fixed delay between the transmitter and the receiver. Since far more short packets than long packets can be transmitted per unit of time, the overall throughput of a switch is always stated on the basis of the quantity of the smallest Ethernet packets to be transferred (64 bytes). However, these short packets are the ones that cause a switch to approach the limits of their own processing capability.

Elimination of Bottlenecks in the Servers

The biggest area of application for Ethernet Switches is in straightforward client/server environments. In these installations a multitude of 10 Mbit/s clients communicate with one or more 10 Mbit/s server ports. The greater the number of clients communicating simultaneously with the server port, the greater the likelihood of a bottleneck occurring on the server side. This has led to the development of special adapter cards which can operate simultaneously as server ports. These cards each support one MAC interface on the Physical layer. Special software (e.g., NLM) enables these MAC interfaces to act as a single MAC interface with regard to the higher protocols. The user can therefore install several Ethernet cards in his or her server at the same time and increase the bandwidth according to his or her requirements (10, 20, 30 or 40 Mbit/s). However, the drawback to this solution is that several ports in the switch are occupied by the large number of Ethernet adapters on the servers. An alternative option available to the network operator is Full-Duplex Ethernet (FDE) technology. In FDE, the transmit and receive path in an fiber optic or twisted pair cable operate independently on a straightforward point-to-point connection. This results in a throughput of 20 Mbit/s per port. Several, in this case 4, FDE adapters can be installed in one server, which means that the total throughput can be increased to 80 Mbit/s.

Support for Fast Ethernet

The availability of new, ultra high-speed PC servers based on PCI bus architecture (maximum I/O throughput of 132 Mbit/s) has meant that a new approach to upgrading the traditional Ethernet has become necessary. Fast Ethernet was defined by the High Speed Workgroup of the IEEE 802.3 standardization team in response to the ever increasing demand for higher network performance. The official name for Fast Ethernet is the 100Basex Standard. This new Ethernet standard enables data to be transmitted at a speed of 100 Mbit/s via twisted pair (Category 3 and 5) or fiber optic links. Fast Ethernet uses the traditional CSMA/CD (Carrier Sense Multiple Access with Collision Detection) access mechanism and the same MAC packet format as the 10 Mbit/s Ethernet. The integration of high-speed Ethernet ports in the switch enables high-speed servers and high-speed processors to be connected on the network. This technology also ensures that downward-compatibility to 10 Mbit/s LAN components is guaranteed.

100VG-AnyLAN

As an alternative to Fast Ethernet, Hewlett-Packard and AT&T Electronics have developed the 100VG-AnyLAN standard with a speed of 100 Mbit/s. This standard is able to transmit both Ethernet and Token Ring packets. The 802.12 IEEE Committee was specially set up to standardize this technology. The AnyLAN standard replaces the CSMA/CD access technology with a sophisticated demand priority mechanism, by which collisions that would normally occur on Ethernet are avoided. In 100VG-AnyLAN technology, the hub or the switch has the task of centrally controlling the access of the connected end stations to the network.

High-Speed Data Pipelines

The 100BaseX technology offers an ideal solution for providing the connection between distributed LAN switches. These high-speed data pipelines are used to switch the individual switches together into a large virtual switch. Overall performance in the switched network is increased yet further by these so-called "fat pipes" or high-speed uplinks. If the fat pipes are operated in a full-duplex configuration, collision-free transmission at a speed of 200 Mbit/s can be achieved between the individual switch ports. The maximum distance between two switches can be increased to 2000 meters by using a fiber optic link.

Transparency of Technology

Ethernet switches operate on Layer 2 of the ISO/OSI Reference Model and are therefore able to connect all standard Ethernet components transparently. In client/server applications, the use of Ethernet switches enables the individual devices to be connected as if to their own private Ethernet. Moreover, if the switch ports are able to handle more than 1000 MAC addresses, these switches can also facilitate the connection of complete bus segments. In this case, switches can operate as a substitute for backbone routers. Since switches operate on Layer 2, these devices can subdivide a network or a broadcast domain into subsegments. Subdivision into protocol-specific subnetworks is not possible on this layer, however. This task is reserved for routers. Switches operate like bridges and cannot, for example, filter out broadcast packets.

6.3   Definition of Functions

As with all new technologies, the marketing people at the various vendors make every effort to invent new words to describe their products. These neologisms offer few clues as to the exact nature of the device and its functions. Sometimes it is impossible to escape the feeling that these terms have been created with the sole intention of leaving customers at a loss. In America, this practice of disguising functionality behind imprecise terms is called "the game of specmanship." A closer look at the switching market reveals terms such as port switching, configuration switching, microsegmenting, dynamic switching, learning, aging, software switching, hardware switching, cut-through switches, on-the-fly switching, store-and-forward switching, work-group switches, enterprise switches, 10/100BaseT switches, flow control switches, frame switching, single MAC layer switches, multiple MAC layer switches, MAC layer independent switches, cell switches, etc. The authors feel it is necessary to provide a more detailed explanation of the individual terms and the functions concealed behind them to enable the reader to understand how the various products work.

How Switches Work

The end stations are connected directly to the port on a switch. The data packet transmitted from the end stations on the cable always contains a source and a destination address. The port recognizes which device is being connected to it on the basis of the source address. This address is forwarded, with the relevant port identification, to the central address list of the switch. These common address lists are formed using an address algorithm. The address lists are used as transport tables for the data packets. The switch uses this address pool to determine the receiver (switch port) to which the data packet must be forwarded. If a destination address is not entered in the table, the switch process assumes that this address has not yet actively communicated on the network. In this case, the switching process treats the packet as a broadcast packet and forwards it to all ports. If the as yet unknown device replies to the received data packet, the source address it contains is registered in the address table with the appropriate port. If the switching process finds the appropriate destination address or the switch port for a received data packet in the table, it transports the packet to the destination port via the backplane. The Ethernet controller at the destination port has to forward the packet to the relevant end stations. As with a bridge, the entries in the address table are time-stamped. The time stamp is reset to 0 each time the address occurs. All addresses that have been learned but are currently not being used by a communication partner are aged with a timer. The address tables are always sorted according to the age of the entries. This means that the address currently being used by the switch is always at the beginning of the table and the search process requires relatively little time. This so-called aging time can be configured as required by the network administrator. The following default values have been found useful in practice:

0 - 180 seconds = recent

180 - 300 seconds = medium

300 - 600 seconds = old

If an address is not used within the maximum time set (e.g., 10 minutes), the learning/aging process automatically ensures that this address is deleted from the address list. This mechanism keeps the address lists in the switch relatively small and enables them to be searched very quickly. Some switches even allow addresses to be included in the tables permanently. The network administrator has the option of deactivating the learning mechanism and only entering addresses in the table manually. If this is done the switch can only handle addresses that have been entered manually. Communication between all other addresses or devices is not possible.

Distinction Between Bridging and Switching

All Ethernet bridges operate on the basis of the store-and-forward mechanism only. Because of their field of application, bridges are designed for situations in which some 80% of all data traffic is local and only 20% of data traffic has to be forwarded to one of the connected segments. In a switch, all data traffic is forwarded to one or more of the switch ports. Switches therefore usually have more ports than bridges and the architecture of the switch must be able to transmit all data traffic between all ports. Because a bridge has only a few ports, the forwarding and learning process of a bridge only has to search relatively flat tables. In a switch with a high port density (e.g., 128 ports), a high-speed search mechanism must be provided to enable the tables to be searched very quickly and to ensure that the delay between receiving and forwarding a packet is minimized. A switch must also support parallel connections between a multitude of incoming and outgoing ports.

Table 6.2: Comparison of bridges and switches

Function	Switch	Bridge
Port density	High	Low
Cost per port	Medium	High
Throughput	High	Medium/low
Delay	Low	Medium/high
Parallel connections	Yes	No
Optimized for connection of	Stations	Segments

Port Switching

Two years ago, manufacturers of hubs and cable concentrators introduced a number of terms into the networking world. Port switching, configuration switching, and static switching have nothing to do with actual switching on Layer 2. Most hub systems currently available on the market have a backplane in which several different data busses are supported in parallel. Today, the various products usually support the following data busses via the backplane:

- Several parallel Ethernet segments (IEEE 802.3)
- Several parallel Token Rings (IEEE 802.5, 4 and 16 Mbit/s)

- Several parallel FDDI Rings

- One or more parallel high-speed busses for future applications, such as ATM or Ethernet switching applications

The plug-in cards of hubs are constructed in such a way that the individual ports or port groups of the cards can be statically assigned to the relevant busses via the management system. This static assignment function forms the basis for an electronic patch panel. Instead of the terms port switching or configuration switching, therefore, the term "port assignment" should be used to describe the voluntary assignment of a port to an internal hub bus.

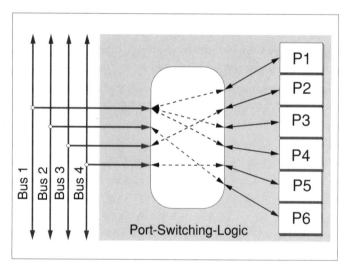

Figure 6.8: Port assignment

Microsegments

The transmission procedure used by Ethernet makes it a half-duplex transmission technology. In practice, this means that the transmitting station checks for the presence of a signal on the transmission medium before it transmits an Ethernet packet. This process is called *Carrier Sense*. If a signal is detected, it means that the medium is occupied, and the transmission process is deferred until later. If no signal is found, then the medium is available, and the data can be transmitted. With this procedure (Multiple Access) a situation can arise in which two stations transmit their data simultaneously. The information signals overlap on the cable, i.e., the data packets collide, and the data contained in them is lost. Collisions are detected by special logic in the receiving station (Collision Detection) and reported to the end station. The devices involved in the collision have to retransmit the data after a waiting period. The Tx part actively transmits the data in the standard Ethernet interface of the transmitting station. All the data is read via the RX part. The data is received at the receiving device via the RX part of the interface. If two stations transmit data onto the network simultaneously, a collision is detected and the Ethernet controller interrupts the data communication.

In Ethernet technologies, such as 10/100BaseT (Ethernet on Twisted Pair) or 10/100BaseF (Ethernet on Fiber Optics), the transmit and receive directions are separated on the cable. The 10/100BaseF and 10/100BaseT technologies are only used in straight point-to-point applications. A switch port only has one end station connected on it. Because the two transmission channels are separate, collisions cannot occur on the transmission medium. Since the Ethernet switch has learned all the addresses connected to the ports, it can set up a direct connection according to the destination and source addresses of the data packet. Every client/server link thus has available an exclusive, collision-free data channel with a 10 Mbit/s throughput rate. By multiplexing several connections on a high-speed internal bus in the Ethernet switch, the throughput rate of the connected Ethernet end stations can be increased to several times that of a traditional LAN segment. The overall throughput rate of the network depends only on the maximum speed of the internal logic and of the bus. The use of Ethernet switches turns every star-type end station connection into a separate, independent microsegment. This technical trick results in an immediate performance improvement in a heavily strained network, without any modification of the network infrastructure being necessary.

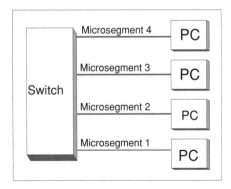

Figure 6.9: Microsegments

Software Switching

Software switches are mainly based on regular high-performance architectures. In these devices the whole switching function is performed via the software. The performance of software switches depends solely on the number of ports per microprocessor, the frequency of the processor, and the quality of the software code. At the moment, most manufacturers of software switches are basing their devices on one or more Intel i960 processors. Because of their construction, Ethernet switches based on RISC processors are unable to process more than 80,000 to 120,000 packets per second. This can lead to a drastic fall in overall performance of software switches. In order to guarantee high performance the number of ports on the switch is limited to six to eight Ethernet ports. Software switches can guarantee an acceptable throughput but, compared with hardware switches, do not have the same ability to transfer data at maximum wire speed where there are a large number of parts per switch. However, software switches do have the advantage that code modifications or performance enhancements can be carried out via a software update.

Most software switches are based on a bridging code which has been expanded to support multiport devices. By integrating a bridge function, software switches provide the following important functions:

- The possibility of filtering out invalid data packets

- Implementation of the Spanning Tree mechanism

Generally speaking, hardware switches are not able to filter out invalid data packets. These packets are forwarded transparently from the transmit port to the receiver port, and are not discarded until they reach their destination.

Hardware Switching

The following note applies to the hardware switch category: the respective manufacturers have each developed a special chip to enable their switches to process data packets. These chips are called ASICs (Application Specific Integrated Circuits). ASICs are specially designed to carry out a specific task. These chips can generally be described as "software molded into hardware." As far as their processing speed is concerned these components are ideal for ultra high-speed processing of data packets. Experts describe this as "full-wire-speed." This means that the ASIC can process the data packets at the maximum speed of the transmission medium. Today's ASICS support up to 100,000 logic elements in one chip. Because of this, the software operates in close proximity to the hardware. This results in a high processing speed (several hundred thousand packets per second). In some ASICs, the processing power of five to ten RISC chips is produced in one chip. The development of ACISs is a very costly and time-consuming process for the manufacturers. Moreover, the development of each new ASIC chip involves a high degree of risk for the manufacturer.

In ASICs, the relevant codes are implemented directly in the hardware. The code is therefore extremely difficult to modify. Every time the code is expanded, a new ASIC chip must be produced. The ASIC debugger devices now available are still very expensive, and the cost of acquiring such devices is often greater than the cost of developing the ASIC. ASICs are very expensive to develop. Because ASIC chips cost relatively little to produce, this technology is resulting in a general fall in the cost of LAN components. At any rate, ASICs are considerably more cost-effective compared with ordinary processors used in software switches. Because of ASICs, switches are becoming cheaper to mass produce, and this results in a competitive retail price. Some manufacturers develop their ASICs in two stages. In the first stage, the switch code is integrated into a so-called FPGA (Field Programmable Gate Array) component. These components are considerably cheaper than pure ASICs. Compared with pure ASICS, however, they have a great drawback; they process the code far more slowly. Modifications to the code can be implemented much more quickly, though.

The first versions of switches from many manufacturers were based on FPGAs. After the switch code has been optimized, these components are replaced with pure ASICs. Several manufacturers (e.g., Madge Lannet) use a separate ASIC for each individual port on a switch. Other manufacturers (e.g., Ornet) have implemented one ASIC as the central component in their switch. Implementing ASICs on the basis of ports makes it easier to construct scalable switches with a high port density. Of course, the large number of ASICs is reflected in the costs. Architectures based on a single ASIC cost far less to produce. Single-ASIC architectures are often used in switches with a lower port density.

Advantages of ASICs

- Direct processing of data/functions.

- An ASIC processes the data in close proximity to the hardware and is therefore much faster than conventional discrete components.

- These components are developed for specific applications.

- A far greater degree of functionality can be integrated in the individual components.

- The use of ASICS means a big reduction in the number of hardware components. This inevitably results in an increase in the MTBF (Mean Time Between Failure) for the whole system.

Table 6.3: Comparison between ASIC switches and processor based switches

Function	ASIC switch	Processor switch
Processor	ASIC	Standard processor
Design	Design specially tailored to requirements	Chipset developed for general requirement
Instruction sets	All instruction sets are implemented in the hardware	Additional software required
Processing speed	High	Low
Modifications	Difficult to implement	Can be implemented by changing the code
Scalability	High	Low scalability
Risk	Very high	Low
Cost	High	Low

Cut-Through Switches

With cut-through switches or on-the-fly switches, the forwarding process of the switch is started as soon as the six-byte destination address is read by the switch controller on the receiving port. This switching method reduces the latency between the receiving and the transmitting port, since the data frame never has to be buffered in its entirety. The great advantage of cut-through switches is the speed of these products. The cut-through products available on the market show a latency between input and output port of 15 µs to 60 µs. This latency is lower than most ATM switches currently available. In communication conducted over a network, the data transmitted on the transport path may be destroyed or corrupted. This results in packet fragments or data packets with an invalid CRC value. A cut-through switch does not buffer the received data packet, and therefore the validity of the data packet cannot be checked. This means that all packets—even ones that are too short, too long, or defective—are forwarded as soon as the destination address is recognized. If there is a high error rate on the network, this results in all defective packets being forwarded to the receiver. The receiver discards these packets and the higher protocols (e.g., TCP/IP) ensure that the discarded packets are sent again by the transmitter. The transmission of defective packets wastes valuable bandwidth. This problem has been recognized by some manufacturers and the following solutions have been implemented in the devices:

- The switch continuously checks the validity of the data packets while the packets are being transferred. If a large number of invalid data packets is detected, the receive port in question either becomes blocked or it switches over to store-and-forward mode. In order to do this, however, the switch must be able to operate in both transmission modes.

- The cut-through switch is configured so that it does not begin to transmit the packet until it has received the first 64 bytes (smallest Ethernet data packet). This guarantees that all packets which are too short are automatically filtered out.

Pure cut-through switches should therefore only be installed in well implemented networks which show a low number of defective packets. Cut-through switches are normally based on straightforward hardware switch architectures.

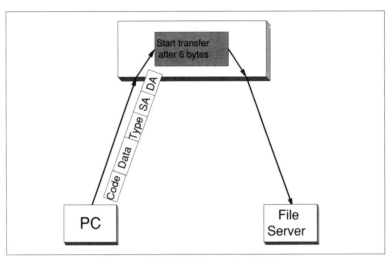

Figure 6.10: Cut-through switching

Store-and-Forward Switching

On closer inspection, Ethernet switches based on store-and-forward technology are revealed as a cross between a switch and a bridge. This type of device could more accurately be described as a "high-performance multiport bridge." These modified bridges offer a far greater bandwidth than ordinary bridges. In terms of their architecture, they still operate mostly within the narrow limitations of a CPU-based device. Store-and-forward switches have a higher latency than hardware-based cut-through switches. The typical latency for store-and-forward switches is between 80 µs and 100 µs. However, hardware switches that operate in store-and-forward mode are now available on the market. The time needed by the switch in order to transfer a data packet between the incoming and the outgoing ports is therefore the same as the time required to send a packet on the medium. The latency of a store-and-forward switch thus depends on the length of the data packet to be transferred.

The latency for the shortest Ethernet packet (64 bytes) is 51.2 µs; for the longest Ethernet packet (1518 bytes) it is 1.21 ms. The latency of store-and-forward switches thus depends on the length of the data packet to be transmitted. In cut-through switches, the latency is constant and does not depend upon the length of the data packet. Most Ethernet switch ports support a transfer rate of 10 Mbit/s in the standard procedure. If the switches are also equipped with faster ports (e.g., Fast Ethernet), the data packet must be transmitted with the store-and-forward technique during the transition between the different speeds (10 Mbit/s <–> 100 Mbit/s).

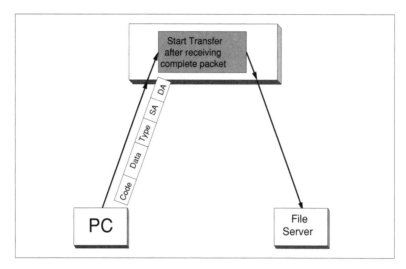

Figure 6.11: Store-and-forward switching

Table 6.4: Comparison between cut-through switches and store-and-forward switches

Function	Cut-through	Store-and-forward
Speed	High	Medium
Latency	Low	Medium
Forwarding after receipt of	6 bytes	whole packet
Complexity	High	Medium
Speed adaptation (10 <–> 100 Mbit/s)	Not possible	Yes
Error filtering	Partial	Yes

Latency

Another distinguishing feature in switches is latency. Latency is measured in microseconds and is defined as the interval that elapses between the receipt of the first bit of a data packet by the switch port to the point at which this bit leaves the destination port of the switch. The difference in latency between store-and-forward components and cut-through devices is several hundred microseconds. Delays can therefore be reduced to a low level in cut-through devices. This is particularly important for applications or protocols which require every data packet transmitted to be confirmed by the communication partner. Another important aspect with regard to latency is whether the duration of the delay is guaranteed or variable. Multimedia applications generally require a low latency. Where possible, this latency should be fixed and should never vary. Voice and data transfer via a network is simplified if there is a predictable, fixed delay between the transmitter and the receiver. Since far more short packets than long packets can be transmitted per unit of time, the overall throughput of a switch is always stated on the basis of the quantity of the smallest transmissible Ethernet packets (64 bytes). However, it is these short packets which cause a switch to approach the limits of its own processing capability.

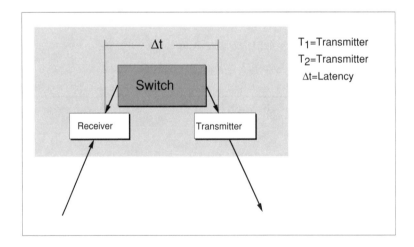

Figure 6.12: Latency

Workgroup Switches

Most workgroup switches are based on straightforward software switch architectures. These switches are used for interconnecting a small number of high-speed workstations (up to eight ports). There are notable exceptions to this rule. Kalpana (Cisco) bases its switches directly on ASIC architecture. Workgroup switches are designed to support only a small number of MAC addresses per port. The FastSwitch 10/100 from Grand Junction was designed for the connection of only one device (one MAC address) per port. The Grand Junction switch is also based on hardware switching architecture and is capable of supporting 100 Mbit/s ports as well as the normal 10 Mbit/s ports. This switch therefore operates in both store-and-forward and cut-through mode.

Enterprise Switches

The main feature of enterprise switches is their ability to support a large number of connected ports. The highest port density is currently offered by the Madge/Lannet switch, with 128 10BaseT-Ethernet ports per device and a total bandwidth of 1.28 Gbit/s. The LanPlex switch developed by 3Com supports 88 ports, while the Ornet switch has only 48 ports per device. The core of the enterprise switch is formed mainly by an ultra high-speed central bus. The available bandwidth of this bus depends upon the bus width (32-bit or 64-bit) and the frequency (16, 20, 32 MHz or higher). The hardware components available at the moment facilitate a maximum throughput rate of 1.28 Gbit/s. This data rate is achieved by running a 64-bit bus at a frequency of 20 MHz. Enterprise switches must also support a large number of MAC addresses per device. A minimum of 1024 MAC addresses is supported by virtually all manufacturers. Some devices, however, can handle 4000 or even 64,000 MAC addresses. Most enterprise switches combine the high-speed bus with one or more FDDI/ATM interfaces. These connections are used for linking an Ethernet domain to one or more high-speed servers or to the campus backbone. If this technology is used the Ethernet data packets must be converted to FDDI or ATM data packets.

10/100BaseT Switches

100BaseT technology provides an ideal solution for connecting 10BaseT ports to high-speed LAN servers or to a high-speed backbone. It is necessary to use store-and-forward technology for switching between a 10 Mbit/s segment and a 100 Mbit/s segment. This disadvantage is balanced by the fact that the data packets no longer have to be converted into a different data format. Another advantage of the 100BaseT uplink is that it operates in full-duplex mode. This enables collision-free transmission with a transfer rate of 200 Mbit/s to be achieved. The length restriction for a 100BaseT connection can be circumvented by using a fiber optic link (2000 meters). The use of low-cost Ethernet technology even in the high-speed area provides a real alternative to ATM technology in the local area.

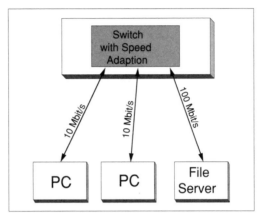

Figure 6.13: 10/100BaseT switch

Flow Control Switches

A flow control system similar to ATM has already been implemented in some of the switches currently available on the market. If a port on one of these switches becomes inundated with too much data, the overloaded port sends a signal to the input port instructing it to reduce the data flow. This ensures that no data packets are lost, even if the load is extremely heavy. However, this technique has a serious drawback in enterprise switches, as demonstrated by the following example: several stations are connected to one port via an Ethernet segment, and some of these stations are communicating with an overloaded output port. If the overloaded port reduces the incoming traffic flow on the input port, this mechanism also affects the stations that are communicating with other output ports which are not heavily loaded. It must therefore be possible to switch the flow control mechanism on and off.

Cellbus Switches

Further development of cut-through switches has resulted in the cellbus switching architecture. A cell is defined as a data block with a fixed size. Data packets of different lengths are split into cells with a defined size. The great advantage of cellbus switching is that these data cells have a defined transmission time. In a cellbus architecture, the switch functions as an exclusive data highway between the transmit port and the receive port. The received cells are transmitted and forwarded to the receiver via this data highway in the same sequence in which they were received.

This gives the original sender the impression that there is always a direct connection with the receiver. Whether or not the receiver is currently occupied is completely irrelevant. The shared memory structure is an integral part of cellbus switching technology. The cell bus switches the individual data cells to the shared memory. The receive port processes the data packets transmitted to it in sequential order. In order to do this, however, this shared memory area must allow a high processing speed and must not become a bottleneck in the architecture. This technology therefore guarantees consistency of performance, whatever the number of ports, the data traffic or the type of data transmitted (unicast, multicast, broadcast). The effective switching bandwidth of an Ethernet switch based on a cellbus architecture is calculated by the following formula: theoretical port performance (10 Mbit/s) x number of ports.

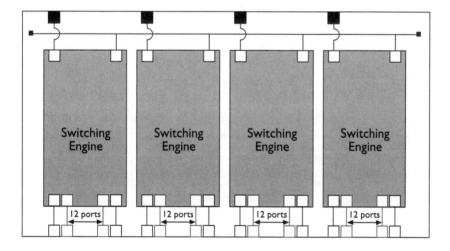

Figure 6.14: Cellbus switch

Single MAC Layer Switches

Single MAC layer switch is the term used for all devices which support only one type of MAC layer protocol. Switches like this are now produced by manufacturers as Ethernet switches (with different interfaces such as AUI, 10Base2, 10BaseT, and 10BaseF), Token Ring switches, and even FDDI switches.

Multiple MAC Layer Switches

Multiple MAC layer switches operate as a straightforward switch between ports with the same MAC layer specification (e.g., Ethernet <—> Ethernet). Between ports with different MAC layer protocols (e.g., Ethernet <—> FDDI) the device operates as a translation bridge.

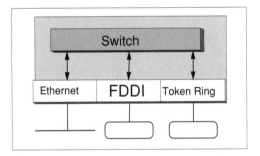

Figure 6.15: Multiple MAC layer switches

Multilayer Switches

In simplified terms, multilayer switches are a combination of switches (Layer 2) and routers (Layer 3). Within a workgroup or a virtual network, all packets are transmitted with the aid of the switching function. However, if data packets have to be transmitted between separate workgroups or between different virtual networks, the routing functions of the switch are called into action.

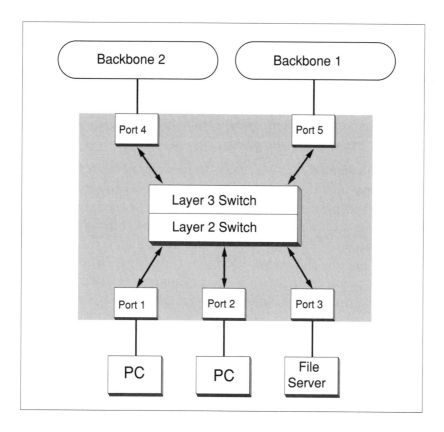

Figure 6.16: Multilayer switches

6.4 General Criteria

The demands on switching technology can be deduced from the functional characteristics of high-speed networks. The information must be transported over the network in the correct sequence and with a high level of quality and reliability. At the same time, it should be possible to incorporate the various speeds of the existing physical network structures and to make the configuration as flexible as possible. Data may be delivered in the correct sequence in data networks, but if it is transported through a network with redundant paths, it is not always possible to guarantee that the data will be delivered in the same sequence. Even the integrity and accuracy of the transported data can only be partially guaranteed by switches.

Most errors are intercepted by the protocols present on the MAC layer. However, these parameters fundamentally affect the overall performance of the system and are therefore among the most important requirements of switches. The internal switching and forwarding of information between the input and output parts of the switch places considerable demands on the performance of the switch. Since switching in the LAN area is a relatively new technology, appropriate measurement techniques for assessing switching performance have yet to be developed.

Assessing the performance of devices is often very difficult for both experts and non-experts alike. Manufacturers make every effort to present their devices in the best possible light. Product brochures sometimes present theoretical values as results which have been measured in practice. At present, switch manufacturers measure their devices according to their own criteria. This also explains the sometimes enormous throughput figures and the relatively high deviation from these by the products in practice. The following four features are particularly important when assessing a switch product:

- Actual aggregate bandwidth

- Latency

- Throughput under maximum load

- Stress situations

Actual Aggregate Bandwidth

The actual total bandwidth provided by a switch can be measured on the basis of the ports which are active at the same time. Operating all ports in parallel in this way must not cause a performance bottleneck to develop in the switch. It must therefore be possible, inside a switch, for information to be transferred between any inputs and outputs without bottlenecks forming. This situation means that this information from the various input ports requires common resources. The switching of these incoming data streams places a high demand on the bandwidth and the performance capacity of the switch.

A detailed examination of the devices available on the market reveals that some manufacturers advertise their products with enormous throughput figures. These figures frequently refer to the backplane data rate. Some manufac-

turers' marketing strategies consist of meticulously adding together the theoretical transfer capacities of all the backplane pins and converting the resulting total capacity into the throughput for the device. In some cases, this figure
is then multiplied again—by the earth's curvature or the DM/US dollar
exchange rate. For practical purposes, the values stated in the glossy brochures
do not in any way mean that the entire bandwidth of the backplane can be
used by the available ports. Nor do the bare transmission rates for bits or packets per second provide any indication whatsoever about the quality of the individual switches and their architectures. If throughput rates measured under
realistic conditions are available (for example the rates determined by the
European Networks Lab (ENL) under the management of Bob Mandaville—see
Section 6.6), then the user is able to work out, on the basis of the total available bandwidth, how the network will deal with network-intensive applications and the transfer of large data quantities between ports. In all but a very
few switches on the market, "worst case" conditions—i.e., when all ports on
the switch communicate simultaneously at 10 Mbit/s or 100 Mbit/s—lead to
some reduction in total bandwidth. The availability of the Fast Ethernet and
the Full Duplex Ethernet (FDE) transmission mode increases the total throughput per port by a factor of ten. This results in even greater demands being
placed on the actual total bandwidth of the switch.

In simplified terms, the throughput of a switch depends on the components
of its hardware architecture. To obtain clear criteria for assessment purposes,
the switch architectures must be reduced to their bare functionality. At the
IBM laboratories in Zurich, in the quest to find the architecture for IBM's ATM
switches of the future, a study of possible switch architectures and their
throughput behavior was produced. During this investigation, the following
architectural models emerged as possible variants for implementation:

- Crossbar matrix switches with single input buffers
- Crossbar switches with several input buffers
- Self-route with output buffers
- Self-route with input and output buffers
- Self-route with a common output buffer pool
- Multistage queuing

Crossbar Switches with Single Input Buffers

In this architecture, all ports on the switch are interconnected via a matrix. If a data packet from one of the ports is being transmitted on the matrix, the entire switch is occupied. Consequently, no further data can be transmitted from other ports while the packet is being transferred. To overcome this bottleneck, each input port is provided with buffers. If a data packet is already being transmitted on the switch matrix, all new data packets are stored in the input buffers until the switch becomes free to transmit the next data packet.

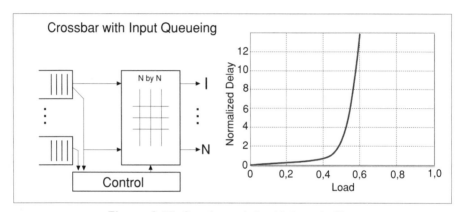

Figure 6.17: Crossbar switch with input buffers

The way in which this switch operates is best explained using the following example based on a simple network structure. Two file servers (Server 1, Server 2) and one workstation (WS-A based on a 10 Mbit/s Ethernet card) are connected to a crossbar switch via point-to-point twisted-pair cables. In addition, two coaxial segments, each with several workstations (WS-B, WS-C, WS-D, WS-E), are connected to different switch ports. In this configuration the following situation can occur:

- Workstation A sends a long data packet (1500 bytes) to Server 1

- At the same time, Workstation B sends a short data packet to Server 1

Since the long data packet requires a relatively large time interval for the data to be read in, this FIFO buffer is blocked. This data packet is then transmitted to the output port of Server 1. During this time the packet from

Workstation B remains in the input buffer, since it cannot be processed any further. After the minimum interval (an interframe gap of 9.6 µs) which must be maintained between two Ethernet packets, Workstation C sends another packet to File Server 2. This packet is stored in the input buffer of the local port behind the packet that is already buffered. The packet from Workstation C to File Server 2 cannot be processed any further, since the switch matrix is already occupied and, what is more, another packet is awaiting processing ahead of it in the queue in the FIFO buffer. As far as the packet from Workstation C is concerned, the switch remains blocked until all packets ahead of it in the FIFO buffer are transmitted. The latency in the FIFO buffer thus depends on the size of the packet which has caused the switch to be blocked.

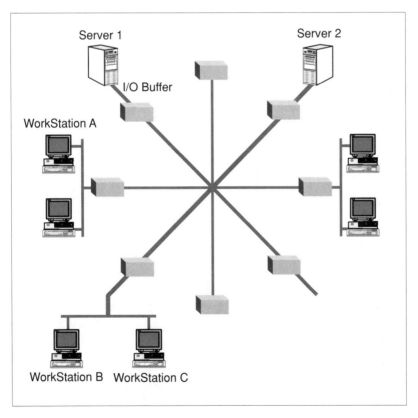

Figure 6.18: Crossbar switch in use

In networks with a low load, the crossbar with input buffers architecture achieves a relatively short delay between the individual packets. However, this delay is increased to extreme levels as the load becomes heavier. This phenomenon is called the "head of the line phenomenon." The upper limit of the operating range is around 58%. If the load continues to grow the delay between packets is increased considerably.

Advantages of the Crossbar with Input Buffers Architecture

- Comparatively low hardware costs
- Cost-effective
- Easy to modify
- Ideal for use in workgroups with a low load
- Ideal architecture for transmitting broadcasts and multicasts

Disadvantages of the Crossbar with Input Buffers Architecture

- Long delays if the throughput rate exceeds 58%
- Not suitable for connecting segments
- Architecture cannot be used in full-duplex mode
- Low scalability

Crossbar Switches with Several Input Buffers

The only logical option for expanding the crossbar with input buffers architecture is the integration of several parallel input buffers. The received packets are each stored in a buffer on the port via an internal mechanism. The switch would prioritize the individual data packets for transmission via the cross-matrix using additional control logic. This architecture would certainly afford the maximum in terms of performance, but the complexity of the hardware and software would make it too expensive to develop. This would mean that products based on this architecture would not be competitive on the market.

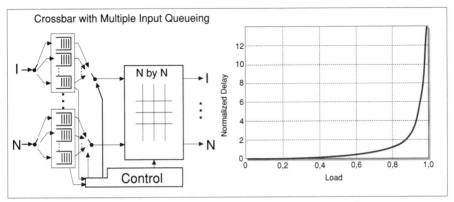

Figure 6.19: Crossbar switch with several input buffers

Self-Route with Output Buffers

In this architecture, input buffers are completely eliminated. This means that the phenomenon described under the heading "Crossbar with input buffers architecture," in which a data packet in the FIFO buffer can block the transfer of another data packet, does not arise. However, this architecture does require that all data packets (of any size) can be transmitted between the input ports and the output buffers without delay with the aid of a very fast switching fabric. The data packets are not buffered for onward transfer to the output port until they reach the output buffer. This means, though, that the output buffer must be relatively large (several Mbytes) and that mechanisms for accessing this memory must be optimized. High efficiency in this switch can be guaranteed only by the direct interaction of the switching fabric with the optimized output memory.

The great advantage of this architecture is that the delay between the individual data packets remains the same even if the network load becomes heavier and the number of ports is increased. In practice, the efficiency achieved by the switch is close to the optimum throughput of 99.xx%.

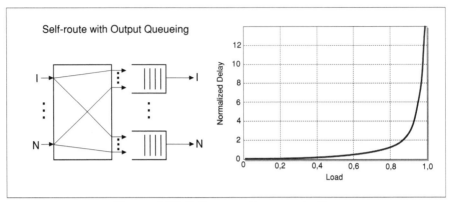

Figure 6.20: Self-route with output buffers

Advantages of Self-route with Output Buffers Architecture

- Easy to modify

- Ideal for use in workgroups and central applications

- Consistent delay times up to a throughput rate of almost 100%

- Architecture can also be used in full-duplex mode

- Suitable for connecting segments

- Ideal architecture for transmitting broadcasts and multicasts

- High scalability

Disadvantages of Self-route with Output Buffers Architecture

- Relatively complex hardware structure

- Costs increased by complex hardware structure

- Large output buffer and optimized memory management are necessary

Self-Route with Input and Output Buffers

This architecture differs from the self-route with output buffers architecture in that it uses both input and output buffers. Because input buffers are used, the "head-of-the-line" blocking phenomenon described above can occur if several stations are connected to one port, though the effect of this blockage is somewhat alleviated by the output buffers. However, delay times are increased dramatically as data traffic becomes heavier and the number of stations grows.

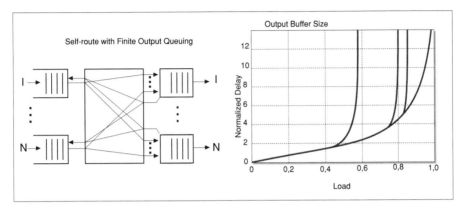

Figure 6.21: Self-route with input and output buffers

Self-Route with a Common Output Buffer Pool

This architecture differs from the self-route with input and output buffers architecture because the parallel output buffers are replaced by a common output buffer pool. Because input buffers are used, the "head-of-the-line" blocking phenomenon described above can occur if several stations are connected to one port, though the effect of this blockage is only marginally reduced by the common output buffer. However, delay times are increased dramatically as data traffic becomes heavier and the number of stations grows.

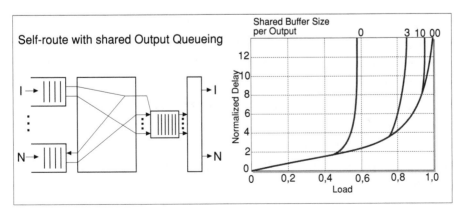

Figure 6.22: Self-route with common output buffer pool

Multistage Queueing

In this architecture, a number of input buffers with a separate switch are available to a port or group of ports. When a data packet is received on a port, its destination address is ascertained. The data packet is then forwarded to the destination port with the aid of the switch. If the receiver is located at a port on the local switch, the data packet is transmitted directly to the destination port. If the receiver is located on a different switch however, the entire data packet must be forwarded to the destination switch in the next stage.

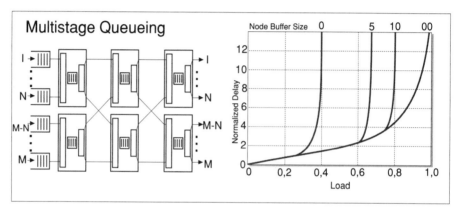

Figure 6.23: Multistage queueing switch

This principle on which this architecture is based is best described using an example of a 16-port Ethernet switch. This switch is based on a 4-ASIC architecture. Each of the ASICs is responsible for transferring data from four Ethernet ports. As shown in Figure 6.24, the data is transmitted between the individual ASICs via 10 Mbit/s high-speed simplex connections. Each ASIC has the following two memory areas: the Content Addressable Memory (CAM) and the standard RAM.

Identical address tables are stored in each CAM. The address tables contain all the addresses for all active end stations connected on the network. When a data packet is received on a port, its destination address is ascertained by means of the CAM. The packet is then buffered in the memory on the destination port. In a broadcast, the data packet is transferred to all three ASICs. Since the ASICs are interconnected via serial connections, the packet is trans-

mitted three times. This results in an enormous transfer overhead. The resulting time delay can sometimes be higher than in switches based on store-and-
forward technology. If the port density in this type of architecture is even higher (e.g., 36 or more ports), the overhead for broadcasts and multicasts is
increased even more substantially. Moreover, the latency varies between ports
connected to the same ASIC and ports served by different ASICs. This also
explains the difference in response times for transmission between local ports
and ports that can be accessed via one or more additional switches.

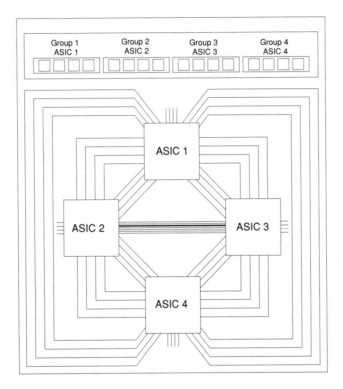

Figure 6.24: ASICs connected via serial cables

Advantages of the Multistage Queueing Switch

• Good architecture for workgroups with a low load

• Suitable for connecting segments

Disadvantages of the Multistage Queueing Switch

- Relatively high hardware costs

- This drives costs up to extremely high levels

- Modifications are very difficult to implement

- Low scalability

- High throughput rates and a large number of users can lead to considerable delays

- Architecture cannot be used in full-duplex mode

In a network, there are a number of defined criteria that can cause a switch to become extremely heavily loaded and possibly overloaded. The following are factors in these critical situations:

- Invalid data packets

- Broadcasts/multicasts

- Overload situations

Invalid Data Packets

In communication conducted over a network, the data transmitted on the transport path may be destroyed or corrupted. This results in packet fragments or data packets with an invalid CRC value. A cut-through switch will forward a packet to the destination device as soon as it recognizes a valid destination address, without further checking. The receiver (the end station) detects the error in the packet and discards this data packet. Most protocols in the higher protocol layers (IPX, TCP/IP, DECnet) ensure that the discarded data packet is automatically retransmitted. However, the switch wastes valuable bandwidth by transmitting defective packets. The switch ports should therefore be able to filter out all invalid data packets sent to the switch by the end station. In store-and-forward switches the forwarding mechanism automatically ensures that the whole data packet is received, a CRC check is carried out, and the packet is then forwarded to the destination port. However, this mechanism results in a dramatic increase in latency compared with cut-through switches.

A cut-through switch is not able to filter out so-called runt or jabber packets. Runt packets are all data packets with a length of less than 64 bytes. These packets, which are too short, are the result of a collision. Runts or collisions are always occurring in heavily loaded network segments. This is why, when connecting segments to cut-through switches, it is important to ensure that as few stations as possible operate on the network segment. For this reason, some manufacturers have incorporated a so-called look-ahead or fragment-free mode. This mode can be individually configured for each port. In look-ahead mode, the port waits until it has received at least 64 bytes (the minimum size of a valid data packet) before it forwards the packet to the receiver by means of the forwarding process. Of course, this waiting for the first 64 bytes increases the latency between the input and output port. The great advantage of this mechanism, however, is that any packets that are too short are not transmitted.

The occurrence of jabbers (excessively long data packets) can be traced to a defective end station. A jabber packet like this can possibly contain the broadcast address or an unknown unicast address as the destination address. A cut-through switch always transports the data on the basis of the first 6 bytes, which contain the destination address of the packet. Since a cut-through switch does not check the whole data packet before processing it further, this sort of switch will forward all data packets (runts and jabbers) that contain a valid destination address. This also means that the data is forwarded to all the ports on the switch if the destination address is unknown or is a broadcast address.

Cut-through switches with integrated CRC checking are a myth. Some manufacturers claim that their switches carry out a CRC check. This statement is correct, but the marketing strategies of these companies do not include explaining to the users what happens with the CRC check. Cut-through switches are able to check the whole data packet during the forwarding process and then carry out a CRC check. Since the CRC check sum is always transmitted at the end of a data packet, the switch port in question can tell that the CRC check has detected an error. However, the packet has already been switched to the destination port and, in most cases, has left the output buffer as well. If a CRC error has been ascertained, the port can forward this error to the management module. On the basis of this information, the management function is able to build up a set of port-related CRC statistics. If errors in the network are suspected, the network administrator has the task of checking the individual statistics and identifying the defective port.

Meanwhile, some manufacturers have gone over to making devices in which the ports can be configured to enable the switched packets to be continuously checked for errors. Certain threshold values can be defined via the management function; if these values are exceeded, the corresponding receive port is blocked or switched over to store-and-forward mode. In store-and-forward mode, the switch operates as a normal bridge. In this mode all packets are buffered in full before being forwarded. The advantage of this is that all invalid data packets (e.g. CRC errors) can be filtered out directly at the receive port. In order to do this, however, the switch must be able to operate in both transmission modes. Unfortunately, these devices switch over to store-and-forward mode if the threshold value (x% of defective packets per unit of time) is exceeded, but no mechanism has yet been implemented for automatically switching back to cut-through mode if the figure falls below a lower threshold value.

Broadcasts/Multicasts

All Ethernet switches operate on Layer 2 of the ISO/OSI Reference Model and are able to connect standard Ethernet components transparently via twisted-pair cables. For this reason switches can divide up the load handled by a large network, but the separate microsegments still form a closed broadcast domain. Subdivision into separate broadcast domains is not possible on this layer. This task is reserved for routers and the functions of virtual networks (see also the section on virtual networks). Switches operate like bridges and cannot, for example, filter out broadcast packets. If broadcast or multicast packets are sent from an end station, the switch has the task of forwarding this information to all ports or to a group of ports. This increases the load on the switch's internal communication paths to an extremely high level. In some switches, these packet types have a serious impact on overall performance. Multicast packets (group addresses) present another problem for switches. This type of address enables a server, for example, to send information to all clients programmed on this multicast address. The great advantage of group addresses is that the server does not have to know its clients. The information is sent onto the network and only certain receivers copy the information from the network. The DECnet protocol, for instance, frequently uses multicast mechanisms for communication. Although the clients receive the data packets from the network via the multicast addresses, they send their reply with their own unicast address. This means that the switch does not have any chance to learn the receiver port for the multicast packet. Inevitably, multicast addresses are always treated as broadcasts and sent to all ports. Some manufacturers have now incorporated an option that allows the network administrator to configure the address tables of the switch via the management function, thus enabling the multicast addresses for certain ports to be configured manually. This inevitably means that the multicast packets are only switched to the ports that are configured for the multicast address in question. This mechanism works in favor of all ports which do not support this multicast address, since the number of packets unnecessarily transmitted to those ports is drastically reduced.

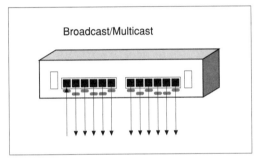

Figure 6.25: Broadcasts/multicasts

Overload Situations

Ethernet switches can, in practice, also be connected to Ethernet segments. Several hundred end stations can be connected to these segments. In practice, a situation can arise in which a large number of users wish to access this one port. This port has available a theoretical throughput of 10 Mbit/s. However, this throughput is divided among the devices communicating via this port. If a large number of data packets (possibly with the maximum data rate) are sent to this one port by a large number of processors on the switch, this inevitably leads to an overflow or backlog of data packets (increase in latency). An overload situation such as this also allows conclusions to be drawn as to the quality of the switching architecture.

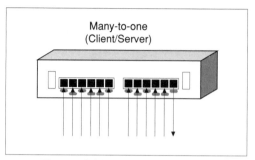

Figure 6.26: Overload situations

If a large number of data packets are transmitted to one output port (e.g. the server connection) by a large number of ports, this can cause resources to become overloaded even if the port has a large output buffer. What this means in practice is that the port cannot accept any more data packets. These new data packets are discarded if the output buffer is full. It is the task of the higher layers (Transport layer) to retransmit these "lost" data packets. This does not cause any problems in connection-oriented protocols such as TCP or SPX. If a UDP or LAT service is used however, this situation can very quickly cause the connection to be interrupted. Some manufacturers have therefore integrated a flow-control mechanism. If a full output buffer is registered, it sends a signal to all input ports. For each data packet to be transferred, the ports check (on the basis of the destination address) whether sufficient resources are available for the transmission. If a full output buffer is detected, a collision is automatically generated (within the first 64 bytes of the data packet). This causes the transmitter to cancel the transfer and retransmit the data according to the Ethernet backoff algorithm. This collision mechanism has a great advantage in that no modifications whatsoever are required in the protocols in order to implement effective flow control on the Physical layer. Since no data packets are lost during transmission from Transport layer to Transport layer, switches with this mechanism never lose any data or block the data path between transmitter and receiver.

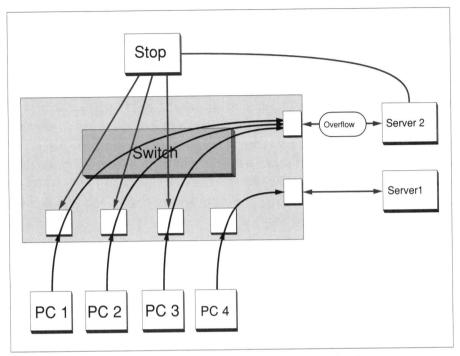

Figure 6.27: Principle of the flow-control mechanism

At first glance, this collision mechanism seems impressive. However, as with so many things in technology, it too has a drawback. In the following example, two servers (Server A and Server B), a number of workstations (Stations 1, 2, 3, 4, 5), and a complete segment with one server (Server C) and Workstations 6, 7, and 8, are connected to one switch. All the connected devices use the TCP/IP protocol. Workstations 1, 2 and 3 communicate with Server A. Workstation 5 communicates with Server B via the switch. Since Server A is a relatively slow machine and the three workstations create a high network load, server switch port A becomes overloaded. This port uses the flow-control mechanism (collision) to reduce the input load. Workstation 5 or even Workstations 6, 7 and 8 can still communicate, unimpeded, with Server B.

If Workstation 6, for instance, communicates with Server C for the first time, no connection is achieved. Although Workstation 6 only wishes to communicate via the local segment, the flow-control mechanism causes this communication to be affected. The link here is not immediately apparent. What is happening here at the bit level? Since Workstation 6 uses the TCP/IP protocol for communication, the 32-bit IP addresses must be converted into 48-bit Ethernet or IEEE addresses. The dynamic mapping of the two address forms takes place in the TCP/IP protocol with the aid of the ARP protocol. Before a datagram is transmitted the IP protocol checks the ARP cache table to establish whether a hardware address for the destination IP address has already been entered in this table. If an entry is found in the table, the datagram can be sent directly onto the network. If there is no entry in the table, however, the hardware address of the destination device is ascertained with the aid of the Address Resolution Protocol. This ARP request is always sent via a packet which contains a broadcast address.

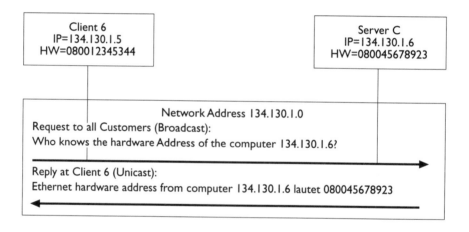

Figure 6.28: ARP Function

Only processors with an entry for this IP address reply to this request. The reply (ARP reply) to the ARP request is stored in the ARP cache.

Since the ARP request is sent via the segment, this packet also reaches the switch port on which the cable is connected. However, since server port A has signalled an overload situation and a broadcast packet must be transmitted to all ports, a collision inevitably occurs. This results in the ARP request being discarded owing to the collision signal. The sender of the ARP request will retransmit the same packet after a short waiting period. If the overload on the server port has not been eliminated in the meantime, the fresh ARP request is again discarded due to a collision. In a situation like this, there is no way out. The only remedy is to replace server port A with a faster processor or a 100 Mbit/s interface, or to break up the segment and connect all the stations in this segment to the switch in a star-type configuration.

6.5   Components of a Switch

Because all microsegments (and thus all end stations) are concentrated in one or more central components, the hardware and software configuration of switches must be designed to ensure that switch component failure is a very rare occurrence, or the basic components must be duplicated in the configuration (redundancy). For example, the power supply in a switch must be installed so that it can be replaced quickly and easily by a service technician. It is also necessary to ensure that the switch does not have to be taken out of service while work on the power supply is being carried out. By designing the switch with redundant power supplies, the availability of the switch is greatly increased. Moreover, the hardware configuration of the individual modules in a switch must be designed so that these can be replaced on the spot without reconfiguration. Of course, this process must be possible during normal operation. As a result the service engineer's work is greatly simplified, costs are reduced, and network availability is considerably increased.

The hardware configuration of a switch depends on the architecture of the switch. Since all the switches on the market are configured with different architectures, the individual modules are described on the basis of a fictitious Ethernet switch. The individual function modules can be found in every switch in one form or another.

The following function modules interoperate in a switch system:

- Input controller,
- Control process,
- Switching element and
- Output controller

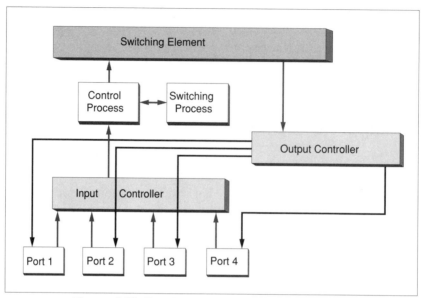

Figure 6.29: Function modules of an Ethernet switch

Input Controller

The input controller ensures that data transmitted to the switch is properly transferred. The task of this function module is to receive the data packets and to forward them to the control process. In a cut-through switch, the input controller attempts to forward the data to the control process as soon as it recognizes the 6-byte long destination address. In some architectures (see also Section 4.4 General Criteria), the switch may have buffering on the receive side. Depending on the availability of the switching element and the output controller, the data may have to be buffered at the input port and its forwarding to the control process deferred until later. Some switches also have a facility for filtering out defective packets on the receive side. Some cut-through switches can be configured so that they do not begin to transmit the packet until they have received the first 64 bytes (smallest Ethernet data packet). The information must therefore be buffered in the input controller until at least 64 bytes of information have been received. This guarantees that all packets which are too short are automatically filtered out. Some cut-through switches can even check the validity of the data packets continuously while the packets are being transferred. If a large number of invalid data packets is detected, the receive port in question either becomes blocked or it switches over to store-and-forward mode. In pure store-and-forward switches, the whole data packet is received by the input controller and an error check carried out before the packet is forwarded to the control process. This means that the latency in store-and-forward switches depends on the packet length. The delay for the shortest Ethernet packet (64 bytes) is 51.2 µs; for the longest Ethernet packet (1518 bytes) the latency is 1.21 ms.

Flow-Control Process

Another function of the input controller is the operation of the manufacturer-specific flow-control mechanism. If one of the output ports becomes over-loaded (e.g., because too many clients are communicating with one server port) and the quantity of data packets received can no longer be handled, the incoming data packets must be discarded. It is the task of the higher layers (Transport layer) to retransmit these "discarded" data packets. This does not cause any problems in connection-oriented protocols such as TCP or SPX. If a UDP or LAT service is used however, this situation can very quickly cause the connection to be interrupted. If a bottleneck is detected on the output port, the output controller for the switch ensures that this status is signalled to the transmission process. The transmission process registers this overload status. The transmission process signals this overload status to the relevant input controller for each new packet to be sent to that port. The input controller therefore recognizes that the output port for this packet does not have sufficient resources available. The input controller thereupon automatically generates a collision on that port within the first 64 bytes of the data packet. This causes the transmitter to cancel the transfer and retransmit the data according to the Ethernet backoff algorithm. This collision mechanism has a great advantage in that no modifications whatsoever are required in the protocols in order to implement effective flow control on the Physical layer. Since no data packets are lost during transmission from Transport layer to Transport layer, switches with this mechanism never lose any data or block the data path between transmitter and receiver.

Control Process

The entire control process is divided into the following tasks:

- The transmission process
- The learning process
- The forwarding process and
- The flow-control process

Transmission Process

After the destination address (the first six bytes of a data packet) has been recognized the transmission module of the switch checks the address table to establish whether this address has been entered. The switch uses this address pool to determine the receiver (switch port) to which the data packet must be forwarded. If no entry relating to this source address is found in the address table, it means that the receiving device in question has not yet communicated with the switch. If the switch has not been manually configured and if broadcasting to unknown addresses is activated, the switching process treats the packet as a broadcast packet. The packet with the unknown address is therefore forwarded to all ports. In this case the switching process assumes that the unknown end station will respond to this packet in the form of a reply. If the as yet unknown end station replies to the received data packet, the source address it contains is registered in the address table with the appropriate port. If the switching process finds the appropriate destination address or the switch port for a received data packet in the table, it transports the packet to the destination port via the backplane.

Learning Process

If the source address of a switch interface is already in the address table, only the timer for the address entry is reset. If the source address of the switch interface is not in the address table, this address is entered, with the relevant port identification, in the central address list of the switch. At the same time the aging timer for this new address entry is started. This time stamp is reset to 0 each time the address occurs. All addresses that have been learned but are currently not being used by a communication partner are aged with a timer. The address tables are always sorted according to the age of the entries. This means that the addresses currently being used by the switch are always at the beginning of the table and the search process requires relatively little time. This so-called aging time can be configured as required by the network administrator.

Forwarding Process

After the transmission process has established the destination port of the switch to which the received data packet must be sent, the forwarding process actually transfers the data via the backplane of the switch. Depending on the backplane technology used and the transmission mechanism across the back-plane, the information received is switched to the output process as a complete data packet in the case of frame switching. If a cell switching procedure is used, the data packet must be split into separate cells and the individual cell fragments must be given a fragment number. These cells are then switched to the output process.

- Treatment of unicasts

  The forwarding process uses the port identification from the address table as the header information for the data packet or cells to be switched. The information is forwarded to the output process according to the header information.

Ethernet Packet	Source Port 1	Destination Port 5	Type Uni

Figure 6.30: Header information of the forwarding process for unicasts

A unicast packet is therefore switched to the exact port on which the receiver of the packet is located. If an entry for a destination address is not found in the address table, it means that the receiving device in question has not yet communicated with the switch. If the switch has not been manually configured and if broadcasting to unknown addresses is permitted, the unicast packet is forwarded to all ports on the switch. The header information entered is therefore no longer the destination port, but the internal broadcast address. In this case the forwarding process assumes that the unknown end station will respond to this packet in the form of a reply. If the as yet unknown device replies to the received data packet, the source address it contains is registered in the address table with the appropriate port.

Ethernet Packet	Source Port 1	Destination Port 5	Type Broadcast

Figure 6.31: Header information of the forwarding process for unknown unicast addresses

- Treatment of broadcasts

  With a broadcast address (FF-FF-FF-FF-FF-FF), all components in a broadcast domain are addressed. If a packet like this is received by a switch, the forwarding process must ensure that this packet is forwarded to all other ports on the switch. The header information entered is therefore no longer the destination port, but the internal broadcast address of the switch.

Table 6.5: Registered broadcast addresses

Broadcast Address	Type Field	Description
FF-FF-FF-FF-FF-FF	0600	XNS packets, Hello search
FF-FF-FF-FF-FF-FF	0800	IP
FF-FF-FF-FF-FF-FF	0804	CHAOS
FF-FF-FF-FF-FF-FF	0806	ARP
FF-FF-FF-FF-FF-FF	0BAD	Banyan
FF-FF-FF-FF-FF-FF	1600	VALID packets,
FF-FF-FF-FF-FF-FF	8035	Reverse ARP
FF-FF-FF-FF-FF-FF	807C	Merit Internodal (INP)
FF-FF-FF-FF-FF-FF	809B	EtherTalk

- Treatment of multicasts

  With a multicast address, all components in a broadcast domain are addressed. If multicast packets are sent from an end station, the switch has the task of forwarding this information to the group of ports for which it is intended. However, since the receiver has always used its own unicast address when replying to a multicast packet, the switch does not have any chance to learn the receiver port for the multicast packet. Inevitably, multicast addresses must always be treated as broadcasts by the forwarding process and sent to all ports. The header information entered is therefore no longer the destination port, but the internal broadcast address of the switch. Some manufacturers have now incorporated an option that allows the network administrator to configure the address tables of the switch via the management function, thus enabling the multicast addresses for certain ports to be configured manually. This inevitably means that the multicast packets are only switched to ports that are programmed for the multicast address in question. In a case like this the ports released for a particular multicast type are entered in the header information.

Table 6.6: Registered multicast addresses

Multicast Address	Type Field	Description
01-00-5E-00-00-00 to 01-00-5E-7F-FF-FF	0800	Internet Multicast (RFC-1112)
01-80-C2-00-00-00	-802-	Spanning Tree (for bridges)
09-00-09-00-00-01	8005	HP Probe
09-00-09-00-00-01	-802-	HP Probe
09-00-2B-00-00-03	8038	DEC LanBridge Traffic Monitor
09-00-2B-00-00-04	????	DEC MAP End System Hello
09-00-2B-00-00-0F	6004	DEC Local Area Transport (LAT)
09-00-2B-01-00-00	8038	DEC LanBridge Copy packets
09-00-2B-01-00-01	8038	DEC LanBridge Hello packets
09-00-56-FF-00-00 to 09-00-56-FF-FF-FF	805C	Stanford V Kernel, Version 6.0
AB-00-00-01-00-00	6001	DEC Maintenance Operation
AB-00-00-02-00-00	6002	DEC Maintenance Operation
AB-00-00-03-00-00	6003	DECnet Phase IV end node Hello
AB-00-00-04-00-00	6003	DECnet Phase IV Router Hello
AB-00-03-00-00-00	6004	DEC Local Area Transport (LAT)
AB-00-04-01-xx-yy	6007	DEC Local Area VAX Cluster
CF-00-00-00-00-00	9000	Ethernet Loopback

Output Controller

The output controller on the destination port has the task of receiving the packet from the switching element and forwarding it to the relevant end station. The receive process reads the header information of the information packet transferred via the switching element and interprets the relevant port identification from this. This process then forwards the data either to the output buffer of a port group or directly to the output port. In frame switching, the complete data packet is switched to the output process. If a cell switching procedure is used, the output process must reassemble the data packet from the individual cell fragments (on the basis of the fragment numbers) before the packet can be sent to the output port.

Flow-control Process

Another function of the output controller is to monitor the output resources continuously. If a bottleneck is detected in the resources for the output port (memory, connected cable, etc.), the output controller of the switch signals this status to the switching process. The switching process then ensures that no more data is sent by the input or that the data rate with which data is switched by the input port is reduced.

Two different types of Ethernet switch are now available on the market: frame switches and cell switches. These terms define the way in which the data is transferred from the input port to the output port.

Frame Switching

Most Ethernet switches currently available operate according to the frame switching procedure. In this procedure the data packets on the input port are forwarded, unchanged, to the output port via the internal processes of the switch. This method is no different from the transmission method used in multiport bridges. In this method occupation of the internal transmission route between the input and the output port is dependent on the length of the data packet to be transferred. The transmission time for the shortest Ethernet packet (64 bytes) is 51.2 µs; for the longest Ethernet packet (1518 bytes) the latency is 1.21 ms. Since the latency in frame switching depends on the length of the data packet to be transferred, the backplane must operate with high parallelism and at a high frequency to ensure that the system backplane does not become a bottleneck during data transmission.

Cell Switching

In the cell switching method the data packets received on the input port of the switch are split into cells before being transported to the output port. A cell is defined as a data block with a fixed size. The switch splits data packets of different lengths into cells with a defined size. The great advantage of cell switching is that these data cells have a defined transmission time. In a cellbus architecture, the switch functions as an exclusive data highway between the transmit port and the receive port. The received cells are transmitted and forwarded to the receiver via this data highway in the same sequence in which they were received. This method does however require a process at the output port that is capable of buffering the individual cell fragments and then reassembling them into the original packet. In order to do this, however, this memory area must allow a high processing speed and must not become a bottleneck in the architecture. Cell-switching performance is largely independent of the number of ports, the data traffic or the type of data transmitted (unicast, multicast, broadcast). The cell switching method also provides a direct and, above all, very fast way of converting LAN packets into ATM packets.

Table 6.7: Comparison between frame switches and cell switches

Function	Frame switches	Cell switches
Transmission speed required on the backplane	High	Medium
Occupation of backplane dependent on the length of the data packet	Yes	No
Fragmentation necessary	No	Yes
Reassembly necessary	No	Yes
Conversion into other frame formats frame formats	Complex	Very easy

The Backplane

The connection between the individual ports on a switch is conducted via the switching network between the input controller and the output controller. Because of the high parallelism of virtual connections, the internal transmission capacity must be high enough to enable all ports to transport their data streams in parallel for each unit of time, even in full-duplex transmission mode. The internal capacity of a switching network for a 10-port switch (100 Mbit/s) in full-duplex mode (worst case scenario) is 5 x 200 Mbit/s = 1.0 Gbit/s.

The simple technologies for switching information via the backplane use Time Division Multiplexing (TDM). The best known TDM switching method in data communication and computer technology is the bus. Busses are even used in Ethernet switches. The available bandwidth of these busses depends on the bus width (32-bit or 64-bit) and the frequency (16, 20, 32 MHz or higher). The hardware components available at the moment facilitate a maximum throughput rate of 1.28 Gbit/s. The great advantage of the bus method is that this technology has been tried and tested for a long time and switching can take place between any input and output ports in a single stage. For this reason the bus offers a fast and cost-effective solution. As explained above, bus technology currently reaches its upper limits at around 1.2 Gbit/s. However, the bandwidth can be increased by switching the busses in parallel, giving rise to space-division procedures.

Space-Division Procedure

Parallel data busses between the input and output ports form a matrix. The parallel input and output busses are crossed over and the information switched via these busses is transferred from the input busses to the output busses at suitable intersection points. The transfer is effected at the intersection points according to the destination port, by the switching element taking this information, whose destination lies the end of the output bus, from the input bus. In this way, several information blocks can be transported through the matrix in parallel and independently. A condition of this, however, is that different information blocks must use only different input and output busses simultaneously. If two information blocks on different input busses have the same destination, it is necessary to equalize the simultaneous access to the same output bus. This can be solved in two ways:

• The output bus has a higher bandwidth than the input bus. This means that several information blocks can be transported in one time cycle.

- A switching element delays the transport of an information block by buffering it in the input or output buffer for one clock cycle.

The first procedure, however, requires that outputting on the line must also be possible at a higher speed. The problem can be illustrated by an example:

The input-side speed is 100 Mbit/s and the output-side speed is 500 Mbit/s. In this case up to four information blocks from different inputs of one cycle can be outputted on one output controller.

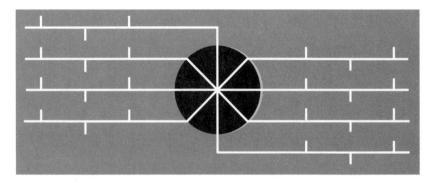

Figure 6.32: Structure of a matrix switch

The structure of a matrix like this requires that every header in an information block is analyzed by every switching element. Compared with the straightforward bus procedure, the matrix procedure is relatively time-consuming. However, the number of transmission points in the matrix procedure increases exponentially in relation to the number of inputs and outputs. This is one of the reasons why developers began to think about alternative structures. This resulted in switching fabrics or switching networks, which manage with far fewer switching elements. The complexity in this case is shifted to the switching elements.

Switching Fabrics

The matrix-type switching procedure provides an interim solution between single-stage solutions such as the TDM bus or ring and the multistage, meshed, space division procedure. A logical approach is to use the switching procedures implemented until now inside switching elements and to combine these via special switching networks. The idea of the switching network is to create special networks and switching elements that allow a greater number of inputs and outputs. In this kind of arbitrarily meshed network with node elements on the switching points, the route from one input point to the corresponding output can lead through various interim stations or, alternatively, can follow just one path.

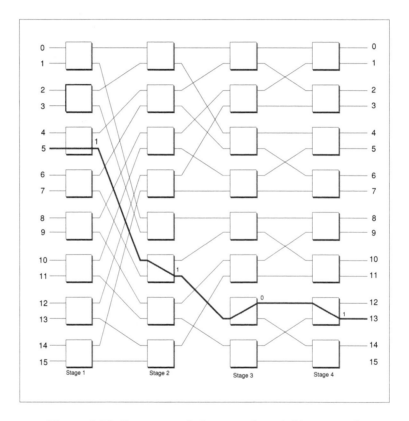

Figure 6.33: Structure and elements of a switching network

The BANYAN switching network is constructed in a tree configuration. Every input controller provides just one route to every output controller. In the BANYAN network, (logk n) stages, in which k corresponds to the number of inputs on the switching elements and n corresponds to the number of inputs, are required in order to do this. For example, if there are 2x2 switching elements and 8 inputs, then log2 8, i.e. 3, switching stages are required. Even with a large number of inputs, this logarithmic dependency of the switching stages makes for switching networks that are comparatively far less complex than those with linear dependency, such as the matrix.

Information Routing in Switching Networks

Two procedures are used for switching information blocks through the switching network:

- Routing tag

  The input controllers have access to all internal routing information and tag this routing information to the header of the information block to be switched.

- Routing tables

  The switching elements use routing tables to decide independently to which of the connected outputs the information block is to be sent.

Routing Tag

If routing tags are used to help select routes for information blocks through a switching network, all the information required to find the route from the input controller to the output controller is integrated in the transport header. This additional header information is called the routing tag. This routing tag is a series of bits in which the decision for a special output of each switching element is coded. However, this routing procedure requires that the input controller knows the complete route through the switching network via which an information block is to be switched. The switching elements on the route between the input and the output controller remove from the header the part of this routing tag intended for them and determine the output from this. The routing tag procedure is very simple and fast since the switching elements, for their part, do not need to have routing information. This simplicity is, however, reflected in a certain additional overhead as a result of the routing tag information.

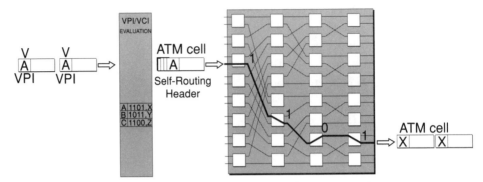

Figure 6.34: Cell routing by the routing tag procedure

Routing Tables

If routing tables are used to help switch information blocks, all switching elements and even the input controller have separate routing information. Each switching element starts a separate route-finding process for each information block received. This route-finding process searches the local routing table for routing information to the output controller and then forwards the information block to one of the outputs. In this procedure it is necessary for each switching network to maintain its own individual routing table. These routing tables must be monitored and adjusted by a central processor. Besides the complexity of monitoring the tables, the cost of operating the tables for each element and for each information block to be transmitted is problematic. The advantage of this procedure, however, is that broadcasts can be distributed more easily since the copying action does not have to be executed until the latest possible point within a switching network.

Using the BANYAN network as an example, there follows a discussion of the problems and solutions presented by this method. The main aspects with regard to the design of switches are as follows:

- Costs

- Distribution of broadcasts/multicasts,

- Contention and

- Blocking.

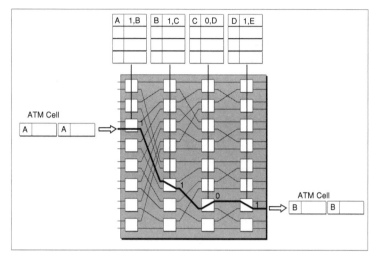

Figure 6.35: Cell-routing via tables in switching elements

Costs

The costs involved in a switching method are an essential factor in the buying decision. Unless installation costs are reasonable, the switching method will not achieve the forecast market penetration. The cost of switching fabrics depends on both the number and variety of elements contained in them. A series of switching stages with similar structures and few elements therefore improves the cost situation of a BANYAN network. Simply by rearranging the elements, the OMEGA switching network is produced.

Broadcasts/Multicasts Distribution

The distribution of broadcasts (to all devices within the broadcast domain) and multicasts (to a defined group of devices) is one of the most complicated tasks performed by a switch. An Ethernet switch no longer has the same broadcast capabilities as a shared Ethernet. By connecting the end stations via point-to-point cables and switching the packets via virtual point-to-point connections the individual information blocks (data packets) must be copied and transported by the switch, via separate routes, to all connected devices or a defined user group. The easiest solution to this problem is to copy the message accordingly to all the possible addressees in the user group. However, this procedure generates a very large overhead since the transmitting input controller would have to transmit a large number of identical packets. This would place an additional burden on the internal switch network. Another possibility is to delay copying the broadcast/multicast packets until the points in the switching network at which the routes to the different destinations divide. A reduction in components can be achieved by cascading specialized units. To enable broadcasts/multicasts to be processed quickly and effectively, the switching networks are first switched to a specially designed COPY network.

Contention

A data jam occurs whenever too many competing demands are made on a limited resource. If the competing data blocks are not to be lost, they must be parked in a queue if a jam occurs. A contention situation occurs in the event of an overload (concentration of a large number of data streams on one resource) in statistical multiplexing.

A contention situation usually occurs on the outputs of switches, since this is where the individual data streams from different transmitters meet. In most cases the external cables (e.g. the connection cable to a server) are much slower than the internal processing speed of the switch (e.g. 1.2 Gbit/s). To avoid contention situations, therefore, the following procedures are used:

Discarding Information Blocks

If the receiver has too many information blocks to be transported and the output resources (cable, end station) are unable to accept this information quickly enough, the overloaded system has no option but to discard the incoming data packets. This process is called frame dropping or cell dropping. In this case it is the task of the higher layers (Transport layer) to retransmit these "lost" data packets. This does not cause any problems in connection-oriented protocols such as TCP or SPX. If a UDP, NetBIOS or LAT service is used however, this situation can very quickly cause the connection to be interrupted.

Buffering

A simple option for bridging short-term bottlenecks is to implement output buffers. If a resource bottleneck occurs on the output, the incoming data is buffered in a queue and processed in sequence. However, if a large number of data packets are transmitted to one output port (e.g. the server connection) by a large number of ports, this can cause resources to become overloaded even if the port has a large output buffer. What this means in practice is that the port cannot accept any more data packets. These new data packets are discarded if the output buffer is full. This practice of discarding data packets has a negative effect on isochronous characteristics. It can cause unwelcome side-effects (distortion, screen flicker, etc.) especially in the case of voice and video data.

Priorities

The ATM method provides the option of prioritizing certain data in the event of a resource bottleneck. This is revealed by the Cell Loss Priority (CLP) anchored in the ATM header. The following strategies are available in ATM:

- The switch can guarantee a certain bandwidth for a virtual channel that switches real time information. This is achieved by allocating the channels with a constant bit rate (voice, video) to an output queue with a high priority. Data streams with variable bit rates (compressed voice or data) are allocated to an output queue with a lower priority. To prevent virtual channels with a low priority occupying bandwidth unnecessarily and possibly influencing other connections, a maximum transmission limit is defined for these channels. For variable bit rates both a maximum transmission limit, and the maximum time in which such a data burst can occur, are defined.

- ATM switches also guarantee that voice information is not interrupted or impeded by data transmission (e.g. IP information) during the transmission process. This takes place through the Usage Parameter Control (UPC) which was defined by the UNI 3.0 specifications. The UPC algorithm has the task of protecting the network from virtual channels that attempt to use more than their allocated bandwidth. With the UPC mechanism, ATM switches guarantee different levels of service quality for constant, variable and non-specific data rates. For constant data rates, a maximum transmission rate is defined for the respective channel. The so-called "leaky bucket" algorithm ensures that all cells which exceed the agreed upper limit are discarded by the switch. In addition, a dual bucket policy ensures that not only the maximum transmission load, but also the maximum duration of a data burst, is observed.

- Switches use yet another mechanism to guarantee that time-critical data traffic is not unnecessarily delayed during transmission via the switch. Cells with a variable or non-specific data rate are discarded as required if the necessary bandwidth for the time-critical traffic is no longer sufficient. This is achieved by placing the cell loss priority bits in the relevant cell headers.

- Traffic management algorithms ensure that a certain bandwidth is kept ready for virtual channels and that cells are discarded on a random basis if the requirement for bandwidth increases. In the default setting, if two virtual channels use the same port, half of the available bandwidth is allocated to each channel. An equality mechanism ensures that each of the two channels can exceed the reserved bandwidth limits if this band-width is not required by the neighboring channel.

However, since these mechanisms are not present in LAN protocols, these strategies cannot be used. Nevertheless, some manufacturers have already implemented proprietary priority mechanisms in their respective switches. The network administrator has the option of allocating priority for certain ports and/or protocols via the network management function. If an output becomes overloaded, the respective data streams are processed according to the defined priorities.

Backlog of Information Blocks

To prevent transmitted information being discarded at the output in the event of an overload, some manufacturers have integrated a flow-control mechanism in their switches. If a full output buffer is registered, it sends a signal to all input ports. This mechanism is called back pressure. For each data packet to be transferred, the ports check (on the basis of the destination address) whether sufficient resources are available for the transmission. If a full output buffer is detected, a collision is automatically generated (within the first 64 bytes of the data packet). This causes the transmitter to cancel the transfer and retransmit the data according to the Ethernet backoff algorithm. This collision mechanism has a great advantage in that no modifications whatsoever are required in the protocols in order to implement effective flow control on the Physical layer. Since no data packets are lost during transmission from Transport layer to Transport layer, switches with this mechanism never lose any data or block the data path between transmitter and receiver.

Blocking

Bottlenecks do not only occur on the outputs of a switching fabric, but can also be created by competing access to internal resources. This bottleneck in a switching fabric is called blocking. An essential feature of a switch is whether it is blocking or non-blocking.

In non-blocking networks the probability of a deadlock forming is reduced to a minimum. If there are too many information blocks to be transported via an internal resource, however, internal blocking occurs on the output port of the switch in spite of all the mechanisms. One possibility, alongside the remedies described above, arises if competing information blocks are not necessarily addressed to a common output, but only their routes cross over at this one point in the switch. These bottlenecks can be avoided using a number of strategies.

Higher Internal Bandwidth

Increasing the internal bandwidth of the switch considerably reduces the risk of jamming. If the internal bandwidth of the switch reaches the total bandwidth of all possible input data, the possibility of blocking is completely avoided.

Sorting the Information Blocks

By sorting the information blocks on the basis of their destination and feeding them into the switching network accordingly, it is possible to avoid critical, parallel accesses to potential bottlenecks. This task is performed by a so-called sorting network. This sorting network is preconnected to the switching network. The sorting network and the switching network are linked via a shuffle network.

This network design is known as the Batcher Banyan Network. The batcher network sorts all information blocks comparatively according to the prefix (routing tag) in the header. This produces collision-free paths in the routing network. If two information blocks are simultaneously headed for one sorting element, the cell with the higher value leaves the sorting element on the path that has been reserved for high values. If there is no value for comparison, the information block is outputted on the output reserved for lower values. The BANYAN network then routes the cells independently on parallel paths.

Multiple Path Network

Switching technology opens up a whole range of different strategies for bypassing blocked switching resources. In the switching networks described above, data is always transferred from the source to the destination along just one path. If redundancy is introduced into this network, however, a way of bypassing occupied resources (switching elements, cables, etc.) can be found. This means that information blocks can be switched between the same inputs and outputs via different paths. This redundancy is provided by multiple path networks. The transferred information blocks can move at different speeds via different paths depending on the condition of the path. In multiple path networks, therefore, it is important to ensure that related information blocks (packet fragments) do not overtake one another.

Multiple Plane Network

The simplest way of developing single path networks into multiple path networks is to switch several single path networks in parallel. The selection of transmission paths takes place outside the parallel-switched networks. If no resources are available in one network when a connection is set up, the path can be laid through an alternative network if necessary. However, rerouting is not possible within the same network if bottlenecks occur dynamically.

The multiple plane switching network also offers a function called "hot standby". If one switching fabric fails, the remaining switching fabrics can take over the function of the failed switching element. This procedure is relatively cost-effective to implement, since straightforward, standard components can be used.

BENES Network

The problem of rerouting within a network leads to redundancy being created in every network. The BENES switching network is an example of a true multiple path network. It comprises two cascaded, mirrored BANYAN networks. Several parallel paths are possible between two points in the network. The paths each cover the same distance (measured in switching elements). This means that no rerouting is necessary and the sequence problem is reduced to a minimum.

If a jam occurs on one output, the corresponding output in the other network can be used. The BENES network can therefore also provide time-neutral secondary paths during dynamic bottlenecks. The higher number of paths, however, is at the expense of an increase in the number of switching stages. If the degree of meshing between the individual stages is increased and if the layout of the switching elements is correspondingly more complex, the number of switching stages can be reduced. This in turn has a positive effect on the processing speed. One example of such a network is the CLOS network.

TWO SIDED CLOS Network

The CLOS network comprises three fully intermeshed switching stages. This circuitry enables each input to be connected with each output in only three stages.

The first stage branches each input to a switching element in the middle stage. Accordingly, each element in the second stage can take over the entire switching operation. The number of these elements therefore corresponds to the number of possible redundant paths in this network. The third stage (output stage) concentrates the alternative paths back down to the output. The structure itself is symmetrical, but the switching elements of the second stage are different from those of the first and third stage. Any further simplification of the CLOS network is in turn accompanied by a higher outlay in the components.

FOLDED CLOS Network

To reduce the number of elements further, the first and third stages of the above TWO SIDED CLOS network have been combined to form the FOLDED CLOS network.

The folding makes it necessary for the inputs and outputs and the connection paths between them to be bidirectional or duplicated in the configuration. This structure does however mean that only one switching process is needed in the best-case scenario, i.e., when the destination and source of an information block are on the same input/output element. This results in a considerable reduction in processing time and in the volumes of data to be switched over the network.

6.6 Switch Tests

When the first MAC-layer bridges were installed 8 years ago, the users did not know what these devices could all do. It was some time until generally accepted measuring and testing methods were established, with which these bridges could be tested. The testing of bridges and also routers is now one of the standard functions supported by every data analyzer. With the aid of two interface cards, the analyzer transmits data from an interface and receives it on the interface. Special measurement programs enable the response times and throughput measurements, and the processing of broadcasts and multicasts, to be easily tested. The network load can be preset by the tester as a percentage. Realistic values in the Ethernet area are 40% for small packets (64 bytes) and 90% for large packets (1512 bytes). As well as "good" packets, these programs are also able to generate defective information and frames (FCS and alignment errors, incorrect preamble). This enables the network operator to establish the efficiency of individual devices (e.g. bridges, routers, etc.) quickly and selectively.

The introduction of switching systems is now provoking renewed discussions about the correct methods for measuring these devices. Traditional bridges normally have only a few ports (2, 4 and sometimes even 8). These bridges were designed so that the ratio between the filtering rate and the forwarding rate is 80:20. This means that some 80% of data traffic is local traffic that does not have to be transported via the bridge. Only 20% of data traffic should be switched from one LAN interface to another using bridges. The hardware and software architecture of most bridges does not allow the data packets to be read in and forwarded to the other network segment with the full network speed (14,880 packets/s). In the case of switches, however, every data packet must be forwarded to one of the ports on the switch. For this reason switch tests and bridge tests must fulfill quite different requirements. The main criteria for testing a switch are to establish:

- Switch performance,

- Latency,

- Address handling and

- General behavior

SwitchScan

The European Network Test Labs (ENL), in collaboration with the company Wandel & Goltermann, have developed the SwitchScan testing procedures for detailed testing of Ethernet switches. The SwitchScan test series can be executed on Wandel & Goltermann DA 30 analyzers and controlled either automatically or manually. In automatic mode, 105 tests are carried out. The results are displayed on the screen in real time. At the same time a spreadsheet file is created for later processing. In manual mode, the individual test procedures can be initiated separately according to the tester's requirements.

SwitchScan 1: Switching Performance Tests

The first group of test procedures checks the transmission capacity of a device during the switching of packets between the input port and the output port. During the test, the test ports transmit and receive bidirectional data traffic. The SwitchScan tests include the option of defining all the main test parameters as variables. The following six parameters can be freely defined:

- Number of ports

- Number of addresses per port

- Packet size

- Load per port

- Burst size

- Broadcast packets

Number of Ports

This test depends on the interface ports available on the device being tested. A two-port device is the minimum that can be defined. Tests with four, six and eight ports give good average values for a tested device. The testing procedure can be adjusted at any time to the maximum number of ports on the device currently being tested.

Number of Addresses Per Port

The number of MAC addresses per port can be set between one and 500 addresses. If automatic mode is selected, eight MAC addresses per port are tested in the default setting.

Packet Size

The packet size can be set between 64 bytes (minimum packet size) and 1518 bytes (maximum packet size) in accordance with IEEE 802.3 specifications. The default value of this test in automatic mode is based on a packet length of 64 bytes.

Load Per Port

The load generated on one port can be set between 0 and 100%. For the shortest packet lengths (64 bytes) and a 100% load, the analyzer generates 14880 packets per second. The load is calculated from an 8-byte preamble, the actual data packet and the interframe gap. A 100% load with a maximum packet size (1518 bytes) results in a transmission rate of 812 packets per second. Loads of 70%, 80%, 90% and 100% are generated in automatic mode.

Burst Size

In burst mode, a defined number of packets with a minimum interframe gap (9.6 μs) are transmitted by the analyzer to the relevant input port. In automatic mode, data bursts with 20, 40, 128, 256 and 500 packets are generated.

Broadcast Packets

Broadcast packets are transmitted from one port to all ports on the device being tested. In automatic mode, between 0, 15, 30 and 50% broadcast packets are mixed among the normal data traffic by the analyzer.

If automatic mode is activated for the test, the user only has to preset three parameters. These three parameters are allocated to the relevant variables by the application. These parameters are: the number of ports, the number of addresses per port and the packet size. The variables for the parameters are:

- Load (70%, 80%, 90% and 100%)
- Burst size (20, 40, 128, 256 and 500 packets)
- Percentage of broadcast packets in total load (0, 15, 30 and 50%)

From these few parameters and values, the automatic test generates a test matrix of 50 test procedures.

Switching Performance Traffic Sample

The SwitchScan test generates random traffic between all the ports on the device being tested. Particular care has been taken to ensure that this data traffic resembles conditions in a real network as closely as possible. The data traffic is switched from a random address on one port to an arbitrary port on which a random address is located. In this way the data traffic is transmitted simultaneously from all the switch ports being tested. The data traffic generated and received for each port corresponds to the load—for example 70% or 100%—that has been defined for this test. The data traffic sample for a 6-port switch looks like this:

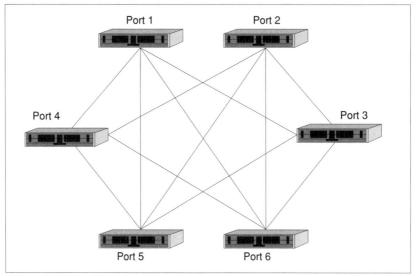

Figure 6.36: X-stream traffic pattern: switching performance

Setting Up the Switching Performance Test

A DA-30 analyzer is connected to each port of the switch being tested. All addresses are initialized at the start of the test procedure. The data generators then begin to transmit the data packets according to the test conditions. The received data packets are automatically stored by the analyzers and compared with the number of data packets transmitted. By implementing the IEEE 802.3 back-off algorithm in the DA-30 analyzers, collisions are not rated as transmitted data packets. The proportion of transmitted and received data packets is expressed as a percentage. Each of the test procedures implemented in the SwitchScan test is run for ten seconds.

Address Handling Tests

In the second test group, the address handling of the switch is tested, i.e., whether the switch is able to support everything from a few MAC addresses to a full Ethernet segment for each port. In this test, data packets are transmitted from half of the switch ports being tested (transmitters) to the other half of the switch ports (receivers). The data traffic is transferred from the transmitter to the receiver in one direction only. The number of MAC addresses per port can be set at between 1 and 500 addresses. In automatic mode, the number of MAC addresses generated per port is as follows: 1, 8, 32, 64, 128, 256 and 500. In an 8-port switch, the test with 128 MAC addresses per port results in a total of 1024 MAC addresses. This corresponds to the maximum number for a complete Ethernet segment in accordance with the IEEE specification. In this test, the number of data packets received is compared with the number of data packets transmitted. The total load of the data traffic is 100% and is generated on the basis of 64-byte packets. In automatic mode, seven separate results are established by this test.

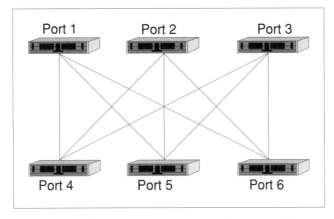

Figure 6.37: Fan-out test pattern: address handling

General Behavior

In the third group of test sequences, the behavior of the switch under extraordinary conditions is tested. These tests check the following conditions:

- The ability of the switch to respond to overloads,

- Blocking by the switch under a heavy load,

- Whether the minimum interframe gap is kept

- The buffer size during the test

- The ability to filter out broadcast packets,

- The ability to filter out invalid data packets.

Overload Test

In the overload test a maximum data stream is transmitted from four ports to one receive port. This is to determine whether, in an overload situation, the switch being tested is able to control the data traffic to the overloaded port by means of a congestion control or a backpressure mechanism.

Blocking by the Switch Under a Heavy Load

This measurement checks whether the architecture of the switch being tested causes it to lose bandwidth. A data stream is transmitted from a transmit port to a free receive port. At the same time another data stream is transmitted from the same transmit port to an overloaded receive port. Depending on the architecture of the switch, the data in the input buffer that was sent to the free port may be unable to be transmitted because of the overload on the other receive port.

Minimum Interframe Gap

In this measurement a receive port is overloaded and the minimum interframe gap (9.6 µs) is measured for the data packets transmitted by this port.

Buffer Size

To establish the buffer size, 64-byte long data packets are transmitted from a transmit port to an already overloaded receive port in a data stream of 32, 64, 128, 256 and 512 Kbit/s, and the data loss is measured on the receive side.

Broadcast Packets

To ascertain whether the switch being tested is able to filter out broadcast packets, a unidirectional data stream is sent to receive ports in which the proportion of broadcast packets is 15%, 30%, 45%, 60% 75% and 100%. The broadcast packets received are compared with the broadcast packets transmitted. The number of filtered broadcast packets is expressed as a percentage.

Invalid Data Packets

To ascertain whether the switch being tested is able to filter out invalid data packets, the following packet types are sent to the destination port:

- Runts (32-byte long packets)

- Jabber (30000-byte long packets)

- 64-byte long packets with an invalid FCS (Frame Check Sequence) field

- 1518-byte long packets with an invalid FCS (Frame Check Sequence) field

Latency

The test procedures establish the latency of a data packet between the input and the output port. The latency for both unicast and broadcast packets is established. A data load of 0%, 50% and 100% is generated over the switch during the test. The latency between two isolated ports during the transmission of 64-byte, 128-byte, 512-byte and 1518-byte packets is established. The established time values have an accuracy of +/- 5 µs.

Most of these test criteria cannot be determined without measuring equipment. However, in order to obtain an impression of a particular device, the following simple tests are recommended.

1. PCs and Novell Netware Test

Equipment required:

- 16 workstations (minimum 486 DX PC),

- 4 high-performance servers (486 DX2/4 PC or higher specification),

- 5 repeaters (if necessary)

- 1 Ethernet switch.

Applications required:

- NetWare 3.xx and

- Novell Perform 3

Test Set-Up

The servers are connected directly to the Ethernet Switch via twisted-pair cables. The 16 workstations are divided between Cheapernet segments in groups of four (WS11 - WS14, WS21 - WS24, WS31 - WS34, WS41 - WS44). Since most Ethernet switches do not have Cheapernet interfaces, a repeater (10Base2 <—> 10BaseT) must be used for conversion from this medium to twisted-pair.

Test 1: The following sessions must then be started:

WS11 - WS14 <—> Server 1,

WS21 - WS24 <—> Server 2,

WS31 - WS34 <—> Server 3,

WS41 - WS44 <—> Server 4

The entire data traffic for a segment is transmitted to one server by all the workstations. The Perform 3 Test Utility is then started simultaneously on all workstations.

The performance results of all sessions should be established by the tester.

If the performance results of the sessions are not equal, the min./max. values should be registered.

Test 2: The following sessions must be started:

WS11, WS21, WS31, WS 41 <—> Server 1,

WS12, WS22, WS32, WS42 <—> Server 2,

WS13, WS23, WS33, WS43 <—> Server 3,

WS14, WS24, WS34, WS44 <—> Server 4.

The data traffic for each of the individual workstations in a segment is sent to a different server. The Perform 3 Test Utility is then started simultaneously on all workstations.

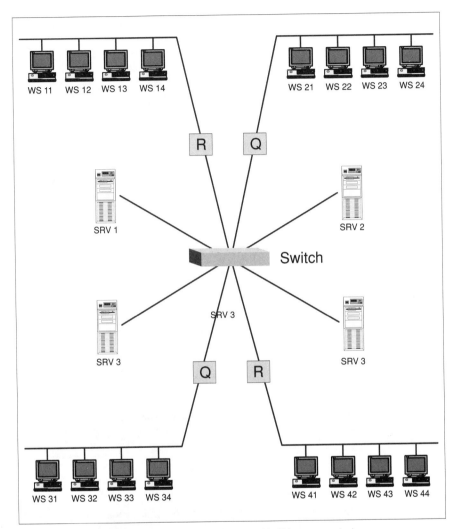

Figure 6.38: Test scenario with Ethernet switch

The Ethernet switch is replaced with a twisted-pair repeater and Tests 1 and 2 should be repeated in this scenario.

The two sets of test results should show marked differences in terms of performance per session and overall performance.

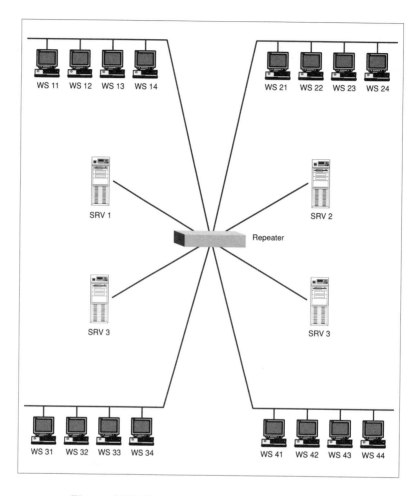

Figure 6.39: Test scenario with twisted-pair repeater

2. PCs and PDCLKSET

Equipment required:

- 16 workstations (minimum 486 DX PC),

- 4 high-performance servers (486 DX2/4 PC or higher specification),

- 5 repeaters (if necessary)

- 1 Ethernet switch.

Applications required:

- PDCLKSET software
- TCP/IP software

The PDCLKSET software is based on the DOS operating system and is available on the Internet as Public-Domain Software. The software generates ping traffic (based on UDP or TCP) between a client and a server. The PDCLKSET utility is configured as follows:

- The PCs must be configured as either server or client,
- the User Datagram Protocol (UDP) or the Transmission Control Protocol must be selected in the test set-up,
- the traffic rate between the client and the server must then be defined. The following parameters can be set:
- the length of the packets
- the interval between two packets.

Test Set-Up:

The servers are connected directly to the Ethernet Switch via twisted-pair cables. The 16 workstations are divided between Cheapernet segments in groups of four (WS11 - WS14, WS21 - WS24, WS31 - WS34, WS41 - WS44). Since most Ethernet switches do not have Cheapernet interfaces, a repeater (10Base2 <—> 10BaseT) must be used for conversion from this medium to twisted-pair.

Test 3: The following sessions must then be started

WS11 - WS14 <—> Server 1,

WS21 - WS24 <—> Server 2,

WS31 - WS34 <—> Server 3,

WS41 - WS44 <—> Server 4

The entire data traffic of a segment is transmitted to one server by all the workstations. The test should be executed with the following packet lengths: 64, 250, 500, 100 and 1518 bytes.

After the test has been started the test report indicates the number of packets lost. A constantly increasing figure indicates constant packet loss.

The performance results of all sessions should be established by the tester.

Test 4: The following sessions must be started:

WS11, WS21, WS31, WS 41 <—> Server 1,

WS12, WS22, WS32, WS42 <—> Server 2,

WS13, WS23, WS33, WS43 <—> Server 3,

WS14, WS24, WS34, WS44 <—> Server 4.

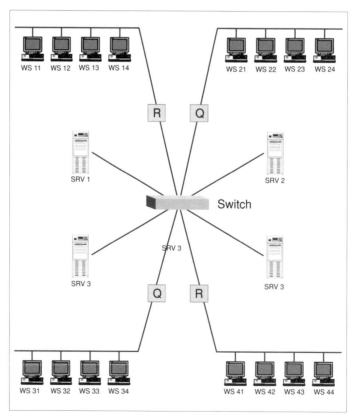

Figure 6.40: Test scenario with Ethernet switch

The Ethernet switch is replaced with a twisted-pair repeater and Tests 1 and 2 should be repeated in this scenario.

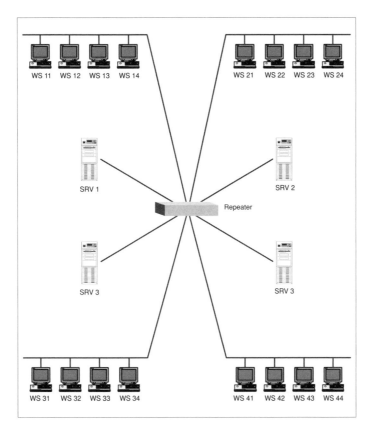

Figure 6.41: Test scenario with twisted-pair repeater

The two sets of test results should show marked differences in terms of performance per session and overall performance.

3. UNIX and TTPC

Equipment required:

- 4 UNIX workstations (minimum performance 11 MIPS)
- 1 repeater and
- 1 Ethernet switch.

Applications required:

- TTCP software

- UNIX and TCP/IP software

The TTPC software is based on the Unix operating system and is available on the Internet as Public-Domain Software. The software functions in a similar way to the FTP program. The great difference between the TTCP and the FTP is that the TTCP program registers the time needed for the data to be transferred from memory to memory, whereas the FTP program registers the time from disk to disk. The traffic rate between the client and the server must also be defined in the TTCP program. The following parameters can be set:

- the length of the packets

- the interval between two packets.

Test set-up

The 4 Unix workstations are connected directly to the Ethernet switch via twisted-pair cables. Four windows are opened on each of the Unix workstations and the following sessions are started:

WS1TX1 —> WS2RX2

WS1TX2 —> WS3RX2

WS2TX1 —> WS4RX1

WS2TX2 —> WS1RX1

WS3TX1 —> WS4RX2

WS3TX2 —> WS1RX2

WS4TX1 —> WS2RX1

WS4TX2 —> WS3RX1

The entire data traffic for one [port] is forwarded by the switch to a different destination port in each case. The test should be run over a period of three minutes. The test should be executed with the following packet lengths: 64, 250, 500, 100 and 1518 bytes.

The performance results of all sessions should be established by the tester.

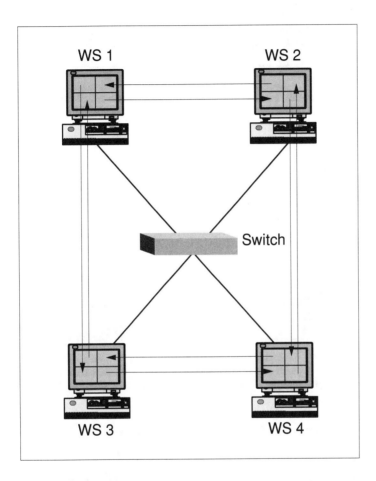

Figure 6.42: Test scenario with Ethernet switch

The Ethernet switch is replaced with a twisted-pair repeater and the test should be repeated in this scenario.

The two sets of test results should show marked differences in terms of performance per session and overall performance.

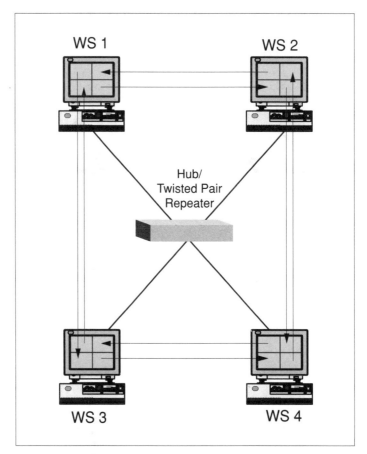

Figure 6.43: Test scenario with twisted-pair repeater

The Public Domain Utilities PDCLKSET and TTCP can be obtained either via the Internet (various servers) or by contacting Elon Littwitz of Ornet DCT (Email: elon@ornet.co.il).

7 Switched LANs

Owing to the cost structures involved, when planning WAN networks it was necessary to take both required and available bandwidth into account. In the past, there was no shortage of bandwidth available to LANs and bottlenecks were unknown. Bottlenecks were more likely to develop in the components connected to the network (the network software, the processing performance of the CPU and the disk access time). The problem of shared bandwidth is solved by switching technology. In workgroup computing, the continually rising demand for bandwidth is met by microsegmenting. The available bandwidth no longer depends on the number of stations in the network, but rather on the throughput of the switches in the network. New LAN technologies (Fast Ethernet, ATM, etc.) and new superfast workstations have enabled new network structures to emerge. The widespread use of these modern transmission methods (Ethernet, Token Ring, and FDDI) means that they are unlikely to disappear from the scene in the foreseeable future. The transitions between the individual technologies as well as the ability to integrate virtual networks require an in-depth understanding of the new capabilities offered. Bridges, switches, and routers will continue to have a role in ensuring the effective utilization of LAN/WAN resources.

Switch Applications

In recent years LAN and computer components have improved dramatically and applications have become ever more network-dependent. As a result, available bandwidth is increasingly proving to be a brake on the efficient utilization of the capacity of resources. At present anyone planning a network chiefly faces the problem of providing the bandwidth required today, while protecting yesterday's investment and keeping the door open for the developments of tomorrow. Some reasons for the growing demand for bandwidth in a LAN:

- LANs represent the backbone of a company's infrastructure (more users, more data).

- The shift from mainframes to client/server architectures is progressing at a very rapid pace.

- Even end stations at simple workplaces are being equipped with graphical user interfaces (Windows, X-Windows, etc.).

- Multimedia applications (voice mail, high resolution imaging, video, etc.) are now finding their way into corporate computing.

Apart from providing an ever-increasing amount of bandwidth, a LAN architecture has to be constantly adaptable to the changing requirements within an enterprise. In the past most companies built up LAN and PC infrastructures on the departmental level. These LAN resources were usually acquired without any kind of control or coordination under an enterprise-wide, integrated system management. The inevitable result of this development was a veritable "mish-mash" of different network topologies and servers spread all over the place. Over time most of these "computer islands" came to be interconnected by means of a campus or building LAN. Quite apart from time and money constraints, there was simply insufficient knowledge to implement a comprehensive planning and network concept. We have now reached a stage where the important applications (software programs which are increasingly crucial for the success of a company) are forcing a revision of network structures and the integration of management systems. The necessary corollary of this development is the greater centralization of distributed resources (e.g., network servers) and the restructuring of cabling systems. Only in this way can LAN resources be better protected, monitored, and managed. In terms of cabling, this will mean a return to a physically centralized topology. The applications that use these physical structures will follow the trend to more distributed architectures, however. Changes in corporate organization will also result in a change in the workgroup concept, with the result that maintaining data traffic in a network will become more and more difficult. It will consequently be necessary to set up high-performance virtual workgroups within a physically centralized architecture.

7.1 Multimedia Applications

Multimedia is synonymous with the future of computer technology. In particular, audio and video communications are providing boundless scope for our imaginations, and it is no longer just the computer buffs who dream of the multifunctional computer. Buzzwords such as "video on demand" and "interactive video applications" have become generally accepted descriptions of new computer applications. These visions are the driving force behind the trend of making centrally stored information available to all users in a network. Many multimedia applications, such as online training courses, videoclip databases, and documentation systems, will therefore have to be accessible to the various workgroups in a company. New applications such as desktop videoconferencing have forced companies to network their computers. Multimedia applications make very heavy demands on today's LAN technology and have led to an inexorable burgeoning of data traffic on networks. Transmission of video and audio data between two parties requires an isochronous data stream. Video data is fundamentally different from other data such as that used for word processing or for accessing databases. Video and audio data is transmitted in the form of a continuous data stream which must arrive at the receiving application at a particular point in time. Today's LAN systems and their attached computer resources are capable of transmitting short bursts of large data streams. If, however, several time-critical and continuous data streams are to be transmitted simultaneously over the network, then these systems very soon reach the limit of their capabilities and become very slow. Audio and video data streams have to be assigned a high priority by the operating system and the computer resources for processing and transmission over the network. In other words, an isochronous data stream describes a stream with a precisely-defined interval between two data blocks. In order to obtain clear, distortion-free image and sound quality in the transmission, the individual data blocks have to be sent virtually synchronously from the transmitter to the receiver.

There are three types of network video services currently available:

- Video file service

- Video object service

- Stream management service

Video File Service

Technically the most straightforward mode of transmitting video and audio data is called video file service. This service requires only a store-and-play function, i.e., a simple file service for videos. This video file service supports only the recording, retrieval, and playback of videos. The digital information is stored statically. Delays and longer access times can be tolerated to a certain extent during video playback. In terms of their technology, the video file service systems currently on the market are similar to today's file servers.

Video Object Service

Implementing network-wide support for video object services represents a much greater technical challenge. These applications enable the interactive interconnection of several audio/video databases. The video resources available in the network can be combined freely with each other. For example, a user can edit individual videos and intercut them to produce a new video. This service requires fast access to resources and simultaneous access to a large number of information objects.

Stream Management Service

The implementation of stream management services in a network presents the greatest technical challenge. This service enables a user to access a number of live videos simultaneously. The range of applications supported includes both desktop videoconferencing and interactive distance learning per video transmission. Video stream management services allow the parallel transmission of a wide variety of live videos on the same network. Depending upon the application and the content, it would even be possible for the individual videos to be transmitted at different rates.

Today's LAN systems built up on the basis of repeaters were designed only for use in data and file sharing systems. The applications running on these LAN systems are mainly used to transmit simple text and graphics files. To be capable of handling audio and video services, these networks will have to be overhauled and restructured. The use of audio and video services on a LAN places the following constraints on the transmission system:

- The enormous size of the video files

- The isochronous transmission mode

These demands are further compounded exponentially if this information is to be made available to many users simultaneously across the network from one or more file servers. In order to reduce the large volumes of data transmitted between servers and clients to manageable proportions, the video data is compressed. A large number of compression mechanisms have since been developed to compress video and audio data. The most widely known compression mechanisms are: JPEG, DVI, MPEG, QuickTime, and P*64. Since even the best compression mechanism can only reduce the enormous amount of video data, the system still has to be capable of providing a very large transmission bandwidth. Video communication over a network requires a constant transfer rate of 2 to 6 Mbit/s. This means that it is necessary to send between 7.2 and 21.6 Gbytes of data information net per hour over the network for each video session.

If, for instance, 20 workstations with video applications were connected to a digital video server, it would be necessary to transport very high data streams over the network. Users expect videos to arrive at their computers the instant they call up the video application. In a best case scenario for video applications running on the network, one could expect a continuous data stream of 2 Mbit/s per workstation. At the video server end this would result in an overall throughput of 20 parallel data streams. The aggregate transfer rate of 40 Mbit/s would have to be handled by the network and processed simultaneously by the server.

On the Physical Layer, a network (Ethernet, FDDI or Token Ring) treats all data alike. It is not possible to set priorities for the data packets transmitted, nor is it possible to define specific bandwidths for the transmission. Transmission of video information is dependent upon a fixed chronological sequence of continuous images. Other information streams on the medium cannot therefore be allowed to interfere with the video data stream over the LAN. However, normal LANs share the available bandwidth between all the active users connected. In some circumstances this could lead to tolerable limits being exceeded during the transmission of the video data stream. In an extreme case, playback of a data stream transmitted across a shared network would be completely distorted and would run at slow-motion speeds.

The transmission of videos over the network must always be assigned a high priority to ensure that this data always arrives at the receiver at the correct time. In ordinary LANs (Ethernet, Token Ring) there are a number of bottlenecks that influence the above-mentioned requirements for video/audio data transmission. Neither personal computers nor networks were developed to cope with the demands of these multimedia applications. A number of bottlenecks can slow down the continuous data stream, or even interrupt it entirely, en route from the hard disk on which the video is stored to the desktop computer on which the video/audio transmission is to be played back. Examples of such potential bottlenecks are the disk drives, the processor buses, the processors, the network protocols, and the network interfaces. Since a network is designed for a variety of applications, it must be ensured that audio and video data streams do not affect other network applications (e.g., email, word processing, databases, etc.).

Replacing an existing network structure with more high-powered equipment will only bring short-term success. If an existing Ethernet is replaced by 100 Mbit/s fast FDDI, then not only is this solution expensive, it merely shifts the problem on the time axis. The additional bandwidth gained will simply postpone the struggle for transmission capacity until the time when network components will again have to compete for more transmission time. Response times will lengthen as the number of active network components increases. The time-critical demands of audio and video data will not have gone away. In many cases modern networks are capable of meeting the demands set out above. Each client workstation requires only 2-5 Mbit/s bandwidth for transmitting a video data stream. This does not require any special network hardware for the client computer and existing 10BaseT Ethernet controllers can continue to be used. On the server side, connection of 20 clients would result in a data stream of 40–100 Mbit/s. Since it is not possible for a 10 Mbit/s fast Ethernet to handle such large data streams, bottlenecks are inevitable. Only the use of Fast Ethernet technology could help here.

If one assumes a star cabling topology, then an exclusive data path exists between the client and the interconnection component (hub, repeater, etc.). Since with this type of cabling the transmitting and receiving paths are separated between two wires in each case, there are never any collisions on these lines. If hubs or repeaters are used as interconnection components, then the bandwidth is reduced immediately on the cables connected. The cards in the hubs are usually based on repeaters. The job of a repeater is to forward all information from the one LAN (e.g., internal bus of the hub system) to the connected segments within the respective collision domain. The democratic nature of the networks as defined under the Ethernet standard, with the available bandwidth being shared between the attached stations, makes it difficult to guarantee the time window required for videos to be transmitted cleanly and reliably. As a consequence, the bandwidth available in each case decreases as the load and the number of stations in the network increase.

If multiport bridges are used in the hub instead of repeater cards, then two store-and-forward components are integrated between the input port and the output port. An Ethernet bridge always copies all the data packets into the buffer of the local Ethernet controller. The bridge then checks the destination address of each packet received. The bridge decides on the basis of this destination address whether this data packet is to be forwarded to a connected LAN or whether it is local data traffic. If a data packet has to be forwarded to another LAN segment of the bridge, this information is passed to the memory of the sending Ethernet controller. The controller sends the data packet as soon as the network is available for transmission. The store-and-forward function of the bridge requires a relatively large amount of time for processing.

The technical term for this delay is latency. By definition, latency describes the delay between the time the first bit of a data packet is received at the bridge port and the time this bit leaves the destination port of the bridge again. In normal bridges the latency is approximately 150–300 ms. This delay is of particular significance for multimedia applications since communication over two bridges (latency per bridge = 200 ms) would result in an overall delay of 400 ms between two packets. One further important aspect of latency is the difference between guaranteed and variable delay times. Multimedia applications require a low latency.

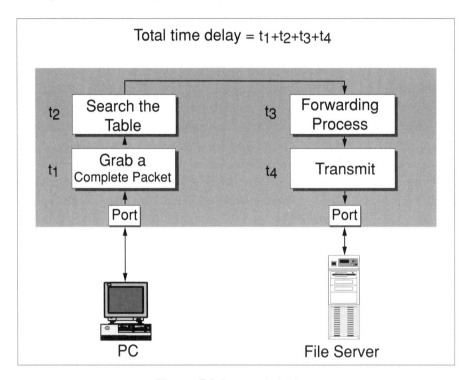

Figure 7.1: Latency in bridges

The solution is to use Ethernet switches. From the point of view of load separation, latency and the number of stations connected per port (available bandwidth), cut-through-forwarding switches provide the ideal starting point for implementing multimedia applications based on standard LAN technology. With cut-through switches the forwarding process is started immediately the six-byte long destination address has been read by the switch controller. This switching method reduces the delay between the receiving and the sending port because it is never necessary to buffer the complete frame. By definition, latency describes the delay between the time the first bit of a data packet is received at the switch port and the time this bit leaves the destination port of the switch again. The difference in latency between store-and-forward compo-nents and cut-through devices is several hundred microseconds. Using cut-through switches therefore, latency can be reduced to a low level (14–52 ms). As already mentioned, multimedia applications require a low latency. When switches are used, this latency is a defined fixed value which does not vary during transmission. The biggest problem is still the concurrency of the paral-lel video connections between the clients and the server. It is not possible to transmit more data than the maximum bandwidth permits over a standard 10 Mbit/s Ethernet port.

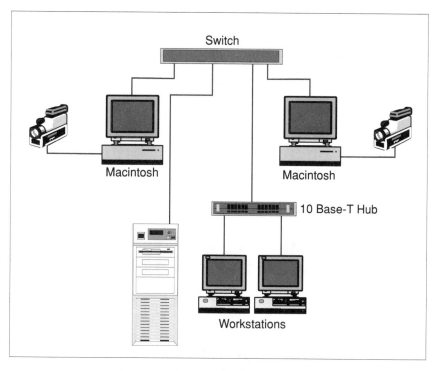

Figure 7.2: Multimedia using switches

It is now possible to upgrade the server ports of the Ethernet switch to 100 Mbit/s using Fast Ethernet technology. Since the standards are mutually com-patible, it is only a question of clock rate conversion as to how many 10 Mbit/s clients can communicate with a 100 Mbit/s video server. If this is still not enough bandwidth, then the server connection can be run in full-duplex mode.

This will provide a total bandwidth of 200 Mbit/s for the file server. The integrated load separation of the switches ensures that the video data stream can flow unimpeded from the client to the server. Since this type of transmission via switches provides an exclusive data channel for each end station connected, there are never any collisions. Transmission of voice and data over a network is simplified and the application benefits from predictable fixed delay times between the transmitter and the receiver.

7.1.1 Multiport Server Connections

The increasing prevalence of client/server systems in corporate environments is one of the main reasons for the rise in demand for greater network bandwidth. As the trend to distributed applications strengthens, networks are becoming more and more the cornerstone of reliability and performance. Unfortunately in the past, most departmental LANs were set up without much forward planning or integration in an overall concept. New stations and servers were simply connected to the LAN when required.

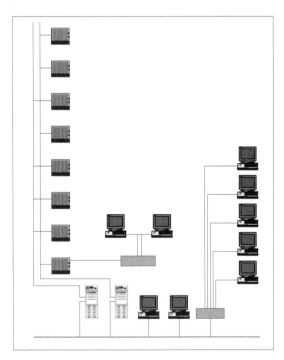

Figure 7.3: Typical server structure in a LAN

To implement these server structures, several network adapters must be installed in the individual file servers. The clients in the individual segments communicate with the respective server interface over the cable. This set-up has the following inherent problems:

- The available performance is shared between the connected clients (performance sharing).

- If the cable fails, all the stations attached to the network will fail as well (low reliability).

- Some of the processing power of the server is wasted on routing data packets between the various network segments.

- In many cases it is also necessary to support different network adapter cards (different manufacturers or technologies) in the servers. For the network/server administrator, this entails management and maintenance of the different drivers and their individual management functions.

- The integration of central management is immensely difficult due to the cascading of LANs.

- Any upgrading or expansion is time-consuming and ties up a large amount of staff resources.

If the LAN is replaced by structured cabling in conjunction with a high-speed Ethernet switch, the performance bottlenecks of the LAN are immediately eliminated. The failure (breaking) of a cable will no longer cause several stations to fail. Full network performance is available on every file server via every server connection. In the case of Full-Duplex Ethernet, double the bandwidth is also available. It is therefore possible to dispense with the parallel LAN adapters installed on the servers. There is no need to route the data traffic between the network segments. The server performance increases, since the servers are now only responsible for carrying out actual server tasks. Logically then, the performance of the workstation computer will increase as well since each client has a direct connection to each server. Roundabout routes via interposed routing servers are eliminated. Centralization of the cabling and the end stations allows management of the overall resources to be readily implemented. This greatly simplifies monitoring and control over the network. Neither the integration of new stations nor the relocation of end stations in the network poses any particular difficulty.

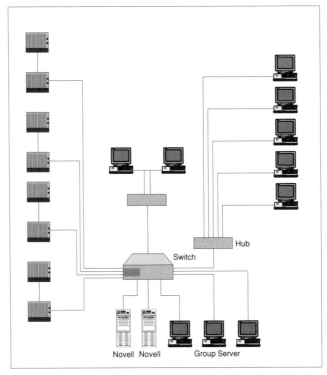

Figure 7.4: Typical server structure in a switched LAN

If the performance of the server connections is still inadequate, either the LAN and switch adapters can be replaced by Fast Ethernet adapters (see Chapter 5, High-speed workgroups), or several parallel Ethernet adapters can be installed in the server.

Parallel Ethernet Adapters in the File Server

The solution outlined above does of course have some pitfalls. The failure of a cable leading to one of the servers will automatically lead to the complete unavailability of this important network resource. Also the performance of the individual adapters in the file servers has inherent limits. The greater the number of clients accessing the server, the less bandwidth will be available to each individual station. Migration of LAN adapter cards to Fast Ethernet is not possible in all cases. For example manufacturers do not offer any Fast Ethernet adapters for ISA and Micro Channel architectures. These architectures are not suitable for the high throughput rates here. Migration from ISA bus servers to Fast Ethernet would necessitate completely rebuilding the servers with faster architectures (EISA or PCI).

For this reason the only viable solution here is the installation of several parallel Ethernet adapters in the file servers.

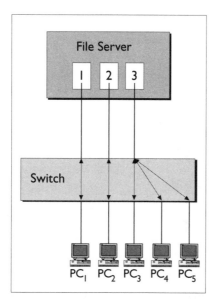

Figure 7.5: File server connection via parallel Ethernet adapters

These additional connections do not deliver the anticipated improvements. If this network is based on TCP/IP protocols, then a separate IP address must be defined for every adapter in the server. Each IP address thus represents a separate IP network on Layer 3. Clients can now be distributed over the different IP networks. As a consequence, however, the failure of an adapter or a cable would lead to the breakdown of communications between clients and the server within this network. A similar function prevents the use of parallel connections in Novell networks (IPX/SPX).

For this reason, some manufacturers have found a way to solve this dilemma. An additional driver can be used in the file server to combine several adapter cards to form one virtual adapter. This adapter acts like a single card (only one MAC address) for the server. The switches from these vendors ensure that groups of ports can be interconnected to form a single network resource. This produces a virtual path between the file server and the switch with a bandwidth equal to the sum of the bandwidth from the available connections.

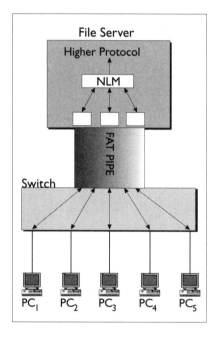

Figure 7.6: Virtual channel between server and switch

This function offers the network operator the following additional benefits:

• The current network load is distributed over the individual connections (load sharing).

• The bandwidth between server and switch is dynamically scalable.

- If an adapter or connection path fails, the load is distributed over the remaining communication paths.

- The use of Full-Duplex Ethernet adapters doubles the bandwidth of the virtual connection.

- The service life of existing network resources is extended and past investment in the network is protected.

7.1.2 High-Speed Workgroups

A number of different solutions have been developed for high-speed workgroups. Nearly all these solutions are based on switches as the core network component. The subdivision of a network into several mutually independent segments not only achieves a maximum of network performance for the individual station, it means that if a fault develops, it will only affect a single point-to-point connection. Since servers and clients in a network only communicate across a contention-free channel, only the bandwidth available in the server needs to be shared between the clients currently communicating with the server. If this bandwidth is insufficient, then it is possible to migrate to Fast Ethernet between servers and switches when it becomes necessary. Network operation does not need to be interrupted for migration, nor does the entire network need to be reinstalled. Moreover, the greatest advantage of this technology is that it delivers the dramatic improvements cited using the existing network layout and the existing cabling.

The publication of the 100BaseX standard as a fixed part of the IEEE 802.3 solutions (IEEE 802.3u) means that there are no longer any barriers to the spread of this new technology. The majority of adapter card and switch manufacturers already support Fast Ethernet solutions. The manufacturers are agreed that the bus architectures used in the past (ISA and Micro Channel) do not provide sufficient performance for fast processor architectures such as have become available with the emergence of Pentium and Alpha-AXP processors. The PCI architecture is increasingly the standard at the high-end of the market. With a bandwidth of 132 Mbyte/s, this architecture represents the ideal basis for overcoming bottlenecks in fast computers. A large number of drivers are now available for the Fast Ethernet board (ODI, NetWare 386, NetWare 4.x, NDIS, Windows NT, etc.). The manufacturers of RISC workstations are now also catching up and are beginning to integrate Fast Ethernet adapters in their product ranges.

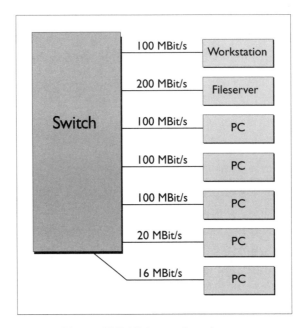

Figure 7.7: High-speed workgroup

This high bandwidth in the file servers and in the workstations also requires support for this technology in the switches. Some manufacturers have built their switches in the following configuration:

- Many standard 10 Mbit/s ports
- Few 100 Mbit/s Fast Ethernet ports

Although these configurations enable high-speed file servers to be realized, if workstations are gradually switched over to 100 Mbit/s Ethernet then it will be necessary to replace the entire switch. Also, some manufacturers have only implemented support for a single MAC address per port on these low-end switches. This means that no segments can be connected to these devices.

The following requirements therefore apply to high-speed workgroup switches:

- It should be possible to operate all ports in 10/20 Mbit/s and in 100/200 Mbit/s mode.

- Switching over between 10, 20, 100, and 200 Mbit/s mode should be automatic. According to the Fast Ethernet standard, the ports of the end station (PC, computer) and the switch should automatically negotiate the transmission rate using the autonegotiation function.

- The switching function between two identical ports (same transmission rate and mode) should be executed in store-and-forward or in cut-through mode. The administrator should be able to specify the mode of operation of the switch. In the store-and-forward mode, the switch acts like an ordinary bridge. In this mode all packets are buffered completely before being forwarded. The advantage of this method is that all invalid data packets (e.g., CRC errors) can be filtered out directly at the receiving port.

- The administrator should be able to define for the switch that data received will be passed on to the destination port only after at least 64 bytes of the packet have been received. This mechanism ensures that any packets that are too short (fragments or collisions) will not be passed onward through the switch.

- The switch should have a high-speed uplink port for attachment to the building backbone. Gateways to ATM or a fast proprietary mechanism are conceivable here.

7.2 Migration from 10 to 100 Mbit/s Ethernet

Networks are undergoing changes as a result of the availability of fast network technologies. In the extensive and diverse product ranges of vendors and manufacturers of network products, for every problem and for every application, there is always one product purporting to be the unique answer to all problems. Technical buffs love talking about technology. They usually fall prey to the subtle techniques of sales staff and end up extolling the virtues of the technology offered as the means of solving the problem. It is then often overlooked that some of the products offered are not as technically mature as state-of-the-art products. Moreover, the solution offered is usually restricted to the product range of one manufacturer. Slogans such as open system, SNMP-compliant, 100BaseX standard, and migration capability are used to sell all of these products. If one does not allow oneself to be dazzled by hollow marketing-speak, and examines these products objectively, one will discover that many of them are not truly open or they do not meet all one's requirements. Unfortunately, the implementation of the 100BaseX standard does not actually indicate whether the card in question can also be operated in 10, 20, or 200 Mbit/s mode. In many cases only a subset of the available standards was integrated in the chipsets. Support for the 100BaseX standard means nothing more than that the card can be operated in 100 Mbit/s mode. It provides no indication as to whether the card supports automatic negotiation of the rate using the autonegotiation function or not. In a worst case scenario, the user would have to remove the card in question and switch it over to the desired speed either manually or using a DIP switch. Consequently, before migrating from 10 Mbit/s Ethernet to 100 Mbit/s Fast Ethernet technology, a detailed migration plan should be drawn up. For this exercise, the network operator should answer the following questions:

- How much bandwidth do the individual network components require?

- How is the demand for bandwidth distributed over a full working day?

- What maximum, continuous, and minimum loads are anticipated?

- What increases in load can be expected over the next 6 to 24 months?

- Can parts of the network continue to operate with the existing 10 Mbit/s technology in the short-to-medium term?

- What components would have to be exchanged in the network for migration to 100 Mbit/s technology?

- What computers (servers and clients) have the bus architecture to support the new planned technology?

- Is it possible to continue to use already installed 10 Mbit/s components at other network sites?

- Can the new components be integrated in the existing network management concept?

- Which manufacturers offer a complete migration solution for software and hardware components?

- How high are the costs for a partial or total migration of the network?

The most important aspect of migration planning is however the examination of the existing cable infrastructure. 100BaseTx, 100BaseT4 and 100BaseFx technology is available for supporting the different cables.

100BaseTx

Only Category 5-compliant cable (according to ISO/IEC 11801) is used for transmitting data in the 100BaseTx standard. The 100BaseTx standard prescribes the use of two wire pairs for transmitting the data. On these wire pairs, the data rate is reduced from 100 Mbit/s to 33.333 MHz through the use of MLT-3 encoding. This ensures compliance with the American FCC Class B Regulations and the even more stringent European standard EN 55022B for electromagnetic radiation at a transfer rate of 100 Mbit/s. The impedance of the unshielded twisted pair (UTP) and shielded twisted pair (STP) cables used in the 100BaseTx standard is 100 Ohm ± 15%. Owing to the maximum permissible attenuation of 13 dB at 12.5 MHz, the length of a twisted pair segment is only 100 meters. RJ-45 technology (8-pole RJ-45 socket) was specified as the standard connector for the 100BaseTx standard. This connector is available in both shielded and unshielded versions. The individual contacts of the 8-pole RJ 45 are assigned as follows:

Contact	Signal
I	Transmit+
2	Transmit-
3	Receive+
4	Not used
5	Not used
6	Receive-
7	Not used
8	Not used

100BaseT4

An 8-wire unshielded twisted pair (UTP) cable with an impedance of 100 Ohm ± 15% or 120 Ohm was specified as the standard cable for 100BaseT4 technology. The 100BaseT4 standard prescribes Category 3 cables (according to ISO/IEC 11801) or better for transmission. In comparison with Category 5 cables, Category 3 cables have a much poorer response characteristic and exhibit crosstalk. For this reason the 100BaseT4 standard specifies the use of four wire pairs for transmitting the data. An 8B6T code is used to transmit the data. With this code eight bits are converted into a six-digit code in each case. Each code group is transmitted separately on one of the three data lines. The effective data rate on each data line is therefore 33.333 Mbit/s. With the 6/8 code, the 100 Mbit/s data rate is split between the three wire pairs in 25 Mbit/s communication channels in each case.

The splitting of the data transmission between several parallel wires ensures compliance with the American FCC Class B Regulations and the even more stringent European standard EN 55022B for electromagnetic radiation at a transfer rate of 100 Mbit/s. In addition, the data is transmitted over the cable unidirectionally. In practice the 100BaseT4 standard can only ever be used in point-to-point connections. Owing to the maximum permissible attenuation of 13 dB at 12.5 MHz, the length of a twisted pair segment is only 100 meters. RJ-45 technology (8-pole RJ-45 socket) was specified as the standard connector for the 100BaseT4 standard. RJ-45 connectors are available in both shielded and unshielded versions. The individual contacts of the RJ 45 connector are assigned as follows in the 100BaseT4 standard:

Contact	Signal
1	TX_D1+
2	TX_D1-
3	RX_D2+
4	BI_D3+
5	BI_D3-
6	RX_D2-
7	BI_D4+
8	BI_D4-

100BaseFx

The 100BaseFx specifications are based on the standards (ISO 9324-3) defined for FDDI technology. The 100BaseFx standard relates to optical fiber as the medium for transmitting the data (graded-index 50/125mm or 62.5/125m fibers). Owing to the propagation time, the length of a fiber optic segment is only 400 meters. If the connections are between two 100BaseFx bridges or switches, then the length of the fiber optic segment can be extended to 2000 meters. A range of different connectors are available as standard connectors for the 100BaseFx standard:

- Duplex SC connector according to ANSI X3T9.5 LCF-PMD Revision 1.3.

- Media Interface Connector (MIC). The MIC connector must always be coded as an M-connector with the 100BaseFx standard.

- ST connector.

Migration at the Desktops

In the majority of cases network migration to a new faster technology will take place in a number of phases. Migration can be accomplished quickly and cost-effectively using the multi-phase model set out below.

Phase 1

In the first phase of migration to 100BaseX technology, only new devices to be installed are equipped with 10/100 Mbit/s-capable adapter cards. Since these are backwards-compatible with the 10 Mbit/s standard, use of these devices allows the overall network infrastructure (hubs, repeaters, bridges, etc.) to be retained. The higher speed of the cards does, however, permit switching over to the higher transfer rate at any time. This protects investment in the new technology in the long-term.

Advantages of Migration Phase 1

- New end stations are automatically prepared for the new higher transmission rates.

- Investment in new equipment is protected in the long-term.

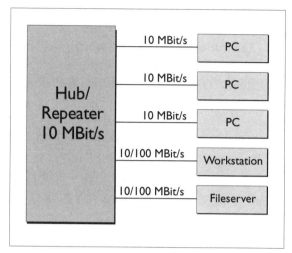

Figure 7.8: Phase I

Phase 2

If the demand for bandwidth increases then the 10BaseT hub to which the end stations are connected can be replaced by a 10/100 Mbit/s switch at any time. The end stations that are already fitted with 100 Mbit/s adapter cards operate in the Fast Ethernet mode and the throughput of the network automatically increases. The older devices continue to communicate at a transfer rate of 10 Mbit/s. The workgroup switch automatically converts the different rates. It is also possible to connect any remaining Cheapernet segments directly to the switch. This cabling does not need to be changed in this migration phase.

Advantages of Migration Phase 2

- The introduction of switching technology enormously increases the bandwidth available to the individual stations.

- 100 Mbit/s end stations can utilize the higher bandwidth immediately.

- Connections between 10 Mbit/s and 100 Mbit/s end stations are accomplished using the integrated speed matching function (store-and-forward mode) in the switch.

- Existing network segments (10Base5 or 10Base2) can be connected to the switch without modifying the cabling structure.

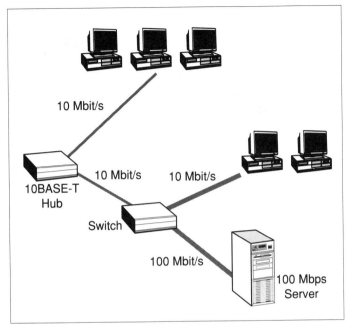

10 Mbit/s

10BASE-T
Hub

10 Mbit/s   10 Mbit/s

Switch

100 Mbit/s

100 Mbps
Server

Figure 7.9: Phase 2

Phase 3

In phase 3, all the end stations connected to the workgroup switch are converted to 100 Mbit/s technology. This requires the entire cabling structure of the workgroup to be reconfigured into a star topology. The central workgroup switch can utilize its full capacity in phase 3 and can interconnect all end stations in the cut-through mode.

Advantages of Migration Phase 3

- The conversion of all end stations to 100 Mbit/s technology and the reconfiguration of the cabling into a star topology makes the full bandwidth available to every end stations.

- Delay between the individual components is reduced since the switch transmits the data packets in cut-through mode between all connected components.

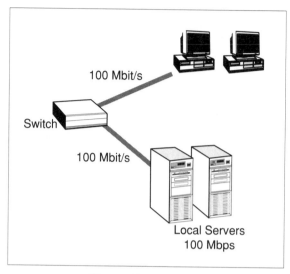

Figure 7.10: Phase 3

Migration at the Backbone

The backbone sections of networks have been undergoing change like no other part of the network. The scope of changes is also wider than ever before, ranging from new features, services and functions through to further developments in the traditional backbone components (bridges and routers). One of the most important reasons behind these changes is the performance problems posed by installed shared media LANs and by combined voice, data, and image applications. In addition, aspects of administration (management) and the resulting operating costs (cost of ownership) are coming more to the forefront.

From the point of view of administration and also cost/benefit aspects, distributed LAN structures are no longer justifiable. For this reason, so-called collapsed backbone structures are now on the ascendancy. With a collapsed backbone structure in a building, all floor distributors in a building distributor are connected directly over separate cables. All cables are then run to the respective subdistributors from this central distribution center, creating a pure point-to-point connection on this segment. If there are enough wires available on the segment, then several parallel LANs can be attached without difficulty and it is even possible to use different parallel LAN technologies (Ethernet, Token Ring, FDDI, etc.). If hubs or repeater components are installed at the center or on the floors, then the overall data load is distributed across all these cables and end stations connected to the LAN. The result of this is that bandwidth is reduced as the number of end stations increases. Connecting several file servers or other computer resources to the central distributor at the central point does not in itself produce any performance improvement for the individual components.

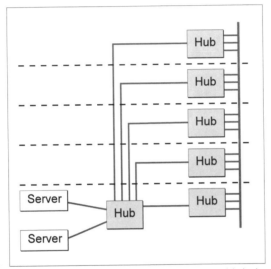

Figure 7.11: Collapsed backbone structure with hubs and centrally connected computer resources

Migration Strategies

Using switches also offers the following migration strategies for solving the performance bottlenecks in the backbone section:

- Replacement of the central hub by a switch
- Replacement of the workgroup hubs by switches
- Replacement of all hubs by switches

Replacement of the Central Hub

The central hub of the collapsed backbone structure of a building is replaced by an Ethernet switch. Since the hubs are retained on the floors, the workgroups are interconnected via the central switch. The total data load is spread over the individual workgroups. With this solution, the file servers on the floors or other computer resources can be connected in the collapsed backbone switch. If required, the central components (servers and computers) can already be equipped with 100 Mbit/s interfaces. This increased bandwidth benefits throughput if several clients from different workgroups access them simultaneously. The failure of a point-to-point connection between the switch and the floor distributor will cause the entire communication segment to fail. If necessary, therefore, redundancy should be provided for this connection. In most of the switches available today, the Spanning Tree mechanism is implemented. As long as operations remain fault-free only the primary connection is active and the backup line is only activated if this connection fails.

Advantages of the Central Collapsed Backbone Switch Solution

- Relatively cost-effective migration solution since only the central hub has to be replaced by a switch.

- Existing components on the floors do not have to be exchanged.

- Throughput between the individual floors is increased. The latency of the bridges is reduced to the minimum latency of the switch.

- The servers and all other computers can be set up centrally. If required, these systems can be equipped with 100 Mbit/s interfaces.

Disadvantages of the Central Collapsed Backbone Switch Solution

- All the data traffic of a workgroup always has to be transmitted to the central switch. Given a large number of end stations, this can result in bottlenecks in the backbone connection (between floor hub and switch).

- Individual end stations on the floors cannot be migrated to Fast Ethernet technology.

Replacement of the Workgroup Hubs by Switches

As described in the section on migration at the desktops, the hubs and end stations in a workgroup can be gradually changed over to switching technology. In a collapsed backbone structure with a central hub this means that all switching functions will be provided at the workgroup level. The individual workgroups are interconnected via the central hub. Since the ports of the hub are based on repeater technology, the entire backbone represents a single collision domain. In relation to performance in the backbone, this means that cross-workgroup communication takes place over a shared medium. If the load on the backbone increases, the number of collisions will also automatically rise. Longer delay times and even further reduced bandwidth are the inevitable results. To reduce the network load on the backbone, the file servers and other computer resources cannot be connected in the collapsed backbone hub in implementing this solution. Consequently, computers must be connected directly to the workgroup switches. The failure of a point-to-point connection between the workgroup switches and the central hub can also be covered by providing redundancy over this segment (Spanning Tree mechanism).

Advantages of Replacing Workgroup Hubs by Switches

- The individual workgroups can be upgraded to switching technology when required.

- Existing components in the backbone do not need to be exchanged.

- Throughput on the floors is dramatically increased.

- Individual end stations on the floors can be migrated to Fast Ethernet technology.

Disadvantages of Replacing Workgroup Hubs by Switches

- Relatively expensive migration step if all floor hubs are to be replaced by workgroup switches.

- All the data traffic between the individual workgroups is routed over the entire backbone (single collision domain).

- Given a large number of workgroups and a high volume of interworkgroup traffic, the shared backbone structure can lead to bottlenecks.

Replacement of all Hubs by Switches

Replacing all hub components on the central backbone and in the workgroups is currently the best solution that can be adopted for Ethernet. The end stations at the desktops can then be gradually upgraded to 100BaseX technology. The central resources can be installed either on the floors or at a central point. By providing switching functions throughout the network, each connection is forwarded from the end station to the receiver without loss of bandwidth. Since such a configuration supports different transfer rates (10, 20, 100 and 200 Mbit/s), the switches must be able to operate both in store-and-forward and in cut-through mode. In practice however, this configuration poses some problems.

- If the end stations on the floors are operated in 100/200 Mbit/s mode, then all backbone connections between the central switch and between the workgroup switches should also be correspondingly upgraded. The prerequisite for this is that both the workgroup switches and the central switch can communicate without bottlenecks at all ports with the high data rate.

- If all computer resources are concentrated in a central communications room (e.g., directly at the central backbone switch), each data packet has to be routed over the connection lines between the workgroup hubs and the central hub. A high concentration of end stations on the floors can lead to the bandwidth of the high-speed uplinks being insufficient to meet user demand. One should therefore consider providing gateways to ATM or a fast proprietary transmission mechanism here.

The introduction of switching technology throughout the building can present the ideal solution to the segmentation problems experienced with earlier technologies.

In switching technology, a distinction is drawn between frame switching and cell/ATM switching. Frame switches are used mainly in Ethernet and Token Ring environments. The characterizing feature of this technology is that conventional Ethernet or Token Ring frames are used for transporting information. When installing end station adapter cards and driver software, this has the advantage that these components can be retained when it comes to the changeover to switching technology.

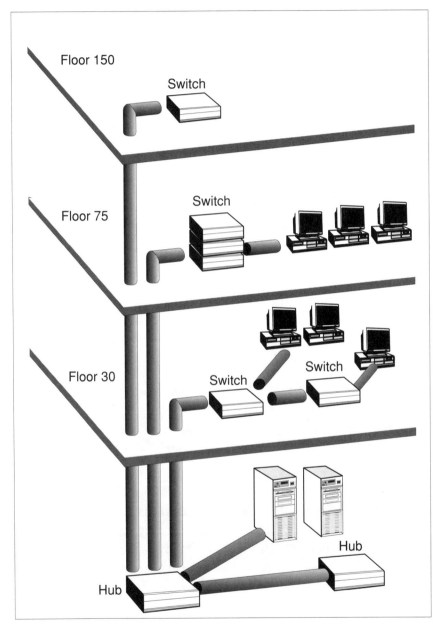

Floor 150

Switch

Floor 75

Switch

Floor 30

Switch

Switch

Hub

Hub

Figure 7.12: Collapsed backbone structure with workgroup switches

By integrating "fat pipes" or "big pipes" in the switches, the network operator is able to operate at different speeds in the same network. For instance, connections with 10 Mbit/s (Ethernet) or 16 Mbit/s (Token Ring) can be implemented (switched or shared) at the end stations, and 100 Mbit/s Fast Ethernet or ATM technology (155 Mbit/s or 622 Mbit/s) can be used for the backbone connections. This means, for instance, that several subscribers can simultaneously access the backbone or central network resources, such as servers and routers. This restructuring results first and foremost in improved performance in the region of the end stations as well as at the backbone connections of the collapsed backbones. This substantially reduces the traditional bottlenecks on the heavily-used connections.

In terms of administration, the installation of switches opens up completely new application areas. Switches allow what are termed virtual networks to be set up (see also section 5.5). This virtual network capability allows physical connections (end stations) to be combined on a logical level to form individual groups. It does not matter at all at what point of the network the individual user is located. The data packets of an end station are only ever sent to computers belonging to the same virtual workgroup. Network administration is simplified essentially by two factors:

- The existence of virtual networks avoids the problem of subnetworks being formed by routers. The router then only has the task of establishing the connections between the virtual networks. The router function can consequently be integrated in the switch as a "virtual networking router."

- New management applications can handle, for example, cable routing and allocation to the various virtual networks at the management console. It is no longer necessary for engineers to make the respective changeovers manually. This saves many working hours, especially when a department moves or the network structure is changed, and it reduces the operating costs of the network.

Advantages of Complete Migration to Switches

- The individual workgroups can be upgraded to switching technology when required.

- Throughput in the overall network is dramatically increased.

- Individual end stations in the network can be migrated to Fast Ethernet technology.

- Individual end stations can be grouped to form virtual networks from the management console.

- Router functions can be integrated in the central switch as a software process.

- The operating costs for the network are reduced by virtue of the new flexibility.

- Easy migration route to ATM.

Disadvantages of Complete Migration to Switches

- Relatively expensive migration step because all hubs have to be replaced with switches.

- Since there is no agreed standard for defining virtual networks, the network operator will have to purchase switching components from the same manufacturer.

Rules for Implementing a 100BaseX Topology

The functions of repeaters are also defined in the Fast Ethernet standard. The Fast Ethernet repeater operates on the Physical layer. Since repeaters are hardware-oriented products, these devices serve to extend and connect Fast Ethernet segments (100BaseTx, 100BaseT4, and 100BaseFx). The maximum expansion of the segments depends primarily upon the round trip propagation time. This value defines the maximum extent a network construct may have and still detect a collision within the transmission time window (collision window) as a valid value. This is also referred to as the collision domain. Different collision domains constructed using Fast Ethernet or standard Ethernet components can be connected to one another using bridges or switches. The Fast Ethernet standard distinguishes between the following two classes of repeaters:

- Class I repeater

- Class II repeater

Class I Repeater

A Class I repeater is a repeater which has a maximum latency between the input port and the output port of 168 bit times. Class I repeaters are always used wherever communication is required between different physical standards (e.g., 100BaseTx <—> 100BaseFx, 100BaseTx <—> 100BaseT4). Only one Class I repeater may be connected on a communication path between two Fast Ethernet end stations with the maximum cable length.

Class II Repeater

A Class II repeater is a repeater which has a maximum latency between the input port and the output port of 92 bit times. Class II repeaters are used in configurations where only one physical standard (e.g., 100BaseTx) is used. Owing to the low propagation times of Class II repeaters, two Class II repeaters may be connected on a communication path between two Fast Ethernet end stations with the maximum cable length.

Table 7.1: Maximum extent of collision domains

Medium	Maximum no. of phys. per segment	Maximum segment length (in m)	Maximum delay through medium per segment (in ns)
Copper link segment: 100BaseT	2	100	1140
Fiber-optic link segment: 100BaseT	2	400	4080

By reducing the cable paths between the individual components, the maximum delay can be reduced to such an extent that further repeater components can be inserted on the communication path between two Fast Ethernet end stations. A core value for verifying a valid network configuration is the worst case Path Delay Value (PDV). A network configuration with several repeaters must therefore be calculated using the following formula:

PDV = (sum of all link delays) + (sum of all repeater delays) + (sum of all MII cable delays) + (sum of DTE delays) + reserve

The values in the formula are calculated as follows:

- The sum of all link delays comprises the values of all delays (Link Segment Delay Value, LSDV) including all interrepeater links.

LSDV = 2 x segment length x delay for this segment.

The segment length defines the distance between the PHY interface of the repeater and the most distant end stations and also the length of the inter-repeater link.

Table 7.2: Delay times of Fast Ethernet components

Component	Delay in bit times per meter	Maximum delay in bit times
Two DTEs	-	100
Cat. 3 cable	0.57	114
Cat. 4 cable	0.57	114
Cat. 5 cable	0.556	111.2
STP cable	0.556	111.2
Fiber-optic cable	0.501	408
Class I repeater	-	168
Class II repeater	-	92

- The sum of all repeater delays is calculated from the latency times specified by their specific manufacturers. If the user does not know the respective repeater latency values, then they should be calculated using default values. (Repeater Class I = 168 bit times, repeater Class II = 92 bit times.)

- The length (in meters) of all MII cables in the communication path gives the total delay over these cables (in bit times).

- Since the end station introduces a delay in the communication path when transmitting onto the cable, this value must also be incorporated in the above formula. If the manufacturers in question do not publish the time values of individual components, then they should be based on the default delay times for DTEs (100 bit times).

- One should always allow a certain minimum reserve on a communication path (e.g., for poor connections, long connecting cables). The standard recommends a reserve of 4 bit times here.

If the result of calculating the PDV is less than or equal to 511 bit times, then this is a valid configuration.

If late collisions or CRC errors occur during operation, one can assume that the maximum delay in the communication path of 511 bit times has been exceeded.

- The maximum distance between a switch port and the end station over UTP cable is 100 meters.

- The maximum distance between two MAC interfaces (switch-to-switch or end station-to-switch) is only 400 meters over fiber-optic cable (half-duplex mode).

- If a single repeater is used (one hub or repeater per floor and optical fiber between the repeater and the switch), a maximum of 185 meters of fiber-optic cable and 100 meters of UTP cable may be laid in the cascade.

- If two repeaters are used, then the UTP cable length in a end station-repeater-repeater-end station constellation may not exceed a total of 205 meters.

- Greater distances can only be covered between two bridges/switches/routers in the full-duplex mode of 100BaseFx technology. In this case, the distance between two internetworking devices may be up to 2000 meters.

7.3 Switches in Hubs/Concentrators

As a result of the introduction of structured cabling systems, hubs and concentrators have become the most frequently installed network components. A hub is an active modular device connected directly to the individual outgoing data cable. Connecting the lowest layer (physical medium) to the hubs ensures that the cables are included in the overall concept. Basically a hub system is a housing into which individual modules for supporting the respective cable medium or the access mechanism are plugged (Ethernet, Token Ring, FDDI, and ATM on optical fiber, coaxial cable or twisted pair). The following function modules interact in a hub system:

- The card modules

- The backplane
- The system controller

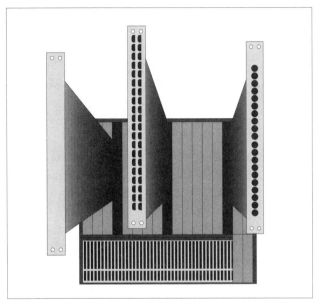

Figure 7.13: Principle of a hub system

Card Modules

Numerous cards are now available for the various hub systems. The following cards and variants are currently available for the different hub systems for Ethernet, Token Ring, and FDDI: AUI repeater modules, AUI end station modules, 10Base2 repeater modules, twisted pair modules, fiber-optic modules, network management modules, local/remote bridge modules, local/remote router modules, end station server modules, ring in/ring out modules, lobe modules, dual attachment modules, single attachment modules, and also switching modules. The card modules match the cable to the hub system and also provide medium-specific services. In addition, a wide variety of additional modules (switches, bridges, routers, end station servers, gateways, etc.) which have also implemented higher protocols are available to the user. Its modular design allows the hub to be tailored to the requirements of the user using individual card modules.

Backplane

Most hub systems currently on the market have a backplane with parallel support for several different data buses. The different products usually support the following data buses over the backplane:

- One or more parallel Ethernet segments (IEEE 802.3).

- One or more parallel Token Rings (IEEE 802.5, 4 and 16 Mbit/s).

- One or more parallel FDDI rings. The individual buses can be configured as a primary or backup ring depending on the application.

- One or more parallel high-speed buses for future applications such as ATM or Ethernet switching applications for example.

- One or more parallel, completely mutually-independent management buses.

Tasks of the Management Bus

If the hub system supports a separate management bus, then this bus handles the following functions:

- Automatic detection of all card modules installed.

- Monitoring of the LAN data traffic and the module status.

Hardware Architecture of the Card Modules

The hardware architecture of the card components features the following three main components:

- Bus interface

- Processor logic

- Network interface

Bus Interface

The bus interface serves as the interface between the card module (processor logic) and the specific data bus over which the data packets are sent to other card modules. The bus interface can be configured in such a way that it switches the data onto the respective transmission bus (primary or/and backup bus) of the backplane either on the basis of the LAN interface port (port switching) or on the basis of a group of LAN interfaces. In addition, it is possible to configure the bus interface in such a way that only the respective card module is supplied with power. In this case, the entire card module acts purely as a repeater or MAU and transmits the data only between the activated LAN ports of the card.

Processor Logic

The job of the processor logic is to process and send the data packets received via the bus or LAN interfaces. A further task of the processor module is to configure the individual hardware and software functions of the card module. The module can be configured either using the jumpers and DIP switches on the card itself or by using the management functions.

LAN Interfaces

The LANs/end stations connected to the card module communicate with each other via the LAN interfaces. Both the electrical characteristics and the functions of LAN interfaces differ depending on the particular LAN technology employed (Ethernet, Token Ring, FDDI). The LAN interface modules also handle the switching on and off of ports or specific functions. The data traffic on the connected networks is also scanned for errors (e.g., short-circuit, no terminating resistor, data packets too short, erroneous signals). Thus it is possible to switch off a port exhibiting excessive error rates so that these faults do not affect the overall network. This automatic isolation of the faulty network segment is termed partitioning. Once the fault has been rectified, the partition will be removed again automatically. This means that once switched off, a port will remain deactivated until no further erroneous information is received over the connected interface for a defined period of time. By analyzing the data traffic and automatically detecting errors, the module is able to activate specific redundancy functions. For instance, two ports could therefore be configured on one or separate access modules as a redundant pair. The functioning of these parallel redundant connections is then continuously monitored. If the line fails on one port, the other port automatically takes over.

The card modules of a hub must meet the following system requirements:

- Reliability

- Automatic fault isolation

- Fault tolerance

- Manageability

Reliability

The reliability of a card module can be increased by selecting suitable components. As a result of the progressive trend to integrating circuits on chips and the availability of customized chipsets (ASICs), the industry is capable of manufacturing card modules with a guaranteed low error rate. This low error rate is expressed as a Mean Time Between Failure (MTBF) figure. The MTBF defines the period of time (in hours) that can elapse before a fault develops on the board or module.

Automatic Fault Isolation

The LAN- and the hub-internal bus interfaces are equipped with a wide range of automatic measuring and analysis functions. If errors occur (e.g., jabber, collision, spurious pulses, etc.) at the respective interface, this port is automatically deactivated by the card module. This ensures that errors on the connected segments/networks or bus systems have no influence on the network as a whole. This port then remains deactivated either until the card is enabled again by the network administrator or until no further incorrect data is received over the connected interface. Analysis of the data traffic and automatic detection of errors enable the module to activate specific redundancy functions.

Fault Tolerance

One of the most important tasks of a hub card module is to provide fault tolerance functionality. The failure of a port, transmission bus, or cable segment (backbone connection) must not be allowed to result in the non-availability of important network resources. Previously, many redundancy functions could only be activated by commands issued by the network administrator. Manufacturers of hub systems have since gone over to implementing these redundancy functions on the hardware level. Thus, alternative paths or redundancy functions are activated automatically when errors occur.

Manageability

A significant aspect of modern network design is manageability. It must be possible to manage the card modules of a hub and all their integrated functions with the aid of a management system. The individual hub modules should also be constructed in such a way that they, too, can be operated without a management system. In this case, it must be possible to enter specific configurations by setting jumpers or DIP switches. The management system should be able to override the hardware configuration of a card module at any time. When a card module is exchanged, integrated management enables the previously-stored configuration values to be loaded on the new card. This greatly simplifies the work of the service team, reduces costs, and significantly increases the availability of the network.

Port Switching

Port switching allows the network operator using a management system to assign a particular port of the hub to a specific bus in the hub. Port switching is therefore sometimes referred to as configuration switching. In many cases, this substantially increases the bandwidth available per collision domain. However this approach does not utilize the total bandwidth of the network, since many stations of a workgroup are usually connected via a hub-internal bus. These stations must share the available bandwidth equitably. If many stations are assigned to the internal bus, the bandwidth of the individual stations is reduced to the number of end stations simultaneously accessing the medium. Port switching can therefore only deliver short-term performance gains. If the network load rises (due to new applications), then the connected end stations will again suffer from the narrow bandwidth limits of a shared medium. Port switching is consequently not a solution in the same way as true switching. The individual port can only be assigned to the respective bus of the hub dynamically from the network management station console. It would therefore actually make more sense to call this function port assignment.

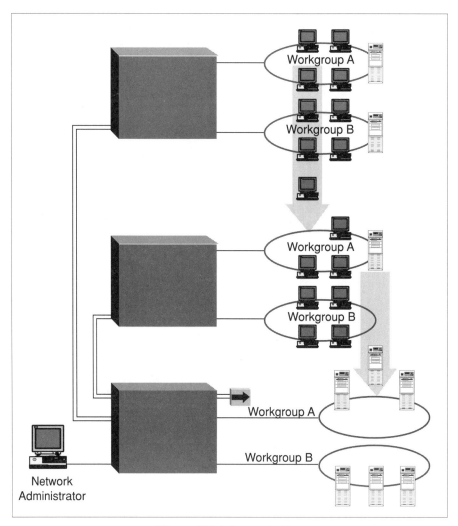

Figure 7.14: Port switching

Noticeable increases in throughput for workstations can be achieved by microsegmenting networks. Modern cabling systems are able to support such a strategy without difficulty. Carefully selecting a suitable cable system will allow different LAN technologies to be implemented in parallel within the overall concept. This solution offers particular advantages when used in networks with heterogeneous system environments. Star-topology cabling from the hub at the center allows targeted microsegmenting to be carried out at any time required by installing switch modules, and the use of switch technology will mean that all the bandwidth can be made available to the connected end stations.

Switching Modules in the Hub

A hub only becomes a switching hub if true switching functions are integrated. It is completely immaterial whether the switching system uses an on-the-fly or a store-and-forward (buffer switching) switching mechanism. The internal circuitry of the respective switch card module ensures that the end stations can communicate over the full bandwidth. In practice, of course, the different switch mechanisms have an effect on the delay time, fault isolation, performance, flexibility, and reliability of the network.

Third-generation hub systems offer parallel support for several data networks on the backplane. Assigning subscribers to one of the hub-internal buses enables differentiated segmenting, effectively shielding users and applications from one another. Most of the hub systems currently on the market state a theoretical bandwidth of inconceivable proportions in their literature. The Advanced Media Center hub system developed by the German company Hirschmann is currently in the lead where total bandwidth is concerned. This system is said to be capable of transmitting data at the incredible rate of 18.66 Gbit per second over internal symmetrical high-speed matrix buses. This total bandwidth is calculated as follows:

- The maximum physical bandwidth is 622 Mbit/s per slot using ATM.

- Each of the three passive matrix bus systems can support a maximum of 10 card modules. (10 x 622 Mbit/s = 6.22 Gbit/s)

- Since three independent matrix buses are supported in the Advanced Media Center, this results in the following theoretical total bandwidth: 3x 6.22 Gbit/s = 18.66 Gbit/s.

In addition to the three main buses, the following buses are also supported:

- One management bus (20 Mbit/s)

- One hub status bus for transferring the I/O signals

- One Ethernet bus (10 Mbit/s)

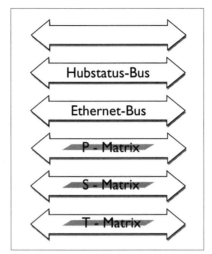

Figure 7.15: Advanced Media Center bus

At first glance this variety of buses may seem confusing. We will therefore briefly discuss the deeper significance of the Ethernet bus and the matrix backplane. It is only possible to implement traditional Ethernet on the 10 Mbit/s Ethernet bus. It is used for communications between the single interface cards developed by Hirschmann. These cards are usually considered to be an interim solution until group switching cards become available. The protocol-independent matrix-backplane (P, S, and T matrix) can support 15 parallel networks. This means that Ethernet, Token Ring, FDDI, or ATM modules can be operated in parallel. With communication over matrix buses, in future all information, even LAN data packets, will be switched as ATM cells. Each card module can be configured to communicate with four networks.

As can be seen from the example, the availability of an integrated fast bus (or several buses) does not mean that the individual buses can be used by the modules available now. The claim of another manufacturer offering a high-speed bus with a total bandwidth of 1.2 Gbit/s for Ethernet switching must also scrutinized thoroughly. Purely theoretically, up to 128 parallel microsegments can be created using this high-speed bus. This manufacturer also offers a number of different switching cards. The difference lies in the current number of ports and the maximum speed per card. The following configurations are offered:

Number of ports	Throughput of card module	Throughput per port
4	40 Mbit/s	10 Mbit/s
1	100 Mbit/s	100 Mbit/s
8	10 Mbit/s	1.25 Mbit/s
4	10 Mbit/s	2.5 Mbit/s

Since the hub system has 15 available slots, given a total bandwidth of 1.2 Gbit/s, only the following number of end stations is possible:

Number	Type	Total no. of ports	Total bandwidth
12	100 Mbit/s card	12	1.2 Gbit/s
15	40 Mbit/s card	60	600 Mbit/s
15	10 Mbit/s card	120	150 Mbit/s
15	10 Mbit/s card	60	150 Mbit/s

As can be seen from this example, the bandwidth made available on the backplane can only be utilized if Fast Ethernet cards are used. However, since these card modules support only one port per card, the flexibility and the number of ports that can be implemented is very limited.

The product brochures of another manufacturer of hubs state that in future it will be possible to connect all switching modules to one another using one or more internal FDDI rings. This must be a marketing joke, since this hub system does not support a high-speed bus. Ethernet and Token Ring data packets can only be converted into FDDI packets using a translation bridge. These components are relatively complicated to configure, and their processing speed is relatively slow. Since the switching modules communicate via an internal shared LAN, readers can work out for themselves the amount of bandwidth that will be available to the respective switch port if many switch interfaces are communicating with one another.

As these examples demonstrate, in many respects the hub architectures available today are still in their infancy and are not yet ready to support switching technologies. This new LAN technology and the concomitant demand for scalable speed have yet to develop. Only once the new architectures are in place will there be full support for switching right through to ATMs. As a result, it will be possible to combine several buildings to form one backbone network and the required bandwidth will be made available to individual users when required from the management console.

Fault-Tolerant Data Networks

Today's workplace is increasingly dominated by information technology systems. New application profiles of the various departments within an enterprise, such as new processor generations or high-resolution graphics applications, for example, are placing a heavier and heavier workload on the data network. At the same time, networks are expanding and becoming denser as more and more staff need to be hooked up to this communication infrastructure. As a consequence, the ability of a company to function properly has become increasingly dependent upon the availability of the network. Failure of a network could prove very costly. Long-term studies in data networks have shown that networks are down for approximately 6% of the total time. This is mainly attributable to cable faults, non-compliance with the relevant specifications, and component failures. Comparing these figures with other critical resources in a company, the failure rate of telephone systems and the power supply is less than 0.1%. The most important objective of installing a product must therefore be to make the overall network behavior predictable, and hence as protected and reliable as other resources in the company. A local data network (LAN) must therefore develop from a fault-prone system into a fault-tolerant system.

A fault-tolerant data network is implemented gradually in a number of phases:

Phase 1

The first step is to construct the data network in a fault-tolerant manner. To do this, redundant cabling structures with redundant interconnection elements (hubs or switches) must be integrated in the subnetworks. A structured cabling system forms the ideal basis for a redundancy concept of this type. For this, the communications infrastructure is set up as a hierarchical cabling system with the following levels:

- Access cabling (cabling between the switches and the connection sockets for the end stations).

- Building cabling (cabling between the workgroup switches and the central switch within a building).

- Site cabling (cabling between individual buildings).

The application-independent infrastructure of the network makes it much more comprehensible, any extensions can be integrated quickly and subnetworks can be assigned specific areas of responsibility. There is no such thing as an absolutely error-free communication system. There will always be a certain residual probability of the occurrence of system failures. Minimization of this failure probability entails additional complexity in the structure of the network and hence additional costs. The operator of a data network is thus forced to make a compromise between the desired level of reliability and the cost. One major area of network planning is therefore concerned with preventing any errors that occur from leading to the complete failure of the network, but rather only to the failure of one part of it at most. With the levels of structured cabling set out above, there are three ways of gradually increasing reliability and protection:

- *Route redundancy*
  Redundant routing of the connections over separate paths.

- *Component redundancy*
  Redundant provision of access or interconnection modules.

- *Switch redundancy*
  Redundant design of cabling centers and crosspoints.

Phase 2

Fault tolerance on the access level can be realized using the following functions:

- *Route redundancy*

The connections between the switches and the end stations must be designed to be redundant. It must be ensured that the connecting cables are run over different routes. In the event of a fault (cable break, sabotage), these separate routes can then be automatically used as an alternative path. This also requires a redundant design of the network controller in the end station or—in the case of Ethernet systems—the use of redundant transceivers. At the switch end therefore, two connections are configured as redundant. The system software automatically triggers the switchover in the event of a failure.

- *Component redundancy*

Route redundancy does not protect against the failure of the access module in the switch system. Component redundancy is achieved by using two access modules in each case. In the event of a fault, the redundant access module takes over the functions of the failed module or port.

- *Switch redundancy*

Connecting the end stations to different switches offers the greatest level of protection. These switches must be set up in different cabling centers. This provides protection not only against the electrical failure of a switch but also against the destruction of the cabling center following sabotage or accidents.

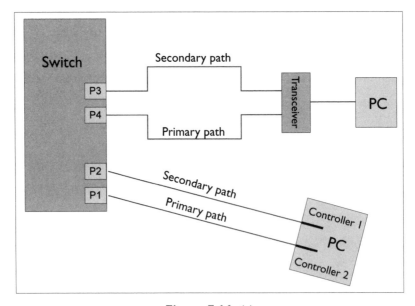

Figure 7.16: (a)

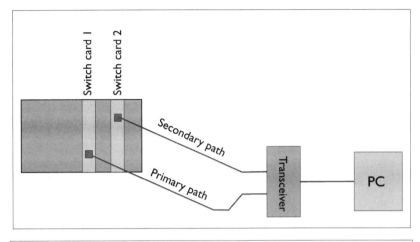

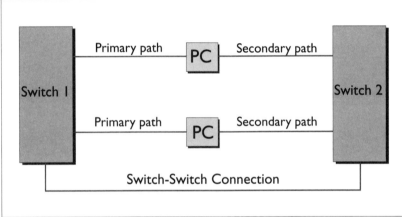

Figure 7.16: (b)

Phase 3

As on the access level, fault tolerance in the building cabling can also be gradually improved:

- *Route redundancy*

The connection between the central switch and the workgroup switches is conducted over two separate paths to two inputs of an access module in the respective switch in each case. These ports are configured redundantly to one another. Since most switches employ the Spanning Tree mechanism, one of the connections is linked passively. If the primary connection is interrupted, the entire data load is routed over the redundant path.

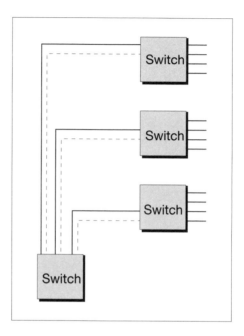

Figure 7.17: Route redundancy in building cabling

• *Component redundancy*

The different connection paths terminate at two access modules of the respective switches. The same redundancies as for route redundancy are possible in terms of functionality. The failure of one card module in the switch then no longer causes the entire backbone connection to be interrupted.

• *Switch redundancy*

For this solution two collapsed backbones are set up. The backbones are installed in different rising ducts in the building. Both backbones terminate at one or more central switches. The central resources (servers, computers, routers, etc.) can be connected directly to these switches.

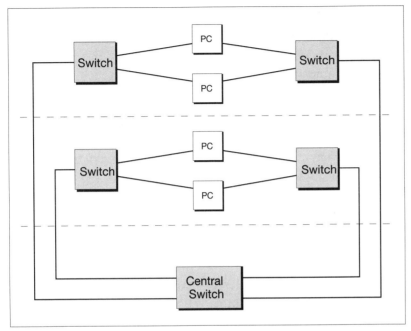

Figure 7.18: Switch redundancy in building cabling

Phase 4

Fault tolerance between the individual backbones of a building or the backbones of different buildings can be improved through additional measures.

- *Route redundancy*

Several connections must be set up between the individual buildings. In the simplest case, this can again be achieved by a ring structure, but any kind of mesh structure is also possible. The simplest way to provide the building cabling with redundancy is to use the Spanning Tree mechanism of the switches. Installing an ATM backbone between buildings makes it possible to provide any number of redundant configurations with a high transmission capacity.

- *Component redundancy*

Several backbone modules for attachment to the site cabling are integrated within a central switch.

- *Switch redundancy*

Access to the building cabling is possible from different points in the building by the provision of several switches. If the building cabling is already designed with redundancy, then each backbone is connected to the site network via a separate switch.

With today's technology it is possible to greatly reduce the residual probability of failures of data networks or parts of them and hence increase their availability to the operator. The examples cited should give network operators or planners helpful hints on how to play through the cost aspects of the individual models and arrive at system solutions that meet their reliability requirements.

7.4 Network Management in the Ethernet Switch

In modern companies, all data and information can be retrieved from any location. Naturally this makes users more reliant on the availability of data networks and the end stations connected to them. Failure of a crucial component would incur substantial costs. For this reason the availability of a suitable network management system has become indispensable to a company. Data networks are therefore also usually managed from a central point. Over the last five years, network management has become firmly established in the computer and data communications world. The task of network management is to reduce network downtime and to prevent network failures as far as possible by taking appropriate preventive measures. The availability of generally agreed standards in computer communications (OSI and TCP/IP) has led to the development of a range of function modules which can be combined in an overall system to handle the tasks of network management. These function modules of a management system can be specified as follows:

- An interface via which the user can retrieve information in a simple way.

- A report generator to furnish the user with practical information to be acted on.

- A function which allows flexible alarm criteria to be defined.

- A preventive mechanism which identifies potential sources of error before the system is affected by these errors.

- A database system in which all this information is stored.

These function modules provide specific information about the network and all the events that have occurred in it and allow an administrator to exercise control over the individual components. These tools have been defined by the International Standards Organization (ISO) in the form of objects and attributes. An object always defines an abstract entity onto which a component in the data network is mapped. This abstract entity can have a large number of attributes (parameters). If this object can be integrated in a management system, then it is referred to as a manageable object. A management function is simply a series of parameterized operations on an object. The collection of all manageable objects is termed the Management Information Base (MIB). The network management station always communicates with the manageable objects by means of so-called agents. Agents are implemented in all manageable devices and translate the commands (queries) of a network management station into action. Open Systems Interconnection (OSI) defines the following five mutually-independent functional areas (specific management functional area) for network management:

Configuration Management

The configurations of the devices to be monitored must be stored and monitored in the network management station. The network manager is then able to register changes in the network. Ideally, this would cause an alarm message to be generated each time a new device was connected to the LAN. This change within the network would then have to be actively confirmed by the respective network manager before the new device can participate in communications.

Performance Management

The network management application should be capable of reacting automatically to certain errors (automatic isolation of a faulty segment). A capability for providing the manager with the greatest possible support (statistics, CPU capacity utilization, memory utilization, etc.) should also be in place to enable speedy and targeted fault localization.

Fault Management

Network management must be capable of automatically analyzing all the data traffic (data throughput and error rate). If required, alarm messages must be generated at the network management station. Alarm or fault indications should be color-coded. It should be possible for the individual network manager to define alarm priorities. It should also be possible to store all alarms together with all their associated data in a database so that if absent, the network manager is able to reconstruct any problems at later point in time, and possibly then take steps to prevent the same happening again in the future.

Accounting Management

One important function of network management is the collection of user-specific data. It should be possible to store this information in a central database so that the costs of using the network can be apportioned.

Security Management

Network management should monitor access to the data network and access to particular resources and services. This requires certain monitoring mechanisms and rules, such as passwords, access privileges, etc.

Very early on the ISO/OSI organization began to specify a complete network management protocol. These specifications were called CMIP (Common Management Interface Protocol). In practice the CMIP specifications turned out to cover too wide a functionality, requiring enormously complicated software for implementing the protocols. The computer industry went to great lengths to implement this standard in its systems. However, it proved economically inviable for conventional computers and LAN devices to process this unwieldy code.

The TCP community adopted a different practical approach to network management based on the Simple Gateway Monitoring Protocol (SGMP). The actual tasks of the SGMP protocol were limited to monitoring functions implemented on IP routers. The Internet Team, which was responsible for the implementation of the SGMP protocol, was commissioned by the Internet community to develop a successor with more functions. This development resulted in the Simple Network Management Protocol (SNMP). Since the

Internet community has always supported international published standards, it was natural that the work of the ISO/OSI Organization served as the basic framework for the development of the SNMP standard. For this reason SNMP was defined in Abstract Syntax Notation One (ASN.1) and contains a Management Information Base (MIB) and the Structure of Management Information (SMI). Two years of development time, during which the protocol was tested in practice, elapsed before the first official SNMP standard was agreed by the Internet Architecture Board (IAB). In 1990, the SNMP protocol was raised to the status of a Recommended TCP/IP protocol and went on to change the history of network management in its favor.

Although the OSI/CMIP specifications were never a commercial success, for technical and political reasons quite a number of fundamental OSI management concepts were integrated in the SNMP model. The developers of SNMP intended to make migration to OSI possible at any later point in time if desired. This is why the protocol-independent "Structure and Identification of Management Information" (SMI) specification was integrated. In addition the individual variables (MIBs) were defined to be completely device- and protocol-independent. At the same time, an OSI migration path (CMIP over TCP/IP, also known as CMOT) was documented in a Request for Comments (RFC).

From the point of view of SNMP development, the SNMP protocol was clearly positioned as merely an interim solution which was to be replaced by an OSI-based solution as soon as practicable. In reality, the process got bogged down in emotional and political discussions with the result that the process of integrating the two protocols came to a complete standstill. The upshot of this was the decision to allow the two protocol communities to lead their own lives in future and to continue to develop them completely independently of one another.

The SNMP protocol is based on a very simple model, the query-response model. The client, called the "manager" in SNMP jargon, issues all queries. The SNMP server (the device that responds to the queries) is referred to as the "agent." The SNMP protocol allows a network management station to read the parameters of an agent according to the rules of the SNMP, and also to modify them (write). In addition, the SNMP allows agents to send an unsolicited alarm message to the management station in certain situations. These alarm messages are known as "traps" or "events."

SNMP uses the familiar TCP/IP protocols as standard communication protocols. SNMP sits directly on top of the Transport layer and communicates directly with its peer using the User Datagram Protocol (UDP) and the Internet Protocol (IP). The protocol standards for the Simple Network Management Protocol (SNMP) are drawn up by the American "Internet Architecture Board" (IAB) and are published as valid standards in the Requests for Comments (RFCs). The following RFCs contain information about the SNMP standard:

RFC 1052   General recommendations of the IAB on the management of heterogeneous networks.

RFC 1155   Defines the Structure and identification of the Management Information (SMI).

RFC 1157   Defines the SNMP communication protocol used between the management entities.

RFC 1213   Defines the database for manageable objects (MIB II).

The syntax of the Management Information Base (MIB) is based on the "ASN.1" (Abstract Syntax Notation One) notation defined by OSI. ASN.1 allows objects to be defined in a system-independent way and identifies each object using unique numbers. These numbers are termed object identifiers. The object identifiers allow full modularity and extensibility within the protocol. The object identifier has a tree structure (Figure 7.19). The term "internet" in this tree includes the TCP/IP protocol family (including SNMP). The management tree below the internet root branches into the following four object classes: directory objects, management objects, experimental objects and private objects.

Directory Objects

Directory objects are not used at present and are reserved for future applications.

Management Objects

Management objects are prescribed in every SNMP implementation. These objects contain all the details defined in MIB II. The MIB I version from an earlier version of the standard contains a subset of MIB II and is no longer used today. From the outset the MIBs have offered the following three options for dynamic expansion: the publication of a new MIB specification, the use of the experimental group, and the use of the private object group in the management subtree. All MIBs that were available as so-called Internet drafts and could be used as an interim solution by means of this branch were put in the experimental group until these objects and object groups could one day be included in the standard MIB. If an experimental MIB became officially standardized, the manufacturers had to provide a software update for all their products which would integrate these objects in the standard MIB tree.

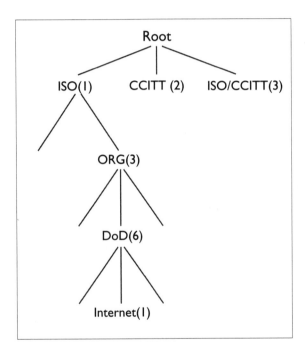

Figure 7.19: The MIB tree

Planning of a MIB III was abandoned for the sake of flexibility. Instead, MIB II has been substantially extended over the years. Within MIB II all objects and variables made available by the system, its interfaces, and the information from the lower protocol structures are defined. The functions of the SNMP protocol today go far beyond those of the pure TCP/IP protocol. In the course of evolution of SNMP, besides the traditional Ethernet, a variety of other LAN transmission mechanisms, such as Token Ring, Fiber Distributed Data Interface (FDDI), AppleTalk and SNA for example, have also been supported. SNMP has now become a generally accepted standard on the market and is used in all market sectors of the communications industry.

Table 7.3: Extended MIB II

System Objects Group
Interface Objects Group
Address Translation Objects Group
Internet Protocol Objects Group   • IP Forward Objects Group
Internet Control Message Protocol Objects Group
Transmission Control Protocol Objects Group
User Datagram Protocol Objects Group
Exterior Gateway Protocol Objects Group

Transmission Objects Group
  • Ethernet Objects Group
  • FDDI Objects Group

Simple Network Management Protocol Objects Group
RMON Objects Group
Bridge Objects Group
Repeater Objects Group.

Experimental Objects

Experimental Objects are only used for trials on the internet (testing new objects) and are reserved for future developments.

Private Objects (Private MIBs)

The Private Group (Enterprise Subtree) enables manufacturer-specific objects to be included. Each manufacturer has the option of implementing any number of so-called private MIBs in addition to the generally accepted MIB information. With many products, a whole range of company-specific information and functions is implemented in the standard as a sort of optional addition. Consequently, the user must know exactly which network management station fully supports which private MIBs in order to be able to utilize the full functionality of the products used. Within the strictly hierarchical management tree, each manufacturer can reserve certain trunks and branches using an individual company identifier. The company identifier is assigned centrally by the IAB.

Since the Simple Network Management Protocol (SNMP) was born from practice, all unnecessary ballast was deliberately avoided. For this reason the SNMP protocol supports only three types of command: GET, SET, and EVENT (trap).

GET REQUEST

The GET REQUEST command allows a management system to interrogate a particular variable in the MIB of an agent.

GET NEXT

The GET NEXT command allows several successive variables of a MIB to be interrogated.

GET RESPONSE

The GET RESPONSE command represents the answer of an agent to a query made using GET REQUEST or GET NEXT.

SET REQUEST

The SET REQUEST command enables variables within a MIB to be changed. This command is also acknowledged by the agent with a GET RESPONSE.

Trap

While all communications generally originate from the management station, the EVENT (trap) command allows an agent to send an unsolicited message to the management station in certain situations (alarm).

Although the SNMP protocol is supported by almost every manufacturer today and consequently is set to become even more widespread, the current version of SNMP is to be replaced by an even more powerful enhanced SNMP specification (referred to as SNMPv2). This work is being coordinated world-wide by the Internet Engineering Task Force (IETF) and is being implemented in various SNMPv2 working groups. This work on the new SNMP standard has been coordinated worldwide by the Internet Engineering Task Force (IETF) and has been implemented in various SNMPv2 working groups. Like its predecessor, SNMPv2 is also based on the SGMP (Simple Gateway Monitoring Protocol) of 1987 (RFC 1028). On the long road to becoming a standard, the protocol had to go through various phases and include the practical experiences of the past. The protocol mechanisms defined in the original SNMP specifications and the area of security represented the driving force behind the modifications to the simple network management protocol. An SNMP security variant, referred to as the Secure SNMP Proposal, was briefly published as an RFC. This paper defined an independent authentication and encryption mechanism. The greatest criticism leveled at the Secure SNMP Proposal was that it did not guarantee backwards compatibility with the existing SNMPv1 version. This would have meant replacing or upgrading all installed SNMP products.

On April 2, 1993 the IETF published a completely revised Internet Draft (Proposed Standard) as SNMP Version 2. This new draft was based on practical experience with SNMPv1 and considerably extended the functionality of network management. The reason for enhancing the SNMP protocol was the greatly increased demands being made on network management and its concomitant functionalities. The support for management functions in a wide range of complex devices (gateways, bridges, routers, end station servers, etc.) allows a substantially greater amount of more detailed information to be provided than was ever originally anticipated.

SNMPv2 lays the foundations for all requirements of a modern management protocol. The SNMPv1 protocol provided only relatively simple configuration and monitoring functions. Since the SNMPv1 protocol supported only a few commands and was implemented over a connectionless transport protocol (UDP), it was possible to integrate it in every device, and it required comparatively little memory. The success of SNMPv2 will depend upon how simple this protocol is to implement in comparison to SNMPv1.

Table 7.4: SNMPv2 Standards

RFC 1452	Coexistence between Version 1 and Version 2 of the Internet-standard Network Management Framework
RFC 1451	Manager-to-Manager Management Information Base
RFC 1450	Management Information Base for Version 2 of the Simple Network Management Protocol (SNMPv2)
RFC 1449	Transport Mappings for Version 2 of the Simple Network Management Protocol (SNMPv2)
RFC 1448	Protocol Operations for Version 2 of the Simple Network Management Protocol (SNMPv2)
RFC 1447	Party MIB for Version 2 of the Simple Network Management Protocol (SNMPv2)
RFC 1446	Security Protocols for Version 2 of the Simple Network Management Protocol (SNMPv2)
RFC 1445	Administrative Model for Version 2 of the Simple Network Management Protocol (SNMPv2)
RFC 1444	Conformance Statements for Version 2 of the Simple Network Management Protocol (SNMPv2)
RFC 1443	Textual Conventions for Version 2 of the Simple Network Management Protocol (SNMPv2)
RFC 1442	Structure of Management Information for Version 2 of the Simple Network Management Protocol (SNMPv2)
RFC 1441	Introduction to Version 2 of the Internet-standard Network Management Framework

The administrative framework of SNMPv2 is also based on the SNMP definitions with only minor enhancements. The differences are to be found mainly in the extended authentication and authorization functions. In the SNMP protocol a community string contained in each SNMP packet is compared with the configured SNMP community string in the agent. Engineers conversant with the internal characteristics of the SNMP can therefore readily identify the packets and their contents. Armed with this information, they can then generate their own management messages without difficulty. The Secure SNMP working group was concerned with addressing this not inconsiderable gap in security in the SNMP standard. SNMPv2 incorporated some of the proposed solutions, for example by providing for the integration of the MD5 algorithm for authentication. From a kind of checksum and a timestamp, the MD5 algorithm forms a 16-byte long individual fingerprint for each SNMPv2 packet. On the basis of this fingerprint the receiver is able to verify the originator of a message and whether it was transmitted without corruption. There is also an encryption option which can be used to prevent a network observer understanding the message transmitted. As a further security feature, time-stamps for the lifetime of an SNMP message have been integrated. These are aimed at preventing a valid message being repeated at a later time. If this is still not enough security, there is an option to encrypt all data. The DES (Data Encryption Standard) of the National Bureau of Standards is provided as the encryption mechanism. Owing to export restrictions of the US government, no software containing the DES algorithm may be freely sold, although the algorithm is available as public domain software. For non-American users or licensees, this means that they use with the SNMPv2 version without this addition.

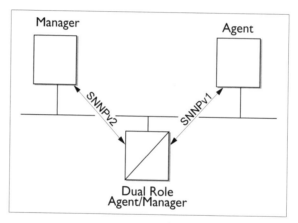

Figure 7.20: Hierarchical network management concept

The individual security and authentication mechanisms can be configured by the network administrator using so-called parties. Parties permit individual definition of the different access privileges, i.e., the views of the Management Information Base. Several network management stations can access an agent. One specific part of the MIB tree is configured (MIB view) for each of the parties (in our case the NM stations) so that one station can read or write only the objects for which it has authorization. In order to accommodate these functions in the protocol, it was necessary to completely revise the standard MIB. At the same time, a further criticism of the SNMP was also addressed. The rigid distinction between an agent and a network manager was dropped. With SNMPv2, a network manager can act both as an agent process and as a server process. This function enables manager-to-manager communication (realized by means of a manager-to-manager MIB) in SNMPv2.

Following the vision of a multi-protocol internet, SNMPv2 was designed in such a way that it can be used on a number of different transport protocols. Besides transport mapping on the basis of the User Datagram Protocol (UDP) already implemented in the SNMP standard, an access point was defined in RFC 1449 (title: "Transport Mappings for Version 2 of the Simple Network Management Protocol") for the following other protocols: SNMPv2 on OSI, SNMP on DPP and SNMP on Novell-IPX.

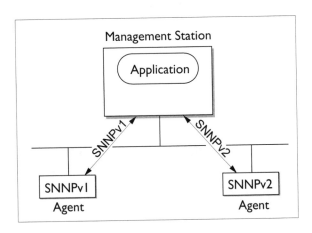

Figure 7.21: Bilingual SNMP implementation

Besides the new features described above, SNMPv2 also introduces a number of changes to format and operation. The GetBulk Request was introduced in addition to the original SNMP commands (Set Request, Get Request, GetNext Request, and Response). GetBulk makes it possible to read out an entire MIB tree with only one request. Since this greatly reduces the volume of data to be processed, it also frees up the transmission capacity of the network for other data. Remote Network Monitoring (RMON), developed in parallel with SNMPv2 and based on the RMON MIB, automatically benefits from the new functions. End stations (agents) which have an integrated RMON MIB can function as quasi-intelligent analyzers in the network. They are consequently able to record any data traffic. The large volumes of data transported over the network using this function, coupled with the necessity of making this data accessible only to certain people (passwords, etc.) for security reasons, are forcing network operators to implement SNMPv2 as soon as possible.

As a transitional solution, until there is full migration of all products to SNMPv2, all these codes are being implemented in "bilingual" form. This allows SNMPv2 agents to communicate directly with their management stations, while SNMPv1 stations need to go via an SNMP translator. In the long-term the SNMPv1 version will in any case die out, so that sooner or later full migration to SNMPv2 is inevitable. The new SNMP version does have an effect on other management protocols, such as CMIP, for example. Since SNMPv2 now offers greater flexibility, this protocol will be used by more and more new companies and in new product fields (Wide Area Networking). In the future, however, network management systems will have to support more than one network management protocol. As a long-term strategy, it will probably be possible to run the SNMP protocol parallel to other protocols within one station. This approach will offer the user a multifunctional environment under a uniform user interface. The either/or war fought by many proponents of the ISO philosophy will therefore eventually fizzle out since in the long run the functionalities of the various protocols will inevitably converge.

Ethernet Management

As with all technical developments, the translation of standards into available products moves at a very slow pace. The necessity of manageable Ethernet components was recognized very early on by the TCP/IP community and these have already been implemented where necessary. There are already a whole range of subspecifications for Ethernet products:

RFC 1623   Definitions of Managed Objects for the Ethernet-like Interface Types.

RFC 1493   Definitions of Managed Objects for Bridges.

RFC 1516   Definitions of Managed Objects for IEEE 802.3 Repeater Devices.

RFC 1515   Definitions of Managed Objects for IEEE 802.3 Medium
             Attachment Units (MAUs). (1993 September)

Ethernet Interface MIB

In May 1994 the Ethernet-like Interface Type MIB was published in RFC 1623. The Ethernet MIB enables the management and administration of devices that support the Ethernet (IEEE 802.3) CSMA/CD transmission mechanism. The Ethernet MIB is based on IEEE 802.3 layer management specifications. The following values were defined for the different Ethernet specifications in the Internet-standard MIB (ifType Variable): ethernet-csmacd(6), iso88023-csmacd(7), and starLan(11).

Bridge MIB

The bridge MIB defines the Management Information Base (MIB) that allows an Ethernet bridge to be monitored and configured via SNMP. The bridge MIB is based on draft standard IEEE 802.1d. In addition, the options of supporting both source routing bridging and transparent bridging in the local and remote areas were implemented. The bridge MIB is subdivided into the following object groups: dot1dBase, dot1dStp, dot1dSr, dot1dTp, and dot1dStatic.

Dot1dBase Group

All objects that are compulsory for all bridge types are defined in the dot1dBase Group.

Dot1dStp Group

The dot1dStp Group is only implemented for bridges that support the Spanning Tree protocol. These objects enable monitoring of all bridge Spanning Tree states.

Dot1dSr Group

The dot1dSr Group is only implemented for bridges that support source routing. These objects enable monitoring of all source routing bridging states.

Dot1dTp Group

The dot1dTp Group is only implemented for bridges that support transparent bridging. These objects enable monitoring of all transparent bridging states.

Dot1dStatic Group

The dot1dStatic Group is only implemented for bridges that support destination address filtering. These objects enable monitoring of values relevant to the destination address filtering mechanism.

Repeater Devices

In October 1992, the repeater MIB was published in RFC 1516 as a standard. This specification allows the user to monitor and manage IEEE 802.3 10 Mbit/s baseband repeaters. The IEEE 802.3 baseband repeater is sometimes also referred to in the literature as a hub or concentrator. The repeater MIB corresponds to the "Repeater Unit for 10 Mb/s Baseband Networks" defined in Chapter 9 of the IEEE 802.3/ISO 8802-3 CSMA/CD standard and is based on IEEE Draft Standard P802.3K (Layer Management for 10 Mb/s Baseband Repeaters). The repeater MIB is subdivided into the following object groups: basic, monitor, and address tracking.

Basic Group

The objects in the Basic Group must be implemented as basic information in all repeaters. This group contains the status, parameter, and control objects for all the repeaters, the port groups, and the individual ports.

Monitor Group

The optional Monitor Group contains objects that enable statistics to be collected for all the repeaters and the individual ports.

Address Tracking Group

The optional Address Tracking Group contains objects that enable the MAC addresses of the end stations (DTEs) connected to the ports of the repeater to be recorded.

IEEE 802.3 Medium Attachment Unit (MAU) MIB

Request for Comments 1515 defines the IEEE 802.3 Medium Attachment Unit (MAU) MIB. The MIB definitions are based on Draft 5 of the IEEE-802.3p specifications entitled: "Layer Management for 10 Mb/s Medium Attachment Units." The MAU MIB contains the following new groups: the Repeater MAU Basic Group, the Interface MAU Basic Group, and the Broadband MAU Basic Group.

Repeater MAU Basic Group

This Group combines all the configuration, status, and control variables required for proper management of IEEE MAUs that can be connected to repeaters. Implementation of the repeater MAU Basic Group is mandatory.

Interface MAU Basic Group

All the configuration, status, and control variables required for proper management of IEEE MAU interfaces are combined in the Interface MAU Basic Group. Implementation of this group is mandatory.

Owing to the high concentration of connected network segments in a switch, this is the ideal place to start with network management. For this, every switch manufacturer supports network management based on the Simple Network Management Protocol (SNMP). The integration of an agent module (hardware/software) in the switch allows the management station to address and reconfigure specific individual components of the switch or to switch individual ports. If one of the end stations is connected to the switch (e.g., a PC or computer) fails, the agent module automatically generates alarm messages and sends them to the network manager. An agent module is an intelligent management front-end processor which handles all the network management functions of the switch. The SNMP architecture is based on a very simple concept, namely the query-response model. The manager issues the queries. The SNMP agent of the managed device receives these queries and translates them into responses.

The SNMP protocol allows a network management station to read and also modify the parameters of an agent according to the rules of SNMP. In addition,

SNMP allows the agent to send an unsolicited message to the management station in certain situations (alarm). With the SNMP protocol, the network management station interrogates all the information collected by the agent in a targeted manner. The variables and values managed by the switch agent are defined and encoded on the basis of the "Structure and Identification of Management Information (SMI) for TCP/IP-based Internets" (RFC 1155). A subset of OSI's Abstract Syntax Notation One (ASN.1) notation and the Basic Encoding Rules (BER) are used for encoding. The manageable objects (parameters/attributes) described according to these rules represent part of the network. A management function is therefore simply a parameterized operation on an object. The collection of all managed objects is termed the Management Information Base (MIB). Switch agents are responsible for executing the actions requested by the network management station and for forwarding alarms and event messages to this station. Communication between the management station and the agent takes place using the IP/UDP/SNMP communication protocol. In practice, this means that a management station can only communicate with the agent by means of a read (Get) and a write (Set). UDP port number 161 is always used for communication between a network management station and an agent. Port number 162 is always used to communicate alarms (traps).

7.5   Tasks of the Switch Agent

All functions and activities which can be executed in the switch with the aid of a management system are defined in the agent module. A switch agent processes the requests of the management station, e.g., setting or reading parameters. The agent examines the specific request of the management station and converts it into switch-internal actions. If, for instance, a port of the switch is to be deactivated, the agent sends a specific command to the respective module via the management bus. The module executes this command by deactivating the port. The successful execution of the command is reported to the agent. The agent translates this message into an SNMP message and sends it to the management station over the network. Agent management also defines how the switch can be monitored on a per-port basis. These functions are called management monitoring functions and supply the network manager with the necessary information to be able to fully monitor the connected resources. For instance, the data traffic on a connected network segment can be monitored specifically, and also data traffic statistics and information about traffic volumes (number of data packets, number of bytes transmitted, etc.) can be collected. A whole range of messages (alarms) which the agent can send to the network management stations and their trigger criteria are also defined in the agent. If a particular situation arises, it sends a "trap" type message to the management station. This trick allows the network management station to react to this information immediately. The following generic traps are provided for this in the SNMP protocol:

- Cold start trap

- Warm start trap

- Link down trap

- Link up trap

- Authentication failure trap

- Enterprise specific trap

When an agent is put into service for the first time, the cold start trap is used to signal the network management station that the respective agent is now active on the network. The trap information consists of an ASCII string. This string may include the following data:

- Type of device

- Model designation

- Serial number

- Firmware revision

- Software version

- IP address

Once the network manager has received this basic information, it is able to manage and monitor every parameter of the switch. One of its most important tasks is to provide the protocol-specific functions for sending management data to the management station. This includes the Layer 3 address functions (e.g., IP addresses and broadcast addresses) and, for communications via routers, the respective routing information. For this reason, the agent must have implemented the following protocols: the Internet Protocol (IP), the User Datagram Protocol (UDP), and the Address Resolution Protocol (ARP).

7.5.1 Switch Agent Architectures

The demands on a switch agent module have increased in line with the advances made in management functionality. From the first software solutions, which were more or less piggybacked on the controller module, an SNMP agent specifically optimized for management tasks has been developed. This swapping out of the management processes greatly increases the processing speed. The basic functionality of an agent module is divided into three functional groups:

- The management bus interface

- The process module

- The communication interface

Management Bus Interface

The management bus interface serves as the interface between the agent module and the data bus over which the management information is transferred between the agent and the individual switch modules. The data is transferred via the management bus interface directly from the agent module into the memory of the card module so that the CPU of the card can process this data. Since most bus systems feature asynchronous buses, FIFO buffers are connected between the management bus interfaces and the logic modules of the card. This enables optimum speed of access to the bus.

Process Logic

The core tasks of process logic are the processing of the management information (commands, queries, collecting statistics, generating traps, etc.), transporting the data over the management bus to the respective modules and communicating with the management station via the LAN interface. To transport the information over the management bus, the agent must append a separate header (addresses of the respective modules, ports, etc.) to the data, or conversely strip this header information from the data received over the management bus. This information is then made available to the individual processes in the agent module for further processing. The agent module is also responsible for translating the collected and prepared SNMP information for the communication protocol used. The SNMP data blocks are provided with the respective header information (Layer 4 to Layer 2) and are converted into a bitserial data stream. This data stream is then passed to the communication interface.

Communication Interface

The communication interface represents the link between the process logic of the agent module and the communication bus via which management data is exchanged between the agent and the network management station. The data blocks supplied by the agent are furnished with the specific protocol headers and sent to the respective communications controller in the switch. The electrical characteristics and the functions of the LAN interfaces differ depending upon the particular communication bus used (Ethernet, Token Ring, FDDI). The data of the management station is also received via the communication interface. In the receiving direction, the interface strips out the bus-specific header information and passes the data to the IP protocol process in the agent module.

The architecture of switch agent modules is divided into the following two classes:

- Monolithic agents
- Distributed agents

Monolithic Agent Architecture

The simplest way of integrating an agent in a switch system is to implement the agent functions centrally on a card module. Consequently, this type of design is also referred to as a monolithic agent architecture. With this design, all management parameters and management functions are processed in a central module. The concentration of all management functions in a central module results in a relatively complex software structure. All MIBs of all supported card modules must be implemented in each agent. This complex MIB structure inevitably means that the development of the agent software is comparatively slow. Therefore, a relatively long time is required before a new management standard is supported or new management parameters are implemented (e.g., for a new card module). Since the development costs for a monolithic agent are comparatively high, owing to the complex MIB structures, some manufacturers offer optimized agent modules for only one network family (Ethernet, Token Ring, FDDI). These agents only support all MIBs and parameters for a particular card module family. If support is to be provided for several different networks in one switch, then the corresponding number of specific agent modules must be integrated. This means that valuable card slots are lost. Furthermore, every agent module requires its own IP address to communicate with the management station.

Advantages of a Monolithic Agent Architecture

- No management functions need be implemented on the card modules of the switch.

- The development and manufacture of switch card modules become less expensive, since the card modules do not support any management functions.

Disadvantages of a Monolithic Agent Architecture

- The concentration of all agent functions and management variables on one module makes the development of a monolithic agent relatively complicated.

- New management standards or support for new management parameters can only be provided by replacing all the agent software.

- Monolithic agents are usually optimized for only one network structure (Ethernet, Token Ring, FDDI).

- In some circumstances relatively high network loads can arise.

Distributed Agent Architecture

A considerably more flexible way of setting up switch management is to construct a distributed switch management architecture. In this case, the management functions are no longer inflexibly implemented on one card module. Instead, the required agent processes are integrated on each switch card module. Depending upon how the SNMP is implemented, one of the agents or a special agent card module acts as the master in this configuration. All other hierarchically-subordinate sub-agents communicate with the master agent in a master-slave relationship. In a hierarchical agent structure, the SNMP commands of a management station are sent only to the master agent. The master automatically forwards the command to the respective sub-agent. The sub-agent processes the SNMP command and then sends the desired information back to the master agent. The latter in turn passes this data on to the network management station. The network management tasks are swapped out to the card modules, and processing takes place in situ on the module. A distributed switch agent architecture offers the following advantages:

- Only the management functions specific to the card need be implemented on the individual card modules.

- These subagents can be dynamically assigned to the master agent.

- Communication between the master and slave implementations can be based on proprietary mechanisms.

- The data encoding scheme between the subagent and the master agent can be freely defined by the manufacturer, which makes it possible for existing encoding methods to be supported as well.

- Switch management can be automatically adapted to new situations simply by inserting modules into the switch.

In a modular management environment, distributed management is capable of automatically adapting to new conditions and reconfiguration. In practice this means that modular expansion of management functionality is possible by inserting new card modules. However, the prerequisite for this distributed agent functionality is that the card modules have integrated network management logic (hardware and software) so that certain network management tasks can be processed directly where they originate/take effect. This extended functionality automatically increases the costs for developing and manufacturing individual card modules.

7.5.2 RMON in the Ethernet switch

The functions of the Simple Network Management Protocol (SNMP) today go far beyond simply the management of TCP/IP data. In the course of evolution of SNMP, besides the traditional Ethernet, a large number of other LAN transmission mechanisms and protocols, such as Token Ring, Fiber Distributed Data Interface (FDDI), AppleTalk, DECnet, and SNA, for example, have also been supported. By extending SNMP to include the Remote Network Management Information Base (RMON MIB), it is now also possible to integrate measuring and diagnostic functions on the Physical layer with SNMP. The RMON MIB standard was published by the Internet Engineering Task Force (IETF) in Request for Comments (RFC) 1271 under the title "Remote Network Monitoring Management Information Base." This SNMP substandard allows management of the lowest layer of the ISO/OSI reference model. Consequently, for the first time it is now possible to use a management tool on the actual wire of the data network itself.

7.5.3 RMON MIB

The RMON MIB was published in 1992 as a supplement to the SNMP standard. The aim of this specification was to create a standard platform which network managers could use to monitor local and remote data traffic from a central network management station. The RMON MIB considerably extends the management functionality of the MIB II standard and supports comprehensive error diagnostic and statistics functions. These enable the network operator to monitor network performance and make network expansion as simple as possible. The RMON MIB subset of the SNMP variables extends the monitoring of remote LAN segments to include a large number of hitherto unavailable new functions. A complete RMON MIB agent is able to detect errors in data packets, filter out individual data packets for analysis, generate traffic statistics and trend graphics, and also to activate user-definable alarm thresholds. The RMON standard divides the RMON MIB into the following groups:

1. The Statistics Group gives an overview of all current network activities. The collected data provides information about packet lengths, error states, number of octets transmitted, etc. Generally speaking, the Statistics MIB provides a snapshot of the current state of a LAN.

2. The History Group links the data collated by the statistics MIB over a longer period of time. RMON management software can be configured in such a way that the network administrator can obtain an overview of the different network segments with the aid of the History MIB. For example, RMON can be configured to poll several interfaces for their statistics every 30 seconds and to display these statistics virtually in real time. Another option is to poll a single interface for its average value over 60 seconds and to store this for later analysis. The polling intervals can be specified individually by the administrator. They are then referred to as buckets.

3. The Alarm Group is used for rapid identification of problems in the network. A network administrator can define specific threshold values for the alarms. If the data traffic exceeds or falls below a particular threshold, the RMON agent sends a message to the network management station. The individual values can be defined either as absolute values or as the difference between two values. To monitor broadcast packets for instance, an alarm (trap) is generated when the upper limit defined by the administrator is exceeded and the network management station is informed of this anomaly in the data traffic.

4. The Host Group records the known computers in a table for each interface of the RMON station. The Host MIB enables statistics to be compiled individually for each computer. The collected information may contain information on transmitted or received data packets/octets, transmission errors, broadcast, and multicast packets. For instance, if the error rate in a network segment rises sharply, it is relatively easy to identify the cause on the basis of the computer address.

5. The HostTopN Group enables information to be collected specifically on the basis of individual computers. The criteria for collection can be specified by the network administrator. A ranking of computers per network segment can be drawn up using these criteria (for example, trans-

mitted or received data packets/octets, transmission errors, broadcast and multicast packets). The HostTopN Group is a tool that should not be underestimated for isolating network problems.

6. The Matrix Group allows the network administrator to identify the communication structures between the individual computers. A specific table is assigned to each interface. All computer addresses with which this computer has communicated are recorded in the destination table and in the destination source table.

7. The Filter Group contains freely definable packet filters and channels. The filters can be used to isolate specific data packets, which are then forwarded over a channel. The ChannelDataControl variable defines whether a data packet is to be copied into the packet store or whether an alarm is to be triggered. The ChannelMatches variable counts the data packets written to a channel. The combination of the two variables enables the administrator to monitor the data traffic individually as required and define the alarm criteria accordingly.

8. The Packet Capture Group handles the buffering of the information collected from the individual channels. The respective data stores can be individually configured so that when the maximum buffer capacity is reached, data collection is halted or the data packets stored first are overwritten. In the event of an error, the packet capture function allows the network manager to access the actual data packets transmitted. To record a large volume of data, it is also possible to store only specific header information.

9. The Event Group permits the definition of individual actions of the RMON agent in response to a given network status. This means that an alarm can be triggered if the threshold value of the data stream on a channel is exceeded, or if certain traffic situations arise in the network. These alarms can lead to an action being triggered within the RMON device. These actions could be, for instance, automatic creation of a log file, sending a trap, or switching a channel on or off.

Like all other SNMP substandards, the individual RMON groups can be extended at any time and adapted to the individual application areas of the RMON agent.

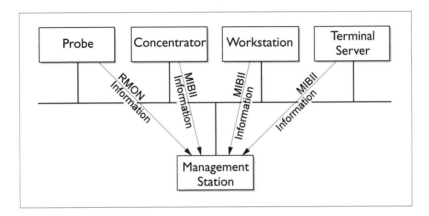

Figure 7.22: Communication between the network management station and probe/agent

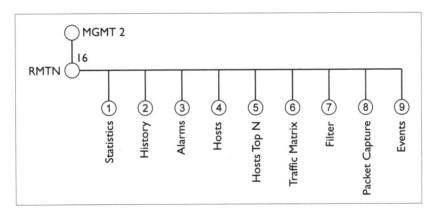

Figure 7.23: The RMON MIB

RMON Functionality

Correct use of the complex functions and function groups of the RMON MIB demands an in-depth understanding of these functions from the user. RMON standardizes the format of the data to be collected. The management stations are consequently able to display this information on the respective user interface. Since it is not compulsory for all RMON groups to be supported, vendors can implement the individual parts in a RMON agent as they see fit. Consequently, a wide variety of RMON monitors optimized for specific tasks are already available. These devices are designed quite differently with respect to performance, processing speed, and memory capacity. The RMON MIB is supported by all these devices. However, this does not signify anything more than that certain parts of the RMON MIB have been implemented.

In principle, RMON enables cooperation with different management stations in the network. This allows organizational distribution of the management tasks. For instance, all statistical data can be sent to the normal operator workstation, while all alarms and panic messages can be sent to a catastrophe management system.

Besides simply collecting data on the network, a RMON agent is able to filter out certain data and compare this information with previously-defined values. This can make it easier, for example, to identify the LAN devices handling the most traffic. A RMON agent can also be configured for monitoring and automatically detecting potential network problems and fault conditions. If a fault condition occurs, then the agent registers this event and signals it to the SNMP management stations. In day-to-day operations, diagnostic functions can be used to record the performance data of a network or segment in order to collate long-term statistics.

Proxy Management

Normally each SNMP station periodically polls the end station to be managed according to the query-response model. In large networks this can lead to these data packets constituting the majority of the data traffic. Inevitably this has a negative effect on performance and the bandwidth available in the data network. The Proxy Management function of the RMON MIB reduces the amount of data traffic, particularly in applications in Wide Area Networks (WANs). In these applications the RMON MIB functions as a sort of network management station and sends the management information to the management center only at user-definable intervals. RMON devices can be operated in the following modes: OFF Line, ON Line, and On Demand.

Online Mode

In the Online mode all of the data collected at the RMON agent is automatically sent to the network management stations. Since a lot of data can be collected in a network, this function requires a certain amount of transmission bandwidth.

Offline Mode

The RMON agent collects all the data and stores this information. The network management stations establish a connection to the RMON agents in the network at a specified time and pick up the stored information. Offline mode is ideal for RMON agents installed in a remote network (connected by a WAN).

On Demand Mode

In On Demand mode, the following two options are possible:

- The management station continuously interacts with the RMON agent. If a fault results in the interruption of the connection between the RMON agent and the management station, the monitor can be programmed to collect all the data until the connection is re-established.

- As with the OFF Line mode, the RMON agent does not require a connection to a management station. Communication does take place after a value has been exceeded (threshold value, alarm situation).

Flexibility

The flexibility of the RMON standard means that all data can be collected on the lowest layer and passed to the management station. Ultimately the functionality depends only on the particular implementation. For example, it is possible to mark threshold values for a large number of events for nearly all devices (probes). Exceeding a threshold generates an alarm. The network operator is therefore made aware of a problem in plenty of time to take targeted countermeasures if required. Grading alarm messages according to freely definable priorities frees the operator from an unmanageable flood of information. Collecting statistics continuously and defining threshold values allows the "normal" behavior of a network to be individually characterized. For example, certain data (number of packets/octets, broadcasts/multicasts, etc.) can only be written into a log file, whereas real errors, such as packets too small, packet fragments, CRC/alignment errors, jabber, packets too large, and collisions for example, can cause the color of the respective icon to change at the console. By coupling the alarm with an acoustic signal or a paging system, the network management system can alert the operator to a critical situation.

Performance Analysis

The RMON MIB is structured in such a way that it optimally supplies performance data for communications between SNMP management stations and SNMP agents. In practice this means that the data can be transported much more quickly over the network while at the same time, less network overhead is produced. Each row in a table with MIB variables is indexed. This value is used to identify the row uniquely. The tables managed by the RMON MIB always begin with the index 1 and are then progressively incremented. When the management station accesses the RMON MIB, it can consequently access a range of index types. The data contained therein is transferred to the management station in a single data packet. The function of the statistics and alarms are illustrated in the example below. The basic characteristics for a network are defined during configuration. The normal load on the network is 15% per minute on average. An alarm is to be triggered if the average load (per minute) exceeds 40%. The normal statistics are gathered by the RMON probe and are passed to the network management station from time to time, depending on the specified interval. If an alarm occurs, the network manager is notified of the event immediately by means of a trap (alarm). Using the TopNTalker function, the manager can then determine which of the computers is generating the data traffic. If necessary, the filter function can be used to reroute some or all of the data traffic. The manager is able to analyze all the data transmitted on all layers of the ISO/OSI reference model using decoding software at the management station. The source of the problem can be targeted and quickly identified with the aid of these tools and can be rectified without difficulty by reconfiguring the network.

Management of Legacy Devices

Many older LAN devices have no integrated management so they cannot be included in a global management concept. In practice this means that these devices are not manageable. A RMON agent extends the functionality of the data network and indirectly supports these devices as well. For these devices the network operator can define special filters and statistics which gather all the information pertaining to the respective device and pass it to the network management station. The availability of RMON transforms an unmanageable device into a quasi-manageable end station.

RMON Architecture

In the widest sense of the word a RMON application represents a cost-effective measuring instrument. This measuring instrument always comprises a RMON application and one or more RMON probes. The RMON application is always installed on a computer (client), while the server software resides on the individual probes in the network.

RMON Application

The RMON application can be set up either as a stand-alone tool or as an add-on to a common network management application (e.g., HP-OpenView, SunNet Manager). The most important tasks of the RMON application can be described as follows:

- Collection of RMON SNMP information

- Preparation of the collected information

- Graphical representation of the data (statistics)

RMON Probe

A RMON implementation on a RMON server can be realized as a hardware and as a software solution.

Hardware Probe

The extensive functionality of the RMON MIB means that it requires a powerful hardware platform for collecting and processing the data. The hardware and software of the RMON probe must never lose information transported over the connected networks. For this reason, most of the currently-available hardware platforms for probes are based on a RISC architecture. In order to be able to process and store the data satisfactorily, this probe must have a large memory (2-16 Mbytes). The size of the memory depends on the number of LAN interfaces available. The hardware probe may either be an independent device (standalone probe) or an additional module integrated in the Ethernet switch.

Software Probe

With some manufacturers the server version of the RMON MIB can also be distributed to workstations (e.g., SUN) by downloading over the network. In this case the workstation is functioning as a temporary probe. In comparison with a hardware probe, this application has the disadvantage that the functionality and the maximum number of data packets that can be processed are limited.

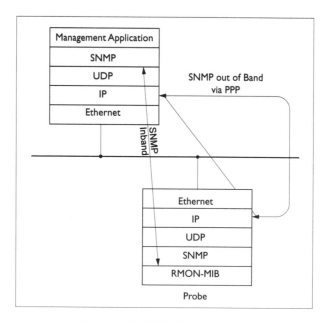

Figure 7.24: RMON architecture

Extensibility

The RMON MIB was originally designed only for use in Ethernets. A standard for supporting Token Rings has been available for quite some time; FDDI networks and WANs are to be supported in the near future. RMON is designed in such a way that this MIB can be extended at any time to facilitate adaptation to the realities of the marketplace in the form of upgrades. For example, further application areas are already conceivable today, e.g., creating inventories, automatic protocol, and address identification, as well as network security, etc. As yet there is no end in sight to this rapid development process.

Table 7.5: Comparison of MIBs

Parameter Group	MIB II	RMON MIB	HUB MIB	Bridge/ Switch MIB	Host MIB
Interface	X				
Statistics					
IP Statistics	X				
TCP Statistics	X				
UDP Statistics	X				
SNMP Statistics	X				
Host Job Counts					X
Host File System Information					X
Link Tests			X	X	X
Data Traffic Statistics		X	X	X	
Host Statistics		X	X		
History Statistics		X			
Spanning Tree Performance			X		
Thresholds For Each Area		X			
Configuration		X			
Statistics					
Traffic Matrix		X			
Top Talkers		X			
Packet Analysis		X			
Distributed Logging Logging		X			

7.6 Migration from Ethernet to ATM

The technology behind the term Asynchronous Transfer Mode (ATM) is being hailed by all network companies as the technology that will deliver hitherto undreamed of functionality and flexibility to the networking community. With ATM, bandwidths of up to 155 Mbit/s can be made available to specific individual end stations as and when required. Once transmission has been completed, this bandwidth is then immediately freely available to other communication processes again. This makes ATM the ideal transmission technology for transferring the sporadic transmission loads (data bursts) typical of local area networks. Above all, ATM bandwidth is to be used for transporting bandwidth-hungry video applications over the network. Since ATM technology provides an enormous amount of bandwidth per station, connection paths remain free of bottlenecks even at times of peak data volume. For this reason, some overzealous prophets are advising companies to get rid of their enterprise LANs completely and replace them with new networks employing ATM technology throughout. Nothing is more constant than change in the world of information technology; however, changing over immediately to this new high-speed method is not advisable for all users and network operators. Throughput-thrashing ATM is not necessarily the sensible option to have right through to every end station. Immediate changeover to the wonderful new world of ATM is usually unjustifiable from a business point of view, since investment in the network technologies installed to date has not yet been written off. This conflict can only be solved by a planned migration to high-speed ATM technology. Only proper planning will guarantee that the bandwidth, throughput, and cost realities in the individual network sections will not be ignored.

Currently, switching and the concept of virtual networks are seen as the cure-all for all types of network problems. Switching can indeed solve many problems, and many new network concepts are being developed. In practice, however, these buzzwords are robbing some network operators of their senses. No prophet can predict exactly what throughput loads future networks will have to carry. When transmitting pure LAN data, end stations are usually well served by 100 Mbit/s. Even for transmitting voice over a network, the demand for bandwidth is still well within bounds. Using modern compression techniques, only approximately 8 kbit/s to 32 kbit/s is now required for high-quality voice transmission. The real bandwidth-crunching applications are the transmission of complex graphics or even the transmission of desktop videos. With the aid of powerful compression methods such as JPEG (Joint Photographic Expert Group) or MPEG (Motion Picture Expert Group), however, video data volumes are being reduced to occupying a bandwidth of from 3 to 10 Mbit/s.

With Ethernet switching, the full 10/100 Mbit/s bandwidth is available to the end stations. Structured cabling can readily provide the user with dedicated communication services such as voice, video, and data communications at the workstation. This cabling structure also offers the network operator the security of being able to change over to another technology (such as ATM, for example) if the demand for bandwidth rises. This facilitates the embedding of ATM in enterprise-wide networks and offers protection against high additional investment. Category 5 twisted pair cable is already supported by a large number of manufacturers. In the backbone sector, fiber-optic cable has long been established as the standard. The ATM specifications for transmission rates of 100 Mbit/s (TAXI) or 155/622 Mbit/s (SONET/SDH) on 50 mm or 62.5 mm multimode fiber have long been the norm.

Bandwidth demand in the backbone will rise much more rapidly than in the workgroups. It is here that data traffic with all its different types of data (voice, graphics, and video traffic) will be concentrated. If the backbone is constructed as a collapsed backbone, the user will have the flexibility to change over to ATM transmission (SONET/SDH or TAXI) later without having to make changes to the cabling. If it is necessary to lay cable lengths of more than two kilometers—to connect several buildings on an enterprise backbone for instance—ATM transmission can also be realized on monomode optical fiber. For this medium, too, the ATM Forum has already created reliable standards for covering distances of up to 40 kilometers using ATM. By combining monomode and multimode fibers in one ATM switch system, two or more buildings can thus be connected using ATM.

From LAN Switching to ATM Switching

Manufacturers of ATM and of LAN components have learned that these two worlds are inseparable, and they will continue to converge. LAN switching makes the full bandwidth (10, 16 or 100 Mbit/s) available to every connected end station on Layer 2.

End stations (clients and servers) are connected directly to an ATM network with the aid of different ATM adaptation layers (AAL). These layers enable matching to service-specific requirements and provide the necessary functions. The AAL is located between the ATM layer and the higher application layers. Since in contrast to Token Ring, Ethernet, or FDDI, ATM technology operates over dedicated channels, a method of transmitting broadcast information over an ATM network had to be found. At a gateway between a LAN and an ATM network, the conventional LAN packets must be converted into ATM cells. At this gateway the Ethernet, Token Ring, or FDDI packets are divided up into 48-byte long cells and a 5-byte ATM-specific header is attached. If two LANs are connected via an ATM transit network, then the LAN packets have to be reconstituted from the ATM cells.

LAN Emulation

For direct connection between the LANs and ATM networks, the ATM Forum defined the exact interface and its functions under the name LAN emulation User-to-Network Interface (LUNI). The LUNI specification ensures that the connectionless services of a LAN are mapped onto a connection-oriented ATM connection using a LAN emulation. The LAN-to-ATM converter ensures that the LAN packets are received, an identification header is placed in front, and the respective checksum (frame check sequence) is removed from the data stream. The LAN information is then passed to the ATM network as an AAL type 5 PDU. The AAL layer subsequently splits the packets into cells. Once the cells reach the destination LAN, the cells are reassembled to form the original data packet under the control of the ATM adaptation layer.

The LAN emulation makes it possible to connect up several separate LANs of the same type. Conversion between the different network systems is handled by a bridge or a switch.

The following services must be provided at the gateway between the LAN and the ATM network:

- The switch/bridge must check whether a virtual channel (Virtual Channel Connection, VCC) already exists for the respective 48-bit long MAC address. If a virtual channel is found, the data can be forwarded directly to the receiver. The respective MAC addresses are assigned to the channel in question in a table of the switch.

- If no VCC channel is found in the table for the respective MAC address, the ATM controller must establish this virtual channel. This takes place in the following two phases:

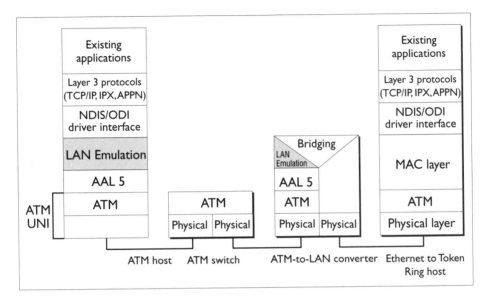

Figure 7.25: Conversion from a LAN into an ATM network

1. The ATM address of the destination network (switch providing access to the LAN in question) is determined with the aid of an address resolution process.

2. A virtual channel is then established to this switch using ATM signalling. This specific information is stored in the local address table.

   - Once the VCC has been established, a 2-byte long emulation header is placed in front of the data packet, and it is then transported across the network according to ATM rules.

   - At the ATM receiver, the individual ATM cells are reassembled into the original data packet and are forwarded to the actual receiver in the LAN.

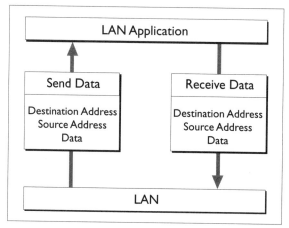

Figure 7.26: Transmitting processes at the gateway between a LAN and an ATM network

The LAN emulation is a composite of the concept of LAN Emulation Clients (LECs) and LAN Emulation Services. The LAN Emulation Client software can be implemented in the ATM-LAN switch/bridge or as a permanent part of a network server connected to the ATM network. The principal task of this software is to convert MAC addresses into ATM addresses. This address resolution function is termed LE_ARP. The software that performs the LAN Emulation Service is divided into the following three logical servers: the Configuration Server (COS), the LAN Emulation Server (LES), and the Broadcast and Unknown Server (BUS).

In practice however, a LAN Emulation Client (LEC) must first know the ATM address of the LAN Emulation Server (LES). The LEC can only partici-pate in the services if it is assigned to an emulated LAN. This incorporation in an emulated LAN can take place in the following ways:

1. The client initially uses the Interim Local Management Interface (ILMI) and tries to read the address of the COS out of an ATM switch table.

2. If this connection is not set up, the client then attempts to determine another COS via the ILMI.

3. If no address is found, the client uses a "Well Known ATM Address" defined as standard for each network;

a) or the client searches for a VPI/VCI pair that has a link to a virtual connection to the BUS which has already been established;

b) or the client searches for a preconfigured LES address or a predefined PVC between the client and the configuration server.

Once the client has determined the address of the LES, the type of LAN emulated and the maximum permitted frame size must be agreed between the two devices. Once this information exchange has been completed, the LEC joins the emulated LAN. For this purpose a bidirectional control connection is established to the LES by the LEC. The LEC then sends a LE_JOIN_REQUEST to the LES. This request contains the ATM address, the LAN type, the maximum frame size, and a proxy flag. The LEC uses the proxy flag to signal that it is functioning as a gateway for other end stations. As a response to the LE_JOIN_REQUEST, the LES transmits a LE_JOIN_RESPONSE to the LEC. As a result of this response, either the client is registered in the emulated LAN or the join request is rejected.

The Address Resolution Process

If a LAN packet is to be transmitted over an ATM network, the switch/bridge checks whether a virtual channel already exists for the respective 48-bit long MAC address. If no entry is found in the ARP table, an address resolution process (LE_ARP) is used to determine the ATM address of the destination network. This ARP_Request is transmitted by the LEC to the LES over the VCC (known as the control direct VCC) established during the assignment to the emulated LAN. If the LES is unable to resolve the received ARP request, it sends this request on to all the LESs known to it. This forwarding of the request could be handled by special control direct VCCs between the LESs. Since the use of many parallel VCCs would constitute an enormous waste of network resources, however, so-called point-to-multipoint connections (control distribute VCCs) are established between LES components. The address information is sent to the requesting LES and then later back to the requester LEC via these connections.

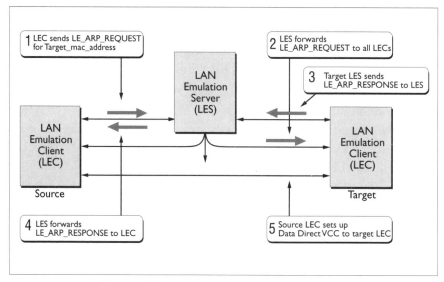

Figure 7.27: LE_ARP request in ATM network

After this the data connections to the destination network can be set up. This connection is termed a "channel" and consists of a point-to-point data connection between the clients, via which the entire data traffic between these parties is exchanged.

If broadcast or multicast information is transmitted by the client into the ATM network, then a large number of different channels are not opened. Instead these special packets are transmitted directly over a separate channel (unidirectional connection) to the Broadcast and Unknown Server (BUS). The broadcast or multicast transmission is distributed by the BUS to the stations for the respective packet type.

LAN switch systems can communicate directly with ATM components using LAN emulation. The benefits of ATM technology can consequently be fully exploited in the backbone and the network operator need not change existing LAN resources over to the new technology immediately. A gradual, well-planned changeover allows bandwidth to be successively increased wherever it no longer suffices.

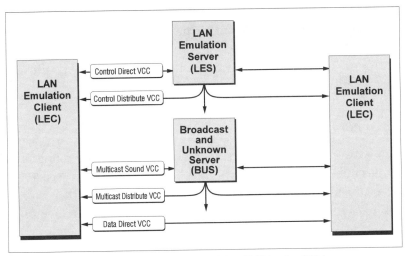

Figure 7.28: Principle of the BUS in the ATM

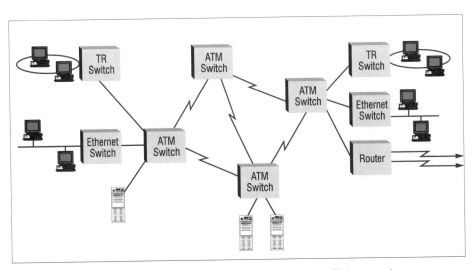

Figure 7.29: Connections between LANs and ATM networks

7.7 Virtual Networks

Switches not only deliver significantly increased bandwidth and reduce delay times in the network, they also enable the introduction of dynamically definable workgroups. This free definition of group allocations in the network is generally known as the integration of virtual networks. In a switched network, the network administrator can use this function to group the ports into logical workgroups. This free assignment and its advantages will be illustrated by the following example:

Single Domain Hub Concept

Thirty end stations (clients, servers, routers, and bridges) are connected to one another via a hub. The 10BaseT ports are all operating on the basis of repeaters. For this reason, all devices are communicating with each other over a single bus. As the load increases, this leads to less bandwidth per end station being available to the individual stations.

Advantages: Single Domain Hub Concept

- Flat network hierarchy

- Inexpensive components

- Simple configuration

- Central resources (file servers, application servers) can be connected directly

Disadvantages: Single Domain Hub Concept

- The available bandwidth is shared between the active stations

- Changeover or upgrading to 100BaseX technology is not possible without using bridges

Multiple Domain Hub Concept

The end stations are assigned to a particular bus in the hub with the aid of the port switching function. The number of end stations per collision domain is consequently reduced. The stations within a collision domain must share the available bandwidth equitably. If many stations are assigned to the internal bus, the bandwidth of the individual stations is reduced to the number of devices simultaneously accessing the medium. Port switching can therefore only deliver short-term performance gains. If the network load rises (due to new applications), then the connected end stations will again suffer from the narrow bandwidth limits of a shared medium. A connection between the individual physical workgroups is only possible via bridges or routers. The use of bridges has the disadvantage that in the case of unknown packets; the device will simply send the information out to all ports and will consequently let the traffic pass in an uncontrolled manner. If a router is used instead of the bridge, the connection will be set up on the protocol-specific layer. The individual buses of the hub are consequently divided into logical subnetworks.

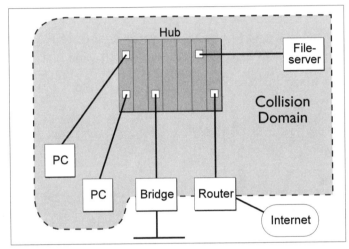

Figure 7.30: Hub with end stations

A necessary side effect of this solution is that the router port of a special subnetwork will need to be physically connected directly to the respective bus in the hub. The splitting of workgroups into different subnetworks means that users cannot work in distributed physical workgroups. Furthermore, if a user moves into a different workgroup, it will necessitate changing this subnetwork address.

Advantages: Multiple Domain Hub Concept

• Flat network hierarchy

• Inexpensive components

- Simple configuration

- Reduction of the load within a collision domain

Disadvantages: Multiple Domain Hub Concept

- Communication between the different collision domains is only possible via routers or bridges (subnetting)

- The available bandwidth is shared between the active stations

- Changeover or upgrading to 100BaseX technology is not possible without using bridges

- Since general access to central resources is not possible, each collision domain must have its own file servers/application servers

- Moving individual workstations is only possible by reconfiguring the subnetwork numbers.

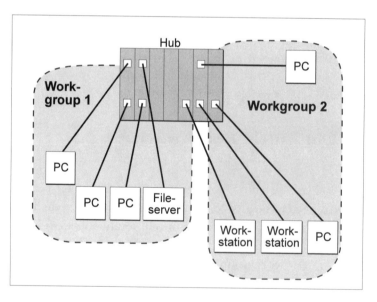

Figure 7.31: Hub with reduced load due to division into workgroups

Single Domain Switch Concept

Thirty end stations (clients, servers, and routers) are connected to one another via a switch. The 10BaseT ports of the switch all operate according to the switching functions (store-and-forward or cut-through) on Layer 2. The devices still together form a single broadcast/multicast domain. Consequently, this decouples the load between the individual ports. However an increase in broadcast/multicast load significantly reduces the bandwidth available per end station. Since each station can access every end station, data protection functions must be realized on a higher layer. Splitting into workgroups is not possible on the Physical layer.

Advantages: Single Domain Switch Concept

- Flat network hierarchy

- Decoupling of load between end stations

- Inexpensive components

- Simple configuration

- Central resources (file servers, application servers) can be connected directly to the switch

- Changeover or upgrading to 100BaseX technology is possible without using bridges

Disadvantages: Single Domain Switch Concept

- The available bandwidth of the active stations decreases as the broadcast or multicast load rises

- Not possible to implement data protection functions

Virtual Workgroup Switching

With few exceptions, the data traffic within a workgroup is relatively self-contained. Workgroup subscribers normally communicate only with each other. The respective central resources (servers, hosts, gateways) are available to this workgroup without restriction. The following requirements exist for the smooth network operation of such different workgroups:

- The workgroups must be dynamically definable.

- It must be possible for individual members of a workgroup to move easily and inexpensively.

- The definition of individual logical workgroups must not be limited to only one switch.

- It must also be possible to set up the logical workgroups in an internet (e.g., campus network).

- If required, it must be possible to use central resources from several workgroups.

- It must be possible to implement access or data protection between the workgroups.

- It must be possible to establish a connection between individual distributed workgroups when required.

The availability of switch technology brought with it the new concept of virtual networks. A virtual network is characterized by the fact that individual subscribers within such a virtual network need not correspond to physical end stations of a hub or switch. A virtual network is produced by the deliberate assignment of an end station to a logical network. It is completely immaterial whether a virtual network comprises a single switching component, a building network, or a campus network.

The virtual networks are defined using a management application. The principle of splitting physical ports into logical virtual workgroups will be illustrated using the example of a 30-port switch.

Stations 1 to 5, 6 to 10, and 11 to 15 are split into three virtual networks with the aid of the network management application. This is done by means of an internal table of the switch.

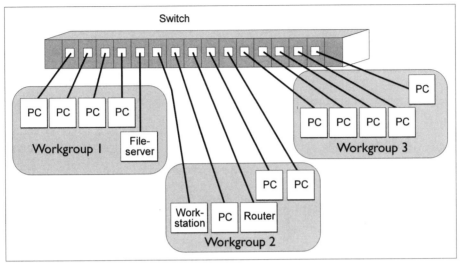

Figure 7.32: Switch with 15 end stations

Example table

Port	Virtual network
1	1
2	1
3	1
4	1
5	1
6	2
7	2
8	2
9	2
10	2
11	3
12	3
13	3
14	3
15	3

The data packets transmitted by the end station onto the cable always contain a source address and a destination address. The source address tells the respective port which device is attached to it. This address is forwarded together with the respective port identifier to the central address list of the switch. This common address list is formed using an address algorithm. These address lists are then used as transport tables for the data packets. Using this address pool and the table for the virtual networks, the switch determines to which receiver (switch port) the data packet is to be forwarded and to which receivers this packet must not be forwarded.

The additional virtual network table is used to determine which port or end station is located in the collision/broadcast domains in question. If no entry is found for a destination address in the address table, the switch process assumes that this address has not yet actively communicated on the network. In this case, the switching process will treat the packet as a broadcast packet and send it to all ports in this virtual workgroup. If the hitherto unknown device responds to the received data packet, then the source address it carries is added with the associated port to the address table. If the switch process finds the associated destination address or switch port for a received data packet in the address table and in the virtual network table, then the switch process transports the packet via the backplane to the destination port. If the switch process does not find the destination address in the address table and it finds out that the destination port does not belong to the virtual network of the device in question, then it does not forward this packet. Consequently, only switch ports in the same group can communicate with one another. As a result of this mechanism, a user can be moved into a different virtual workgroup by redefining the group assignment at the management station.

before: Port 8—> Virtual network 3

after: Port 8—> Virtual network 2

In addition, shared resources (e.g., mail servers, network printers, etc.) can be made available to several virtual networks using the management application.

Port 8 (printer) —> Virtual network 2, 3

Allocation to virtual networks on the basis of the individual port identifiers does pose the following problems however:

- Lack of flexibility for supporting network segments

- Security problems

It is possible to attach not only individual devices, but also complete LAN segments to a switch port. The result of reducing assignment to virtual networks simply to a port basis is that only the switch ports can be used as a criterion for creating virtual networks. For this reason, in addition to the respective ports, the MAC address or the respective address pool must also be recorded in the network tables. Defining virtual groups on the basis of the MAC address solves some of the security problems within networks as well.

If the assignment to a workgroup is determined solely on the basis of the respective port, the user can swap end stations or the individual Ethernet card at any time and will then already belong to the workgroup in question. As a result of this extension of the definition of virtual networks, it is possible to permit network access only to known devices already on the lowest layer. It is therefore no longer possible for devices with unknown MAC addresses to communicate with the switch or one of its connected resources.

Example of extended table

MAC address	Port	Virtual network
080002001234	1	1
080002002234	2	1
080002003234	3	1
080002001244	4	1
080002001235	5	1
080002001236	6	2
080002001237	7	2
080002001238	8	2
080002001239	9	2
080002001240	10	2
080002001241	11	3
080002001242	12	3
080002001243	13	3
080002001344	14	3
080002001245	15	3

In practice, however, the advantageous security mechanisms can turn out to be disadvantageous, too. When an Ethernet controller is exchanged, its burnt-in MAC address (ROM) also change. This means that the tables of the local switch will have to be modified before the new card can communicate with the switch.

Since LAN switches can also operate in a switch network (backbone), it is also advisable to make the respective definitions unique across switches as well. For this reason, in addition to the respective ports and the connected MAC addresses, the individual switch identifiers (switch IDs) should also be included in the network tables. This extension enables security functions to be incorporated in a switched distributed network.

Example of extended table:

MAC Address	Port	Switch ID	Virtual Network
080002001234	1	1	1
080002002234	2	3	1
080002003234	3	2	1
080002001244	4	1	1
080002001235	5	1	1
080002001236	6	2	2
080002001237	7	2	2
080002001238	8	2	2
080002001239	9	2	2
080002001240	10	3	2
080002001241	11	1	3
080002001242	12	3	3
080002001243	13	3	3
080002001344	14	3	3
080002001245	15	3	3

Extending the group assignments on the basis of MAC addresses reduces the amount of work involved when moving a station into another workgroup simply to a matter of redefinition at the management console.

before: 080002001245   Port: 15   Switch: 3   Virtual network: 3

after: 080002001245   Port: 15   Switch: 3   Virtual network: 2

The assignment of MAC addresses to the individual groups and switch IDs need not necessarily be realized by a fixed assignment to one port. The introduction of a "Don't Care" function (X) in the table enables the following combinations:

• If the defined MAC address occurs at one of the ports of a switch with the ID = 1, then this address is assigned to virtual network 1.

Example:

MAC address	Port	Switch ID	Virtual network
080002001234	x	I	I

- All MAC addresses of port 5 within the switch with the ID =1 are assigned to virtual network 1.

Example:

MAC address	Port	Switch ID	Virtual network
x	5	I	I

- The defined MAC address at a particular physical port is assigned to virtual network 1 irrespective of the switch in question.

Example:

MAC address	Port	Switch ID	Virtual network
080002001234	5	x	I

Advantages: Virtual Switch Concept

- Flat network hierarchy
- Load decoupling between end stations
- Increasing broadcast or multicast load in a virtual network has no effect on other virtual networks at all
- Inexpensive components
- Simple configuration
- Central resources (file servers, applications servers) can be connected directly to the switch
- Changeover or upgrading to 100BaseX technology is possible without using bridges
- Advanced security functions

Disadvantages: Virtual Switch Concept

- High administrative outlay

- In distributed switching concepts, sufficient bandwidth resources must be provided between the individual switches

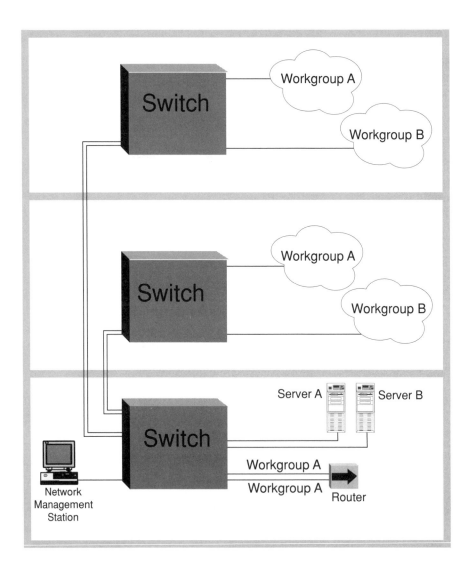

Figure 7.33: Example of a virtual network with logical workgroups

If the correct backbone technology is selected, there are no limits to the expansion of a virtual network. Individual end stations in a virtual network are addressed according to the mechanisms outlined above. An end station can therefore change its physical location but still remain a member of the same virtual network. The individual members of a workgroup consequently become location-independent, and reconfiguration of the network is unnecessary.

In a large distributed switched network with virtual workgroups, the backbone technology used is of particular importance. The backbone must be able to carry many virtual networks simultaneously. There are two ways of implementing distributed virtual workgroups (networks):

- Proprietary frame encapsulation method, or

- ATM technology.

Proprietary Frame Encapsulation Method

On the Physical layer, Fast Ethernet (200 Mbit/s) or FDDI can be used for high-speed backbone connections. Neither technology supports any way of identifying the respective virtual group within the Ethernet or FDDI data frame. For this reason, some manufacturers have implemented this function in the backbone ports of the switches they produce. The great disadvantage of this solution is, however, that these components can then only be purchased from one manufacturer. To date, there has been no discussion as to standardization of these Ethernet and FDDI extensions among international standardization organizations.

ATM Technology

Besides scalable bandwidth one of the most important features of ATM technology is support for several mutually-independent logical connections on one physical line. For this reason, ATM currently offers the ideal prerequisites to be used as the standard technology for implementing virtual networks in the backbone sector. Use of ATM networks is not restricted to a building backbone or a campus backbone; it also allows direct connection of LANs and WANs.

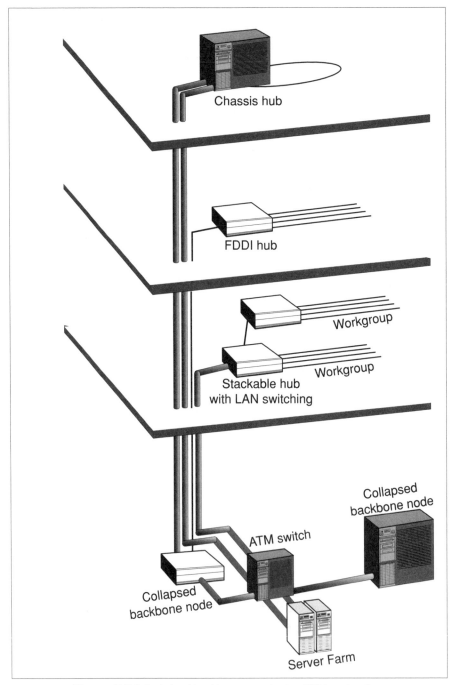

Figure 7.34: Switched backbone employing ATM technology

How Much Bandwidth Does a Virtual Backbone Require?

LAN switching technology is dependent upon sufficient bandwidth being available between the connected subscribers of a workgroup to transport information quickly and efficiently between the subscribers. In the local area, the fast backplanes of the switches will ensure that bottlenecks never develop. However, if several switches are interconnected on one backbone to form one large virtual switch, this can quickly lead to a shortage of available bandwidth. The phenomenon of insufficient bandwidth is discussed in detail below with reference to examples.

Ethernet Backbone

A switched network with a collapsed backbone is constructed in a building. All connections in the backbone sector are implemented in Fast Ethernet technology (100BaseFx). The connections between the central switch and the floor switches are set up redundantly to provide protection. For administrative reasons, all file servers of the workgroups are installed at the central switch (in the computer center). Different numbers of subscribers work in the individual virtual workgroups. The individual workstations are allocated as follows:

Floor 1:
Workgroup 1 with 8 users @ 10 Mbit/s
Workgroup 2 with 2 users @ 10 Mbit/s
Workgroup 3 with 4 users @ 10 Mbit/s
Workgroup 4 with 1 user @ 10 Mbit/s

Floor 2:
Workgroup 1 with 4 users @ 10 Mbit/s
Workgroup 2 with 2 users @ 10 Mbit/s
Workgroup 3 with 6 users @ 10 Mbit/s
Workgroup 4 with 1 user @ 100 Mbit/s

Floor 3:
Workgroup 1 with 3 users @ 10 Mbit/s
Workgroup 2 with 6 users @ 10 Mbit/s
Workgroup 3 with 5 users @ 10 Mbit/s
Workgroup 4 with 5 users @ 10 Mbit/s

Floor 4:
Workgroup 1 with 2 users @ 10 Mbit/s
Workgroup 2 with 2 users @ 10 Mbit/s
Workgroup 3 with 4 users @ 10 Mbit/s
Workgroup 4 with 1 user @ 10 Mbit/s

Since all workstations are operating in client/server mode, the following loads can arise in the respective backbone under worst-case conditions:

Central switch <—> Floor 1: 150 Mbit/s
Central switch <—> Floor 2: 220 Mbit/s
Central switch <—> Floor 3: 190 Mbit/s
Central switch <—> Floor 4: 90 Mbit/s

As these throughput figures reveal, 100 Mbit/s connections in the backbone are no longer sufficient. Further growth would only be conditionally possible and performance problems would intensify. If video or audio services were to be implemented on this backbone as well, then these services could not be provided at the desired quality level.

How can bandwidth in this network be dynamically increased? Since a parallel connection (100 Mbit/s) already exists between the switches, use of this resource would be the first logical step. Unfortunately, in an Ethernet only unique connections are permitted between two stations. If two active connections exist, packets are duplicated and the entire transmission mechanism no longer functions. To prevent the failure of a transmission path, a mechanism has been implemented in Ethernet switches to ensure that connection redundancy can be set up. This connection redundancy is achieved with the aid of the Spanning Tree mechanism. This mechanism ensures that, of two parallel paths, only one single connection is activated at one time. The other connection is automatically switched to passive by the Spanning Tree mechanism and this one is only activated if the primary connection fails. As a result, although double the transmission capacity is theoretically available on the Physical Layer, only one path can be used at any one time.

For this reason some manufacturers are already exploring the possibility of providing a fast broadband connection between the switches by defining so-called fat pipes. The parallel connections (e.g., based on Fast Ethernet technology) between the switches are combined to form one virtual channel. Depending upon the bandwidth required, individual transmission resources can be activated or deactivated. This fat pipe appears to the end stations as a single Ethernet transmission path. This means that individual users get their desired bandwidth and no change of any kind is required at the end stations (drivers, hardware). By virtue of the high transmission capacity in the backbone, a distributed data network becomes a switched virtual LAN which combines any collection of end stations from different LAN segments to form one logical unit with a faster speed and less delay.

ATM Backbone

The switched network described above is constructed as a collapsed backbone employing ATM technology. For administrative reasons, all file servers of the workgroups are installed at the central switch (in the computer center). Twenty subscribers work in each of the virtual workgroups. The individual workstations are allocated as follows:

Floor 1: Workgroup 1 with 8 users @ 10 Mbit/s
Workgroup 2 with 2 users @ 10 Mbit/s
Workgroup 3 with 4 users @ 10 Mbit/s
Workgroup 4 with 4 users @ 10 Mbit/s

Floor 2: Workgroup 1 with 4 users @ 10 Mbit/s
Workgroup 2 with 2 users @ 10 Mbit/s
Workgroup 3 with 6 users @ 10 Mbit/s
Workgroup 4 with 6 users @ 100 Mbit/s

Floor 3: Workgroup 1 with 4 users @ 10 Mbit/s
Workgroup 2 with 6 users @ 10 Mbit/s
Workgroup 3 with 5 users @ 10 Mbit/s
Workgroup 4 with 5 users @ 10 Mbit/s

Floor 4: Workgroup 1 with 6 users @ 10 Mbit/s
Workgroup 2 with 10 users @ 10 Mbit/s
Workgroup 3 with 5 users @ 10 Mbit/s
Workgroup 4 with 5 users @ 10 Mbit/s

Since all workstations are operating in client/server mode, the following loads can arise in the respective backbone under worst-case conditions:

Central switch <—> Floor 1: 180 Mbit/s
Central switch <—> Floor 2: 720 Mbit/s
Central switch <—> Floor 3: 200 Mbit/s
Central switch <—> Floor 4: 260 Mbit/s

As these throughput figures reveal, in extreme conditions, the 155 Mbit/s connections on the backbone are insufficient. As a result of the high throughput rates of the ATM, the bandwidth can be drastically increased from 155 Mbit/s to 622 Mbit/s by exchanging a card module. In an extreme case, however, this great bandwidth will not help when attaching floor 2. The ability of ATM to specify a particular bandwidth for certain services (information streams) makes it possible to define certain upper and lower limits of guaranteed available bandwidth for the individual virtual networks. The network administrator therefore has scope for a differentiated response to the specific requirement in question. The following three mechanisms are possible:

- The switch can guarantee a particular bandwidth to a virtual channel. This is done by assigning the channels with a constant bit rate to an output queue with a high priority. Data streams with variable bit rates are assigned to an output queue with a lower priority. To prevent virtual channels with a low priority from unnecessarily occupying bandwidth, and possibly also influencing other connections, a maximum transmission limit is defined for these channels. For the variable bit rates, both a maximum transmission limit and the maximum time during which such a data burst can be transmitted are defined.

- The ATM switches also ensure that the particular information of a virtual network is not disturbed or hindered by the transmission of other data of other virtual networks. This is achieved by a Usage Parameter Control (UPC) algorithm defined by the UNI 3.0 specifications. The job of the UPC algorithm is to protect the network from virtual channels that attempt to use more of the available bandwidth than they are entitled to. By means of the UPC mechanism, ATM switches guarantee the various qualities of service for constant, variable, and non-specific data rates. In the case of constant data rates a maximum transmission rate is defined for the respective channel. The so-called leaky bucket algorithm is used to ensure that all cells over and above the agreed upper limit are discarded by the switch. A dual bucket policy furthermore ensures that not only the maximum transmission load limit, but also the maximum duration of a data burst is not exceeded.

- Switches employ a further mechanism to guarantee that time-critical data traffic is not delayed unnecessarily when transmitted over the switch. In this case, cells with variable data rates or non-specific data rates are rejected if there is no longer sufficient bandwidth for the time-critical traffic. This is achieved by setting the cell loss priority bit in the respective cell headers.

By managing the bandwidth of ATM, the network administrator is able to assure individual user groups a guaranteed bandwidth under heavy load conditions. Consequently, the backbone need not be designed for the maximum load occurring, only for the available resources to be shared between the connected virtual networks according to defined criteria. The individual virtual networks are allocated the required bandwidth and, depending upon the application and their overall importance ranking, they must live with longer delays at peak times.

Connection Between the Virtual Networks

By separating networks into different broadcast domains, two stations from different virtual networks can no longer communicate with each other. Each station is unaware that the other exists. Connections between different broadcast domains are only possible using routers. For this, the virtual networks must be supplied with different addresses on Layer 3. Figure 7.35 illustrates a switch with one external router. The router has the task of switching all packets between the connected "virtual" IP networks.

In a large network with many virtual workgroups, the situation can therefore arise where two stations connected to the same physical switch will always have to send their packets via a distant router. If the backbone connection is carrying a heavy load and if the router is not working quickly enough, noticeable delays can develop between the communicating stations.

ATM Routing

To solve this problem, some manufacturers have developed special ATM routers. One or more routers in the network are equipped with one or more OC-3 interfaces (155 Mbit/s). With optimized software and protocol modules, the routers are able to process more than 100 000 packets/s. This therefore avoids router bottlenecks in a distributed switched network as well.

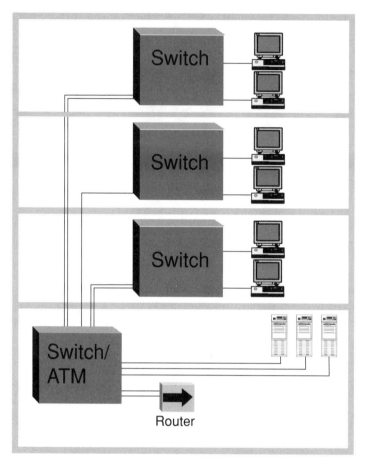

Figure 7.35: Switch with connected router

7.8 Ethernet Switches and Support for Other Technologies

Networks have been around for over twenty years now. During this time, the world of data communications has undergone radical changes. From a niche product known only to a few insiders, networks have now become commonplace. The 1980s saw great changes to communication structures in the office and administration sectors. Up until this point these sectors had employed only special hardware and software solutions based around a strictly hierarchical central system. Central computing was gradually replaced by systems in which many independent devices were linked to each other by Local Area Networks (LANs) or Wide Area Networks (WANs). This development rapidly led to a quantum leap in the performance of data processing end stations, both quantitatively and qualitatively. Open Systems Interconnection (OSI) was the watchword under which new communication technologies emerged with which it was possible to manage effectively large volumes of data and distribute the available information (office automation).

Non-proprietary universal solutions based on international standards became available both for communications software and for the hardware components of the network. The resulting availability of comparable devices greatly accelerated the general fall in prices and provided the foundation for the widespread use of LAN components. Today, local data networks are a permanent part of the communications landscape. LANs enable mainframes, end stations, and PCs to be integrated in a common network with distributed processing power which can in principle be utilized by all the end stations.

Over the last twenty years the computer industry and the communications industry have become the motor of economic development in the western world, and there is still no end to this turbulent development in sight. Particularly in workstation environments, Ethernet has become firmly established for peer-to-peer communications. New generations of processors and new application profiles such as multimedia, high-resolution graphics in desktop publishing (DTP), and archiving systems, for example, are placing ever greater demands on the available bandwidth of data networks. For this reason, data networks and communication networks will have to become more and more powerful, secure, and reliable. Internationally these structural changes in data processing were recognized very early on, and the industry moved over to switching technology. Following years of dispute as to which was the better transmission method—here chiefly fought between proponents of Ethernet and those of Token Ring networks—16 Mbit/s Token Ring, FDDI, and ATM technology has become available, and the choice has become largely a matter of personal preference. For users, it is the application itself that counts, not the method of transport employed. Today, no network operator can allow himself the luxury of basing a network structure on one system alone. New technologies must therefore always be able to offer a migration path to the alternative technology. The different transmission mechanisms of the individual data networks are located on the two lowest layers of the 7-layer or ISO Reference Model. Only the Data Link Layer (Layer 2) and the Physical layer (Layer 1) are defined for all the methods (Ethernet, Token Ring, Token Bus, and FDDI).

Table 7.6: The lower layers of the ISO Reference Model

Layers 3-7	Higher protocols			
Layer 2B	IEEE 802.2			
Layer 2A	Ethernet MAC	Token Ring MAC	Token Bus MAC	FDDI MAC
Layer I	Ethernet	Token Ring	Token Bus	FDDI

The most important other standards relevant to Ethernet switching include Fast Ethernet, Token Ring, FDDI, and ATM technology.

7.8.1 High-Speed Ethernet

At the end of 1992 Ethernet users were surprised by the announcement of communications giants Hewlett-Packard (HP) and AT&T Microelectronics of their proposal for a new generation of Ethernet. This proposal was called 100BaseVG and was based on an Ethernet-like transmission mechanism (with a data rate of 100 Mbit/s). In November 1992, this proposal was submitted to the IEEE standards committee. Since the 100BaseVG standard has a completely different MAC layer concept, subgroup 802.12 was set up within the IEEE to define this standard. The 100BaseVG proposal was deliberately positioned as the high-speed successor to Ethernet 10BaseT technology. The twisted pair star structures and the RJ45 connector familiar from the 10BaseT specification were carried over. The designation VG stands for voice grade and defines the requirements the cables must satisfy. 100BaseVG specifies Category 3 and Category 5 cables for transmission. Owing to the considerably poorer transmission characteristics and crosstalk susceptibility of Category 3 cables, this standard specifies the use of four (4!!!) wire pairs for transmitting data. The splitting of the data transmission between several parallel wires ensures compliance with the American FCC Class B Regulations and the even more stringent European EN 55022B regulations for electromagnetic radiation at a transfer rate of 100 Mbit/s. In addition, the data is transmitted over the cable unidirectionally.

In practice, the 100BaseVG standard can only be used in point-to-point connections. A station can either send or receive, never both simultaneously. Collisions are consequently impossible. The packet format of the Ethernet (IEEE 802.3) standard was also retained. However, this is where the similarity ends.

Owing to the unidirectional transmission of data and the need for significant improvements in the efficiency of bandwidth utilization, the complete
Ethernet MAC protocol had to be rewritten. Access to the medium is realized
by the integration of additional logic in the hub. A 100BaseVG station may
only transmit when it is requested to do so by the hub. This mechanism is
referred to as demand priority. Each end station signals its send request to the
hub together with an indication of its priority. The hub allocates permission
to send on the basis of these priorities. The end station can then seize all four
line pairs and transmit the data to the hub. Since the hub is responsible for
allocating the send permissions, it can guarantee a defined bandwidth for time-
critical applications. With the 100BaseVG standard the hub does not function
as a repeater; it actually switches packets. The system is therefore able to forward the data packets only on the line to which the respective end station (destination address) is attached. In contrast to CSMA/CD, the packets are not
broadcast to all stations, and it is therefore not possible for an analyzer to lis-
ten within the star-topology access domain of a hub. Use of the Manchester
code for bit synchronization has also been dropped completely from
100BaseVG. Instead, a more bandwidth-efficient encoding method (5B/6B
encoding) is used.

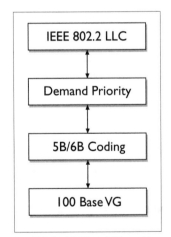

Figure 7.36: 100BaseVG architecture

At almost exactly the same time as the 100BaseVG specification was published, a counter-proposal to this standard was drawn up by the Fast Ethernet
Alliance. The Fast Ethernet Alliance is a consortium comprising approximately 64 companies, including such well known names as 3Com, Bay
Networks, Cabletron Systems, Cogent Data, Data General, DEC, Grand
Junction, Hughes LAN Systems, Intel, National Semiconductors, ODS,
Hirschmann, Racal Datacom, SMC, Sun, Unisys, etc. This new standard is
being examined by the IEEE 802.3 committee in the 100BaseX group. The
100BaseX standard comprises, put simply, a combination of the known
CSMA/CD mechanisms and some parts of FDDI technology. On the Physical
layer, both optical fiber (100BaseFx) and twisted pair cable (100BaseTx and
100BaseT4) are supported. The 100BaseTx and 100BaseT4 specifications
include support for Category 5 and Category 3 shielded twisted pair (STP) and
unshielded twisted pair (UTP) cables. The familiar CSMA/CD mechanisms are
used above the Physical layer. Using 100BaseX components also guarantees
backwards compatibility, protecting previous investment in the cable infrastructure.

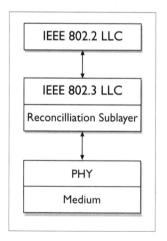

Figure 7.37: 100BaseX architecture

A further advantage of the 100BaseX standard is the use of known standards.
This substantially reduces the time required to agree a standard and greatly
speeds up the introduction of the "new" technology. The scalability of

100BaseX technology has already been demonstrated. Since nothing has been changed on the logical level of the 100BaseX standard, the software employed in the past can continue to be used. This applies equally to the drivers of PC adapter cards and to the software in bridges and routers; everything continues to run as before, only ten times as fast.

Comparison of 100 Mbit/s Standards

	100BaseVG	100BaseX
Speed	100 Mbit/s	100 Mbit/s
Access mechanism	Demand priority	CSMA/CD
Priorities	Yes	No
Point-to-point connection	Yes	No
Connector type	RJ45	RJ45
Number of wires	8	4
Cable category	3 and 5	3, 4 and 5
Backwards-compatible	No	Yes

The first 100 Mbit/s Fast Ethernet products have been available since the Networld + Interop 1994 in Paris. The two camps of 100 Megabit Ethernet groups (the Fast Ethernet Alliance and the 100BaseVG Forum) are still fighting it out, but the consortium around the manufacturers of the Ethernet MAC-compatible 100BaseX standard are now putting words into action. A large number of new and inexpensive products are being launched on the market. This applies above all to the three areas of adapter cards, hub systems, and Ethernet switches.

Especially in the field of PC adapter cards, the fast PC bus architectures (EISA and PCI) are dominant. These system architectures also benefit from the new standard. The entire sector is anticipating rapid migration to the 100 Mbit/s standard, particularly in the server connection sector.

Today users who are faced with the decision of acquiring new adapter cards for end stations should consider whether they will need to support fast data transmission at the end stations in the medium-term. The standard also supports the Full-Duplex 100BaseX mode. This makes it possible to connect servers at an aggregate rate of 200 Mbit/s. With attractive pricing and backwards compatibility to the 10 Mbit/s standard, the manufacturers have high hopes that users will migrate quickly to 100 Mbit/s technology. Where hub systems and Ethernet switch products are concerned, Fast Ethernet has almost become the entry level already. The standard also guarantees support for a range of different media on the interface side. Thus a further sublayer, called the reconciliation sublayer, has been integrated between the MAC layer and the actual Physical layer. The job of this sublayer is the media-independent definition of the higher layers and adaptation to the physical medium below. The standard submitted for final ratification covers the following physical media:

- 100BaseT4 (on Category 3 cables)

- 100BaseTx (on Category 5 cables)

- 100BaseFx (optical fiber)

Automatic detection of the transfer rate (10 or 100 Mbit/s), the repeater functions and management of the lower layers were also defined. The members of the Fast Ethernet Alliance have also considered product compatibility and to this end have set up a laboratory for testing interoperability between the new products and the established standards. Users can therefore be sure that all the products that have passed this test are compatible with the current implementations and will work together with existing network products without any problems.

Parameters of the Fast Ethernet Standard

Parameter	Value
Slot time	512 Bit times
Interframe gap	0.96 μs
Attempt limit	16
Backoff limit	10
JAM size	32 Bit
Maximum packet size	1518 Byte
Minimum packet size	64 Byte
Address size	48 Bit

Table 7.7: Comparison between Ethernet and Fast Ethernet

	Ethernet	Fast Ethernet
Speed	10 Mbit/s	100 Mbit/s
Cost	Low	Twice that of 10 Mbit/s technology
IEEE standard	IEEE 802.3	IEEE 802.3
Medium access control	CSMA/CD	CSMA/CD
Topology	Bus/Star	Star
Cables supported	Coax, UTP, FO	UTP, STP, FO
Twisted pair cables supported	Category 3, 4 or 5	Category 3, 4 or 5
Maximum length of TP Link segments	100 meters	100 meters
Full-Duplex Ethernet (FDE)	Yes	Yes
Media-independent interface	AUI	MII

Details of the 100BaseX Standard

The 100 Mbit/s extension of the Ethernet standard defines several new features in the structure of the lowest two layers. Besides the Medium Access Control protocol (MAC) sublayer and the Physical Medium Attachment (PMA) sublayer, the Physical Signalling (PLS), the Attachment Unit Interface (AUI), and the Medium-Dependent Interface (MDI) were replaced by the following sublayers:

- Reconciliation Layer

- Media-Independent Interface (MII)

- Physical Coding Sublayer (PCS)

- Physical Medium-Dependent (PMD) sublayer

Reconciliation Layer

In the Fast Ethernet standard the reconciliation layer and the Media-Independent Interface (MII) together form the interface to the Physical Layer (PHY). The reconciliation layer represents the logical interface between the MAC layer and the Media-Independent Interface. The job of the reconciliation layer is to convert the MAC/physical line signalling primitives into MII signals.

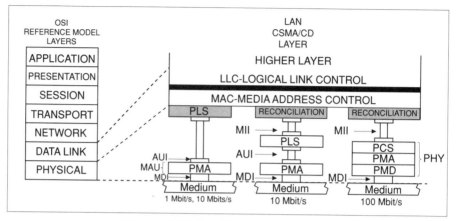

Figure 7.38: Fast Ethernet architecture

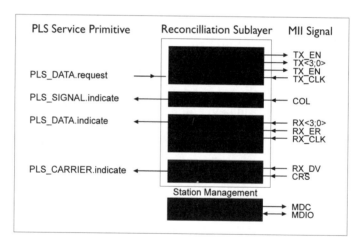

Figure 7.39: Input/output and management functions of the reconciliation layers

Conversion of Physical Line Signalling Primitives into MII Signals
PLS_Data.request (Output-Unit)

The data is transmitted from one MAC layer to all other MAC layers connected to the network using the PLS_Data.request primitive. The Output-Unit parameter can assume the following values: One (1), Null (0), Data-Complete. The Data-Complete parameter signals the fact that there is no further data for transmission from the MAC layer. The individual data bits are transported on the medium with the values 1 and 0. The reconciliation layer converts the Output-Unit parameters 1 and 0 into the signals TXD<3>, TXD<2>, TXD<1>, and TXD<0>. At the same time, the TX_EN signal is set to the value 1 during the transmission of the data. The time is synchronized between the PHY layer and the reconciliation layer using the TX_CLK signal.

PLS_Data.indication (Input-Unit)

The PLS_Data.indication primitive is used by the Physical layer to notify the MAC layer of data transmission. The Input-Unit parameter can assume the values One (1) and Null (0). The reconciliation layer generates the Input-Unit parameters 1 and 0 from the TXD<3>, TXD<2>, TXD<1>, and TXD<0> signals. At the same time, the RX_DV signal is set to the value 1 during the transmission of the data. The data sent to the MAC layer is monitored using the RX_ER signal. The time is synchronized between the PHY layer and the reconciliation layer using the TX_CLK signal.

PLS_Carrier.indication (Carrier-Status)

This primitive signals the MAC layer the current status of the transmission medium. If the Carrier-Status parameter has the value Carrier-Off, the medium is free for the transmission of data. The Carrier-On value indicates that the medium is occupied and no data can be sent from the MAC layer onto the medium. If the signal RX_DV has the value 0, then each transition of the signal CRS from the value 0 to the value 1 causes a change in the Carrier-Status parameter from the value Carrier-Off to the value Carrier-On. Given a signal value of 0 for RX_DV, each transition of the signal CRS from the value 1 to the value 0 causes the Carrier-Status parameter to change from the value Carrier-On to the value Carrier-Off. If the signals RX_DV and CRS have assumed the value 1, then resetting the signal RX_DV to the value 0 will lead to a Carrier-Status value of Carrier-Off.

PLS_Signal.indication (Signal-Status)

Using the Signal-Error parameter, the PLS_Signal.indication primitive signals to the MAC layer that the Physical layer has detected an illegal signal or a collision. The MAC layer indicates that the error state has been rectified with the No-Signal-Error parameter. If the Physical layer sends a COL signal to the reconciliation layer, then the latter converts this signal into a Signal-Error message for the MAC layer.

If the signals RX_DV and RX_ER occur on the reconciliation layer during the reception of a data packet, the MAC layer is notified that a frame check error has been detected by the lower layer.

Media-Independent Interface (MII)

In the Fast Ethernet standard, the Media-Independent Interface (MII) handles the access to the physical medium. In contrast to the Medium-Dependent Interface (MDI) used in Ethernet, this interface is designed uniformly for the different physical media. The Media-Independent Interface (MII) performs the following functions:

- Support for different data rates (10 Mbit/s and 100 Mbit/s)

- Management interface for monitoring/control and for configuring the lower layers

Electrical and Physical Specifications of the MII

The Media-Independent Interface (MII) is based on conventional TTL signal levels. This allows the interface to be inexpensively constructed from standard CMOS logic components. The PHY layer is supplied with a voltage of +5 Volt ± 5% (750 mA) from the end station. The voltage supply must be protected against overload and short-circuiting.

The MII cable comprises twenty individually shielded, symmetrically twisted pairs of wires. In addition, a general cable shield (S = shield) provides protection against external radiation and conversely protects the environment from high-frequency radiation emitted by the data streams. The impedance of the cable is 68 Ohm ±10%. Only wire cross-sections of 28 AWG are used in the Fast Ethernet standard. The maximum delay of the MII cable is 2.5 ns.

Media-Independent Interface Signals

The signals of the MII are based on TTL signal levels. In detail, the interface comprises the following signals: Transmit Clock, Receive Clock, Transmit

Enable, Transmit Data, Transmit Coding Error, Receive Data Valid, Receive Data, Receive Error, Carrier Sense, Collision Detected, Management Data Clock, and Management Data Input/Output.

Transmit Clock

Transmit Clock (TX_CLK) is a continuous clock signal generated by the PHY layer. The timing of the TX_EN, TXD, and TX_ER signals is synchronized using this clock. The TX_CLK frequency is 25 % of the nominal transfer rate. When transmitting data over Fast Ethernet, the clock frequency is 25 MHz; when transmitting data over 10 Mbit/s Ethernet, the clock frequency is 2.5 MHz.

Receive Clock

Receive Clock (RX_CLK) is a continuous clock signal generated by the PHY layer. The timing of the RX_DV, RXD, and RX_ER signals is synchronized using this clock. The RX_CLK frequency is 25 % of the nominal transfer rate.

Transmit Enable

The Transmit Enable (TX_EN) signal indicates that the reconciliation layer has data nibbles ready for sending to the MII. A nibble is the name given to a group of four data bits. The Transmit Enable signal assumes the value 1 when the first data nibble of the preamble from the reconciliation layer is waiting. This signal remains high until the last nibble of a data packet is ready for sending.

Transmit Data

The four Transmit Data (TXD) signals are denoted TXD<3:0>. The data is transferred synchronously with the TX_CLK clock from the reconciliation layer to the PHY layer. The data TD<0> always represents the bits with the least significance (least significant bit).

Table 7.8: Coding of the TXD<3:0>, TX_EN and TX_ER signals

TX_EN	TX_ER	TXD<3:0>	Designation
0	0	0000 to 1111	Interframe Gap
0	1	0000 to 1111	Reserved
1	0	0000 to 1111	Send Data
1	1	0000 to 1111	Send Transmit Error

Transmit Coding Error

If the Transmit Coding Error (TX_ER) signal is set to the value 1 for one or more TX_CLK clock periods, the receiver is signalled that one or more invalid (errored) data symbols were transmitted. If the TX_ER signal is set to the value 1 on a 10 Mbit/s PHY layer, this signal has no influence on data transmission.

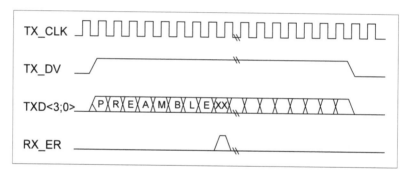

Figure 7.40: Signalling transmit errors with the TX_ER signal

Receive Data Valid

The Receive Data Valid (RX_DV) signal indicates that the PHY layer is transferring data nibbles for transmission to the reconciliation layer. The Receive Data Valid signal assumes the value 1 when the first data nibble of the preamble from the PHY layer is waiting. This signal remains high until the last nibble of a data packet is ready for sending.

Receive Data

The four Receive Data (RXD) signals are denoted RXD<3:0>. The data is transferred synchronously with the RX_CLK clock from the PHY layer to the reconciliation layer. The data RD<0> always represents the bits with the least significance (least significant bit).

Table 7.9: Coding of the signals RXD<3:0>, RX_EN and RX_DV

RX_DV	RX_ER	RXD<3:0>	Designation
0	0	0000 to 1111	Interframe Gap
0	1	0000	Interframe Gap
0	1	0001 to 1101	Reserved
0	1	1110	Invalid Carrier Signal
0	1	1111	Reserved
1	0	0000 to 1111	Normal Data Reception
1	1	0000 to 1111	Incorrect Data Reception

Receive Error

The Receive Error (RX_ER) signal is generated by the PHY layer. If the RX_ER signal is set to the value 1 for one or more RX_CLK clock periods, the receiver is signalled that one or more invalid (errored) data symbols were transmitted.

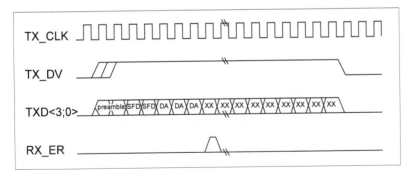

Figure 7.41: Reception of errored data

If the RX_DV signal is not set to the value 1, the PHY layer may indicate an invalid carrier signal by the set RX_ER signal for one or more RC_CLK clock periods.

Carrier Sense

The Carrier Sense (CRS) signal is always set by the PHY layer to the value 1 if the medium is already occupied on the receiving or transmitting path. The CRS signal is set to the value 0 only when the medium is not being used. If Full-Duplex mode is switched on by setting control register 0.8 to the value 1, the CRS signal is no longer significant and may assume any value.

Collision Detected

The Collision Detected (COL) signal is set by the PHY layer to the value 1 when a collision is detected on the medium. If Full-Duplex mode is switched on by setting control register 0.8 to the value 1, the COL signal is no longer significant and may assume any value.

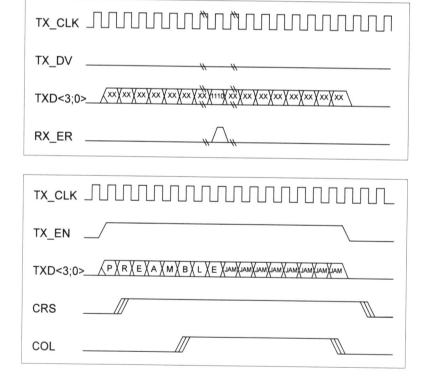

Figure 7.42

Management Data Clock

The Management Data Clock (MDC) is sent by the station management of the end station to the PHY layer. This clock is used to synchronize the timing of the MDIO signal.

Management Data Input/Output

The Management Data Input/Output (MDIO) signals are used to exchange data bidirectionally between the station management and the PHY layer.

MII Data Structure

In comparison with the Ethernet data format, the header of the packet has been changed only slightly in the Fast Ethernet standard. Instead of the CRC field, an end of frame delimiter is used in Fast Ethernet. The overall MII frame has the following format:

<Interframe Gap> <Preamble> <Start Frame Delimiter> <Data> <End Frame Delimiter>

The data octets are transmitted in the form of nibbles. A nibble is a group of four data bits. As shown in Figure cx, a data octet is always divided into two nibbles. Bit 0 to bit 3 are sent in the first nibble. The second nibble is used for transferring the second half of the octet (bits 4 to 7).

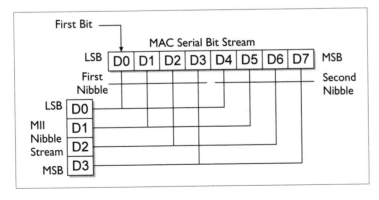

Figure 7.43 Dividing the octet into nibbles

Interframe Gap

The interframe gap is defined as the minimum time that must elapse between two data packets. In the Fast Ethernet standard, the minimum interval between two data packets is 0.96 µs.

Preamble and Start Frame Delimiter

Once the minimum interval (interframe gap) between the packet transferred has elapsed, a data packet can be transmitted on a free medium. The bit-serial data stream begins with the preamble:

10101010 10101010 10101010 10101010 10101010 10101010 10101010

Directly following the preamble is the start frame delimiter:

10101011

If the TX_EN signal is present, the preamble and the start frame delimiter fields are transmitted by the MII as data nibbles as shown in Table 7.10.

Table 7.10: Preamble and SFD nibbles

Signal	Bit values of the nibbles passed to the MII during transmission
TXD0	x I I I I I I I I I I I I I I I I I I D0 D4
TXD1	x 0 0 0 0 0 0 0 0 0 0 0 0 0 0 0 0 0 D1 D5
TXD2	x I I I I I I I I I I I I I I I I I I D2 D6
TXD3	x 0 0 0 0 0 0 0 0 0 0 0 0 0 0 0 0 0 D3 D7
TX_EN	0 I I I I I I I I I I I I I I I I I I I

D0 to D7 represent the first 8 bits of the data of a packet.

When the data is received, if the RX_DV signal is present the preamble and the start frame delimiter fields are passed from the PHY layer to the MII as data nibbles as set out in Table 7.11.

Table 7.11: Receiving SFD data with preamble

Signal	Bit values of the nibbles received from the MII
3Com	x I I I I I I I I I I I I I I I I I I I I I D0 D4
RXD1	x 0 0 0 0 0 0 0 0 0 0 0 0 0 0 0 0 0 0 0 0 0 D1 D5
RXD2	x I I I I I I I I I I I I I I I I I I I I I D2 D6
RXD3	x 0 0 0 0 0 0 0 0 0 0 0 0 0 0 0 0 0 0 0 0 1 D3 D7
RX_DV	0 I I I I I I I I I I I I I I I I I I I I I I I

D0 to D7 represent the first 8 bits of the data of a packet.

In some circumstances the preamble may get lost during transmission. As illustrated in Table 7.12, if the RX_DV signal is present the remaining start frame delimiter field is passed as data nibbles from the PHY layer to the MII.

Table 7.12: Reception of SFD data without a preceding preamble

Signal	Bit values of the nibbles received by the MII
RXD0	x x x x x x x I I D0 D4
RXD1	x x x x x x x 0 0 D1 D5
RXD2	x x x x x x x I I D2 D6
RXD3	x x x x x x x 0 I D3 D7
RX_DV	0 I I I I I I I I I I I

D0 to D7 represent the first 8 bits of the data of a packet.

Data

The data in the data packet comprises the following fields: 6-byte destination and 6-byte source address, two-byte length/type field, 50- to 1500-byte data field and a four-byte long frame check sequence. The n-data octets are transferred as 2n nibbles over the connection.

End of Frame Delimiter

The End of Frame Delimiter (EFD) is indicated during sending by the resetting of the TX_EN signal. The resetting of the RX_DV signal during transmission indicates that no more data follows and the end of frame delimiter has been reached.

Management Functions

The management data of the PHY layer is communicated to the end station via the MII management interface. Management protocol information is exchanged over the two signal wires (MDC, MDIO) of the MII, i.e., the respective registers are written or read. The control register (register 0) and the status register (register 1) are referred to as the base registers. The status and control functions must be supported by all 100 Mbit/s PHY layers. Registers 2 to 7 are referred to as expansion registers. The complete management registers are shown in Table 7.13.

Table 7.13: MII management registers

Register Address	Register Name	Base/Expansion
0	Control	B
1	Status	B
2, 3	PHY Identifier	E
4	Autonegotiation Advertisement	E
5	Autonegotiation Link Partner Ability	E
6	Autonegotiation Expansion	E
7	Autonegotiation Next Page Transmit	E
8 to 15	Reserved	E
16 to 31	Proprietary	E

Control Register (Register 0)

The individual bits of the control register are listed in Table 14. During implementation, the values of the individual registers should be selected so that the PHY layer assumes its normal mode of operation without any management intervention after the device has been powered up or reset.

Table 7.14: Bit definition of the control register

Bit(s)	Name	Description	R/W
0.15	Reset	1= PHY reset 0 = normal mode	R/W SC
0.14	Loopback	1 = loopback mode switched on 0 = loopback mode switched off	R/W
0.13	Rate Selection	1 = 100 Mbit/s 0 = 10 Mbit/s	R/W
0.12	Autonegotiation Enable	1 = autonegotiation process switched on 0 = autonegotiation process switched off	R/W
0.11	Power Down	1 = power down 0 = normal mode	R/W
0.10	Isolated	1 = PHY electrically isolated from MII 0 = normal mode	R/W
0.9	Restart Auto-negotiation	1= restart the auto-negotiation process 0 = normal mode	R/W SC
0.8	Duplex Mode	1 = Full-Duplex 0 = Half-Duplex	R/W
0.7	Collision Test	1 = COL signal test active 0 = COL signal test switched off	R/W
0.6:0	Reserved	Write = 0 Read = ignore	R/W

R/W = read/write   SC = self clearing

Reset

The PHY layer is reset by setting bit 0.15 to the value 1. Following a successful reset, this register assumes the value 0 again. The reset process must be completed within 0.5 seconds after bit 0.15 has been set to the value 1.

Loopback

The PHY layer enters loopback mode by setting bit 0.14 to the value 1. This logically isolates the receiving logic of the PHY layer from the medium, and the MII cannot send any more data on the network. The data of the MII transmit path is automatically sent back on the MII receive path.

Rate Selection

The speed of the Link layer is either agreed using the autonegotiation process or is set manually by the administrator. For manual setting of the rate, the autonegotiation enable bit 0.12 must be set to the value 0. If the autonegotiation enable bit 0.12 is set to 0, setting the rate selection bit 0.13 to the value 1 configures the PHY layer for communication at 100 Mbit/s. Resetting the rate selection bit 0.13 to the value 0 configures the PHY layer for communication at 10 Mbit/s. If the PHY layer indicates in bits 1.15:11 that it can support only one rate, then the value of bit 0.13 represents the current communication speed and cannot be overwritten.

Autonegotiation Enable

The autonegotiation (negotiation of parameters) process is enabled by setting bit 0.12 to the value 1. If bit 0.12 is set, bits 0.13 and 0.8 have no significance for the parameterization of the respective link. In this case the autonegotiation process executes parameterization (Half-Duplex/Full-Duplex mode, rate, etc.) automatically.

Power Down

This parameter, which is dependent upon the respective implementation, enables the power consumption of the PHY layer to be reduced. If bit 0.11 is set to the value 1, then the PHY layer is in the low-power mode.

Isolated

The PHY layer can be electrically isolated from the MII by setting bit 0.10. Only management information is then exchanged between the two layers.

Restart Autonegotiation

Setting bit 0.9 to the value 1 triggers the automatic process for negotiating the parameters.

Duplex Mode

The duplex mode can be set either by the autonegotiation process or by setting bit 0.8 to the value 1 manually. If bit 0.8 has the value 0, this means that the link has been set up for Half-Duplex communication. If the PHY layer indicates via bits 1.15:11 that it supports only Half-Duplex mode, then the value of bit 0.8 represents the current communication mode and cannot be overwritten.

Collision Test

The collision signal (COL) can be tested by setting bit 0.7 to the value 1.

Reserved

Bits 0.6:0 are reserved for future additions.

Status Register (Register 1)

The status register shows the current configurations and states of the respective link. The individual bits of the status register are listed in Table 7.15.

Table 7.15: Bit definition of the status register

Bit(s)	Name	Description	R/W
1.15	100BaseT4	1 = PHY is operating in 100BaseT4 mode 0 = PHY is not operating in 100BaseT4 mode	RO
1.14	100BaseX Full-Duplex	1 = PHY is operating in Full-Duplex 100BaseX mode 0 = PHY is not operating in Full-Duplex 100BaseX mode	RO
1.13	100BaseX Half-Duplex	1 = PHY is operating in Half-Duplex 100BaseX mode 0 = PHY is not operating in Half-Duplex 100BaseX mode	RO
1.12	10 Mbit/s Full-Duplex	1 = PHY is operating in Full-Duplex 10 Mbit/s mode 0 = PHY is not operating in Full-Duplex 10 Mbit/s mode	RO

(continued)

Table 7.15: (continued)

Bit(s)	Name	Description	R/W
1.11	10 Mbit/s Half-Duplex	1 = PHY is operating in Half-Duplex 10 Mbit/s mode 0 = PHY is not operating in Half-Duplex 10 Mbit/s mode	RO
1.10:6	Reserved	Ignored during read	RO
1.5	Autonegotiation Completed	1 = autonegotiation process completed 0 = autonegotiation process not completed	RO
1.4	Remote Fault	1 = remote fault detected 0 = no remote fault detected	RO LH
1.3	Autonegotiation Possible	1 = PHY can perform autonegotiation process 0 = PHY cannot perform autonegotiation process	RO
1.2	Link Status	1 = link up 0 = link down	RO LL
1.1	Jabber Detected	1 = jabber detected 0 = jabber not detected	RO LH
1.0	Expanded Functions	1 = expanded register functions are supported 0 = only base register functions are supported	RO

RO = read only   LL = latching low   LH = latching high

100BaseT4

If bit 1.15 is set to the value 1, then the Physical layer is able to transmit the data according to the 100BaseT4 specifications.

100BaseX Full-Duplex

The Physical layer is able to transmit the data in Full-Duplex mode according to the 100BaseTx specifications only if bit 1.14 is set to the value 1.

100BaseX Half-Duplex

If bit 1.13 is set to the value 1, then the Physical layer is able to transmit the data in Half-Duplex mode according to the 100BaseTx specifications.

10 Mbit/s Full-Duplex

The Physical layer is able to transmit the data in Full-Duplex mode at a rate of 10 Mbit/s only if bit 1.12 is set to the value 1.

10 Mbit/s Half-Duplex

If bit 1.11 is set to the value 1, then the Physical layer is indicating that it is able to transmit data in Half-Duplex mode at a rate of 10 Mbit/s.

Reserved

Bits 1.10:6 are reserved for future additions.

Autonegotiation Completed

If bit 1.5 is set to the value 1, then the register is indicating that the automatic negotiation of parameters has been completed. The information in registers 4, 5, 6, and 7 define the parameterization of the link. If the PHY layer sets the value 0 for the bit 1.5, then this indicates that the autonegotiation process has been disabled. At the same time, bit 0.12 is reset to 0.

Remote Fault

If a value of 1 is detected when bit 1.4 is read, then the PHY layer is indicating that the communication partner has detected a fault. The remote fault bit must always be reset by manager intervention (read register 1 or reset).

Autonegotiation Possible

If bit 1.3 has the value 1, the PHY layer is indicating that automatic negotiation of parameters between the link partners is possible.

Link Status

If bit 1.2 has the value 1, the PHY layer is indicating that a connection has been correctly established between the two link partners.

Jabber Detected

A value of logical 1 for bit 1.1 indicates that jabber has been detected on the network. The jabber bit must always be reset by manager intervention (read register 1 or reset).

Expanded Functions

If bit 1.0 returns the value 1 in response to a read access, then the PHY layer is indicating that expanded register functions have been implemented. The respective PHY layer can perform further management functions with these additional six registers.

PHY Identifier (Registers 2 and 3)

Registers 2 and 3 provide a 32-bit value for uniquely identifying a PHY type. Bit 2.15 contains the most significant bit of the PHY identifier. Bit 3.0 represents the least significant bit of the PHY identifier. The PHY identifier comprises bits 3–24 of the organizationally unique identifier (OUI) assigned by the IEEE to the respective manufacturer, a 6-bit model number and a 4-bit revision number of the manufacturer.

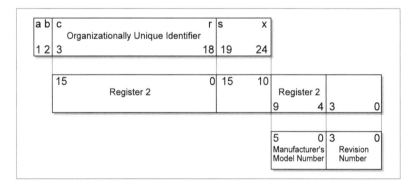

Figure 7.44: Format of the PHY identifier

Autonegotiation Advertisement (Register 4)

Register 4 contains 16 bits which are of significance for the autonegotiation process.

Table 7.16: Advertisement register

Bit	Designation	R/W
4.15	Next Page	R/W
4.14	Reserved	RO
4.13	Remote Fault	R/W
4.12:5	Technology Ability Field	R/W
4.4:0	Selector Field	R/W

Autonegotiation Link Partner Ability (Register 5)

Register 5 contains 16 bits which are of significance for the autonegotiation process.

Table 7.17: Link Partner Ability Register bits (Base Page)

Bit	Designation	R/W
5.15	Next Page	RO
5.14	Acknowledgment	RO
5.13	Remote Fault	RO
5.12:5	Technology Ability Field	RO
5.4:0	Selector Field	RO

Table 7.18: Link Partner Ability Register bits (Next Page)

Bit	Designation	R/W
5.15	Next Page	RO
5.14	Acknowledgment	RO
5.13	Message Page	RO
5.12	Acknowledgment 2	RO
5.11	Toggle	RO
5.4:0	Message/Unformatted Code Field	RO

Autonegotiation Expansion (Register 6)

Register 6 contains 16 bits which are of significance for the autonegotiation process.

Table 7.19: Expansion register bits

Bit	Designation	Meaning	R/W
6.15:5	Reserved		RO
6.4	Parallel Detection Fault	1 = more than one 10BaseT, 100BaseTx or 100BaseT4 PMAs have detected a link 0 = more than one 10BaseT, 100BaseTx or 100BaseT4 PMAs have detected a link	RO
6.3	Link Partner Next Page Able	1 = link partner supports the next page function 0 = link partner does not support the next page function	RO
6.2	Next Page Able	1 = local device supports the next page function 0 = local device does not support the next page function	RO
6.1	Page Received	1 = 3 identical link codewords received in succession 0 = 3 identical link codewords were not received in succession	RO
6.0	Link Partner Autonegotiation Able	1 = link partner supports the autonegotiation function 0 = link partner does not support the autonegotiationfunction	RO

Autonegotiation Next Page (Register 7)

Register 7 contains 16 bits which are of significance for the autonegotiation process.

Table 7.20: Next Page register bits

Bit	Designation	R/W
7.15	Next Page	R/W
7.14	Acknowledgment	RO
7.13	Message page	R/W
7.12	Acknowledgment 2	RO
7.11	Toggle	RO
5.10:0	Message/Unformatted Code Field	R/W

PHY-Specific Register

Register addresses 8–15 are reserved for future additions. Register addresses 16–31 can be used individually by manufacturers.

Management Data

The management data which is communicated over the MII to the PHY layer has the following format:

Table 7.21: Data structure of management packets

							Data fields	
	PRE	ST	OP	PHYAD	REGAD	TA	Data	Idle
Read	I	I	0I	I0	AAAAA	RRRRR Z0	DDDDDDDDDDDDDDDD	Z
Write	I	I	0I	0I	AAAAA	RRRRR I0	DDDDDDDDDDDDDDDD	Z

Idle

There is always a value of 1 at the MDIO pin during the idle signal.

Preamble

A sequence of 32 bits with the value 1 is always sent over the MDIO interface at the commencement of transmitting management data. The MDIO signals are accompanied by 32 clock cycles of the MDC signal for receiver synchronization.

Start of Srame

The beginning of a management packet is indicated by the bit sequence 01.

Operation Code

The operation code specifies whether the management function is a read (bit sequence: 10) or a write (bit sequence: 01) access.

PHY Address

The individual physical interfaces of the device can be uniquely identified on the basis of the PHY address. The five-bit long PHY address allows 32 individual PHY addresses to be represented. The first PHY interface always has PHY address 00000.

Register Address

The five-bit long register address allows 32 individual registers to be represented per PHY address. The individual registers of the interface can be uniquely identified on the basis of the register address. The first register always has register address 00000 and contains the control register. The second register always has register address 00001 and contains the status register.

Turnaround

The turnaround time denotes a 2-bit time between the register address field and the data field. This ensures clear definition of the signals during the read operation.

Data

The length of the data field is 16 bits. The data field contains the actual management information for the respective register.

The Autonegotiation Process

The full Ethernet standard supports Half-Duplex or Full-Duplex mode. This allows devices to be attached at rates of 10, 20, 100, and 200 Mbit/s. Backwards compatibility to the 10 Mbit/s standard offers users a rapid migration path to 100BaseX technology. With twisted pair cable, the standard provides for automatic configuration of the link segments with the aid of the negotiation process. Consequently, users can install all Fast Ethernet or 10 Mbit/s products in a network without difficulty and do not need to take account of the specific configurations of already installed components. The autonegotiation process allows two components attached to a link segment to exchange parameters and set the basic communication values supported in each case on the basis of these parameters. The autonegotiation process is based on a modified form of the link integrity test pulse sequence known from the 10BaseT standard. The autonegotiation process is available only for the 10BaseT, 100BaseTx, and 100BaseT4 standards. The link integrity test pulse mechanism is termed the Fast Link Pulse (FLP) burst. If a device supports this mechanism, then after powering up, it initiates the FLP process, either via the management system or by manual intervention. Each device derives a link codeword from the bits of the FLP burst. The receiver determines the parameters and the functions of the link communication partner using this sequence.

The IEEE has defined the following objectives for the autonegotiation function:

- Compatibility with the existing 10BaseT standard
- 10BaseT devices need not therefore support this additional function
- Inexpensive and simple implementation
- The code must support a large number of functions

It must be possible to integrate additions at any time.

- It must be possible to transmit remote fault signals.
- It must be possible to negotiate parameters bidirectionally.
- It must be possible to overwrite the dynamically negotiated parameters by means of manual configuration or management intervention.

The mechanism must ensure that it does not cause any malfunction even if there is interference (noise) on the UTP cable.

Compatibility with Existing 10BaseT Devices

A device in the process of autonegotiation generates a Fast Link Pulse (FLP) burst every 16 ± 8 ms. The FLP burst in turn contains a number of pulses (time interval 62.5 ±7 µs in each case). The time conditions of the FLP burst ensure that a regular 10BaseT device recognizes the FLP sequence as a pure link integrity test pulse and consequently remains in the link test pass mode. On the basis of the Normal Link Pulse (NLP) transmitted from a 10BaseT device, a device that supports the autonegotiation process recognizes that the link partner is not able to interpret the FLP bursts. As a result of the NLP information received therefore, transmission of the FLP bursts is halted and the 10 Mbit/s communication mode is entered.

Autonegotiation Functions

If a device supports autonegotiation functions, it decodes the base link codeword from the FLP burst information, and from that it derives the parameters jointly supported by both link partners. Both link partners then confirm the received parameters by means of an FLP burst with the acknowledgment bit set. In addition, it is also possible for optional extensions (pages) to be negotiated between the two link partners. Once the autonegotiation function has been completed, the communication partners initialize themselves to the highest common parameter values and are able to exchange regular data packets over the connection.

Transmission of Link Pulses

The link integrity test pulses already defined in the 10BaseT standard serve as the basis for exchanging autonegotiation functions. These Normal Link Pulses (NLP) are emitted by the link partners regularly every 16 ±8 ms. If a device supports the autonegotiation function, then the NLP sequence is substituted by a Fast Link Pulse (FLP) burst.

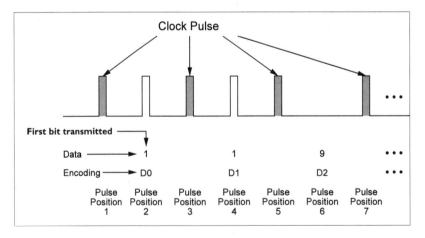

Figure 7.45: Relationship between FLP burst sequence and NLP sequence

FLP Burst Coding

A Fast Link Pulse comprises 33 successive pulses. The 17-odd pulses contain the link pulses and the clock information. The remaining 16 even pulses define the data information of the pulse. The information is encoded as follows:

1. If an even pulse is detected between two clock pulses, then this pulse represents a logical one.

2. If no even pulse is detected between two clock pulses, this missing pulse represents a logical zero.

The first pulse in an FLP burst is defined as the clock pulse. The individual clock pulses always have an interval of 125 ±14 µs. If an information pulse contains a logical one, then this pulse occurs 62.5 ±7 µs after the clock pulse. If an information pulse contains a logical zero, then no information pulse occurs within 111 µs after the clock pulse.

Table 7.22: Summary of all FLP timers

#	Parameter	Min	Type	Max	Unit
T1	Width of data pulse	-	100	-	ns
T2	Clock pulse to clock pulse interval	111	125	139	µs
T3	Clock pulse to data pulse interval	55.5	62.5	69.5	µs
T4	Pulses in burst	17	-	33	-
T5	Burst width	-	2	-	ms
T6	FLP burst to FLP burst interval	8	16	24	ms

Encoding the Link Codewords

The base link codeword (base page) is always transmitted as the first code over a link. Implementation of the autonegotiation function in a device can allow support for further pages. This function is called the next page function. The base link codeword has the following structure:

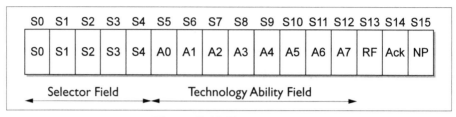

Figure 7.46: The base page

Selector Field

Selector fields S0 to S4 allow 32 messages to be encoded. At present, only the IEEE 802.3 and IEEE 802.9a messages are supported.

Table 7.23: Selector field

S0	SI	S2	S3	S4	Description
0	0	0	0	0	Reserved
I	0	0	0	0	IEEE 802.3
0	I	0	0	0	IEEE 802.9a
I	I	I	I	I	Reserved

Technology Ability Field

The 8 bits (A0 to A7) of the Technology Ability Field define the technology currently supported by the PHY layer.

Table 7.24: Technology ability field

Bit	Technology
A0	I0BaseT
AI	I0BaseT Full-Duplex
A2	I00BaseTx
A3	I00BaseTx Full-Duplex
A4	I00BaseT4
A5	Reserved
A6	Reserved
A7	Reserved

Remote Fault

Bit D13 is reserved for the remote fault function. Setting this bit to the value 1 indicates that the remote communication partner has detected a fault.

Acknowledge

The receiver uses bit D14 to signal that it has received the full base page. If no next page information is agreed, then the ACK bit is set to the value 1 after three FLP bursts have been successively received. If next page information is negotiated between the partners, then the ACK bit is set to the value 1 after three FLP bursts have been successively received and the link codeword has been stored. Once the complete acknowledgment mode has been entered, the link codeword is sent 6 to 8 times in succession over the link.

Next Page

The next page function is indicated using bit D15. With next page, information beyond that of the base page can be negotiated between the link partners. The next page function is split between message page and unformatted page. A dual acknowledgment mechanism was developed for the next page function. The normal acknowledgment (ACK) confirms that the data has been received. The acknowledgment (ACK2) confirms to the sender that it was possible to execute the information contained in the message. Completion of the negotiation of next page information is signalled by both partners resetting bit D15 to the value 0.

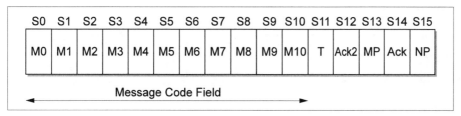

Figure 7.47: Next page coding

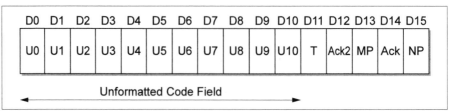

Figure 7.48: Unformatted page coding

Next Page

The Next Page (NP) bit defines whether this page is the last page transmitted or whether further pages follow.

0 = last page

1 = more pages follow

Acknowledgment

With bit D14, the receiver signals that it has received the complete base page. If no next page information is agreed, then the ACK bit is set to the value 1 after three FLP bursts have been received in succession. If next page information is agreed between the partners, then the ACK bit is set to the value 1 after three FLP bursts have been received in succession and the link codeword has been stored. Once the complete acknowledgment mode has been entered, the link codeword is sent 6 to 8 times in succession over the link.

Message Page

The Message Page (MP) bit is used to differentiate between message pages and unformatted pages.

0 = unformatted page

1 = message page

Acknowledgment 2

With the acknowledgment 2 (ACK2) bit the receiver signals that it supports the information contained in the message.

0 = does not support message

1 = supports message

Toggle

The Toggle (T) bit is used for synchronization between the two link partners when they are exchanging next page information. The T-bit always assumes the opposite value of the preceding link codeword. The T-bit relates to bit 11 of the link codeword.

0 = the value of the preceding bit 11 in the link codeword corresponded to logical 0

1 = the value of the preceding bit 11 in the link codeword corresponded to logical 1

Message Page Coding

The message pages contain message codes defined by the IEEE. The message page code fields are defined with bits M0 to M10. At present the following definitions have been agreed:

Message	M M M M M M M M M M	Description
Code	0 1 2 3 4 5 6 7 8 9 10	
1	0 0 0 0 0 0 0 0 0 0 0	Reserved
2	1 0 0 0 0 0 0 0 0 0 0	Null message
3	0 1 0 0 0 0 0 0 0 0 0	One page higher with following technology ability field
4	1 1 0 0 0 0 0 0 0 0 0	Two pages higher with following technology ability field
5	0 0 1 0 0 0 0 0 0 0 0	One page higher with following binary coded remote fault
6	0 1 1 0 0 0 0 0 0 0 0	Two pages higher with following binary coded remote fault
4096	1 1 1 1 1 1 1 1 1 1 1	Reserved

Unformatted Page Coding

The unformatted pages can be defined by the respective manufacturer. The unformatted page code fields are defined using bits U0 to U10.

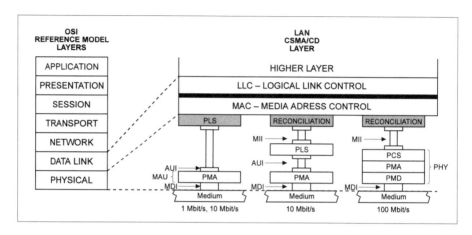

Figure 7.49: Autonegotiation state diagram

Physical Attachment (PHY)

The Physical Attachment (PHY) layer comprises the Physical Coding (PCS), Physical Medium Attachment (PMA), and Physical Medium-Dependent (PMD) sublayers. These sublayers define the physical and logical conditions of the lowest layer in the Fast Ethernet standard. The specifications of the PHY layer depend on the respective substandard used (100BaseT4, 100BaseTx, or 100BaseFx). The respective specifications are given separately in Chapter 4.

Table 7.25: Comparison between Fast Ethernet PMDs

Function	Standard		
	100BaseT4	100BaseTx	100BaseFx
Transmission medium	Twisted pair	Twisted pair	Optical fiber
Number of wires/fibers	8	4	2
Encoding	8B6T	4B5B	4B5B
Maximum distance in meters	100	100	400

100BaseX

The 100BaseX substandard supports the transmission of 100 Mbit/s data both over twisted pair lines (100BaseTx) and over optical fiber lines (100BaseFx). The 100BaseTx standard is divided into the following areas:

- Physical Coding Sublayer (PCS)

- Physical Medium Attachment (PMA) sublayer

- Physical Medium-Dependent (PMD) sublayer

Physical Coding Sublayer (PCS)

The Physical Coding Sublayer (PCS) is the uppermost sublayer of the PHY layer and represents the direct interface to the Media-Independent Interface (MII). The following interface signals to the MII are supported: MDIO, MDC, RXD<3>, RXD<2>, RXD<1>, RXD<0>, RX_DV, RX_CLK, RX_ER, TX_ER, TX_CLK, TX_EN, TXD<0>, TXD<1>, TXD<2>, TXD<3>, COL, and CRS. The Physical Coding Sublayer performs the following functions:

- Encoding/decoding the data nibbles in 4B/5B code groups

- Generating carrier sense and collision detect signals

Upon presentation to the medium, the data nibbles passed from the MII to the Physical Coding Sublayer (PCS) are encoded according to the 4B/5B technique already used in FDDI technology. The data nibbles (4 bits) are converted into a 4B/5B code group. Each code group comprises 5 bits, i.e., 1 bit more than would be necessary for encoding a data nibble. This means that there are 32 combinations available per code group rather than 16. Given an effective data rate of 100 Mbit/sec therefore, data is actually transmitted on the medium at a baud rate of 125 Mbit/s. This type of encoding is known as a block code. The expansion of a data byte into 5 bits serves several purposes:

- It provides additional code groups which can be used for special purposes (signalling) along with the code groups used for transmitting the payload data. Confusion with data code groups is eliminated.

- Error detection: the remaining codes are defined as illegal (violation symbols). The occurrence of such code groups is an unmistakable sign of transmission errors. This provides encoding redundancy, which helps to monitor the quality of a transmission link.

- The encoding of the code groups is selected so that the run length of bit patterns is limited, and the code is referred to as run length-limited. This technique ensures that for any given code group combination there are never more than a maximum number of zeros or ones transmitted in succession. This ensures that enough timing information is retained in the data stream so that the receiver can reconstruct the 100 Mbit/s data rate again. The encoding technique used for Fast Ethernet therefore has an efficiency of $100/125 = 80\%$. To compare, the Manchester code used for 10 Mbit/s Ethernet has an efficiency of only 50%.

- Minimization of baseline wander

A baseband transmission code should be constructed as much as possible in such a way that direct current voltage cannot form on the line. Direct voltage is produced on the line if on average more zeros than ones or vice versa are transmitted. This DC offset, which depends on the length of the packets transmitted, is also referred to as "baseline wander." If possible, the baseline wander should be zero. 4B5B encoding is not free of DC voltage, however. A maximum limit of 10% is not exceeded, even when transmitting packets of maximum length. The baseline wander influences the ability of the receiver to receive data correctly. The input stages can only operate properly within a given voltage range. A DC voltage component thus reduces the sensitivity of the receiver. In an extreme case, the receiver is pushed so far off its optimum operating point that reception is no longer possible.

The FDDI 4B/5B codes defined in the ISO 9314-1 document are used for the 100BaseX standard. Note here, however, that not all code groups are used with the 100BaseX standard, or some have a different meaning.

- S and Q code groups
  The S and Q code groups are not used and are always evaluated as illegal combinations.

- R code group

The R code group is used as the second code group of the end of stream delimiter. (With FDDI this symbol signals the reset condition.)

- H code group
  In the 100BaseX standard the H code group signals receive errors. (With FDDI this symbol signals the halt line state.)

	PCS code-group [4:0] 4 3 2 1 0	Name	MII(TXD/RXD) <3:0> 3 2 1 0	Interpretation
D A T A	1 1 1 1 0	0	0 0 0 0	Data 0
	0 1 0 0 0	1	0 0 0 1	Data 1
	1 0 1 0 0	2	0 0 1 0	Data 2
	1 0 1 0 1	3	0 0 1 1	Data 3
	0 1 0 1 0	4	0 1 0 0	Data 4
	0 1 0 1 1	5	0 1 0 1	Data 5
	0 1 1 1 0	6	0 1 1 0	Data 6
	0 1 1 1 1	7	0 1 1 1	Data 7
	1 0 0 1 0	8	1 0 0 0	Data 8
	1 0 0 1 1	9	1 0 0 1	Data 9
	1 0 1 1 0	A	1 0 1 0	Data A
	1 0 1 1 1	B	1 0 1 1	Data B
	1 1 0 1 0	C	1 1 0 0	Data C
	1 1 0 1 1	D	1 1 0 1	Data D
	1 1 1 0 0	E	1 1 1 0	Data E
	1 1 1 0 1	F	1 1 1 1	Data F
C O N T R O L	1 1 1 0 1	I	undefined	IDLE; used as inter-Streamfill code
	1 1 1 1 1	J	0 1 0 1	Start-of Stream Delimiter, Part 1 of 2; always used in pairs with K
	1 1 0 0 0	K	0 1 0 1	Start-of Stream Delimiter, Part 1 of 2; always used in pairs with J
	1 0 0 0 1	T	undefined	End-of Stream Delimiter, Part 1 of 2; always used in pairs with R
	0 0 1 1 1	R	undefined	End-of Stream Delimiter, Part 1 of 2; always used in pairs with T
I N V A L I D	0 0 1 0 0	H	undefined	Transmit Error; used to force signaling errors
	0 0 0 0 0	V	undefined	Invalid code
	0 0 0 0 1	V	undefined	Invalid code
	0 0 0 1 0	V	undefined	Invalid code
	0 0 0 1 1	V	undefined	Invalid code
	0 0 1 0 0	V	undefined	Invalid code
	0 0 1 0 1	V	undefined	Invalid code
	0 0 1 1 0	V	undefined	Invalid code
	0 1 0 0 0	V	undefined	Invalid code
	1 0 0 0 0	V	undefined	Invalid code
	1 1 0 0 1	V	undefined	Invalid code

Figure 7.50: 4B/5B conversion code table

Idle Code Groups

The Idle code group (I) is generated in the 100BaseX standard as padding information between streams. This technique is employed by the sender and receiver to ensure that their clocks always remain synchronized.

Control Code Groups

The control code group is always used in code pairs (JK, TR). These special codes signal the beginning and end of MAC data packets.

Start of Stream Delimiter

The Start of Stream Delimiter (SSD) comprises the code pairs JK and signals the beginning of a MAC data packet. The first 8 bits of the preamble are replaced by the SSD code group.

End of Stream Delimiter

The End of Stream Delimiter (ESD) comprises the code pairs TR and signals the end of a MAC data packet.

Illegal Code Groups

In the 100BaseX standard the illegal code group H signals a receive error.

Encapsulation

In the 100BaseX standard, the PMA layer is continuously sending information to its link partner. The code groups passed from the PCS layer to the PMA layer are called 100BaseX Service Data Units (SDUs). The PMA layer then encapsulates the data into 100BaseX Protocol Data Units (PDUs) for transport. With the exception of the start of stream delimiter, the data within an SDU is not interpreted by the Physical layer.

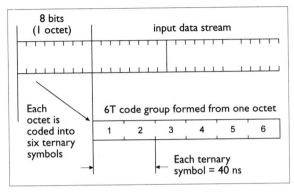

Figure 7.51: PCS encapsulation

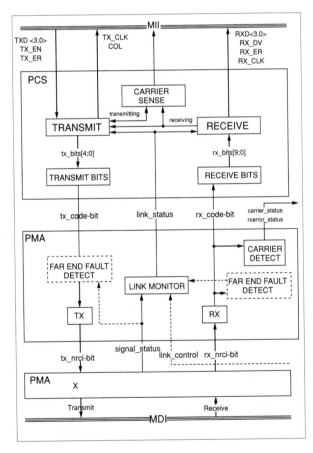

Figure 7.52: Block diagram of PCS/PMA in the 100BaseX standard

Physical Medium Attachment (PMA)

The Physical Medium Attachment sublayer provides the functional interface to the medium and performs the following functions: transmit, receive, carrier detect, link monitor, and far end detect fault.

- Transmit function:
  The transmit function ensures that the code groups provided by the PCS layer are sent over the transmit lines. During sending, the code groups are transmitted using NRZI encoding. NRZI (non return to zero inverted) means that a logical 1 with a change of line level (voltage level) is encoded, but a logical 0 does not cause any transition. The sender must, however, ensure that not too many sequences of 0 are transmitted, as otherwise insufficient timing information would reach the receiver. This prerequisite is met in the 100BaseX standard by the use of 4B5B symbol encoding.

- Receive function:
  The receive function ensures that the signals coming from the PMD layer over the respective receive lines are received and processed. The receiver extracts the timing information from the receive signal, decides whether the incoming signal is strong enough (Carrier Detect), and converts the data from serial NRZI format into 4B/5B code groups. The receiver also has to establish the symbol boundaries using the JK symbol pair. If this bit pattern is detected, all the following bits are passed to the PMA layer using the PMD_Unidata.indicate function.

- Carrier detect:
  The carrier is defined as follows in the 100BaseX standard: if two non-successive zero code bits arrive within 10 rx_code bits (10 bit code window) and if no start of stream sequence was detected, then the Carrier_Status signal is switched from Off to On. If ten successive ones code bits (idle) are detected within the data stream, the carrier status is set to the value Off.

- Link monitor function:
  A fixed part of the 100BaseX standard is the continuous checking of the reliability of the receive channel. Since data is being transmitted continuously between the two link partners with the 100BaseX transmis-

sion method, the receiver is able to keep a close watch on activities on the medium. The link status signal is set to the value On if data is received on the link within 330 to 1000 1s.

- Far end fault detect function:
  The far end fault function continuously monitors the rx_code bit stream of the receive process. If three successive ones code groups are received after the last zero is received, the link partner detects a fault.

Physical Medium-Dependent (PMD) Sublayer

According to the ISO Reference Model, the Physical Medium-Dependent (PMD) sublayer represents the lowest level of the Physical layer. On this sublayer the data is converted into electrical or optical signals. In the 100BaseX standard, the Physical layer is differentiated as follows:

- Fast Ethernet on twisted pair lines (100BaseTx)

- Fast Ethernet on optical fiber (100BaseFx).

Fast Ethernet on Twisted Pair Lines (100BaseTx)

The 100BaseTx specifications are based on the standards (ANSI X3T9.5 TP-PMD/312, Revision 2.1) defined for FDDI technology. The 100BaseTx standard is based on transmission over Category 5 cables (according to ISO/IEC 11801). In comparison with Category 3 or 4 cables, Category 5 cables have much improved transmission characteristics and crosstalk behavior. The 100BaseTx standard prescribes the use of two wire pairs for transmitting the data. On these wire pairs, the 100 Mbit/s data rate is reduced to 33.333 MHz through the use of MLT-3 encoding. This ensures compliance with the American FCC Class B Regulations and the even more stringent European EN 55022B regulations for electromagnetic radiation at a transfer rate of 100 Mbit/s. The impedance of the unshielded twisted pair (UTP) and shielded twisted pair (STP) cables used in the 100BaseTx standard is 100 Ohm ± 15%.

Owing to the maximum permissible attenuation of 13 dB at 12.5 MHz, the length of a twisted pair segment is only 100 meters. The maximum propagation delay of such a link segment is 570 ns. RJ-45 technology was specified as the standard connector for the 100BaseTx standard. An 8-pole RJ-45 socket is available as the standard 100BaseTx interface. This connector is known from telephone technology and is available in both shielded and unshielded versions. It is attached using insulation displacement with a special crimping tool. The individual contacts of the 8-pole RJ 45 connector are assigned as follows:

Contact	Signal
1	Transmit+
2	Transmit-
3	Receive+
4	Not used
5	Not used
6	Receive-
7	Not used
8	Not used

The most important characteristics of the 100BaseTx standard are:

Table 7.26: Chief characteristics of the 100BaseTx standard

4-wire 100 Ohm twisted pair cable (Category 5)
Signalling technique: baseband
Maximum transfer rate: 10 Mbit/s
Encoding: 4B5B
Topology: star
Maximum segment length: 100m
Monitoring of link segments by idle signal
Connector: 8-pole RJ-45

Fast Ethernet on Optical Fiber (100BaseFx)

The 100BaseFx specifications are based on the standards (ISO 9324-3) defined for FDDI technology. The 100BaseFx standard uses optical fiber cable for transmitting the data.

Owing to the propagation delay, the maximum length of a fiber optic segment is 400 meters. The maximum propagation delay of such a link segment is 570 ns. A range of standard connectors are possible for the 100BaseFx standard:

- Duplex SC connector according to ANSI X3T9.5 LCF-PMD Revision 1.3.

- Media interface connector (MIC). The MIC connector must always be coded as an M-connector with the 100BaseFx standard.

- ST connector.

Table 7.27: Chief characteristics of the 100BaseFx standard

2-wire optical fiber cable (62.5/125 1m or 50/125 1m)
Signalling technique: baseband
Maximum transfer rate: 10 Mbit/s
Encoding: 4B5B
Topology: star
Maximum segment length: 400m
Monitoring of link segments by idle signal
Connector: ST, SC or MIC connector

Table7.28: Comparison of FDDI and 100BaseX

FDDI	100BaseX
Bypass	Not used
Connection Management (CNT)	Unknown
Halt line state	Not used
Master line state	Not used
Maximum packet size	Maximum stream size
9000 symbols	3054 code groups
PHY service data unit	Stream
Preamble	Interpacket idles
Quiet Line State (QLS)	Not used
Station Management (SMT)	Unknown
Symbols	Code groups

Fast Ethernet on Category 3 cable (100BaseT4)

The 100BaseT4 substandard is one of the new Ethernet specifications that have been defined in the course of the activities around Fast Ethernet. Some structures and definitions (twisted pair cabling, RJ45 connector) already familiar from the 10BaseT specification have been retained in the 100BaseT4 standard. The designation T4 refers to the transmission cable requirements. The 100BaseT4 standard prescribes Category 3 cables (according to ISO/IEC 11801) or better for transmission.

In comparison with Category 5 cables, Category 3 cables have a much poorer response characteristic and are susceptible to crosstalk. For this reason the 100BaseT4 standard specifies the use of four wire pairs for transmitting the data. An 8B6T code is used to transmit the data. With this code, eight bits are converted into a six-digit code in each case. Each code group is transmitted separately on one of the three data lines. The effective data rate on each data line is therefore 33.333 Mbit/s. With the 6/8 code, the 100 Mbit/s data rate is split between the three wire pairs in 25 Mbit/s communication channels in each case.

The splitting of data transmission between several parallel wires ensures compliance with the American FCC Class B Regulations and the even more stringent European EN 55022B regulations for electromagnetic radiation at a transfer rate of 100 Mbit/s. In addition, the data is transmitted over the cable unidirectionally. In practice, the 100BaseT4 standard can only ever be used in point-to-point connections. A station can either send or receive, never both simultaneously.

The 100BaseT4 standard is divided into the following areas:

- Physical Coding Sublayer (PCS)
- Physical Medium Attachment (PMA) sublayer
- Medium-Dependent Interface (MDI)

Physical Coding Sublayer (PCS)

The Physical Coding Sublayer (PCS) is the uppermost sublayer of the PHY layer and represents the direct interface to the Media-Independent Interface

(MII). The following interface signals to the MII are supported: MDIO, MDC, RXD<3>, RXD<2>, RXD<1>, RXD<0>, RX_DV, RX_CLK, RX_ER, TX_ER, TX_CLK, TX_EN, TXD<0>, TXD<1>, TXD<2>, TXD<3>, COL, and CRS. The Physical Coding Sublayer performs the following functions: reset, transmit, receive, error sense, carrier sense, and collision presence. The data nibbles passed from the MII to the Physical Coding Sublayer (PCS) are encoded on the medium using 8B6T encoding. The symbols produced as a result of encoding are called ternary symbols. This code comprises three values (–1, 0 and 1). A total of six ternary symbols are grouped in one 6T code group.

Table 7.29: 6T code table

Data octet	6T code group	Data octet	6T code group	Data octet	6T code group	Data octet	6T code group
00	+-00+-	40	+0+00-	80	+-+00_	C0	+-+0+-
01	0+-+-0	41	++-0-0	81	++-0-0	C1	++-+-0
02	+-0+-0	42	+0+0-0	82	+-+0-0	C2	+-++-0
03	-0++-0	43	0++0-0	83	-++0-0	C3	-+++-0
04	-0+0+-	44	-0++0-	84	-++00-	C4	-++0+-
05	0+--0+	45	++0-00	85	++--00	C5	++--0+
06	+-0-0+	46	+0+-00	86	+-+-00	C6	+-+-0+
07	-0+-0+	47	0++-00	87	-++-00	C7	-++-0+
08	-+00+-	48	000+00	88	0+000-	C8	0+00+-
09	0-++-0	49	000-++	89	00+0-0	C9	00++-0
0A	-+0+-0	4A	000+-+	8A	0+00-0	CA	0+0+-0
0B	+0-+-0	4B	000++-	8B	+000-0	CB	+00+-0
0C	+0-0+-	4C	000-+0	8C	+0000-	CC	+000+-
0D	0-+-0+	4D	000-0+	8D	00+-00	CD	00+-0+
0E	-+0-0+	4E	000+-0	8E	0+0-00	CE	0+0-0+
0F	+0--0+	4F	000+0-	8F	+00-00	CF	+00-0+
10	+0+--0	50	+0+--+	90	+-+--+	D0	+-+0-+
11	++0-0-	51	++0-+-	91	++--+-	D1	++--+0
12	+0+-0-	52	+0+-+-	92	+-+-+-	D2	+-+-+0
13	0++-0-	53	0++-+-	93	-++-+-	D3	-++-+0

(continued)

Table 7.29: (continued)

Data octet	6T code group	Data octet	6T code group	Data octet	6T code group	Data octet	6T code group
14	0++--0	54	0++--+	94	-++—+	D4	-++0-+
15	++00--	55	++0+--	95	++-+--	D5	++-+0-
16	+0+0--	56	+0++--	96	+-++--	D6	+-++0-
17	0++0--	57	0+++--	97	-+++--	D7	-+++0-
18	0+-0+-	58	+++0--	98	0+0--+	D8	0+00-+
19	0+-0-+	59	+++-0-	99	00+-+-	D9	00+-+0
1A	0+-++-	5A	+++--0	9A	0+0-+-	DA	0+0-+0
1B	0+-00+	5B	++0--0	9B	+00-+-	DB	+00-+0
1C	0-+00+	5C	++0--+	9C	+00--+	DC	+000-+
1D	0-+++-	5D	++000-	9D	00++--	DD	00++0-
1E	0-+0-+	5E	--+++0	9E	0+0+--	DE	0+0+0-
1F	0-+0+-	5F	00-++0	9F	+00+--	DF	+00+0-
20	00-++-	60	0-0++0	A0	0-0++-	E0	+-0++-
21	--+00+	61	00-+0+	A1	00-+-+	E1	0+-+-+
22	++-0+-	62	0-0+0+	A2	0-0+-+	E2	+-0+-+
23	++-0-+	63	-00+0+	A3	-00+-+	E3	-0++-+
24	00+0-+	64	-00++0	A4	-00++-	E4	-0+++-
25	00+0+-	65	00_0++	A5	00--++	E5	0+--++
26	00-00+	66	0-00++	A6	0-0-++	E6	+-0-++
27	--+++-	67	-000++	A7	-00-++	E7	-0+-++
28	-0-++0	68	-+-++0	A8	-+-++-	E8	-+0++-
29	--0+0+	69	--++0+	A9	--++-+	E9	0-++-+
2A	-0-+0+	6A	-+-+0+	AA	-+-+-+	EA	-+0+-+
2B	0--+0+	6B	+--+0+	AB	+--+-+	EB	+--+-+
2C	0--++0	6C	+--++0	AC	+--++-	EC	+0-++-
2D	--00++	6D	--+0++	AD	--+-++	ED	0-+-++
2E	-0-0++	6E	-+-0++	AE	-+--++	EE	-+0-++
2F	0--0++	6F	+--0++	AF	+--0++	EF	+0--++

(continued)

Table 7.29: (continued)

Data octet	6T code group	Data octet	6T code group	Data octet	6T code group	Data octet	6T code group
30	+-00-+	70	-++000	B0	0-000+	F0	+-000+
31	0+--+0	71	+-+000	B1	00-0+0	F1	0+-0+0
32	+-0-+0	72	++-000	B2	0-00+0	F2	0-00+0
33	-0+-+0	73	00+000	B3	-000+0	F3	-0+0+0
34	-0+0-+	74	-0+000	B4	-0000+	F4	-0+00+
35	0+-0+-	75	0+-000	B5	00-+00	F5	0+-+00
36	+-0+0-	76	+0-000	B6	0-0+00	F6	+-0+00
37	-0++00-	77	0+-000	B7	-00+00	F7	-0++00
38	-+00-+	78	0--+++	B8	-+-00+	F8	-+000+
39	0-+-+0	79	-0-+++	B9	--+0+0	F9	0-+0+0
3A	-+0-+0	7A	--0+++	BA	-+-0+0	FA	-+00+0
3B	+0--+0	7B	--0++0	BB	+—0+0	FB	+0-0+0
3C	+0-0-+	7C	++-00-	BC	+—00+	FC	+0-00+
3D	0-++0-	7D	00+00-	BD	--++00	FD	0-++00
3E	-+0+-	7E	++---+	BE	-+-+00	FE	-+0+00
3F	+0-+0	7F	00+--+	BF	+--+00	FF	+0-+00

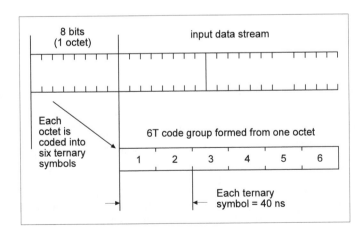

Figure 7.53: Conversion of data octets into 6T code groups

The ternary symbols are then passed on from the Physical Coding Sublayer to the Physical Medium Attachment (PMA) sublayer for data transmission.

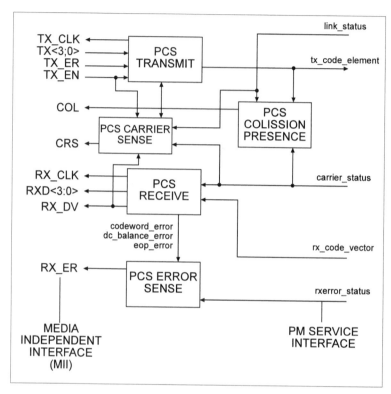

Figure 7.54: PCS block diagram

Transmit Function

In each case two nibbles (8 bits) are written by the Physical Coding Sublayer into the transmit shift register (tsr). If the TX_EN signal is present, the tsr sends out the following information within the first 16 TX_CLK clock cycles: SOSA, SOSA, SOSA, SOSA, SOSA, SOSB, SOSB, SOSB. This sequence replaces the preamble of the MAC header. The individual SOSA and SOSB symbols are then passed on to the output holding registers (ohr). The ohr registers are written cyclically in succession. Before the SOSA and SOSB symbols are loaded into the ohrs associated with the BI_D3 and BI_D4 lines, the sequences P3 and P4 are appended at the head. The actual data is then written into the respective output holding registers (ohr 1, ohr 3, ohr 4) and passed to the PMA layer with the PMA_Unitdata.Request Message function. After the complete MAC packet has been transmitted, the TX_EN signal is reset. This causes the tsr to transmit the following information during the next 10 TX_CLK clock cycles: EOP1, EOP2, EOP3, EOP4, and EOP5. This sequence signals to the receiver that transmission of the data packets has been completed.

If the signals TX_ER and TX_EN are set to the value 1 after the first 16 clock cycles (after the TX_EN signal has been set to High), then the tsr assumes that an error is present. It then automatically generates the Bad_Code constant.

If the TX_EN signal is set to the value Low, then the tsr automatically transmits the Zero_Code constant.

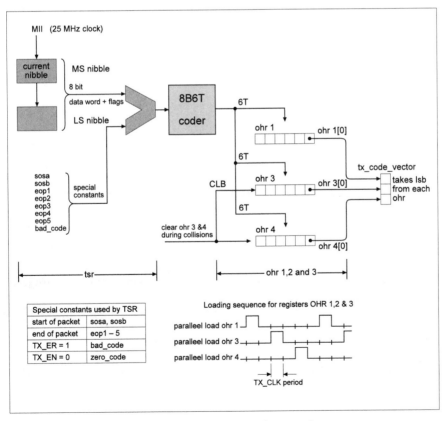

Figure 7.55: PCS transmit reference diagram

Special PCS Constants

SOSA

The SOSA constant comprises six ternary symbols. These symbols are encoded as follows: 1 -1 1 -1 1 -1

SOSB

The SOSB constant comprises six ternary symbols. These symbols are encoded as follows: 1 -1 1 -1 -1 1

EOP1

The EOP1 constant comprises six ternary symbols. These symbols are encoded as follows: 1 1 1 1 1 1

EOP2

The EOP2 constant comprises six ternary symbols. These symbols are encoded as follows: 1 1 1 1 -1 -1

EOP3

The EOP3 constant comprises six ternary symbols. These symbols are encoded as follows: 1 1 -1 -1 0 0

EOP4

The EOP4 constant comprises six ternary symbols. These symbols are encoded as follows: -1 -1 -1 -1 -1 -1

EOP5

The EOP5 constant comprises six ternary symbols. These symbols are encoded as follows: -1 -1 0 0 0 0

Bad_Code

The Bad_Code constant comprises six ternary symbols. These symbols are encoded as follows: -1 -1 -1 1 1 1

Zero_Code

The Zero_Code constant comprises six ternary symbols. These symbols are encoded as follows: 0 0 0 0 0 0

P3

The P3 constant comprises two ternary symbols. These symbols are encoded as follows: 1 -1

P4

The P4 constant comprises four ternary symbols. These symbols are encoded as follows: 1 -1 1 -1

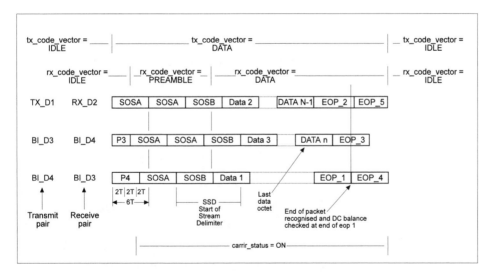

Figure 7.56: PCS/PMA sublayer data structure

Receive Function

The data is passed from the PMA layer to the PCS layer (rx_code=Data) with the PMA_Unitdata.Indicate Message function. The information of the individual transmission channels is forwarded to the input holding registers (ih2, ih3, and ih4). The ihr registers are written cyclically in succession. If there are more than 6 data messages in the ihr registers, then conversion of the ternary symbols into data nibbles (from the start of frame delimiter) commences. The transfer of nibbles from the PCS layer to the MII is indicated using the RX_DV signal. If an error occurs during transmission, then the PCS interface indicates this error using the RX_ER signal.

Error Sense Function

The error sense function enables the PCS layer to notify the MII of transmission errors. If the rxerror_status parameter is set to the value Error by the PMA layer, then an RX_ER signal is generated to the MII.

Carrier Sense Function

When the medium is busy, the PCS layer uses the carrier sense function to notify the MII of this state. If Link_Status = OK is registered by the PMA layer, then the CSR signal is present at the MII when one of the following conditions occurs:

- rx_crs=On
- TX_EN = 1

If Link_Status not OK is registered, then the CSR signal is present at the MII when the parameter rx_crs=On is reported.

Collision Presence Function

The occurrence of a collision on the medium is reported by the PCS layer in the form of a COL signal to the MII when the following conditions occur:

- tx_code_vector = Not idle
- carrier_status = On
- Link_status = OK

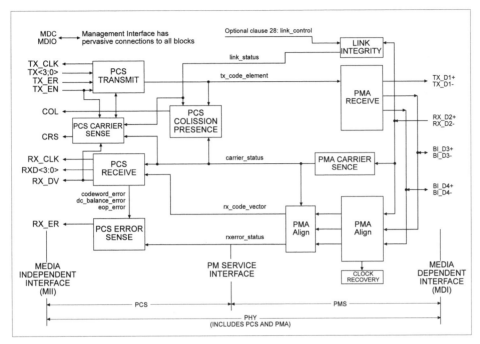

Figure 7.57: Subdivision of the 100BaseT4 PCS and PMA functions

Physical Medium Attachment (PMA)

The Physical Medium Attachment sublayer provides the functional interface to the medium and performs the following functions: reset, transmit, receive, carrier sense, link integrity, align, and clock recovery.

- Reset function:
  The reset function is triggered only when the end station is switched on (or attached to the MII) and also via the management mechanisms. All PMA mechanisms are reset to their default values by the reset functions.

- Transmit function:
  The transmit function ensures that the 6T symbols provided by the PCS layer are transmitted over the corresponding signal lines (TX_D1, BI_D3 and BI_D4). Idle signals (TP_IDL_100) are transmitted during the periods in which no data is awaiting transmission.

- Receive function:
  The receive function ensures that before transfer to the PCS layer, the 6T symbols provided by the MDI layer over the respective signal lines (TX_D1, BI_D3, and BI_D4) are converted into formats which can be processed by the align function.

- Carrier Sense:
  This function is used to check whether a signal is already present on the medium. The Set PMA_Carrier parameter is set to the value On if as a result of the RX_D2 signal the following levels are present during two successive ternary symbols:

  One signal < 467 mV followed by one signal > -225 mV followed by one signal < 467 mV

  The Set PMA_Carrier parameter is set to the value Off if seven successive ternary symbols with the value CS0 are received via the RX_D2 signal.

- Link integrity function:
  The line connection test is a defined part of the 100BaseT4 standard. Since this transmission method over twisted pair lines is simplex only, it must be ensured that the connection between the two end stations is active in both directions. The link integrity function of the receiver checks the RX_D2 signals. Link integrity signals (ternary symbols -1, 1) are transmitted from the 100BaseT4 end station at regular intervals (1.2 ms ± 6 ms) to the respective other end stations.

- Align function:
  The receiver uses the align function to ensure that it is synchronized with the clock frequency of the sender while receiving data. This operation is considered to be finished once the complete preamble has been received. Only then are ternary symbols passed to the higher layer.

Medium-Dependent Interface (MDI)

The Medium-Dependent Interface represents the physical interface to the transmission medium. An unshielded twisted pair (UTP) cable with an impedance of 100 Ohm ± 15%, or 120 Ohm, of Categories 3, 4, and 5 was prescribed as cable for the 100BaseT4 standard. Owing to the maximum permissible attenuation of 13 dB at 12.5 MHz, the length of a twisted pair segment is only 100 meters. The maximum propagation delay of such a link segment is 570 ns. RJ-45 technology was specified as the standard connector for the 100BaseT4 standard. An 8-pole RJ-45 socket is available as the standard MDI interface. This connector is known from telephone technology and is available in both shielded and unshielded versions. It is attached using insulation displacement with a special crimping tool. The individual contacts of the 8-pole RJ 45 connector are assigned as follows:

Contact	Signal
1	TX_D1+
2	TX_D1-
3	RX_D2+
4	BI_D3+
5	BI_D3-
6	RX_D2-
7	BI_D4+
8	BI_D4-

If two 100BaseT4 ports are connected directly to one another, then a twisted pair crossover cable must be used. This cable has the following appearance:

The most important characteristics of the 100BaseT4 standard are:

Table 7.30: Chief characteristics of the 100BaseT4 standard

8-wire 100 Ohm twisted pair cable (Categories 3, 4, and 5)
Signalling technique: baseband
Maximum transfer rate: 10 Mbit/s
Encoding: 8B6T
Topology: star
Maximum segment length: 100m
Monitoring of link segments by idle signal
Connector: 8-pole RJ-45

7.8.2 Fiber Distributed Data Interface

For many years Fiber Distributed Data Interface (FDDI) networks was project-
ed to be the future solution to meet the ever increasing demand for available
bandwidth from new applications and processor generations. With a nominal
data rate of 100 Mbit/s, FDDI was the ideal technology for use on backbones
and for connecting central servers or complete subnetworks (Ethernet or
Token Ring). In the 7-layer ISO Reference Model, FDDI is located on the lowest two layers. For this reason, the standard covers only the MAC layer (Layer
2) and the Physical layer (Layer 1). In the region of the trunk FDDI is based on
a dual optical fiber ring. In the region of the tree, the FDDI network is set up
singly. End stations (servers, computers), or even other networks via
bridges/switches/routers, can be attached in both parts of the network.

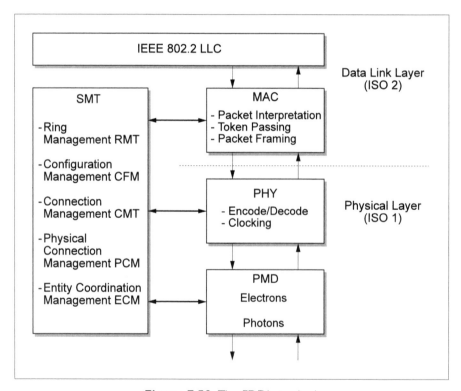

Figure 7.58: The FDDI standard

A data signalling rate of 100 Mbit per second is used for communication on an FDDI network. In the backbone area and for connecting important end stations, an FDDI network is always constructed as a dual closed optical fiber ring. Up to 500 end stations (bridges, routers, gateways, or hosts) can be connected to this backbone. Two FDDI stations can be located at up to two kilometers from one another. The ring radius of a fiber distributed data interface (FDDI) network may be up to 100 km. The smallest FDDI configuration comprises two FDDI stations connected to one another via the Physical Layer (PHY). Connection to the physical medium is controlled by the access and removal algorithm of the Station Management (SMT) software. The FDDI standard is subdivided into four substandards: the Physical Medium-Dependent (PMD) layer, the Physical Layer (PHY), the Medium Access Control (MAC) layer, and Station Management (SMT).

Physical Medium-Dependent Layer

Substandard ISO 9314-3 describes the lowest layer (1a) of an FDDI data network. This layer is called the Physical Medium-Dependent layer and is abbreviated to PMD.

The PMD layer defines the optical/electrical characteristics, the jitter and the rise and fall times. The specification of the connector is also part of the Physical Medium-Dependent (PMD) layer. Since FDDI technology was initially only used on fiber optic segments connecting individual FDDI computers, the PMD standard only defines support for graded-index optical fibers with a diameter of 50/125 μm or 62.5/125 μm. The wavelength of light used with FDDI is 1300 nm. Since the PMD standard would have become too inflexible by too narrow a definition of the optical fiber standard, new extended PMD layers were defined. These include the single mode fiber standard (SMF-PMD) for supporting 9/125 μm monomode fibers, the low cost fiber standard (LCF-PMD) for graded-index fibers having a light wavelength of 820 nm, and the twisted pair standard (TP-PMD) for supporting shielded and unshielded twisted pair cables. As a result of these new developments, FDDI technology can now be employed by a variety of physical media.

Physical Layer

Substandard ISO 9314-1 describes the topmost layer of the Physical layer (Layer 1b) of an FDDI data network. This layer is called the Physical layer and is abbreviated to PHY. The Physical Layer defines all the transmission characteristics of the FDDI. The PHY also defines the type of data encoding. 4B/5B encoding is used with FDDI, so-called because four data bits are converted into a 5-bit value. In comparison with the Ethernet Manchester code, the 4B/5B code is much more efficient and permits the transmission of 100 Mbit/s at an aggregate bandwidth of 125 Mbaud. Besides the encoding and FDDI timing functions, the PHY layer continuously checks the line state between neighboring FDDI stations.

Medium Access Control

Substandard ISO 9314-2 describes the lowest layer (Layer 2a) of the Data Link Layer of an FDDI data network. This layer is termed the Medium Access Control layer and is abbreviated MAC. The Medium Access Control protocol defines the FDDI packet format, network access, FDDI address recognition, token management, and token timing. If stations are connected as active participants in the FDDI ring, the entire data stream of the ring passes through the MAC layer and is forwarded from the network input to the network output. If the MAC layer wishes to send data itself, then it must wait until it receives a token. The token is removed from the ring, and in its place the FDDI controller sends the FDDI data packet onto the ring. Following this, another token is generated, and the data is relayed from the network input to the network output.

Daten Frame									
	Preamble Idles	Start Delimiter	Frame Control	Destination Adress	Source Adress	Information Block	Frame Check Sequence	End Delimiter	Frame Status
# of Symbols	12 -16	2	2	4 - 12		0-08956/8972	8	1	3
# of Bytes	6 - 8	1	1	2 - 6		0-04478/4486	4	0,5	1,5

Figure 7.59: The FDDI data format

Station Management

Station Management (Draft 7) defines the control of the FDDI protocol layers. The Station Management (SMT) detects the errors, such as token loss, no optical signal or optical signal too weak, or CRC error for example, that can occur on an FDDI network. This information is collected by the Station Management software, evaluated, and, if necessary, required responses to the particular error are triggered. If a connection (primary ring) between two FDDI computers is interrupted, the Station Management software automatically reroutes the data path onto the secondary ring. If a token is lost the Station Management software handles the reinitialization of the ring and the generation of a new token. Since Station Management must be implemented in every FDDI controller, each station reacts individually to errors and responds dynamically to the particular data load on the ring. One other function of SMT is the continuous gathering of statistical data. This data can then be passed up to the higher protocol layers for optimizing data throughput or for management purposes. All variables managed by Station Management are defined in a so-called SMT MIB (MIB = Management Information Base). By integrating a management agent, the information collected by the FDDI SMT can be integrated into an SNMP (Simple Network Management Protocol) system readily.

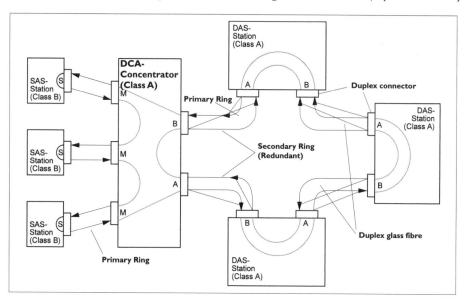

Figure 7.60: FDDI ring in normal mode

FDDI operation

A Fiber Distributed Data Interface network is always constructed with a dual ring topology. In the normal mode (standard) all the data is transmitted over the primary ring. If a fault occurs (line break), the FDDI stations nearest to the source of the error automatically switch over onto the secondary ring and close the FDDI ring again. Once the line break or fault has been rectified, they switch back onto the primary ring again immediately.

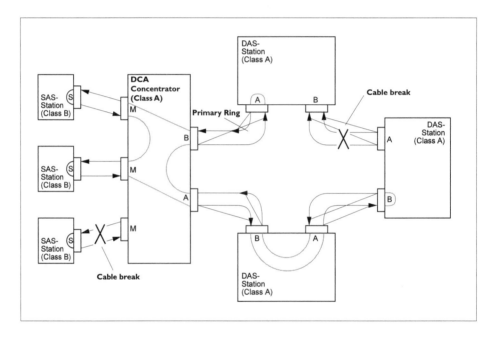

Figure 7.61: FDDI ring in a fault situation

The access units (stations) that can be connected to an FDDI data network are divided into two classes in the FDDI standard. Class A stations include dual attachment stations, while Class B includes single attachment stations.

Class A

All FDDI stations that can be connected directly to the FDDI ring belong to FDDI Class A. These devices are known as Dual Attachment Stations, abbreviated to DAS. The Physical layer protocol (PHY) is implemented twice in DAS. All Class A stations are capable of rerouting their entire data traffic from the primary ring onto the secondary ring in the event of a fault. In this case, the Station Management (SMT) protocol identifies the particular faulty segment or the malfunctioning station and removes it from the ring. The FDDI network remains fully operational even if a line is interrupted. Concentrators are a special type of Dual Attachment Station which allow one or more single attachment units to be connected to the ring.

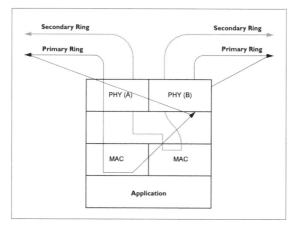

Figure 7.62: Dual attachment station

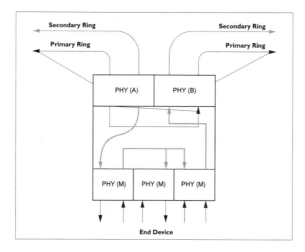

Figure 7.63: FDDI concentrators

Class B

All FDDI stations that cannot be connected directly to a dual FDDI ring belong to FDDI Class B. These devices are termed Single Attachment Stations (SAS). Single Attachment Stations are always connected to the FDDI network via concentrators. In contrast to Dual Attachment Stations, only one physical connection (PHY) is implemented on Single Attachment Stations. Single Attachment Stations permit the inexpensive connection of many simple end stations to the network.

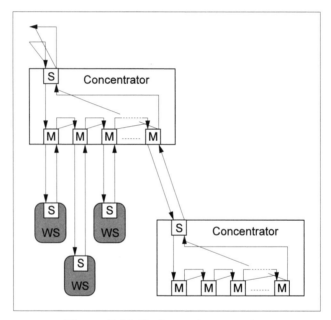

Figure 7.64: Single attachment station

FDDI data networks are nowadays deployed primarily as high-speed data highways (backbone) between existing slower data networks. The various data networks are usually attached via routers or via so-called translation bridges. With both methods, the Ethernet and Token Ring packets are converted directly into FDDI packets on the different layers. FDDI computers are usually connected directly to the network by means of concentrators, since this permits a favorable price per FDDI connection.

Transition from Ethernet switch to FDDI

In general only transparent bridges are used in FDDI networks for interconnecting LANs on Layer 2. The data traffic is routed between the LANs on the basis of the address tables automatically learned by the bridge.

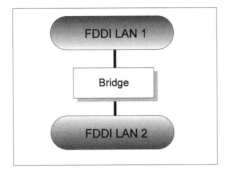

Figure 7.65: FDDI-FDDI bridge

FDDI-LAN Bridges

An FDDI network and an Ethernet LAN are connected on Layer 2 by means of translation bridges. The translation bridge handles the conversion of the various address, protocol, and packet formats. The Ethernet and the IEEE 802.3 methods do not differ in terms of their physical parameters. The principal difference between the two standards is in the frame format. Both data formats begin with a seven-byte long preamble. This is followed by a start frame delimiter as a further signalling byte. In both the Ethernet and in the 802.3 packet, this is followed by a 6-position (byte/octet) destination address and a 6-position (byte/octet) source address. Following the two address fields there is a 2-byte field where the Ethernet standard (V.2) differs substantially from IEEE 802.3. This field is interpreted as the "Type Field" in the Ethernet standard. This type field identifies the following protocol by means of a unique code (e.g., 08-00 hex for the internal protocol). With the IEEE 802.3 version, the length field indicates the length of the data information contained in the following data part in bytes. The standard defines here a minimum packet size (64 bytes) and a maximum packet size (1518 bytes). The complete LLC data area and the subsequent data part containing all the protocol headers and information is included in the computation of the packet length.

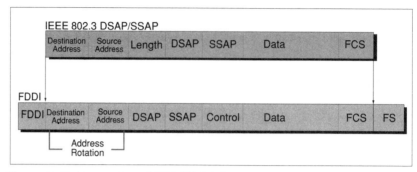

Figure 7.66: Conversion of IEEE 802.3 DSAP/SSAP packet into an FDDI packet

While in the Ethernet standard the data field begins after the type field, in the IEEE packet the fields for Logical Link Control (LLC) defined in the IEEE 802.2 standard follow here. In the IEEE standard, data exchange between two stations is realized by the Logical Link Control (LLC). This means that a minimum of three further fields (of 1 byte each) follow the length field. These fields are termed the DSAP (Destination Service Access Point), SSAP (Source Service Access Point), and control fields. In the past, the encoding of the Link Service Access Points (LSAP) made it possible to use some other external protocols.

Table 7.31: Link service access points

Decimal	Description
0	Null LSAP
2	Indiv LLC sublayer mgt
3	Group LLC sublayer mgt
4	SNA path control
6	Reserved (DOD IP)
14	PROWAY-LAN
78	EIA-RS 511
94	ISI IP
142	PROWAY-LAN
170	SNAP
254	ISO DIS 8473
255	Global DSAP

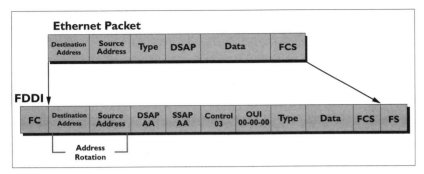

Figure 7.67: Conversion of IEEE 802.3 SNAP packet into an FDDI packet

In practice this method proved to be inflexible since, for instance, of the large family of TCP/IP protocols only the Internet Protocol (IP) has an LSAP identifier. Other protocols, such as the Address Resolution Protocol (ARP), were not included here. For this reason, the existing LLC header (IEEE 802.2 SAP; Service Access Point) had to be extended to include a SNAP header (IEEE 802.3 SNAP; Subnet Access Protocol). All the data is sent as LLC type 1 (unnumbered information) in pure datagram procedures. If the 802.2 SNAP format is used, the DSAP and the SSAP fields are set to the value 170 (AA hex). The control field is always set to the value = 0. This is followed by two further fields which indicate the organization code (OUI) (3 bytes) and contain the Ethernet-type field (2 bytes). This trick makes it possible to use protocols that do not even have a DSAP/ SSAP definition. The FDDI method uses an LLC header on Layer 2b. Depending upon the higher protocol (e.g., IP), the LLC header is then followed by a SNAP header.

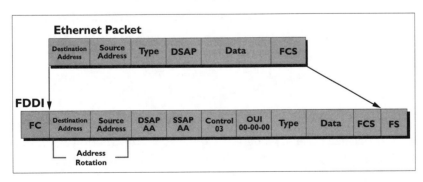

Figure 7.68: Conversion of Ethernet packet into an FDDI packet

In principle every Ethernet packet can be translated into an FDDI packet format. The size of an Ethernet packet is between 64 and 1518 bytes. The length of an FDDI packet may be between 17 and 4495 bytes. These specifications ensure that every Ethernet packet can be converted into an FDDI packet. The opposite direction (FDDI to Ethernet/IEEE 802.3) does pose some problems. At present, no standardized data link fragmentation method is defined with which it is possible to split large FDDI packets on Layer 2 into several Ethernet packets. For this reason, when they are to be relayed over an Ethernet, the size of an FDDI frame is limited to the maximum size of an Ethernet packet.

Operation of a Translation Bridge

The translation of FDDI into Ethernet/IEEE 802.3 packets was defined by the Network Working Group in Request for Comments 1042 (title: A Standard for the Transmission of IP Datagrams over IEEE 802 Networks). This method is also sometimes referred to as the RFC 1042 method. However, in practice, some problems were experienced when converting AppleTalk packets into FDDI packets. AppleTalk 1 uses the Ethernet format, while AppleTalk 2 protocols use pure IEEE 802.3 packets for transmission. The established convention was that all packet formats with an OUI field of 00-00-00 were converted into pure Ethernet packets upon exiting the transit network. The result of this was that the translation algorithm of the translation bridges only produced Ethernet packets and not IEEE 802.3 packets. As a consequence, it was not possible to transmit AppleTalk 2 packets over FDDI.

The IEEE 802.1d committee addressed this problem and extended the bridge standard. The bridge decides on the basis of selective translation tables implemented in it whether a data packet is to be translated into an Ethernet or an IEEE 802.3 format. To differentiate between regular Ethernet frames and IEEE 802.3 packets, the OUI value 00-00-F8 was defined.

Receiving from Ethernet

A translation bridge receives a data packet whose information is destined for the connected FDDI network.

1. IEEE 802.3/LLC/SNAP packet format:

   The translation bridge translates packets received in the 802.3 format directly into FDDI packet formats.

2. Ethernet format:

   If a translation bridge receives an Ethernet packet, it searches for its packet protocol type in the selective translation table.

   – If an entry is found for the packet in question, it is converted into an FDDI packet (LLC/SNAP) and the OUI field is set to 00-00-F8.

   – If no entry is found, the packet is converted into an FDDI packet (LLC/SNAP) according to the RFC 1042 rules and the OUI field is set to 00-00-00.

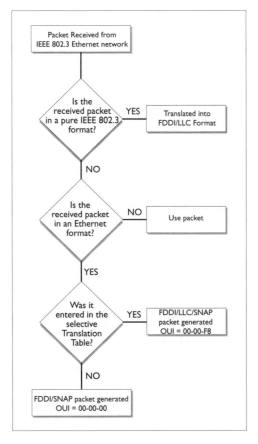

Figure 7.69: Sending from Ethernet/IEEE 802.3 network onto FDDI network

Table 7.32: Relaying an Ethernet/IEEE 802.3 packet on an FDDI network

Is the received packet in a pure Ethernet format?

Was the packet type entered in the selective translation table?

Yes:

- The packet is translated into an FDDI format with the following additions:

  - DSAP = SNAP

  - SSAP = SNAP

  - OUI = 00-00-F8

No:

- The packet is translated into an FDDI format with the following additions according to RFC 1042:

  - DSAP = SNAP

  - SSAP = SNAP

  - OUI = 00-00-00

Is the received packet in a pure IEEE 802.3 format?

- The packet is translated into an FDDI format with an LLC header.

Receiving from the FDDI Network

A translation bridge receives a data packet whose information is destined for the connected Ethernet/IEEE 802.3 network.

1. Initial situation: IEEE 802.3/LLC packet format
   If the packet contains only a pure LLC header (without further SNAP codes), then the packet is translated into an IEEE 802.3/IEEE 802.2 format.

2. Initial situation: IEEE 802.3/LLC/SNAP packet format
   If this packet is encoded according to RFC 1042, then the value of the protocol field is checked.

   - If an entry is found in the selective translation table, the packet is translated into an RFC 1042-compliant format.

   - If the translation bridge does not find an entry, it generates an Ethernet packet.

3. Initial situation: Ethernet packet format (OUI value = 00-00-00)
   If the OUI field was set to the value 00-00-00, the translation bridge searches for the packet protocol type in the selective translation table.

   - If it finds an entry for this protocol identifier, it generates an IEEE 802.3 packet.

   - If no entry is found, it generates an Ethernet packet.

4. Initial situation: Ethernet packet format (OUI value = 00-00-F8)
   If the OUI field was set to the value 00-00-F8, then this packet is in a specially coded format. This packet is therefore converted back into a pure Ethernet packet.

Table 7.33: Relaying an FDDI packet on an Ethernet/IEEE 802.3 network

Does the received packet need to be relayed onto the connected Ethernet/IEEE 802.3 network?
Was the OUI field set to the value 00-00-F8 in the received packet?
Yes: translate into an Ethernet packet format.
No: does the packet conform to the RFC 1042 format?
Is the protocol identifier in the selective translation table?
Yes: translate into an IEEE 802.3 format.
No: translate into an Ethernet packet format.
Does the received packet have pure LLC encoding?
Yes: translate into an IEEE 802.3 format.

This mechanism ensures that by means of the OUI field value 00-00-F8, AppleTalk 1 packets can be transmitted transparently over the FDDI network. After being relayed across the FDDI network, this packet is converted back into an Ethernet format. As a result of the RFC 1042 encoding, after transit AppleTalk 2 packets are converted into IEEE 802.3 packets.

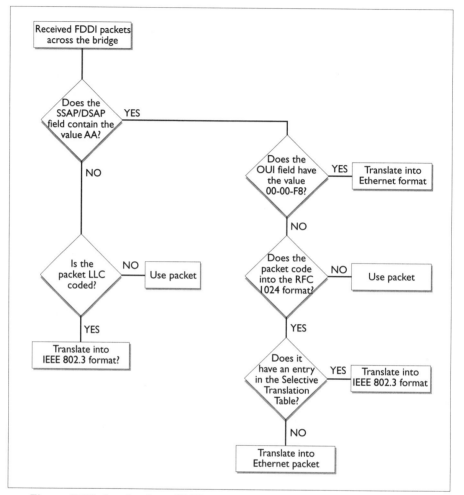

Figure 7.70: Sending from FDDI network onto Ethernet/IEEE 802.3 network

Box: Functions of a Translation Bridge

The following functions are performed when an Ethernet packet is sent over a translation bridge:

Transmitting

- The translation bridge checks whether the destination unit (destination address) is located in the local network (Ethernet) or on the other side of the bridge (FDDI network).

- If the destination unit is on the FDDI network or a further network connected to it, the received data packet is processed further.

- The bit representation of the Ethernet/IEEE 802.3 source and destination addresses is converted. Recall that in Ethernet/IEEE 802.3 packets, the least significant bits are always transmitted first, whereas with FDDI and Token Ring the most significant bits are transmitted first.

- The length and type field and the padding bits in the Ethernet packet are deleted.

- If it is an Ethernet packet, then an LLC SNAP header must be formed automatically.

- The selective translation table is searched for the respective packet protocol type.

- If an entry is found for the packet in question, it is converted into an FDDI packet (LLC/SNAP) and the OUI field is set to 00-00-F8.

- If no entry is found, the packet is translated into an FDDI packet (LLC/SNAP) according to the RFC 1042 rules and the OUI field is set to 00-00-00.

- If the received packet is in the 802.3 format, the translation bridge translates the packet directly into an FDDI packet format.

Receiving

- The translation bridge checks whether the destination unit (destination address) is located in the FDDI network or on the other side of the bridge (Ethernet).

- If the destination unit is on the Ethernet or a further network connected to it, the received data packet is processed further.

- The bit representation of the FDDI source and destination addresses is converted.

- If the packet contains only a pure LLC header (without further SNAP codes), then the packet is converted into an IEEE 802.3/IEEE 802.2 format and a length field is generated.

- If this packet has RFC 1042-compliant encoding, the value of the protocol field is checked.

- If an entry is found in the selective translation table, the packet is translated into an RFC 1042-compliant format and a length field is generated.

- If the translation bridge does not find an entry in the selective translation table, then the EtherType field of the SNAP headers is converted into a type field and an Ethernet packet is generated.

- If the OUI field was set to the value 00-00-00, the translation bridge searches for the packet protocol type in the selective translation table.

- If it finds an entry for this protocol identifier, an IEEE 802.3 packet is generated and a length field is generated.

- If no entry is found in the selective translation table, then the EtherType field of the SNAP header is converted into a type field and an Ethernet packet is generated.

- If the OUI field was set to the value 00-00-F8, then this packet is in a specially coded format. This packet is therefore converted back into a pure Ethernet packet with a type field.

Ethernet Switches with FDDI Ports

Only a translation bridge is possible at the interface between Ethernet switch ports and FDDI. This component must adapt the different data formats on the MAC layer to one another according to the rules set out above. Since this component operates in the store-and-forward mode, it automatically introduces a delay into the communication path. The throughput of the translation bridge is also dependent upon the number of stations attached to the ring and on the respective network load.

FDDI Backbones between Switches

Since the FDDI network has a relatively wide span, it is naturally the preferred method at the moment for constructing large switched LANs. This method can be used if it is ensured that the load on the FDDI is not too high. As an alternative to FDDI, however, the use of ATM for the high-speed backbone should be considered.

7.8.3 Asynchronous Transfer Mode

Currently, the magic word used to conjure up the future of networking is ATM (Asynchronous Transfer Mode). ATM technology has become indispensable in the planning of future networks, both for workgroup/departmental LANs and for backbones. As a consequence of modern data- and processing-intensive applications (such as computer-based audio- and videoconferencing, document sharing, electronic publishing, computer-based training, and other multimedia applications for example), it is predicted that the networks installed to date will not be able to satisfy future demand. Owing to its superior performance, scalable bandwidth, and physical extent, only ATM technology can offer far greater flexibility than the conventional "shared media" networks. For WANs, too, ATM technology offers considerable advantages and is currently seen as the ideal basis for constructing "corporate networks." Its ability to integrate a variety of services, and the fact that it allows—for the first time ever—LANs and WANs as well as voice and data networks to be interconnected using the same technology throughout, means that ATM is ideally placed to revolution-ize communications in the future.

The principal working group defining the ATM standard is the ATM Forum (approx. 500 members) founded in October 1991. The membership of the ATM Forum is comprised of manufacturers, user groups, and other standardization bodies. The objective of the ATM Forum is to promote vigorously the devel-opment and introduction of ATM technology on the market.

Asynchronous Transfer Mode is based on switched connection-oriented LAN and WAN technology. This technology can support a virtually unlimited number of users via dedicated high-speed links with freely scalable bandwidth and a choice of Quality of Service (QoS). With ATM, an exclusive virtual chan-nel is established between the sender and the receiver. The bandwidth for the respective channel can be allocated dynamically depending upon the particu-lar requirement. Moreover, with ATM it is also possible to process a plurality of connections simultaneously with the same ATM bandwidth.

Communication over an ATM network is based on connection-oriented mechanisms. For this, a virtual channel is established between the sender and the receiver over the ATM network. This channel is available exclusively to the two communication partners. Dynamic bandwidth allocation enables the respective channel to request a specific bandwidth with a particular quality of service. Once this connection is set up, the communication partners are assured that they alone can use this channel without any interference, or even interruptions, from other stations wishing to transmit data. It is then possible to transmit continuous data streams such as voice or video information over this fixed virtual channel.

ATM technology allows a large number of simultaneous connections without loss of ATM quality. By way of comparison, with conventional shared network technologies (Ethernet, Token Ring, or FDDI) the entire transmission bandwidth is only available to one station with data to transmit. All other stations wishing to transmit data must wait during this time. Consequently, calculating access times on shared LANs is impossible. Guaranteeing a continuous data stream between the individual stations is also impossible.

The functions of ATM technology can be explained with reference to the ATM layer model. The logical subdivision of the functions required for transmitting, and switching digital signals provides a universal transport infrastructure in the network.

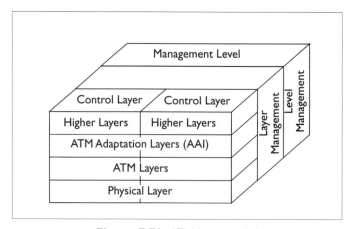

Figure 7.71: ATM layer model

ATM Physical Layer

The lowest layer of the communication model defines the technical functions for transporting the bits on a particular medium. These functions include for instance the bit rate, bit synchronization, line coding, and monitoring functions.

ATM Transport Layer

Located directly above the Physical layer is the ATM Transport layer. This layer provides the ATM-specific cell transport mechanisms. These functions include, for instance, the addressing of the virtual connection, the logical channel number, error correction, priority allocation, bit rate control, and monitoring of the respective agreed bit rate for a channel.

ATM Adaptation Layer

In ATM the adaptation layer provides the functions required for adaptation to the service-specific requirements. In particular, it provides measures for handling signals which compensate for the delay fluctuations or cells lost after transport through the ATM network. This is required, for example, for high-quality voice, music, or video connections. In addition, the adaptation layer supports connections to other transmission methods.

Service Layer

The service layer provides the functions for exchanging service-specific payload information within the ATM connection. It can be used completely freely and transparently by the user.

Control Layer

The control layer is responsible for the functions enabling the exchange of any connection-controlling information between the communication partners on an ATM link. This permits simple implementation of end-to-end signalling.

Decoupling of Service and Transmission Bit Rate

The decoupling provided by ATM of the bit rate required for a service and the bit rate for the transmission path facilitates the adaptation of different services to the network interface. With ATM technology, access to the network is via the User-Network Interface (UNI). If several virtual channels have the same destination, they can be combined to form virtual paths. Redundancy is also provided in the ATM network: if one of the ATM switching units in the network fails, the existing virtual channels are automatically rerouted over other physical paths. The number of services that can be used simultaneously by the user is limited only by the maximum bit rate transmitted on the subscriber line.

Cell Structure

One major feature of ATM technology is that no variable-length data packets are switched. The data to be transmitted is divided into fixed-length cells. This restriction to information of a fixed size has the following advantages:

- The propagation time of a cell through an ATM switch remains small constant, so a cell can be relayed with virtually no delay.

- Due to the cell technique, switching can take place on the hardware layer. This further reduces the processing time in the switch.

Header Format of the ATM Cell

The layer architecture of the ATM Protocol Reference Model is reflected in the structure of the ATM cells. The five-byte long ATM cell header contains all the protocol elements of the Physical layer and of the ATM layer. The information field contains the actual user data (protocol data of the user layers and protocol data of the ATM adaptation layer).

The first four bits of the ATM cell header are used for Generic Flow Control (GFC). This mechanism controls the entry of cells in the ATM data stream from the user to the network depending on the current load on the medium. The GFC is therefore a mechanism for overload/jam control in the ATM network and not an end-to-end controller as is known from other transport layers.

The VPI and VCI identifiers are the destination addresses of the cell and are used for routing the cells through the nodes of the ATM network.

The value of the payload type field indicates the type of data being transported in the ATM cell. The reserved field is unused and is available for any future extensions of the protocol. The Cell Loss Priority (CLP) bit indicates whether the packet may be discarded in the event of unfavorable conditions, such as overloading of the switches or the lines. The CLP depends upon the Quality of Service (QoS) agreed when the connection was set up. The Header

Error Control (HEC) byte is used—as described above—for error correction, i.e., it is comparable with a CRC value. The HEC value is calculated and inserted by the Physical layer.

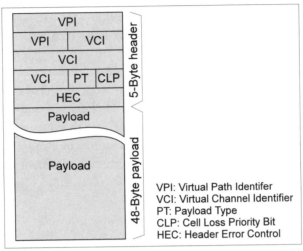

Figure 7.72: Structure of an ATM cell

Physical Access to ATM

The ATM technology supports a number of different physical access types. Both electrical and optical connections are possible, and one can choose from a wide range of different transmission types and transfer rates. Thus the entire digital hierarchy (SDH, Synchronous Digital Hierarchy) from 155.52 to 2488.32 Mbit/s is offered. Several such communication connections are simultaneously possible over an ATM switch. Irrespective of how many stations are connected to a switch, the possible throughput per connected station remains constant. The lowest layer of the ATM Protocol Reference Model is called the Physical Layer. This layer is in turn subdivided into the Physical Medium (PM) sublayer and the Transmission Convergence (TC) sublayer. The role of the PM sublayer is to transmit the bits. Accordingly, the PM sublayer is dependent upon the actual medium used. This sublayer is also responsible for translating signals between the different media.

The following Physical layer standards are defined:

Type	DS-3	STS-1	TAXI	STS-3	STS-3	STS-3
Bandwidth	45 Mb/s	51 Mb/s	100 Mb/s	155 Mb/s	155 Mb/s	155 Mb/s
Comment	OF	TP Cat 3	FDDI PMD	CCITT	Multimode fiber	TP Cat 5
			4B/5B	standard	8B/10B	

The Transmission Convergence (TC) sublayer uses the services of the PM sublayer. This layer is responsible for transmitting the ATM cells, maintaining synchronization between the ATM nodes, and checking that the cell has been correctly received. The TC sublayer is—as all further layers—independent of the transmission medium. In order to send cells, they must be inserted into the ATM data stream. This function is performed by transmission frame adaptation.

ATM Switching Principles

The switching technique of an ATM network is based upon the multiplexing method of transmission. With ATM switching, the cells are switched on the basis of information in the header. Facilities in the switching elements evaluate the header information and control the transport of the cells accordingly. In an ATM network, the cells arrive at the switch at varying intervals. This may be because the source itself generates discontinuous cells or because the traffic intensity of other connections using the same facility (e.g., switching network, multiplexer) varies. As a result of these variations, collisions between cells on different connections simultaneously wishing to use the same facility in the node cannot be ruled out. In order to avoid cell loss, it is therefore necessary to employ buffers in which cells can wait irrespective of the load.

Switching Procedure

The procedure is as follows: each switch has line-specific translation tables containing the address of the ATM cell on the outgoing line. The cell is provided with the new address and routed via the corresponding destination exit to the next switch. This procedure, which is comparable with a time-slot interchange in circuit-switching networks, is repeated until the cell has reached its destination. The translation tables are loaded once when the connection is established and are deleted again when the connection is cleared. These services are provided by the ATM layer. The ATM layer also performs the following four functions:

- Multiplexing cells of a Virtual Path (VP) or Virtual Channel (VC) into the cell stream (network access).

- Mapping the identifiers of received VP and VC cells onto corresponding VP or VC identifiers at the transmitting end (routing).

- Demultiplexing the cells into their Virtual Path or Channel (receiving).

- Generating and removing the ATM header.

An ATM end-to-end connection is a defined sequence of Virtual Channels. These Virtual Channels are defined at connection establishment and are entered in the routing tables of the ATM switches.

Virtual Channel

The concept of a Virtual Channel (VC) describes the unidirectional transport path of ATM cells between two VC switches. A VC is identified by a Virtual Channel Identifier (VCI).

Virtual Path

The concept of a Virtual Path (VP) describes the unidirectional transport of ATM cells from different VCs which are grouped under one Virtual Path Identifier (VPI). VC and VP use the transmission path. Individual VP or VC links are combined on the ATM layer to form VP or VC connections (VCC/VPC) and form an ATM end-to-end connection.

The high bandwidth and the short delay times of ATM switches are usually considered to be the special features of ATM switches. With clever traffic management, ATM switches are able to process different information streams (voice, video, and data) in parallel and respond individually to the specific requirements in question. In ATM switches currently on the market, the following four mechanisms have been implemented to prevent a constant bit rate voice transmission being influenced by a simultaneous high data burst.

- The switch can guarantee a Virtual Channel transmitting real-time information a particular bandwidth. This is done by assigning the channels with a constant bit rate (voice, video) to an output queue with a high priority. Data streams with variable bit rates (compressed voice or data) are assigned to an output queue with a lower priority. To prevent Virtual Channels with a low priority from unnecessarily occupying bandwidth and therefore possibly influencing other connections, a maximum transmission limit is specified for these channels. For the variable bit rates, both a maximum transmission limit and the maximum time in which such a data burst can occur are defined. Note here that the standards for transmitting variable bit rates over ATM have not yet been agreed by the ATM Forum.

- During transmission the ATM switches also ensure that the voice information is not degraded or interrupted due to the transmission of data (e.g., IP information). This is handled by the Usage Parameter Control (UPC), defined in the UNI 3.0 specifications. The UPC algorithm has the task of protecting the network from virtual channels that attempt to use more available bandwidth than they are allotted. By means of the UPC mechanism, ATM switches guarantee the various qualities of service for constant, variable, and non-specific data rates. In the case of constant data rates, a maximum transmission rate is determined for the respective channel. An algorithm known as the leaky bucket algorithm is used to ensure that all cells that exceed the agreed maximum limit are discarded by the switch. A dual bucket policy ensures adherence not only to the maximum transmission load, but also to the maximum duration of a data burst.

- By means of a further mechanism, the switches guarantee that time-critical data traffic is not delayed unnecessarily while being relayed over the switch. In this case, cells with a variable data rate or non-specific data rate are discarded if the bandwidth necessary for the time-critical traffic is no longer sufficient. This is achieved by setting the cell loss priority bit in the respective cell headers.

- The implementation of traffic management algorithms ensures that a particular bandwidth is made available for virtual channels, and cells are discarded according to the random principle if the demand for bandwidth increases. If two virtual channels are using the same port, then in the default setting, each channel is allocated half the available bandwidth. An equality mechanism ensures that each of the two channels may exceed the reserved bandwidth limits if this bandwidth is not required by the neighboring channel.

ATM Adaptation Layer

Building on the features of the ATM layer, the Adaptation Layer provides the functions required for adaptation to the service-specific requirements. The ATM Adaptation Layer (AAL) is situated between the ATM layer and the higher application layers and is subdivided into the following two sublayers:

- Segmentation And Reassembly (SAR) sublayer

- Convergence Sublayer (CS)

The task of the SAR sublayer is to split the Protocol Data Units (PDU) of the higher application layers into ATM format units and correspondingly reassemble the information from the incoming ATM cells to form PDUs. The CS sublayer adapts the different services to the SAR sublayer and accordingly must be realized in a service-specific manner. The protocol information of the AAL is not transported in the header of the ATM cell, but rather in the information field. Functions that support error detection and correction as well as time monitoring are also integrated in the AAL. These functions are matched to the quality of service of the AAL type. The AAL type characteristics are defined on the basis of the different variants of the following parameters:

- Timing relationship between sender and receiver

- Variability of bit rates

- Connectionless or connection-oriented mode

The ATM Reference Model provides for five types of ATM adaptation layers. These match the transport characteristics to the various applications to be transmitted and provide ATM with the desired flexibility.

- AAL 1 emulates circuit-switched services with a constant bit rate, such as the primary rate interface in B-ISDN.

- AAL 2 supports applications with variable bit rates, but which require exact time synchronization. These are compressed audio and video transmissions.

- AAL 3 and AAL 4 are designed for services with a variable bit rate that do not require synchronization. This applies to data-only communications. AAL 3/4 allow connection-oriented and connectionless services such as X.25, Frame Relay, UDP, or TCP/IP.

- AAL 5 is an AAL 3/4 service optimized to high-speed transmissions. AAL 5 will probably replace AAL 3/4 in the long term.

Switching Technology

ATM switching systems usually use switching fabrics instead of internal bus systems. Switching fabrics are synchronous switching networks that can process several connections in parallel without hindering the neighboring connections. A control processor controls and monitors the behavior of the switching fabric with respect to operation, administration, and management (OAM) functions and handles the establishment and clearing of connections. It must be ensured that the switch is "nonblocking."

Management

In contrast to previous network technologies, network management has been defined and integrated in ATM from the outset. The ATM structure shows that both plane management and layer management can be implemented in parallel to the various layers of the ATM Reference Model. All management functions relating to the whole system are covered by the plane management. Layer management covers the operation, administration, and maintenance functions. The management protocol employed is usually the widely used SNMP. Owing to its ability to integrate voice and data networks and to use the same technology for LANs and WANs, network management can be greatly simplified with ATM.

Scalability

ATM networks are able to offer applications exactly the data transmission capacity that they currently need. In addition, ATM networks can be expanded at will. Thus, for the first time in the history of communications, it is possible to use one technology both for local and worldwide communications. Today's networks, such as FDDI for example, do not offer this feature.

Connecting LANs

The ATM Forum has also defined the connection of existing LANs (Ethernet, FDDI) to an ATM network via routers, bridges, and switches. These legacy LANs are currently connected to an ATM network via interconnection components in which an ATM card was directly integrated or via an external ATM adapter. These interconnection components with integrated ATM interfaces relay the LAN packets directly to the ATM board. This board converts the LAN packet according to RFC 1483 and sends this data onto the ATM network. Practical tests have shown that all LAN devices can communicate without problems via the interconnection components with all nodes connected directly to the ATM network (workstations, routers).

ATM Routers

Several network segments are combined to form a logical overall network on Layer 3 of the OSI Reference Model. This makes it possible to set up logically structured networks. Only the lowest two layers of the networks used in data communications are defined in the respective standards. All higher protocols are covered by other standards and specifications. All devices operating on Layer 3 belong to the protocol-specific systems. Devices operating on Layer 3 must be able to understand the respective specific Layer 3 protocols in order to interpret correctly the contents of the received data, and, if necessary, forward it to the receiver. Since a router unpacks each network-specific data packet as far as Layer 3, it is ideally suited to connecting different network topologies such as, for example, Ethernet to Token Ring (802.5), FDDI, ISDN, or ATM. On the path between sender and receiver data, packets can be routed over networks whose maximum permitted packet length is less than the length of the datagrams to be transported. This is the case, for example, at an interface between Ethernet (1514 bytes) and ATM (53 bytes).

If a datagram is awaiting transport in a network at a router which is unable to transmit this data packet in its full length, then the original datagram must be split into several parts. This division into smaller data units is generally referred to as fragmentation. Following this, the resulting datagram fragments are of a suitable length for transmission. The fragments are then transmitted as independent data packets. These fragments can be relayed over different routes to the destination network and reach the destination computer in a different order, so the receiver must be able to pass these data fragments on to the higher protocol layer in the correct order. This procedure is referred to as reassembly.

Router Communication over ATM Networks

Asynchronous Transfer Mode (ATM) is considered to be the network service of the future for use in both local area and wide area networks. In Request for Comments (RFC) 1483 the various functions and mechanisms that allow all standard protocols, such as TCP/IP, Novell IPX, and DECnet, for example, to be transmitted over an ATM network via routers are described. The following variants are available for this on the bottom layer of the ATM protocol stack:

- Multiplexing of several higher protocols over an ATM virtual circuit

- Transmission of each individual protocol over a separate ATM virtual circuit

Multiplexing of Several Higher Protocols

With this method, the higher protocols are multiplexed over an ATM virtual circuit. The respective protocol of a data packet is identified by a preceding IEEE 802.2 Logical Link Control (LLC) header. The Asynchronous Transfer Mode (ATM) is based on the switching of cells and assumes that the variable-length data information of the higher protocols has been segmented into defined cell lengths, or reassembled respectively. With ATM, the data packets of the higher protocols are transported in the payload field of the Common Part Convergence Sublayer (CPCS) Protocol Data Unit (PDU) on the basis of ATM Adaptation Layer type 5 (AAL5).

The AAL5 Frame Format

Whatever multiplexing method used, routed or bridged Protocol Data Units (PDUs) are encapsulated in the payload field of an AAL5 CPCS data frame.

The format of an AAL5 CPCS PDU is as follows:

Table 7.34: AAL5 CPCS PDU format

CPCS PDU Payload
(Up to 2^16 - 1 octets)
PAD (0 - 47 octets)
CPCS UU (1 octet)
CPI (1 octet)
CPCS PDU Trailer
Length (2 octets)
CRC (4 octets)

The payload field can contain higher information with a maximum data content of up to 65535 octets. The PAD field is used to match the CPCS PDUs so that they fit exactly into the ATM cells and to ensure that the last 48-octet long cell of the SAR sublayer contains the CPCS PDU trailer in this cell. The CPCS UU field (User-to-User information) is used for transparent transmission of CPSU user information. Since this field has no function at all with multi-protocol ATM encapsulation, it can be set to any value. The CPI field (Common Part Indicator) defines the length of the CPCS PDU trailer as 64 bits, and in this case it should be encoded as 0x00. The length field defines the length of the payload field in octets. The maximum value of the length field is 65535 octets. A length field encoding of 0x00 indicates that the abort function is activated. The CRC field covers the entire CPCS PDU, with the exception of the CRC field itself.

LLC Encapsulation

The LLC encapsulation function is always used whenever several protocols are to be multiplexed onto an ATM Virtual Circuit (VC). To ensure that the receiver can also process the AAL5 CPCS PDU correctly, the payload field must contain all the information that allows the respective protocol to be uniquely identified. LLC encapsulation provides for this information to be encoded in the LLC header. With LLC encapsulation, the respective routed protocol is defined by an IEEE 802.2 LLC header placed in front of the actual data packet. The LLC header is augmented by an IEEE 802.1a SubNetwork Attachment

Point (SNAP) header. When data is transmitted in LLC type 1 mode (unacknowledged connectionless mode), the LLC header consists of three 1-octet long fields:

DSAP	SSAP	Ctrl

The control field (Ctrl) always has the value 0x03 (unnumbered information command).

The LLC header value 0xFE-FE-03 indicates that a routed ISO PDU follows. In this case the AAL5 CPSC PDU payload field is as follows:

Table 7.35: Payload format for routed ISO PDUs

LLC 0xFE-FE-03
ISO PDU|
(Up to 65532 octets)

The routed ISO protocol is defined by the 1 octet-long NLPID field. The NLPID field is part of the protocol data and the respective values are defined by the ISO or CCITT bodies.

Table 7.36: Important NLPID values

0x00	Null network layer
0x80	SNAP
0x81	ISO CLNP
0x82	ISO ESIS
0x83	ISO ISIS
0xCC	Internal IP

Since the NLPID value 0x00 has no significance for LLC encapsulation, this form is not used in an ATM network. Although a separate NLPID value (0xCC) is defined for the Internet Protocol (IP), the IP is treated like all other non-ISO protocols and transported using an SNAP header. The SNAP header is defined in the LLC header by the following value combination: 0xAA-AA-00. The SNAP header has the following format:

OUI	PID

The three-octet long OUI (organizationally-unique identifier) value specifies which organization has defined the respective meaning of the following two-octet long Protocol Identifier (PID) field. An OUI value of 0x00-00-00 indicates that the PID field is to be interpreted as an EtherType field. The format of the AAL5 CPCS PDU payload field for non-ISO protocols is illustrated in the following figure.

Payload Format for Routed Non-ISO PDUs

LLC 0xAA-AA-03
OUI 0x00-00-00
EtherType (2 octets)
Non-ISO PDU
(Up to 65527 octets)

When an SNAP header is used and a following Internet Protocol, the EtherType field is set to the value 0x08-00 in accordance with Request for Comments (RFC) 1042.

Table 7.37: Payload format for routed IP PDUs

LLC 0xAA-AA-03
OUI 0x00-00-00
EtherType 0x08-00
IP PDU
(Up to 65527 octets)

Virtual Circuit (VC) Multiplexing

With Virtual Circuit (VC) multiplexing a separate ATM channel is made available for each higher protocol. In the future, VC-based multiplexing will be used mainly in private ATM networks, since dynamically setting up a plurality of parallel ATM channels is very quick and also very economical. LLC encapsulation is only employed where it is impracticable to open an individual separate channel for each protocol or each application. The method of multiplexing used can either be configured manually (in the case of PVCs) or it can be set by an internal signalling procedure (in the case of switched VCs).

When transmitting data information between two ATM stations using the Virtual Circuit multiplexing technique, a separate channel is opened for each higher protocol. For this reason, it is unnecessary to integrate the respective multiplex information in the payload field of an AAL5 CPCS PDU. Naturally, this reduces both the bandwidth occupied on the medium and the processing overhead considerably.

All higher protocols that are not bridged are transmitted in the payload field of the AAL5 CPCS PDU and have the following format:

Table 7.38: Payload format for routed PDUs

Carried PDU
(Up to 65535 octets)

Switches/Bridges to ATM

Local Area Networks have become firmly established among users as a core data communications concept. Over these networks, users can exchange data at a high speed with any attached computer. However these Local Area Networks are beginning to reach their logical and physical limits. LANs always operate according to the broadcast principle, i.e., information is sent to all stations over the whole network, but only the station with the relevant hardware address actually evaluates the information. This mode of operation automatically means that data traffic increases as the number of connected stations grows. This can lead to network overload and consequently to unacceptably long response times within the applications.

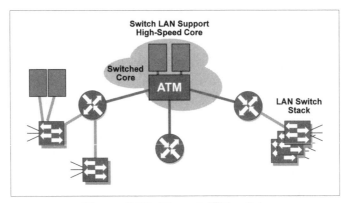

Figure 7.73: Ethernet ATM switch

For transmission of data packets on an ATM network by means of a bridge/switch, the interface to the ATM network must support the following minimum functions:

- Flooding
- Forwarding
- Filtering

Flooding

With the flooding function all data packets are sent to all connected destination addresses. In an ATM environment, this means that these data packets will be relayed over all Virtual Circuits (VCs) present. This is realized by means of a mechanism which ensures that these data packets are transmitted on every VC or that a multicast VC is employed.

Forwarding

In order to transport data packets from one data network to another, the switch/bridge must be able to associate the destination addresses with a VC. In practice, this means that it is not possible to implement a static configuration in which all possible destination MAC addresses are entered manually for each VC. For this reason, the ATM switch/bridge must have a mechanism integrated at the ATM interface which allows it to learn all the destination addresses dynamically without any assistance from the administrator. This learning function can be realized on the basis of the destination address field in the ATM PDU. Using the address algorithm of the switch/bridge, it is possible to recognize all the addresses on the respective network and to create a kind of transport table. If a device on the network tries to establish a connection, a data packet is sent to the receiver. The bridge then reads from this data packet the part of the information containing the destination address and compares this address with the entries in its table.

Filtering

The learning function allows the switch/bridge to transmit only such ATM frames on the network whose destination addresses are located on the connected network. This is performed by looking up the dynamically-maintained transport table. The bridge makes a logical decision whether to transmit a data packet over the switch/bridge or to keep it on the local network. Only data to be relayed over the connected networks actually reaches other subnetworks. This frees the connected subnetwork from unnecessary load.

Customized Filter

An additional mechanism allows bridges to filter data or certain events. The operator of a network is consequently able to put individual communication structures in place.

Connecting Data Networks by Means of a Switch/Bridge

The different functions and mechanisms that enable data packets to be transmitted from bridges over an ATM network are described in Request for Comments (RFC) 1483. The following variants are possible:

- Multiplexing of several higher protocols over an ATM virtual circuit

- Transmission of each individual protocol over a separate ATM virtual circuit

- Multiplexing of several higher protocols

With this method several higher protocols are multiplexed over an ATM virtual circuit. The respective higher protocol of a data packet is indicated by an IEEE 802.2 Logical Link Control (LLC) header placed in front. This method is also known as LLC encapsulation. LLC encapsulation was standardized in the Request for Comments 1209 (The Transmission of IP Datagrams over the SMDS Service). The Asynchronous Transfer Mode (ATM) is based on cell switching, for which the prerequisite is that the variable-length data information of the higher protocols is segmented into defined cell lengths then subsequently reassembled. With ATM, the data packets of the higher protocols are transported in the payload field of the Common Part Convergence Sublayer (CPCS) Protocol Data Unit (PDU) on the basis of ATM Adaptation layer type 5 (AAL5). In the future, VC-based multiplexing will be used mainly in private ATM networks, since dynamically setting up a plurality of parallel ATM channels is very quick and also very economical. LLC encapsulation is only employed where it is impracticable to open an individual, separate channel for each protocol or each application.

- Transmission of protocols over separate ATM channels

This method provides a separate ATM channel for each higher protocol. This method is generally referred to as VC-based multiplexing. In applications in which the data traffic of regular networks is exchanged by means of two ATM stations, the method of multiplexing used can either be configured manually (in the case of PVCs) or in the case of B-ISDN, it can be set by an internal signalling procedure (in the case of switched VCs).

The AAL5 Frame Format

Whether the multiplexing method used is routed or bridged, Protocol Data Units (PDUs) are encapsulated in the payload field of an AAL5 CPCS data frame.

The format of an AAL5 CPCS PDU is as follows:

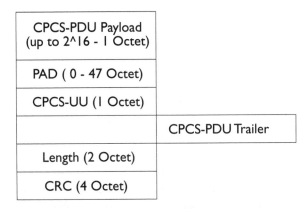

Figure 7.74: AAL5 CPCS PDU format

The payload field can contain higher information with a maximum data content of up to 65,535 octets. The PAD field is used to match the CPCS PDUs so that they fit exactly into the ATM cells and to ensure that the last 48-octet long cell of the SAR sublayer contains the CPCS PDU trailer in this cell. The CPCS UU field (User-to-User information) is used for transparent transmission of CPSU user information. Since this field has no function at all with multi-protocol ATM encapsulation, it can be set to any value. The CPI field (Common Part Indicator) defines the length of the CPCS PDU trailer as 64 bits, and in this case, it should be encoded as 0x00. The length field defines the length of the payload field in octets. The maximum value of the length field is 65,535 octets. A length field encoding of 0x00 indicates that the abort function is activated. The CRC field covers the entire CPCS PDU, with the exception of the CRC field itself.

LLC Encapsulation for Bridged/Switched Networks

The LLC encapsulation function is always used whenever several protocols are to be multiplexed onto an ATM Virtual Circuit (VC). To ensure that the receiver can also process the AAL5 CPCS PDU correctly, the payload field must contain all the information that permits the respective protocol to be uniquely identified. LLC encapsulation provides for this information to be encoded in the LLC header. The data is always transmitted as LLC type 1 (unacknowledged connectionless mode). The LLC header consists of the following three 1-octet long fields:

Table 7.39: 802.2 header

DSAP = AA	SSAP = AA	Control field
I byte	I byte	I byte

The LLC header is augmented by an IEEE 802.1a SubNetwork Attachment Point (SNAP) header. The respective data format of the local network is defined in the SNAP header.

Table 7.40: SNAP header

OUI field	Type field I
3 bytes	2 bytes

When bridging/switching functions are used on an ATM network, the following LLC header values are used: 0xAA-AA-03. Organization code 0x00-80-C2 is used as the value of the OUI field in an 802.1 SNAP header. In the following PID field, a two-octet long code defines the type of bridged network attached. The following values have been defined for this:

Table 7.41: List of all defined values of the OUI 00-80-C2 field

With FCS	Without FCS	Medium
0x00-01	0x00-07	802.3/Ethernet
0x00-02	0x00-08	802.4
0x00-03	0x00-09	802.5
0x00-04	0x00-0A	FDDI
0x00-05	0x00-0B	802.6
	0x00-0D	Fragments
	0x00-0E	BPDUs

In addition, the PID field specifies whether the Frame Check Sequence (FCS) of the original frame to be transmitted is to be retained in the ATM frames or not. Defined PAD information is inserted after the PID field as required so that the user information field is always padded out to the four-octet format. With bridged data information the AAL5 CPCS PDU payload field has the following format:

Table 7.42: Payload format for bridged Ethernet/802.3 PDUs

LLC 0xAA-AA-03
OUI 0x00-80-C2
PID 0x00-01 or 0x00-07
PAD 0x00-00
MAC destination address
(Continuation of MAC frame)
LAN FCS (where PID = 0x00-01)|

Table 7.43: Payload format for bridged 802.5 PDUs

LLC 0xAA-AA-03
OUI 0x00-80-C2
PID 0x00-03 or 0x00-09
PAD 0x00-00-XX
Frame control (1 octet)
MAC destination address
(Continuation of MAC frame)
LAN FCS (where PID = 0x00-03)

The 802.5 Access Control (AC) field has no significance outside an IEEE 802.5 Local Area Network. For this reason it is treated like the last octet of the three-octet long PAD field and can be set to any value.

Table 7.44: Payload format for bridged FDDI PDUs

LLC 0xAA-AA-03
OUI 0x00-80-C2
PID 0x00-04 or 0x00-0A
PAD 0x00-00-00
Frame control (1 octet)
MAC destination address
(Continuation of MAC frame)
LAN FCS (where PID = 0x00-04)

Virtual Circuit (VC) Multiplexing

When transmitting data information between two ATM stations using the Virtual Circuit multiplexing technique, a separate channel is opened for each higher protocol. For this reason, it is unnecessary to integrate the respective multiplex information in the payload field of an AAL5 CPCS PDU. This reduces considerably both the bandwidth occupied on the medium and the processing overhead. The respective multiplexing method can be either manually configured or dynamically activated by a signalling procedure when a connection is established.

VC Multiplexing for Bridged/Switched Protocols

If data is relayed over a bridge onto the ATM field, then this information is likewise transported in an AAL5 CPCS PDU. In contrast to the LLC encapsulation method, only the PID field is inserted into the header. The PID field defines the type of bridged network attached by means of a two-octet code. The same PID field codes as for the LLC encapsulation method are used for this. In this case the AAL5 CPCS PDU payload field has the following format:

Table 7.45: Payload format for bridged/switched Ethernet/802.3 PDUs

PAD 0x00-00
MAC destination address
(Continuation of MAC frame)
LAN FCS (VC-dependent)

Table 7.46: Payload format for bridged/switched 802.5/FDDI PDUs

PAD 0x00-00-00 or 0x00-00-XX
Frame control (1 octet)
MAC destination address
(Continuation of MAC frame)
LAN FCS (VC-dependent)

Table 7.47: Payload format for BPDUs

BPDU as defined by
802.1(d) or 802.1(g)

When transmitting data information of Ethernet, 802.3, 802.5, and FDDI data packets, the respective channel (VC) must define whether the respective LAN Frame Check Sequence (FCS) is integrated in the ATM PDU or not.

7.8.4 Token Ring

The most popular form of a LAN with a ring topology is the Token Ring network. With a ring topology, end stations are interconnected in a physical ring. Each end station has exactly one defined predecessor and one successor. All the devices connected to the ring are loaded equally with the entire data traffic. With the usual access methods all the data is passed through all the individual stations, so not only the failure of the cable, but also the failure of one station leads to a complete communications breakdown. A dual ring is used to counter this serious drawback. Consequently, recovery is possible both from cable faults and from a station failure.

There are also mechanisms for a single ring which allow a defective station to be physically bridged. International standardization of the Token Ring took place in the IEEE 802.5 group. The first generations of Token Ring components operated exclusively at a transfer rate of 4 Mbit/s. At the end of the 1980s the standard was extended to include a further data rate of 16 Mbit/s.

The sole standardized transmission medium for Token Ring at present is four-wire Shielded Twisted Pair (STP) cable. However, demands for a greater transmission range have necessitated the use of fiber-optic converters. For this reason the IEEE is currently endeavoring to unify the various requirements for fiber-optic transmission (IEEE 802.5 Draft J).

The Token Ring topology comprises four star points interconnected in the form of a ring. In turn, end stations are attached to these points in the form of star. In a Token Ring network, the stations are connected in series as a physical/logical ring. Each station therefore has exactly one defined predecessor and one successor. The Token Ring technique is a deterministic access method with which it is possible to calculate exactly the maximum time it will take for a station to send data onto the network. The permission to send is passed here from one end station to the next in the form of a token, so that each end station has a specified amount of time for sending its data onto the network. The token is received by every station. If a station has no data to send, it simply forwards the free token unchanged on the medium. If a station does have data to transmit, it changes the free token into a busy token then sends it back on to the cable immediately followed by its data. The data packet is now read and regenerated unchanged by all the stations until it reaches the receiver. The destination station, which is identified by its physical address, copies the packet into its memory, attaches an acknowledgment flag to it (response bits), and returns it onto the cable. This pattern of bits is then forwarded—again unchanged—until it reaches the station that originally sent the data. This station checks whether the data has been transmitted correctly, removes the data and the busy token from the network, and inserts a new free token on the ring.

The station cannot transmit new data immediately. In the most favorable case, a station wishing to transmit must wait for a complete ring cycle before it may send data on the network again. In the worst case, first all other stations will send data over the network. Due to the frequently unnecessary circulation of the token, however, a lot of bandwidth is lost with the Token Ring technique. In order to get around this disadvantage, newer token access techniques (e.g., FDDI and 16 Mbit/s Token Ring) employ the early token release mechanism. After a data packet is sent, a new free token is generated immediately so that more than one data packet may be circulating on the ring.

Token Ring Bridges

As with Ethernet, Token Ring bridges also operate on the Medium Access Control (MAC) layer. At the same time as it presented the Token Ring in 1985, IBM also put forward an alternative to the conventional transparent transmission of data over bridges, the source routing method. With source routing, information about the transport path is transmitted with the information in the data packet so that the routing decision is then devolved to the end stations. The Ethernet and Token Ring methods use the same address format in the header, which comprises the destination address to which the packet is to be sent (destination) and the source address of the station where the message originated (source). With transparent bridges (Ethernet and FDDI), no further addressing is used. Using the source routing method, the addressing scheme is extended to enable packets to be sent over multiple bridges on the LAN. Since no differentiation between individual and group address (I/G bit) is required in the source address (a packet may be sent to a plurality of stations which have the same group address, but it can never be sent by more than one particular station on the network), the source routing method uses this I/G bit as a Routing Information Indicator (RII).

If the RII is set to the value 1, this indicates that the header contains additional routing information. This additional information may be up to 18 bytes long and describes the complete path that the data packet must travel from the source station to the destination station. In order to utilize this function, every LAN subnetwork must be allocated its own unique network number.

In principle, the routing information is a list of all subnetworks through which the packet must pass. Besides the ring number however, further information is required to describe fully the route between source and destination. In practice the situation may arise where there is more than one bridge for interconnecting two subnetworks. If parallel bridges like this are set up, it is imperative that they are assigned a unique identifier (bridge ID).

Source Routing

The term source routing describes very appositely the technical basis of the method. The sender, also called source, defines exactly the route a frame is to travel between the originator and destination by inserting a routing information field which describes the complete path to the destination into the header of the data packet.

The first two bytes of the routing information field are always control bytes. The first three bits (B) of these bytes contain information about the following LLC header, the L-bits define the length of the following routing information, and the R-bit indicates the direction in which this information is to be interpreted. The F-bits specify the maximum length of the data packet that can be processed on the transmission segment, and the X-bits are reserved for future application-specific information. In general, a routing information field can contain up to 18 bytes of routing information (including the two control bytes). A ring number, which is always a 12-bit value, is combined with a 4-bit long bridge ID to form a 2-byte information unit. In practice, this means that the available 18-byte routing information (minus the two-byte control field) can contain a maximum of 8 ring numbers.

A data packet can therefore be relayed over 8 networks and a maximum of 7 bridges en route between the sender and the receiver. The maximum size of a configuration of Token Rings employing source routing bridges is therefore limited to 7 hops (transfers between subnetworks). In order to be able to relay the data packets correctly, a source routing bridge must receive all data packets on each connected segment.

If the routing information indicator in a packet has the value 0, the bridge knows that the information in this data packet does not contain any routing information and is therefore intended for a station in the local subnetwork. The bridge therefore ignores such packets, i.e., the data traffic remains local and is not relayed onto other subnetworks. If a data packet with a set RII bit is received, the bridge must evaluate the routing information that follows. The bridge checks here whether the connected ring numbers and its own ring number match, i.e., whether this information is represented in the correct order in the routing information field. If all this information matches, this data packet is relayed onto the other subnetwork. All other frames are not relayed. The technical term for this is filtering.

Connection Between Ethernet Switches and Token Rings

A Token Ring network and an Ethernet LAN are connected on the basis of various address, protocol, and packet formats of Layer 2 over store-and-forward bridges.

Encapsulation Bridges

The simplest type of bridge is an encapsulation bridge. This component is only used in cases where the Token Ring network is to be used solely as a transit LAN. These bridges do not analyze or interpret the data traffic in any way. Instead they encapsulate all the received data packets in their entirety into a Token Ring data packet and forward them in transit to a destination bridge. The destination bridge analyzes the Token Ring packet and removes the Ethernet packet from the data field. This packet is then forwarded unchanged on the connected LAN segment.

A typical application for a Token Ring encapsulation bridge described as follow: Two Ethernet switches are interconnected via an existing Token Ring network. A transparent data channel is created between the two LANs over the Token Ring network. The Token Ring bridges encapsulate the data in Token Ring data formats for transport over the Token Ring network. Since there is no generally agreed standard for transparent encapsulation of LAN data in a Token Ring frame, only encapsulation bridges from the same manufacturer can communicate with one another. In practice, this means that all stations (workstations, PCs, file servers, routers) connected to the Token Ring are not able to communicate with LANs connected to encapsulation bridges.

Advantages of Token Ring Encapsulation Bridges

- Quick to install without any great configuration effort
- No conversion of the information into other packet formats required
- No adaptation problems with the different bridging mechanisms (Spanning Tree, source routing)
- Much faster than translation bridges

Disadvantages of Token Ring Encapsulation Bridges

- Proprietary standard
- Products are usually limited to only one manufacturer
- As a rule products cannot be retrofitted with translation bridge functionality
- No communication is possible with end stations connected directly to the Token Ring

Token Ring Translation Bridges

Ethernet data formats are converted directly into Token Ring packets on Layer 2 by means of translation bridges. The translation bridge converts the various address, protocol, and packet formats. Since Ethernet uses the Spanning Tree bridging method and Token Ring uses source routing mechanisms for managing redundant segments, in some circumstances problems may arise if the translation bridge is not configured correctly.

With Ethernet/Token Ring translation bridges, the different lengths of the respective data packets must be taken into account. In principle, every Ethernet packet can be translated into a Token Ring packet format. The size of an Ethernet packet is between 64 and 1518 bytes. The length of a Token Ring packet may be between 32 and 4500 bytes. These specifications ensure that every Ethernet packet can be converted into a Token Ring packet. The opposite direction (Token Ring to Ethernet/IEEE 802.3) does pose some problems. At present no standardized data link fragmentation method is defined with which it is possible to split large Token Ring packets on Layer 2 into several Ethernet packets. The Token Ring frames in the individual stations are therefore restricted by the system configuration to the maximum size of Ethernet packets. This has an effect on performance. It is no longer possible to utilize the full bandwidth, or the maximum packet length, for a file transfer between the Token Ring stations. Consequently, it is necessary to transmit more packets between the two stations to transfer the file.

The Token Ring and the Ethernet/IEEE 802.3 methods both employ the same address formats (6 bytes). With Ethernet, the most significant bit is always transmitted first, whereas with Token Ring the least significant bit is transmitted first. The translation bridge has to expand the address at the gateway between these two media. Since the Token Ring does not have a type field, this field must be inserted at the interface and subsequently removed automatically. The IEEE 802.3 and the Token Ring frame format do not use an LLC header on Layer 2b. It is therefore a relatively simple matter to convert this data. If an Ethernet packet is to be relayed on a Token Ring or vice versa, however, it must be ensured that the translation bridge automatically inserts/discards the LLC header.

At the interface between Ethernet/IEEE 802.3 and Token Ring networks, source routing and transparent bridging methods must be combined with one another. Unfortunately the standardization bodies have not yet developed any techniques for adapting these two incompatible bridge mechanisms to one another. The simplest method is to buffer the source routing information in the translation bridge. The entire data packet is then forwarded transparently on the Ethernet. In this case, the bridge acts as an endpoint for the source routing information. If packets are sent from the Ethernet onto a Token Ring network, the translation bridge examines the respective source and destination addresses. If it is a new connection, then the bridge must dispatch a route discovery frame. If it is an existing connection, then the translation bridge appends the previously buffered source routing information to the header.

7.9 Markets, Trends and Outlook For the Future

As with all new technologies and trends, LAN switching also has its origins in the USA. In Europe the latest developments are not always adopted immediately. Europeans tend to follow a wait-and-see strategy, taking their time to become acquainted with a new development. This reticence is not attributable to any lack of willingness to invest. The market for network components purchased in Europe has since risen to over five billion US$ per annum. Communications technology especially is profiting from the economic recovery, and in many cases procurement managers in companies are again having much bigger budgets at their disposal. All international studies are producing optimistic forecasts, and switching in combination with Fast Ethernet or ATM technology is being acclaimed as a future-proof solution. However increasing the performance of networks is not possible without comprehensively redesigning the infrastructure. At the moment it is not multimedia applications that are overloading networks, the bandwidth is being demanded for the introduction of client/server applications and groupware solutions. Additional applications and network expansion then quickly lead to performance bottlenecks.

According to all predictions, the switching market (LAN and ATM switching) will see explosive growth over the next few years.

A study conducted by the American firm Strategic Networks Consulting (August 1994) states that the following components were sold worldwide in 1993:

- 7 to 8 million Ethernet ports (adapter cards, repeaters, hubs)

- 2 to 3 million Token Ring ports

- 60 to 70 thousand FDDI ports

In total the Ethernet market in 1993 was worth 1.1 to 1.2 billion US dollars. The size of the market for switched LANs (mainly Ethernet) has developed since 1993 as follows:

Year	Sales Volume
1993	100 million US$
1994	300 million US$
1995	900 million US$
1996	2.7 billion US$
1997	3.6 billion US$
1998	7.1 billion US$

These figures assume that the manufacturers of LAN products (hubs, routers etc.) will move over very quickly to supplying switching technology. According to studies carried out by some large hub manufacturers, the costs of a switched network in comparison with a routed network are more favorable by a factor of between 7% and 14%. For this reason, switching technology has a good chance of completely replacing the venerable repeater technology and establishing itself as the standard transmission technology in LANs. Switches today provide all the functions being demanded by network operators. In a survey conducted by Datacom, the German publishers, respondents cited the following criteria:

- Simple migration (77 percent)
- Technical simplicity (74 percent)
- Investment protection (73 percent)
- cost-effective solution (70 percent)

Price Per Port vs. Megabits per $

A favorite ploy of sales and marketing managers is to represent the various given facts in the best possible light. A particular favorite is the price per port calculation. We assume a 10 port device costing, for example, $6,725. The simplest way to differentiate this device from the competition is to declare the lowest price per port ($675) on the market. Since the competition is something like $170 per port more expensive, a customer who does not possess very much detailed knowledge can often be forced into a purchasing decision. If one looks at this device with a critical eye and calculates its effective bandwidth, then one will very quickly discover that despite the higher price, the competitor does have a clear edge. The correct formula should therefore be as follows:

$$\text{Price/performance} \quad \frac{(\text{Price per port})\,(\text{Number of ports})}{(\text{Total throughput})\,(\text{Effectiveness})}$$

. To come back to the example of crossbar matrix switches with input buffers once more, the calculation would be as follows:

$$\text{Price/performance} = \frac{(\$675)\,(10)}{(50 \text{ Mbit/s})\,(58\%)} = \$232.76 \text{ per Mbit/s}$$

Although the competitor's product has a much higher price per port, it has a much better performance due to its completely different architecture. With this device the price/performance ratio is calculated as follows:

$$\text{Price/performance} = \frac{(\$845)\,(12)}{(60\ \text{Mbit/s})\,(99\%)} = \$171 \text{ per Mbit/s}$$

As can be seen from these two examples, with an Ethernet switch it is not just the price per port that counts, the performance of the device is also important.

Bibliography

Steven Baker
Just holding hands, Interoperability Vol 3/ No 2, LAN Magazine, San Francisco October 1992.

Howard Baldwin
Working with an Ethernet, Unix World, June 1990.

Wolfgang Bernau-Kasperki
Strukturierte Verkabelungssysteme [Structured Cabling Systems], Technik-News 8/92, COMPU-SHACK, Neuwied.

Dimitri Bertsekas/Robert Gallager
Data Networks, (Second Edition) Prentice-Hall International Editions, Eaglewood Cliffs, New Jersey 1992.

Uyless Black
OSI: A model for Computer Communication Standards, Prentical-Hall, Eaglewood Cliffs, New Jersey 1991.

Uyless Black
Network Management Standards, McGraw-Hill, Inc., New York 1992.

Uyless Black
TCP/IP and related Protocols, McGraw-Hill, Inc., New York 1992.

Uyless Black
OSI: A model for Computer Communication Standards, Prentice-Hall, Eaglewood Cliffs, New Jersey 1991.

Detlef Borchers
Und der Sieger heißt: NetWare contra LAN Manager [And The Winner Is: NetWare versus LAN Manager], IX Multiuser-Multitasking-Magazin September 1992, Hans Heise Verlag, Hannover.

Petra Borowka
Bridges und Router [Bridges and Routers], Datacom 1992, Datacom Buchverlag, Bergheim 1992.

Petra Borowka
Strukturierung von Netzen mit Brücken und Routern [Structuring of Networks with Bridges and Routers], Ethernet Impulse 1990, Datacomverlag.

Petra Borowka/Mathias Hein
Hub-Systeme, Funktionen-Konzepte-Einsatzgebiete [Hub Systems, Functions, Concepts, Application Areas], November 1994, Datacom Buchverlag, Bergheim 1994.

William Beyda
Basic Datacommunications: a Comprehensive Overview, Simon & Schuster International Group, Hemel Hempstead 1991.

Richard Caruso
Cooperating to achieve global communications, IEEE Communications Magazine, October 1992.

Jeff Case/ Keith McCloghrie/ Marshal Rose/ Steve Waldbusser
The Simple Management Protocol and Framework, CONNEXIONS, The Interoperability Report, October 1992, Interop Company, Mountain View.

Cabletron Systems
Network Management, Cabletron Systems GmbH, 1990.

CCITT
CCITT X.208, "Specification of Abstract Syntax Notation One (ASN.1)," Geneva 1988.

CCITT
CCITT X.209, "Specification of Basic Encoding Rules for Abstract Notation One (ASN.1)," Geneva 1988.

Peter Chylla/Heinz Gerd Hegering
Ethernet LANs, Datacom Buchverlag, Bergheim 1987.

Codenoll
The Fiber Optic LAN Handbook, Codenoll Technology Corporation, Yonkers 1992.

Frank Corr/John Hunter
Worldwide communications and information systems, IEEE Communications Magazine, October 1992.

J.Davis/N.Dinn/W.Falconer
Technologies for global communications, IEEE Communications Magazine, October 1992.

Rick Davis
Fast Packet Switching in Ethernet, LANline 7/92, AWi Aktuelles Wissen Verlags GmbH, Trostberg.

Digital Equipment Corp., Intel Corp, Xerox Corp.
The Ethernet Version 1.0, 1980.

Digital Equipment Corp., Intel Corp, Xerox Corp.
The Ethernet Version 2.0, 1982.

Avi Fogel/Michael Rothenberg
LAN wiring hubs can be critical points of failure, LAN TIMES, McGraw Hill's Network Computing Publication, January 1991.

Avi Fogel/Michael Rothenberg
Why synchronous Ethernet is in your future, LAN Technology, September 1990.

Glaser, Hein, Vogl
TCP/IP Protokolle, Projektplanung, Realisierung [TCP/IP Protocols, Project Planning, Implementation], Datacomverlag, Bergheim 1990.

Gerhard Glaser
(LAN-) Analysatoren und Netzwerkmanagement [(LAN) Analyzers and Network Management], Datacom Netzwerk Management Special, Datacomverlag, Bergheim 1990.

Gerhard Glaser
Kriterien zum Einsatz und Auswahl von LAN-Analysatoren [Criteria for the Use and Selection of LAN Analyzers], Datacom June 1990, Datacomverlag, Bergheim.

Gerhard Glaser/Mathias Hein
Auswahlkriterien für Terminalserver [Selection Criteria for Terminal Servers], Datacom January 1992, Datacomverlag, Bergheim.

Gerhard Glaser/Mathias Hein
Das TCP/IP Kompendium [The TCP/IP Compendium], Datacom 1993, Datacomverlag, Bergheim.

Michael Grimshaw
LAN Interconnections Technology, Telecommunications (North American Edition), February 1991.

Wolfgang Haupt
Moderne Anschlußtechnik, der Weg zur universellen Lösung [Modern Connection Systems, the Way to a Universal Solution], LANline 6/92, Adcomp GmbH, Munich.

John Henshall/Sandy Shaw
OSI Explained, Simon & Schuster International Group, Hemel Hempstead 1991.

Mathias Hein
In Zukunft kein LAN mehr ohne Bridge [No LAN Without a Bridge in the Future], Datacom 5/87 Datacomverlag.

Mathias Hein/Wolfgang Kemmler
FDDI, Standards-Komponenten-Realisierung [FDDI, Standards, Components, Implementation], Thomson Publishing Verlag, Bonn 1994.

Mathias Hein/David Griffiths
SNMP, Simple Network Management Protocol Version 2, Thomson Publishing Verlag, Bonn 1994.

Mathias Hein/David Griffiths
Ethernet Buyers Guide, Datacom Verlag, Bergheim 1994.

Mathias Hein
Fibre Distributed Data Interface, Datacom 5/90 Datacomverlag, Bergheim.

Mathias Hein
Internet Protokoll auf IEEE 802.3 Netzen [Internet Protocol on IEEE 802.3 Networks], Datacom 7/90 Datacomverlag, Bergheim.

Mathias Hein
Protokoll Networking, Datacom 3/91, Datacomverlag, Bergheim.

Mathias Hein
TCP/IP auf FDDI Netzen [TCP/IP on FDDI Networks], Datacom 10/92, Datacomverlag, Bergheim 1992.

Mathias Hein/Dr. Andreas Rendel
Auswahlkriterien für Bridges [Selection Criteria for Bridges], Datacom 10/88 Datacomverlag.

Mathias Hein/Dr. Andreas Rendel
Fehlertolerante Datennetze [Fault-tolerant Data Networks], NTZ Informationstechnik und Telematik für Experten, VDE Verlag, Berlin 11/1991.

Mathias Hein/Dr. Andreas Rendel
Strukturierte Verkabelung, Bausteine zur Realisierung [Structured Cabling, Components for Implementation], Netztechnik 1/92, VTI Verlag, Frankfurt.

Mathias Hein/Dr. Andreas Rendel
Strukturierte Verkabelung, Bausteine zur Realisierung [Structured Cabling, Components for Implementation], Netztechnik 2/92, VTI Verlag, Frankfurt.

Mathias Hein/Dr. Andreas Rendel
SNA-Routing in Wide Area Networks, Datacom 2/92 Datacomverlag, Bergheim.

Mathias Hein/Dr. Andreas Rendel
Beherrschen durch Teilen—LAN Bridges [Divide and Rule—LAN Bridges], Datacom 1/92 Datacomverlag, Bergheim.

Mathias Hein/ Gerd Schliebusch
Modulare Architektur beseitigt Engpässe [Modular Architecture Eliminates Bottlenecks], VMEbus Magazin Nürnberg, 2/90.

Gilbert Held
Ethernet Networks, Design-Implementation-Operation-Management, John Wiley & Sons, Inc., New York 1994.

Gilbert Held
Local Area Network Performance, John Wiley & Sons, Inc., New York 1994.

IEEE 802-1990
IEEE Standard, Overview and Architecture, IEEE, New York 1990.

ISO/IEC 8802-3
ANSI/IEEE Std 802.3, Part 3: Carrier sense multiple access with collision detection (CSMA/CD) access method and physical layer specifications, IEEE, New York 1993.

ISO/IEC 8802-3d
ANSI/IEEE Std 802.3d, Supplement to Carrier sense multiple access with collision detection (CSMA/CD) access method and physical layer specifications, Type 10Base-T Medium Attachment Unit (MAU) (Section 6), IEEE, New York 1993.

ISO/IEC 8802-3j
ANSI/IEEE Std 802.3j, Supplement to Carrier sense multiple access with collision detection (CSMA/CD) access method and Physical layer specifications, Fiber Optic Active and Passive Star-Based Segments, Type 10Base-F (Section 15.18), IEEE, New York 1993.

ISO/IEC 8802-3l
ANSI/IEEE Std 802.3l, Supplement to Carrier sense multiple access with collision detection (CSMA/CD) access method and physical layer specifications, Type 10Base-T Medium Attachment Unit (MAU) Protocol Implementation Conformance Statement (PICS) Proforma (Section 14.10), IEEE, New York 1992.

ISO/IEC 8802-3k
ANSI/IEEE Std 802.3k, Supplement to Carrier sense multiple access with collision detection (CSMA/CD) access method and Physical layer specifications, Layer Management for 10 Mb/s Baseband repeaters (Section 19), IEEE, New York 1992.

ANSI/IEEE Std 802.1D
Information technology—Telecommunications and information exchange between Systems—Local area networks—Media Access Control (MAC) bridges, IEEE, New York 1993.

ISO/IEC 8802-3p
ANSI/IEEE Std 802.3p, Supplement to Carrier sense multiple access with collision detection (CSMA/CD) access method and Physical layer specifications, Guidelines for development of Managed Objects (GDMO) (ISO 10164-4) Format for Layer-Managed Objects (Section 5), IEEE, New York 1993.

Information processing systems
Open Systems Interconnection, "Specification of Abstract Syntax Notation One (ASN.1)," International Organization for Standardization, International Standard 8824, December 1987.

Information processing systems
Open Systems Interconnection, "Specification of Basic Encoding Rules for Abstract Notation One (ASN.1)," International Organization for Standardization, International Standard 8825, December 1987.

Jay Israel, Alan Weissberg
Communicating between heterogeneous networks, Data Communication, March 1987.

Till Johnson
ATM: A dream come true?, Data Communications, March 1992.

Brendan Kehoe
Zen and the art of the Internet, Prentice-Hall, Eaglewood Cliffs 1992.

Wolfgang Kemmler
FDDI Grundlagen [FDDI Fundamentals], Technik-News 3/92, COMPU-SHACK, Neuwied.

Cherryl Krivda
Enterprising Hubs, Interoperability Vol 3/ No 2, LAN Magazine, San Francisco, October 1992.

Franklin F.Kuo
Protocols and Techniques for Data Communication Networks, Simon & Schuster International Group, Hemel Hempstead 1990.

Robin Layland
Put NetBios broadcasts to rest, and get some sleep, Data Communications, May 1992.

Robin Layland
For Routing, Ships in the night should stay at the dock, Data Communications, May 1992.

Robin Layland
The incredible shrinking backbone, Data Communications, March 1992.

Sue K. Lebeck
OSI and the seven layers, the Interoperability Report, Connections 1989.

Daniel Lynch/Marshall T. Rose
Internet System Handbook, Addison Wesley Publishing Company, Inc., Reading 1993.

Thomas Madron
Local Area Networks, new technologies, emerging standards, John Wiley & Sons Inc., New York 1994.

Carl Malamud
Stacks, Interoperability in today's Computer Networks, Prentice-Hall Series in Innovative Technology, Eaglewood Cliffs, 1991.

Carl Malamud
Exploring the Internet, Prentice-Hall Series in Innovative Technology, Eaglewood Cliffs, 1992.

James Martin
Local Area Networks, Prentice-Hall, Eaglewood Cliffs, 1994.

Gregor Mendel
Stern im Netz, was Sternkoppler heute leisten [A Star in the Network, the
Current Capability of Star Couplers], LANline 6/92, Adcomp GmbH,
Munich.

Richard Metz
Vom Netz zum optimalen Netz, Was modernes Netzwerk Management
heute leisten muß [From Network to Optimum Network, the Performance
Nowadays Expected from Modern Network Management], LANline 10/91,
Adcomp GmbH, Munich.

John McHale

Netzwerk Management für 10 Base T LANs, Fehler gar nicht erst entstehen
lassen [Network Management for 10 Base T LANs, Stop Faults from
Occurring in the First Place], LANline 10/91, Adcomp GmbH, Munich.

Mark A. Miller
LAN Protocol Handbook, M&T Publishing Inc.

Paul Newton
CDDI chosen as standard basis, July 1992 Communications Networks,
London.

Radia Perlman
Interconnections, Bridges and Router, Addison Wesley Publishing Company,
Inc., Reading 1992.

Dr. Dietmar Posselt
Multiplex- vs. FDDI-Backbones, die Anwendung ist entscheidend
[Multiplexed Versus FDDI Backbones, the Application is Decisive], LANline
7/92, AWi Aktuelles Wissen Verlags GmbH, Trostberg.

Jerry Rosenberg
Computers, Data Processing & Telecommunications, John Wiley & Sons,
New York 1988.

Sal Salamone
Remote Bridge handles Voice and Fax calls, Data Communications, July
1992.

Patricia Schnaidt
Span the LAN, LAN Magazine, February 1988.

Patricia Schnaidt
Craving LAN Control, LAN Magazine, March 1991.

William Stallings
Handbook of Computer-Communications Standards Vol 2, Howard W. Sams & Company, Indianapolis.

William Stallings
Handbook of Computer-Communications Standards Vol 3, Howard & Company, Indianapolis.

William Stallings
Improving the LAN escape, Interoperability Vol 3/No 2, LAN Magazine, San Francisco, October 1992.

Klaus Stöttinger
Das OSI-Referenzmodell [The OSI Reference Model], Datacom Buchverlag, 1989.

Ralf Syderkum
Grundlagen des Kabelmanagements [Cable Management - Basic Principles], LANline 6/92, Adcomp GmbH, Munich.

Andrew S. Tannenbaum
Computer Networks, Prentice-Hall Verlag, 1988.

Kevin Tolly
SDLC Conversion: We have a winner!, Data Communications, July 1992.

Kevin Tolly
The long goodbye: FEPs and internetworks, Data Communications, July 1992.

Richard Thomas
In Routing, Hardware's only half the battle, Data Communications, May 1992.

B Selection Criteria for Switches

Manufacturer's Details

Name:
Contact:
Address:
Telephone No.:
Fax No.:

Switch product name:

Dimensions of switch (in cm):
Length:
Height :
Width:

Is the switch available in standard commercial 19" rack format?

Yes ❏   No ❏

Can the switch be mounted in a 19″ module rack without modification?

Yes ❏   No ❏

Is the switch supplied with a 19″ mounting kit?

Yes ❏   No ❏

Does the switch have visual indicators that display the hardware status?

Power supply unit:
Data packet received:
Data packet sent:
Collision:
Fault:
Other:

How much power does the switch draw?

Watts:

At what ambient temperature can the switch be operated?

Degrees Celsius:

Does the switch have a built-in temperature sensor?

Yes ❏   No ❏

The basic unit contains the following components:

Power supply unit:
Network interface cards:
I/O interface cards:
Fixed disk:
Diskette drive:

How many optional modules can be fitted in the unit?

Number:

How many ports does the unit support when expanded to full capacity?

Number:

What backup functions can be built in for the hardware components?

Redundant power supply unit:
Redundant network controller:
Redundant I/O interface cards:

Can the switch be configured using function keys on the front panel?

Yes ❑   No ❑

Can the function keys on the front panel be disabled by commands?

Yes ❑   No ❑

From what components can the unit be administered and configured?

Locally via terminal:
Locally via front panel:
Via the network using a special station:
Via the network by any PC:
Via the network by any workstation:
Via the network by a management station:

Does the switch have a serial console port?

Yes ❑   No ❑

Can the console port functions be executed locally (via a terminal or dial-up modem) using out-of-band management?

Yes ❏   No ❏

Which of the following connector styles are supported on the console port?

DB25:
DB9:
RJ11:
RJ45:
Other:

Which of the following terminals can be connected to the console port?

TTY:
VT 100:
VT 220:
VT 320:
Other:

What data rates can be set for the console port?

4800 bit/s:
9600 bit/s:
19200 bit/s:
Other:

Does the switch have a logical administration port?

Yes ❏   No ❏

Can administration functions be executed through any computer connected to the Local Area Network (in-band management)?

Yes ❏   No ❏

Which higher-level protocol must a computer use for communication if administration functions are to be executed via the network?

TCP/IP:
LAT:
XNS:
OSI:
Other:

Which of the following statistical functions are supported by the switch?

CPU capacity utilization:
Buffer capacity utilization:
Throughput in packets/second:
Throughput in bytes/second:
Received/transmitted multicast packets:
Received/transmitted broadcast packets:
Alignment errors:
Collisions on relevant network segment:
Multi collisions:
Lost data packets:
Late collisions:
Network errors (transmission errors, jitter):

How is the operating software of the switch loaded?

From a Network Management Station:
From a UNIX computer:
Via local diskette drive:
By means of static memory (ROM):
By means of dynamic memory (flash EPROM)

Are the addresses of the connected data networks learned automatically?

Yes ❑   No ❑

How many entries in the address tables can the switch handle?

Number:

Can the stored address tables be edited?

Yes ❑   No ❑

Can the learning mechanism be switched off?

Yes ❑   No ❑

Once it has been learned, how long does an address remain in the switch tables? (aging mechanism)

Minutes/hours:

Can the Network Manager define this time interval?

Yes ❑   No ❑

Can the switch be logically switched off in order to inject errors in the network?

Yes ❑   No ❑

Does the switch support filter functions in order to restrict data traffic between connected segments?

Yes ❑   No ❑

Can the filters be defined for each part of the data packet?

Yes ❑   No ❑
The filters offer the following logic operations:
AND functions:
OR functions:
NOT functions:

Freely combinable:

How many different filters can be defined for the switch?

Number:

How many network interfaces does the switch have?

Number:

What is the maximum number of network interfaces with which the switch can be equipped?

Number:

What network interfaces are supported as standard interfaces?

10Base5
10Base2
10BaseT
10BaseFB
10BaseFL
100BaseVG
100BaseTx
100 BaseT4
100BaseFx
ATM
Token Ring
FDDI
Other:

Which switching concept does the switch support?

Store and forward:
Cut-through forwarding:

Does the switch feature the following architecture concept?

Crossbar matrix switches with input buffers:
Self-route with output buffers:
Multistage queuing:

On what is the switch engine based?

RISC processors:
ASIC:

Does the hardware architecture ensure that even in the event of extreme loads, no packets are lost (non blocking)?

Yes ❑   No ❑

Are invalid data packets already screened out at the input port?

Yes ❑   No ❑

Does the switch support a flow control mechanism?

Yes ❑   No ❑

What loop detection mechanism is supported?

Private loop detection mechanism:
Spanning Tree mechanism:
Other:

What is the effective aggregate bandwidth of the switch?

Packet/s:

What is the throughput at maximum load?

Packet/s:

How long is the delay between the input and output port (latency)?

in ms:

By what network management components can the unit be monitored?

Via the network by a special management station:
Via the network by any PC:
Via the network by any workstation:

What Network Management System does the unit support?

IBM Netview/6000:
HP Openview:
SunNet Manager:
SNMPC:
Other:

What version of the SNMP Protocol is supported?

Version 1:
Version 2:

What private SNMP MIBs were implemented?

_____

_____

_____

_____

_____

_____

Are the private MIBs made available on data media?

Yes ❑   No ❑

What MTBF times are stated for the switch?

Years

What warranty period does the manufacturer offer?

Years/months:

What official Approvals have been obtained for the unit?

VDE:
TÜV/GS:
EC/EN:
UL:
FCC:

What documentation is supplied?

Quick Reference Manual:
Administrator Manual:
Hardware Manual:
Software Manual:
Manual for First-time Users:
Network fundamentals:
Network standards:
Switch fundamentals:
Protocol description:
Tips, problem checklist:

C The Spanning Tree Protocol

The use of Ethernet bridges makes it possible to implement redundant network configurations. There may be more than one transport path between two stations in a network. In the event of a fault (e.g., line break or failure of a bridge), the redundant link is activated in order to maintain communication between the stations. Ethernet bridges use the "Spanning Tree Method" as a redundancy mechanism. The Spanning Tree Algorithm (STP, SPA) is used to unambiguously define transmission paths between local bridges in intermeshed Ethernet configurations. This avoids physical network loops at a logical level. In the event of a bridge failure or cable disruption, a new link is automatically restored in the Spanning Tree topology by activating deactivated bridge ports. The "reconfiguring" of the network by the Spanning Tree mechanism takes place within a relatively short period (30 seconds).

The Spanning Tree Mechanism uses bridges to send data packets continuously in order to establish and optimize the Spanning Tree. This bridge-to-bridge communication only constitutes a small percentage of the total network traffic as a rule. The Spanning Tree mechanism is only standardized for local bridges. Some manufacturers also use this mechanism in remote bridges for routing/topology optimization.

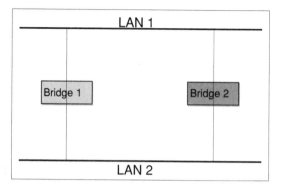

Figure C.1: Redundant connection between two LANs

All Ethernet bridges support the implementation of redundant network configurations. With the transparent bridging method, steps must be taken to ensure that there are no loops and only one unique data path is ever maintained between two networks. In the event of a fault in a redundant network segment, the Spanning Tree Process (STP, SPA) ensures that this redundant network segment is automatically activated. The Spanning Tree algorithm and the associated bridge protocols are specified in IEEE Standard 802.1d. IEEE Standard 802.1d covers the following basic requirements:

- Between two LANs connected by bridges, there is always only one unique data path. In practice, this means that further connections and loops are eliminated at the logical level.

- If the link is broken or if a bridge fails, the Spanning Tree mechanism attempts to establish a link via an alternative path.

- The uniqueness of data paths must be achieved within a relatively short period in order to minimize the interruption of communication paths.

- It must be possible to specify the selected paths and redundant links by means of parameters. This makes it possible for the administrator to determine the relevant paths of data packets in advance during troubleshooting.

- The Spanning Tree mechanism must have no effect on network performance and must be completely transparent to all end stations.

- Bridges must be ready for immediate use with the default settings so that no further configuring is necessary at the time of installation.

- The requirements placed on the memory and CPU capacity of the bridge and individual bridge ports must be as low as possible. In no case shall the performance of the bridge depend upon the number of bridges and LANs in the overall combined network.

Prerequisites for Implementation

The requirements list compiled by the IEEE body for such a bridge-to-bridge protocol formed the basis for devising the Spanning Tree Process. This requirement list defines the following prerequisites:

- To ensure easy identification of all bridges, a unique group address must be specified at the MAC level. All data packets of all bridges connected in the LAN are identified using this group address. The following address was specified as the group address for STP bridges:

- 01-80-C2-00-0010

- Each bridge must have its own non-interchangeable MAC address. The non-interchangeable MAC address is defined by the relevant 48-bit long hardware address of the bridge.

- Each port of a bridge must have a unique user-selectable port designation.

- Its own individual priority can be specified for each bridge and each bridge port.

- Individual path costs can be allocated to each bridge port.

The bridge is identified by means of the bridge address and the relevant priority of the bridge. These values give a unique numerical value (bridge ID) for each bridge. The priority of individual bridges relative to each other is determined by comparing the unique identifiers (bridge IDs) with each other. The definition stipulates the following:

- The highest priority is assigned to the bridge that has the lowest numerical value.

The port designation of a bridge port consists of a port designation and a user-definable variable part. These values give a unique numerical value (port ID) for the relevant bridge port. The priority of individual bridge ports relative to each other is determined by comparing the unique identifiers (port IDs) with each other. The definition stipulates the following:

- The highest priority is assigned to the bridge port that was allocated the lowest numerical value.

Calculating the Active Network Topology

The Spanning Tree algorithm and the bridge-to-bridge protocols are used to establish a unique communication path between the connected LANs starting with an arbitrarily interconnected LAN internetwork. In doing so, the redundant links between LANs are deactivated by automatic communication between the bridges. This is achieved by temporarily deactivating individual bridge ports. The active bridge ports receive all bridge-bridge packets and propagate bridge information through the activated ports. Although deactivated bridge ports receive all bridge-bridge data packets, they do not propagate the bridge information. In practice this means that data packets between two LANs are only transferred via active bridge ports. The deactivated bridge ports operate in hot-standby mode and are only integrated into the LAN internetwork if so required by a change in the network topology (e.g., faulty cables, faulty bridges). This mechanism ensures the unique topology is maintained.

Figure C.2 shows a LAN internetwork established by Spanning Tree bridges. The active path between LAN 1 and LAN 3 takes the following route: bridge 1 port 1 <-> bridge 2 port 1 <-> bridge 3 port 1 <-> bridge 4 port 1.

The passive path between LAN 1 and LAN 3 takes the following route: bridge 5 port 1 <-> bridge 6 port 1 <-> bridge 7 port 1 <-> bridge 8 port 1.

The active LAN topology is determined in line with the following criteria:

- the unique bridge designations (bridge ID) of a bridge
- the path cost of a bridge port
- the unique port designation (port ID) of a bridge port

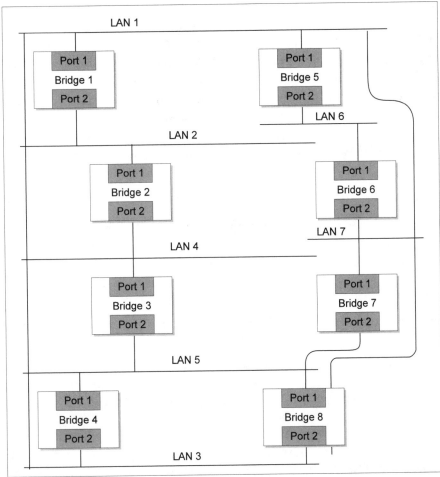

Figure C.2: Bridges in a LAN internetwork

The root bridge always has the highest priority. A unique cost calculation is performed for each bridge port in the LAN internetwork. This root path cost is calculated as the sum of all routing costs incurred for a packet along the path between the root and the port of the relevant bridge. In a bridge, the port having the lowest root routing cost is always used as the active port. If calculations in a combined LAN produce the same value for two or more ports, the bridge number and also the port number decides the weighting of the active path.

Let us assume that one of the bridges in the combined LAN automatically becomes the root bridge. In our example, bridge 1 fulfills this function. The root bridge sends information packets to the connected LANs via both the bridge ports. These packets are received by each of the bridge ports connected to the LAN. The bridges connected to this LAN use these packets to familiarize themselves with the path to the root bridge. The bridge port through which the root information was received is nominated as the designated port for this LAN. The subsequent path to the LANs connected to these bridges is determined via these reports and the root information is passed on.

Propagating the Current Topology

The bridges dynamically swap Bridge Protocol Data Units (BPDUs) with each other in order to calculate the topology. The Bridge Protocol Data Units always use the following SAP address at the LLC level: 01000010. A Bridge Protocol Data Unit has the following format:

Destination Address	Source Address	Length Field	DSAP	SSAP	Configuration Messages

Table C.1: Structure of The Bridge Protocol Data Unit

The BPDUs used to determine the current topology are referred to as configuration BPDUs. The receiving bridge uses the information contained in the BPDUs in order to transfer its own BPDUs to the connected LANs. Each configuration BPDU contains the unique designation of the root bridge (as seen by the sender), the calculated path cost between the transmitting port and the root bridge, the unique designation of the transmitting bridge, and its port designation. Using this information, a receiving bridge is capable of making the following decisions:

- Is the transmitting port more suitable as the designated port for this LAN than the port currently designated at that moment?

- Should the port receiving the message become the root port of the bridge?

The regular sending of configuration BPDUs is initiated by the following three mechanisms:

- A bridge believes it is acting as the root bridge in the LAN internetwork. For this reason the bridge sends configuration BPDUs at fixed time intervals.

- A bridge receives a configuration BPDU. The root port is determined from the information contained in the data packet. The configuration BPDUs are forwarded to all those LANs for which this bridge is the designated port.

- A bridge receives configuration information via a designated port. These packets are answered by sending its own information to all bridges of this LAN.

As a result of these relatively simple mechanisms, the most direct path to the root bridge is disseminated throughout the entire network very quickly. Any other information concerning further root bridges, the parallel equivalent, or better paths results in contradictions and triggers renewed negotiation of the topology.

Reconfiguring the LAN Topology

If a bridge is put out of service (e.g., by a fault) in a LAN internetwork, if a new bridge is installed or if the bridge parameters are modified by Management, the LAN internetwork must be reconfigured. Topology information has a limited life. This is achieved by giving each BPDU an age (time period since the information was sent by the root bridge). Each bridge stores the information concerning the designated port on each supported LAN port and monitors the age of the information. The regular transfer of configuration data by the root bridge ensures that topology information is constantly updated and the timer never expires.

If the topology information for a port stops being updated for any reason, a timeout situation occurs. As a result of the timeout, the port automatically becomes the designated port for the connected LAN. The port also sends the root protocol information received via the root port to the connected LAN.

If a designated bridge fails to receive information from the root bridge for a specific period, the bridge assumes that the root bridge has failed. In this situation, this bridge automatically declares itself the root bridge. If the root bridge fails, all bridges in the combined network receive no new update information whatsoever. As a result, any bridge can become the root bridge for a brief period. The propagation of the new root information very quickly causes the bridges to determine the new root bridge and a new unique network topology is defined.

In practice, the following situation may occur: the path to the root bridge at the time changes. This change can be caused, for instance, by the Network Administrator increasing or decreasing the path costs. This causes a timeout situation on the newly configured bridge. This timeout situation is caused by a discrepancy in the age information. If the path costs were increased, the message contains age information that refers to a point in time prior to the expected arrival time of the message. If the path costs were reduced, the message contains age information that refers to a point in time after the expected time of arrival of the message. In these situations adjacent bridges react directly to the BPDUs that are sent by the quasi root bridge.

In order to ensure that all bridges in a network delete the propagated information using the timeout mechanism, the age accompanies all configuration information initiated by the root. Because one cannot guarantee that all configuration packets will always reach their recipients, a mechanism is required which reduces the number of times a bridge, and hence the network, is reconfigured to a minimum. This is why each configuration BPDU contains an additional time value that represents a multiple of the time interval at which the root bridge sends packets.

Change of Port Status

Because of natural delays that occur in a LAN internetwork, distinguishing between the current topology and redundant configurations is enormously troublesome. For instance, the topology may change at different times in various parts of the LAN. Manual modification of a port status (direct change from inactive to active state) can result in data loops for a short time, and hence duplicated packets on the network or incorrect packet sequences. For this reason, bridge ports must wait to receive new topology information before this information can be propagated to the connected LANs. In addition, the bridges must take into account the age of the information in order to ensure that no old topology information is propagated. Within this brief time, it must also be ensured that entries relating to stations that are no longer present in the LANs are deleted from the local address database of the port. All addresses of new stations also have to be entered in the database within this time.

If the Spanning Tree mechanism is to be used to switch a port from the inactive to the active state, the port must first change to Listening mode. In Listening mode, the port in question is capable of receiving the packets transferred via the connected LAN. Using the information contained in the packets, the bridge checks whether the port is activated completely or whether the port returns to Blocking mode again. If the port remains in Listening mode, after a protocol timer has expired, it changes over to Learning mode. In Learning mode the port transports no more packets. The data packets are only monitored, the station addresses they contain are filtered out, and the address database is updated. After a further timer expires, the port changes to Forwarding mode. In this mode the port is fully opened and packets are transported from and to the connected LAN.

Detection of Topology Changes

In a bridge's operating mode, address information in the filter database need only be modified if stations are removed from the LAN or new devices are connected. Each entry is given a life time in order to keep the address tables up to date. If this address ceases to occur in any packet before this relatively long timer expires, the entry is deleted from the database. As seen by the bridge, a change in the active topology of the LAN internetwork can lead to the impression that certain stations are moving within the network. In order to be able to identify a station unambiguously in a LAN internetwork, it must be ensured that the entire new topology is learned even if only part of the LAN internetwork is reconfigured. The Spanning Tree mechanism is able to detect all changes in the active topology automatically. The bridges included in the LAN internetwork propagate these changes in the direction of the designated bridge. These packets are repeated until the bridge obtains an acknowledgment from the designated bridge. The designated bridge forwards the information using precisely the same mechanism in the direction of the root bridge. In this way, change information slowly spreads as far as the root bridge.

When a root bridge receives a topology change notification, it makes the modified information available to all bridges. In the topology change BPDU, the Topology Change Flag is set to indicate the change in topology. The bridges use this information to update the dynamic entries in the filter database.

Port States

The individual ports of a Spanning Tree bridge can assume various states during the course of operation or due to Management. A series of functions and resulting actions have been defined for each state of the ports. The relevant operating mode specifies how it processes received data packets and which functions must follow the information contained in them. The following five operating modes were stipulated for bridge ports:

- Blocking

- Listening

- Learning

- Forwarding

- Disabled

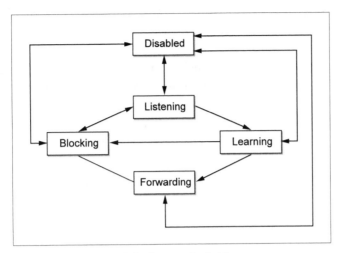

Figure C.3: States of a bridge port

Blocking Mode

In Blocking mode the port of a bridge transfers no data packets. This prevents data packets being transferred in duplicate over the LAN if there are redundant links. The Forwarding process is temporarily completely suspended in Blocking mode. In addition, the Learning process does not accept any new stations (addresses) in the address table.

However, a port that is in Blocking mode must be taken into account when calculating the current network topology. Blocking mode is automatically loaded after the bridge is booted. During operation the port goes through the data contained in the BPDU information in Blocking mode if another bridge or another bridge port is declared the active bridge/bridge port for that path.

The bridge or bridge report remains in this state until a configuration packet notifies it that this port is to be activated. The port then changes to Listening Mode.

Listening Mode

When a port changes to Listening mode, the port prepares itself for transition to active mode.

In this state, the bridge port cannot transfer any data packets. For this reason, no configuration BPDUs can be passed on. This may result in a loop being formed in the LAN internetwork. The Learning process is also switched off in Listening mode, otherwise any changes in the active topology could lead to discrepancies with the filter databases. In this situation the Forwarding process must also pass on no packets. The bridge algorithm must include the relevant port in Listening mode in its calculations. If the bridge receives a configuration BPDU in this mode which defines that this port is not a designated port or root port, the port changes back to Blocking mode. If no configuration BPDU is received, it quits Listening mode after a timer expires and changes to Learning mode.

Learning Mode

Learning mode is reached from Listening mode by a decision made by the Spanning Tree algorithm. In Learning mode, the port resets itself to transfer data packets. Because the possibility of a loop being formed cannot be entirely excluded in this state as well, no regular LAN packets are passed on by the port in question. In order to ensure that the Spanning Tree algorithm is working properly, received BPDUs are sent on. In Learning mode, the port enters all new station addresses in its filter databases. From Learning mode, the bridge port can change over to the following operating states:

- Forwarding mode

After a timer expires, the bridge changes to Forwarding mode.

- Blocking mode

On the basis of information in a BPDU, the port changes to Blocking mode.

- Disabled mode

The Network Administrator can set the port to Disabled mode using a Management command.

Forwarding Mode

Only ports in Forwarding mode transport regular data packets. The Learning process is used to continuously update the port database with new addresses (stations). A port in Forwarding mode is taken into account when calculating the active data path. Received BPDUs are analyzed in this state. Forwarding mode is reached from Learning mode either by a timer expiring or by a decision made by the Spanning Tree algorithm. The port remains in Forwarding mode until it detects, by receiving a BDPU, that a loop has been formed in the network. In this event the port immediately changes to Blocking mode.

Disabled Mode

If a port is in Disabled mode, the port is unable to receive or transport data packets. The port is also ignored when calculating the active and passive paths or ports. The Learning process does not update the address database. A port can only assume this state by means of Network Administrator intervention.

Protocol Parameters and Timers

All bridges included in a LAN internetwork swap information with each other through Bridge Protocol Data Units (BPDUs). The following two types of BPDUs are transferred between bridges:

- Configuration BPDUs
- Topology change notification BPDUs.

Configuration BPDU

It is the configuration BPDU's job to communicate the current topology. Each configuration BPDU contains the unique designation of the root bridge (as seen by the sender), the calculated path cost between the transmitting port and the root bridge, the unique designation of the transmitting bridge and its port designation.

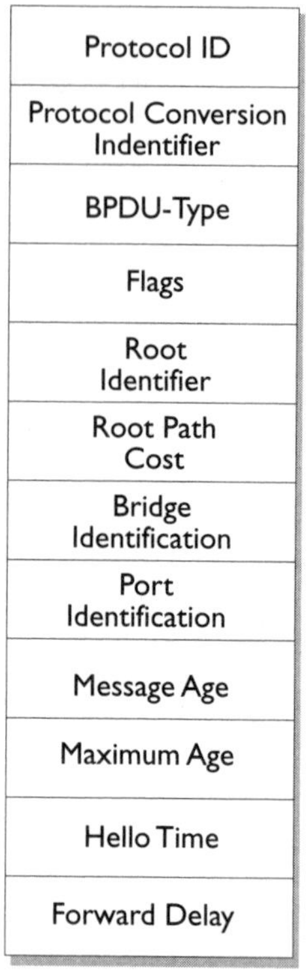

Figure C.4: Configuration BPDU

Protocol Identifier
Length: 2 octets

Contains a 2-byte long identification code for the protocol used. The following value was specified for the Spanning Tree Protocol: 0000 0000 0000 0000.

Protocol Version Identifier
Length 1 octet

This field specifies the current version of the Spanning Tree Protocol. The only Version Identifier so far specified is the value 0000 0000.

Bridge Protocol Data Unit Type
Length: 1 octet

Defines the type of message. The following value was specified as the type for configuration BDPUs: 0000 0000

Flags
Length: 1 octet

This flag field is used to specify the contents of the BPDU in the event of a topology change. The following values have been specified:

0000 0001

This flag is set by a designated bridge in order to confirm a topology change notification BPDU. The root bridge uses this parameter to detect that the active topology has changed.

1000 0000

This flag informs a receiving bridge that the new topology information contained in the BPDU must be stored.

Root Identifier
Length: 8 octets

The unique identification code of the root bridge is reported in this field. The identification number of the current root bridge is made known by the automatic learning of all the bridges in the LAN internetwork.

Root Path Cost
Length: 4 octets

This field contains the current path cost for the path taken by a packet to the root bridge. Using this parameter bridges can determine the least expensive path to the root bridge.

Bridge Identifier

Length: 8 octets

This 8-octet long field contains the unique identifier of the bridge that sends the configuration BPDU. This field forms the basis for the following functions of a bridge:

- If several bridges are to be connected to one LAN, this field is used to determine the least expensive path to the root bridge. The bridge that provides the least expensive path thereby becomes the designated bridge.

- This field is also used to ascertain that a bridge has several ports to the same LAN. The Bridge Identifier information is used to determine which ports should be temporarily switched off.

Port Identifier

Length: 2 octets

This field contains the port designation of the bridge port that sends the configuration BPDU. The value 0 is not used to identify port numbers.

Message Age

Length: 2 octets

Contains time information representing the age of the BPDU. This information represents the point in time at which the root bridge sent the BPDU. The bridge uses this parameter to decide whether the BPDU has exceeded the maximum age.

Max Age

Length: 2 octets

Contains a constant value set by the root bridge. The bridges can use this value to determine the age of a BPDU.

Hello Time

Length: 2 octets

Contains the time interval that expires before the root bridge sends BPDUs.

Forward Delay

Length: 2 octets

The Forward Delay field allows the root bridge to set the bridge Forward Delay parameter of all bridges to a uniform value. This value is used, for example, to implement the ageing process for entries in the filter database.

Topology Change Notification BPDU

A designated bridge of a LAN uses the Topology Change Notification BPDU to inform the root bridge that the active topology has changed. In response to a Topology Change Notification BPDU, the root bridge sets a flag in all configuration BPDUs. All bridges use this flag to detect that the active configuration has changed. The bridges consequently remove all old information from their filter databases.

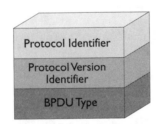

Figure C.5: Topology Change Notification BPDU

Protocol Identifier

Length: 2 octets

Contains a 2-byte long identification code for the protocol used. The following value is specified for the Spanning Tree Protocol: 0000 0000 0000 0000.

Protocol Version Identifier

Length: 1 octet

This field specifies the current version of the Spanning Tree Protocol. The only Version Identifier specified so far is the value 0000 0000.

Bridge Protocol Data Unit Type

Length: 1 octet

Defines the type of message. The following value is specified as the type for Topology Change Notification BPDUs: 1000 0000.

Parameters of a bridge

In order to support the Spanning Tree Protocol, a large number of different parameters are supported in all bridges that are part of a LAN internetwork. The Administrator must configure these parameters before operation under some circumstances. The global bridge parameters are described in detail below.

Parameter: Designated Root

Contains the unique bridge designation of the root bridge at a particular time.

Parameter: Root Path Cost

The Root Path Cost parameter defines the cost of the path from the relevant bridge to the root bridge. This value is equivalent to the designated cost of a root port. In the case of a root bridge this parameter is always set to the value 0.

Parameter: Root Port

Defines the unique port designation of the port for which the lowest path cost was specified. If two or more ports in a bridge have the same path cost, the port with the highest port designation is selected as the root port.

Parameter: Max Age

Defines the maximum age that must be reached before the received information can be deleted.

Parameter: Hello Time

Defines the time interval after which the bridge sends configuration BPDUs.

Parameter: Forward Delay

Defines the period of time for which a bridge retains Listening status in the event of transition from Blocking status to Learning status.

Parameter: Bridge Identifier

Specifies the unique designation of a bridge. This parameter consists of two parts, a unique bridge address and a part that can be used to determine the priority of the bridge. The priority part is modified by a Management function. The following functions are fulfilled by using this identifier:

- Originator identifier

This bridge identifier is included in all configuration BPDUs that are sent by the bridge as originator information.

- Identifier of designated port

This identifier is used in all root bridges or bridges that are in the process of becoming the root bridge as a unique name for the designated port of the bridge.

Parameter: Bridge Max Age

Defines the maximum possible age of a root bridge. This parameter can be modified by the Administrator.

Parameter: Bridge Hello Time

The root bridge uses this parameter to define the longest time interval after which Topology Change Notification BPDUs are sent. The length of this interval is determined by Management.

Parameter: Bridge Forward Delay

Defines the time interval for the Forward Delay. This value is set by Management.

Parameter: Topology Change Detected

This (BOOLEAN type) parameter always has the value = false during normal operation. If a change in the network was registered, this parameter is set to the value = true.

Parameter: Topology Change

This (BOOLEAN type) parameter is used by the Topology Change Flag to request all bridges to note new topology information contained in the BPDU. If the value of this parameter = TRUE, the value of the filtering database aging timer equals the value of the Forward Delay Parameter. This means that dynamic entries that are older than the value of the Forward Delay parameter are deleted from the database.

Parameter: Topology Change Time

Defines the time period during which the root bridge sends BPDUs with a Topology Change Flag set. The value of this parameter consists of the sum of the Bridge Max Age and Bridge Forward Delay parameters.

Parameter: Hold Time

This timer defines the shortest time period that a bridge port has to wait between sending two BPDUs. This parameter is permanently set to the value 1.0 second and cannot be changed.

Bridge Timer

A wide variety of timers are supported in all bridges in order to support the Spanning Tree Protocol. The Administrator must configure these timers before operation under some circumstances. The Bridge Timers are described in detail in the text which follows.

Hello Timer

The Hello Timer ensures that the root bridge sends configuration BPDUs to the connected LANs at periodic time intervals. The standard defines a value between 1.0 and 10 seconds for the Hello Timer. 2.0 seconds is proposed as the default value.

Topology Change Notification Timer

The Topology Change Notification Timer ensures that the designated bridge of a LAN notes every topology change. The value of the Hello Timer is used as the value for this timer.

Topology Change Timer

The Topology Change Timer defines how long the root bridge sends configuration BPDUs with the Topology Change Flag set.

Bridge Port Parameters and Timers in Detail

The individual parameters and timers of a bridge must be matched to each other precisely in order to support the Spanning Tree Protocol. The Administrator must configure these parameters and timers before operation under some circumstances. The bridge port parameters and timers are described in detail below.

Port Identifier

Defines the unique designation of a bridge port. The Port Identifier is an integral part of all configuration BPDUs that are sent by that port. This parameter comprises the following two parts:

- a unique designation of the physical port of a bridge. The designation of the port consists of an integer that is incremented from 1 upwards.

- the priority of a port. The priority of a port is stipulated by the Management System.

State

This parameter defines the current status of a port (e.g., Disabled, Listening, Learning, Forwarding, Blocking). In normal operation this parameter is modified dynamically by the STP algorithm. The Administrator can also use the Management System to alter the value of this parameter.

Path Cost

This parameter contains the itemized cost of the bridge port when this bridge port is acting as the root port. This cost is added to the designated cost when a packet is sent via this port to the root bridge. This cost addition only takes place if the bridge is not simultaneously the root bridge. The Administrator can set this parameter through a Management function.

Designated Root

Contains the unique designation of the root bridge. The designated root bridge is entered in each configuration BPDU by each designated bridge of a LAN. This parameter is used to check the root identifier parameter in a received configuration BPDU.

Designated Cost

This parameter is used to determine the total cost of the path from the relevant designated bridge to the root bridge. This makes it possible to check the total cost contained in a configuration BPDU.

Designated Bridge

Contains the precise designation of the bridge that is acting as the designated bridge for this LAN. The following functions can be fulfilled by means of this parameter:

- Select best port as designated port.

- Check the Bridge Identifier parameter in a BPDU.

Designated Port

Defines the precise port designation of a port that is acting as the designated port for a LAN. The following functions can be fulfilled by means of this parameter:

- Select best port as designated port.

- Manually specify active topology by Management function.

Topology Change Acknowledge

This flag is used to indicate that a topology change must be made.

Configuration Pending

This flag is used to indicate that a configuration BPDU must be sent after the Hold Timer has expired. This ensures that configuration BPDUs are not sent too often and prevents the flow of information from being obstructed.

Message Age Timer

This is used to check the age of the received protocol information of a port. If this parameter assumes a value that exceeds the Max Age parameter, the information is deleted. The standard stipulates a range of values from 6.0 to 40.0 seconds for the Message Age Timer. The default value was defined as 20 seconds.

Forward Delay Timer

Allows a check on the time period during which a port remains in Listening or Learning mode. The standard stipulates a range of values from 4.0 to 30.0 seconds for the Forward Delay Timer. The default value was defined as 15 seconds.

Hold Timer

This timer is used to ensure that configuration BPDUs are not sent too often. The standard value stipulated for the Hold Timer is 1.0 second.

Functions of the Spanning Tree Protocol in Detail

Process: Transfer of Configuration BPDUs

Configuration BDPUs are sent under the following circumstances:

*   As regular information packets

*   In response to a topology change procedure

*   After the Hold Timer has expired

Configuration BPDUs are used to transfer the following information to other bridge ports that are connected to the same LAN:

*   where the designated root bridge is located,

*   what root path costs are incurred,

*   who is acting as the designated bridge,

*   which port is acting as the designated port.

*   In addition, configuration BPDUs are used to transfer the values of timers.

Function:

*   If the Hold Timer of a port was activated, the Configuration Pending Flag is simultaneously set.

*   If the Hold Timer was not activated, a configuration BPDU is sent by the relevant port after the timer expires.

As seen by the transmitting bridge, the following parameters in the configuration BPDUs are set and the following actions are performed:

*   Root Identifier

Contains the name of the root bridge that the transmitting bridge thinks is acting as the root bridge.

- Root Path Cost

Contains the cost that the transmitting bridge has determined for the path to the current root bridge.

- Bridge Identifier

Contains the unique name of the transmitting bridge.

- Port Designation

Unique port designation of the port in the configuration BPDU.

- Message Age parameter

If the sender is the root bridge, the latter must set the Message Age Parameter.

- Max Age, Hello Time, Forward Delay parameters

The values of the Max Age, Hello Time, and Forward Delay parameters contain the current values of the transmitting bridge.

- Topology Change Acknowledgment Flag

The Topology Change Acknowledgment Flag is set to the appropriate value of the transmitting bridge.

- Topology Change Flag

The current value of the Topology Change Flag is set in the BPDU.

- The Configuration Pending Flag is reset.
- The Hold Timer of the port is started.

Process: *Storing the Configuration*

When a bridge first receives a BPDU, the parameters that it contains must be stored. The information must then be compared with the information in any newly-received configuration BPDU and updated if applicable.

During this procedure, the Designated Root, Designated Cost, Designated Bridge, and Designated Port parameters are compared to the BPDU values for Root Identifier, Root Path Cost, Bridge Identifier, and Port Identifier. The Message Age Timer of the port in question is then started. The following situations result in the information being modified:

- The Root Identifier specifies a bridge that has a higher priority than the stored designated root bridge.

- The Root Identifier and Designated Root Bridge match, but the Root Path Cost is lower than the values stored in Designated Costs for a port.

Process: Saving the Configuration Timeout Values

In order to keep the values Max Age, Hello Time, Forward Delay, and Topology Change constantly up to date, the information concerning the root bridge is always immediately saved or updated after the BPDU is received.

Sending configuration BPDUs

Configuration BPDUs allow a bridge to send information to the designated bridge. This process is initiated by the following operations:

- By receiving a configuration BPDU on the root port.

- After the Hello Timer has expired.

- By the Message Age Timer expiring and the bridge being selected as the designated root bridge.

- By a bridge being specified as the designated bridge by Management.

Process: Answering a Configuration BPDU

After a bridge has sent a configuration BPDU to the connected LAN, a designated bridge and a designated port are selected in the answer to this configuration BPDU. This situation occurs when configuration BPDUs from the current root bridge do not reach the transmitting bridge at the right time. The generation of the answer BPDU is equivalent to the process for transferring configuration BPDUs.

Process: Transfer of Topology Change Notification BPDUs

If a bridge has detected a change in the current topology or if the Topology Notification Timer has expired, a Topology Change Notification BPDU (TCN) is generated for the root bridge. Only bridges that do not have root bridge status can generated this BPDU. The TCN BPDU is sent via the root port within the maximum BPDU Transmission Delay.

Process: Updating the Configuration

After receiving a configuration BPDU, a bridge updates its information (this process was described earlier under the heading "Storing the configuration"). Information is also updated in a bridge if a port of a bridge became the designated port for a LAN. This can occur because the Message Age Timer expires or because of Management intervention. The process for selecting the root bridge is used in order to select the designated root, and root port and to calculate the Root Path Cost. The process for selecting the designated port is used to specify a port as the designated port.

Process: Selecting the Root Bridge in a Combined Network

The root port of a bridge has the task of deciding which of all the ports connected in a LAN operate actively in the combined network and which ports must be switched off. The process for selecting the root bridge in a combined network is used to select the designated root bridge and its root port as well as the Root Path Cost. Selection takes place in accordance with the following conditions:

- If the highest priority was assigned to the bridge, it is logged as the designated root bridge.

- If several bridges have the same priority, the bridge with the lowest path cost becomes the root bridge.

- If several bridges have the same priority and if the same path cost was determined for them, the bridge with the highest Bridge Identifier becomes the root bridge.

- If several bridges have the same priority, same path cost, and same Bridge Identifier, the port with the highest port designation of any bridge becomes the designated port.

- If none of the conditions is met by any of the ports, the root port parameter is set to zero and:

- The bridge designation in question is entered in the designated root parameter.

- The value of the root path cost is set to zero.

- If the bridge port was selected as the root port:

- The designated root parameter of the bridge is set to the value of the bridge identifier for the bridge.

- The path cost of the bridge is set to the value 0 and entered in the path cost parameter of the port.

Process: Selecting the Designated Port

Selecting a designated port specifies which bridge port of a LAN may transport packets and which bridge ports are disabled. This bridge-port selection is performed as part of the updating of the configuring procedure. In order to be declared the designated port, the following prerequisites must be satisfied:

- The port in question is already operating as the designated port of a LAN.

- The value of the designated root parameter of the bridge is different to the value currently stored for the port.

- The bridge supports a path to the root bridge that offers a lower path cost than the previous path.

- The bridge offers a path with the same cost, but a higher priority than that of the other bridges was logged for the Bridge Identifier.

Process: Declaration as Designated Port

The basic prerequisite for this function is that a port was selected as the designated port and was allocated appropriate values for parameters that are important for maintaining the active topology. In doing so, this process performs the following functions:

- The designated root parameter of the port is set to the value of the designated root parameter.

- The designated cost parameter of the port is set to the value of the bridge's root path cost.

- The designated bridge parameter of the port is set to the bridge's Bridge Identifier.

- The designated port parameter of a port is set to the value of the port's Port Identifiers.

A port becomes the designated port under the following circumstances:

- After the Message Age Timer expires.

- After the port is declared the designated port by the designated port selection procedure as a result of the configuration update procedure.

- Management intervention makes the change.

Process: *Selecting the Port Status*

The status of a bridge port is defined by the information in configuration BPDUs. The status of a port reveals evidence of its functions. A change of port status occurs under the following conditions:

- After a configuration BPDU is received that updates the old port information;

- After expiration of the Message Age Timer of a port that is to become the designated port for a LAN;

- And/or a change is forced by Management.

If a bridge port becomes the root port, the Configuration Pending Flag and the Topology Change Acknowledge Flag for the port are reset and the Make Forwarding procedure is executed. If the port becomes the designated port for the connected LAN, the active Message Age Timer is stopped, and the Make Forwarding procedure is activated for this port. If the port is to be defined as a backup port, the Configuration Pending Flag and the Topology Change Acknowledge Flag are set and the Make Blocking procedure is activated.

Process: Make Forwarding

By activating this process, a port is able to send data packets actively. When changing to Forwarding mode, a port is set from Blocking mode to Listening mode. At the same time the Forward Delay Timer is started. The port is only fully activated once this timer has expired. This delay time prevents the formation of temporary loops in the network.

Process: Make Blocking

By activating this process, a port terminates the sending of data packets. If a port is not in Disabled mode or in Blocking mode, this process causes the following actions to take effect:

- If the port is in Forwarding or Learning mode, the Topology Change Detection procedure is executed.

- The status of the port is set to Blocking.

- The Forward Delay Timer for the port is stopped.

Process: Topology Change Detection

This process is used to store every change in the network topology. This takes place regardless of whether the change is detected by the bridge in question or whether the change is indicated by Topology Change BPDUs. Before this mechanism is put into effect, one must ensure that the root bridge is already aware of this change in topology. The Topology Change Detection mechanism is triggered by the following actions:

- Reception of a Topology Change Notification BPDU on the designated port of a LAN.

- After the Forward Delay Timer has expired if the designated port of a bridge is in Forwarding mode.

- Transition of a port from Forwarding or Learning mode to Blocking mode.

- After a bridge is declared the root bridge.

When a bridge is given the status of root bridge, the Topology Change Flag in the BPDU is set and the Topology Change Timer for the bridge is started. If the bridge is not the root bridge and the Topology Change Flag is not set, the Transmit Topology Change Notification BPDU procedure is run and the Topology Change Notification Timer is started. In addition, the Topology Change Detected Flag is set.

Process: *Confirmation of a Topology Change*

This process is used to stop the transfer of Topology Change Notification BPDUs. This procedure always follows the arrival from the designated bridge of the LAN of a configuration BPDU that has the Topology Change Acknowledgment Flag set. This resets the Topology Change Detected Flag and pauses the Topology Change Notification Timer.

Process: *Acknowledge Topology Change*

This process is used to acknowledge the receipt of a topology change noted by another bridge. This procedure is always executed after a Topology Change Notification BPDU is received on a designated port of a LAN. After receiving the topology change, the Topology Change Acknowledge Flag is set and the Transmit Configuration BPDU procedure for the port is executed.

D Glossary

ATM Asynchronous Transfer Mode, a high-speed, scalable cell-switching protocol that breaks packets down into fixed 53-byte cells; well-suited for simultaneous transmission of data, voice and video.

BackPressure The technique the Ornet LANbooster uses for notifying end-nodes of a busy condition by sending an Ethernet jam signal requesting that end-nodes refrain from transmitting until buffers are emptied.

Bad packet A corrupted or otherwise damaged (and therefore meaningless) data packet that is often re-transmitted by other Ethernet switches (particularly cut-through switches) chewing up valuable bandwidth.

Bandwidth The transmission capacity of a data channel, often referred to as the network's speed (for Ethernet this is 10 Mbps); can be thought of as the number of open lanes on a highway.

Bottleneck   Any point or intersection in a network, often internet-working devices such as switches, that could cause a data traffic jam when several points of transmission compete for full bandwidth.

Bridge   A relatively unintelligent, MAC-layer device that connects two similar types of networks together to form an internetwork.

Bursty traffic   Characteristic of LAN traffic that requires very high bandwidth for short periods of time and relatively low bandwidth between transmissions.

Client/server   A model of distributed processing in which the client workstation is the requesting machine and the server is the supplying machine; processing is distributed between client and server requiring reliable communication between them for application integrity.

Cross-bar switch   A first-generation switch architecture designed for optimal point-to-point communication that inherently creates bottlenecks and introduces non-deterministic delay; not suitable for multimedia, client/server, or mission-critical environments.

Cut-through switch   A type of switch that examines only the destination address of the Ethernet header before it begins to send the packet on its way; may introduce network errors by forwarding bad packets without checking for errors.

Data packet   A variable-length slice of data formatted with a destination and source address, among other things, that is understandable to all devices supporting a particular protocol, such as Ethernet.

Ethernet   The IEEE 802.3 LAN standard that runs at 10 Mbps bandwidth; Ethernet supports coaxial cable (10Base-5 and 10Base-2), twisted pair (10Base-T), fiber and wireless media; Ethernet relies on a CSMA/CD (Carrier Sense Multiple Access with Collision Detection) algorithm for channel contention arbitration.

FDDI/(CDDI) Fiber (or Copper) Distributed Data Interface; a dual counter-rotating ring, token-passing protocol running at 100 Mbps over fiber (for FDDI) or copper media (for CDDI).

First-generation technology New technology (or the first product of its kind) that has not had the benefit of real-world testing and/or refinement.

Full-duplex Ethernet Ethernet with only two nodes per segment running at double-speed, or 20 Mbps, since nodes have no contention issues and can transmit and receive simultaneously; provides a mechanism for providing higher-bandwidth connections to servers and end-nodes without requiring reconfiguration or new technology deployment.

IEEE 802.1d Spanning Tree algorithm The industry standard for eliminating broadcast storms at the MAC layer in meshed networks that have redundant or cyclical paths.

Inverse multiplexer A device that takes a high-speed link and separates it into several low speed channels to be transmitted over multiple channels: data packets are then reassembled and recombined at the destination.

Jitter A flickering transmission signal or display caused by non-deterministic delay common to packet transmission devices and unacceptable for multimedia or client/server applications.

Latency Delay introduced at any point in a network, due to processing, usually by an internetworking device such as a switch or router; non-deterministic delay causes network jitter, fixed-latency devices introduce small and predictable delays at all levels of traffic load.

MAC layer The second layer of the Open System Interconnect (OSI) Model which bridges and switches use to determine the destination device; by contrast, routers use higher-level information of the OSI Layer 3, or Network Layer, to route data.

Many-to-one A common type of data transmission in client/server environments in which many clients are trying to transmit to one server simultaneously; in switches, successful many-to-one support requires a global shared memory scheme and a high-speed server link, such as full-duplex Ethernet.

Multimedia The simultaneous transmission of voice, video, and data over a shared network to be recombined by a single workstation; very delay sensitive.

Next-generation technology A quantum leap over first-generation technology because it has the benefit of learning from real-world situations and provides enhancements to previously deployed technology.

Non-blocking switch The ability of a switch to continue to accept transmissions from all ports at all times, effectively removing bottlenecks (blocking) at the switch port level.

Non-deterministic delay A variable time period during which data packets are delayed when encountering a network bottleneck or variable-length packets; introduces jitter which is unacceptable in client/server and multimedia environments.

Performance The measure of the processing and packet forwarding power of an internetworking device.

Plug-and-Perform The technology that allows Switches to be installed in existing Ethernet environments without having to make major reconfiguration adjustments or determine traffic patterns through network analysis.

Redundancy Increasing network reliability by providing multiple data paths or components so that a secondary route or device could take over in the event of the primary's failure.

Segmentation Breaking up large Ethernet networks into smaller networks that are then connected by an internetworking device such as a switch, router or bridge; increases overall network bandwidth, isolating traffic by keeping unnecessary packets off segments.

Session time-out   Termination of a communications session due to lack of response from the client; common in mainframe connections when internetworking devices introduce non-deterministic delay.

SNMP   Simple Network Management Protocol, the industry-standard way for devices to communicate with network management platforms.

Store-and-forward   A mechanism in which data packets are received in their entirety by a switch and examined for consistency before they are sent to their destination; reduces network errors by discarding bad packets but increases latency; also required to translate between networks of different speeds or types.

Switch   An internetworking device that intelligently segments networks to increase overall bandwidth, isolate traffic, and provide an interface to high-speed networks.

Virtual collision   A fake collision generated by the LANbooster to implement the BackPressure-based flow control mechanism.

Index